T0338559

The **Convergence** of **Artificial Intelligence** and **Blockchain Technologies**

Challenges and Opportunities

Highly Recommended Titles

Blockchain Technologies, Applications and Cryptocurrencies:
Current Practice and Future Trends
edited by Sam Goundar
ISBN: 978-981-120-526-2

Blockchain and Distributed Ledgers: Mathematics, Technology,
and Economics
by Alexander Lipton and Adrien Treccani
ISBN: 978-981-122-151-4
ISBN: 978-981-122-152-1 (pbk)

Inclusive FinTech: Blockchain, Cryptocurrency and ICO
by David Kuo Chuen Lee and Linda Low
ISBN: 978-981-3238-63-3
ISBN: 978-981-3272-76-7 (pbk)

Artificial Intelligence, Data and Blockchain in a Digital Economy
First Edition
by Infocomm Media Development Authority
edited by David Kuo Chuen Lee
ISBN: 978-981-121-895-8
ISBN: 978-981-121-994-8 (pbk)

Blockchain and Smart Contracts: Design Thinking and Programming
for FinTech
by Swee Won Lo, Yu Wang and David Kuo Chuen Lee
ISBN: 978-981-122-368-6
ISBN: 978-981-122-486-7 (pbk)

Electronic Trading and Blockchain: Yesterday, Today and Tomorrow
by Richard L Sandor
ISBN: 978-981-3233-77-5

Blockchain Economics: Implications of Distributed Ledgers
Markets, Communications Networks, and Algorithmic Reality
edited by Melanie Swan, Jason Potts, Soichiro Takagi,
Frank Witte and Paolo Tasca
ISBN: 978-1-78634-638-4

The **Convergence** of **Artificial Intelligence** and **Blockchain Technologies**

Challenges and Opportunities

Sam Goundar

British University Vietnam, Vietnam

G. Suseendran

Vels Institute of Science, Technology & Advanced Studies, India

R. Anandan

Vels Institute of Science, Technology & Advanced Studies, India

World Scientific

NEW JERSEY · LONDON · SINGAPORE · BEIJING · SHANGHAI · HONG KONG · TAIPEI · CHENNAI · TOKYO

Published by

World Scientific Publishing Co. Pte. Ltd.

5 Toh Tuck Link, Singapore 596224

USA office: 27 Warren Street, Suite 401-402, Hackensack, NJ 07601

UK office: 57 Shelton Street, Covent Garden, London WC2H 9HE

Library of Congress Cataloging-in-Publication Data
Names: Goundar, Sam, 1967– editor. | Suseendran, G., editor. | Anandan, R., editor.
Title: The convergence of artificial intelligence and blockchain technologies :
    challenges and opportunities / Sam Goundar (British University Vietnam, Vietnam),
    G Suseendran (Vels Institute of Science, Technology & Advanced Studies, India),
    R Anandan (Vels Institute of Science, Technology & Advanced Studies, India).
Description: Hackensack, New Jersey : World Scientific, [2022] |
    Includes bibliographical references and index.
Identifiers: LCCN 2021040754 | ISBN 9789811225062 (hardcover) |
    ISBN 9789811225079 (ebook for institutions) | ISBN 9789811225086 (ebook for individuals)
Subjects: LCSH: Blockchains (Databases)--Case studies. | Artificial intelligence--Case studies. |
    Big data--Case studies. | Multiagent systems--Case studies. | Internet of things--
    Case studies. | 5G mobile communication systems--Case studies. |
    Convergence (Telecommunication)--Case studies.
Classification: LCC QA76.9.B56 C674 2022 | DDC 005.74--dc23/eng/20211012
LC record available at https://lccn.loc.gov/2021040754

British Library Cataloguing-in-Publication Data
A catalogue record for this book is available from the British Library.

For any available supplementary material, please visit
https://www.worldscientific.com/worldscibooks/10.1142/11959#t=suppl

Desk Editors: Aanand Jayaraman/Yulin Jiang

Typeset by Stallion Press
Email: enquiries@stallionpress.com

Printed in Singapore

Dedication

Dr. G. Suseendran

We would like to dedicate this book to Dr. G. Suseendran.

Sadly, Dr. G. Suseendran passed away on May 1, 2021 from COVID-19 at the height of the coronavirus pandemic in India. We were in the middle of this book publication process, and it was a big shock to lose him, not only as a Fellow Editor of this book, but also as a research collaboration partner and a dear friend. He was instrumental in preparing the proposal for this edited book, proposal revisions, and all the other work involved to get it approved for publication. His initial involvement in proposing and getting this book off the ground is much appreciated as were his words of encouragement and support. We pay our tribute to this humble computer scientist, husband, father, son, brother, uncle, professor, research supervisor, mentor, friend, colleague, educator, and community leader. He will be sorely missed by all of us.

He was quite active in research, paper publication, and book publications. To date, he had published sixteen books and was working on half a dozen more at the time of his death. According to Google Scholar <https://scholar.google.co.in/citations?user=T2tzt8QAAAAJ, retrieved July 10, 2021>, he has 131 research publications listed with a h-index of 9, i10-index of 7, and 376 citations. His work, teachings, research, publications, and his legacy will live on forever in this book and many of his work that exists in digital form. He was the Editor in Chief of the *International Journal of Innovative Research in Applied Sciences and Engineering*, and the *International of Journal Innovative Research in Pure and Engineering Mathematics*, as well as Associate Editor, Regional Editor, Editorial Board Member, and a Reviewer of many other journals.

Dr. G. Suseendran touched and changed the life of many of his students as an Assistant Professor/Research Supervisor with the Department of Information Technology at Vels Institute of Science, Technology and Advanced Studies, Chennai, India, and all other institutions that he worked at prior. He received his M.Sc., Information Technology and M.Phil., degree from Annamalai University, Tamil Nadu, India and Ph.D., degree in Information Technology-Mathematics from Presidency College, University of Madras, Tamil Nadu, India. As additional qualification, he obtained DOEACC 'O' Level AICTE Ministry of Information Technology and Honor Diploma in Computer Programming. His research interests included Ad-Hoc Networks, Data Mining, Cloud Computing, Image Processing, Knowledge-Based Systems, and Web Information Exploration.

We are thankful for the life of Dr. G. Suseendran who has left us with an everlasting repository of research, understanding, and knowledge of computer science. We also acknowledge that he is now resting in peace. In the same token, we pay our condolences to his wife and daughter.

Professor Dr. Sam Goundar
Editor in Chief
Convergence of Artificial Intelligence &
Blockchain Technologies: Challenges & Opportunities

About the Editors

Sam Goundar is an International Academic having taught at 12 different universities in 10 different countries. He is the Editor-in-Chief of the *International Journal of Blockchains and Cryptocurrencies* (IJBC) — Inderscience Publishers, Editor in Chief of the *International Journal of Fog Computing* (IJFC) — IGI Publishers, Section Editor of the *Journal of Education and Information Technologies* (EAIT) — Springer, and Editor in Chief (Emeritus) of the *International Journal of Cloud Applications and Computing* (IJCAC) — IGI Publishers. He is also on the Editorial Review Board of more than 20 high impact factor journals.

To date, he has 112 publications in total. These publications appear in journals (many of them indexed by Scopus and Web of Science) and as chapters in books. He is currently working (writing/editing) on 16 book projects. Eleven have been published and the other five are expected to be published in 2022. A number of PhD and Master's students have successfully completed their thesis under his supervision.

As a researcher, apart from Blockchains, Cryptocurrencies, Fog Computing, Mobile Cloud Computing, Cloud Computing, Educational Technologies, Dr. Sam Goundar also researches on Management Information Systems, Technology Acceptance Model (TAM), Massive Open Online Courses (MOOC), Gamification in Learning, Cyber Security, Artificial Intelligence, ICT in Climate Change, ICT Devices in the Classroom, Using Mobile Devices in Education, e-Government, and Disaster Management. He has published on all these topics. He was a Research Fellow with the United Nations University.

G. Suseendran was working as an Assistant Professor, Department of Information Technology, School of Computing Sciences, Vels Institute of Science, Technology & Advanced Studies (VISTAS), Chennai, Tamil Nadu, India. He had a PhD degree in Information Technology-Mathematics from Presidency College, University of Madras, Tamil Nadu, India. In addition, he had obtained DOEACC 'O' Level AICTE Ministry of Information Technology and Honor Diploma in Computer Programming. He had 10 years of teaching experience in both UG and PG Level. His research interests were Wireless Sensor Network, Ad-hoc Networks, IOT, Data Mining, Cloud Computing, Image Processing, Knowledge-based Systems, and Web Information Exploration. He produced four MPhil Scholars and six PhD Research Scholars under his guidance and supervision. He had published more than 72 research papers including three SCI publications in various international journals such in Science Citation Index, IEEE Access, Springer Book Chapter, Scopus, and UGC refereed journals. He had presented 20 papers at various international conferences. He had authored 12 books and received six awards.

R. Anandan completed his Doctoral Degree in Computer Science and Engineering. He is IBMS/390 Mainframe professional and he is recognized as a Chartered Engineer from the Institution of Engineers in India and received a fellowship from Bose Science Society, India. He is currently working as Professor, Department of Computing Science and Engineering, School of Engineering, Vels Institute of Science, Technology & Advanced Studies (VISTAS), Chennai, Tamil Nadu, India, which is a Pioneer Institution in Engineering. He has vast experience in the corporate world and at all levels of Academia in Computer Science and Engineering. His knowledge and interests include Artificial Intelligence, Soft Computing, Machine Learning, High-Performance Computing, Big Data Analytics, Image Processing, 3D Printing, and Knowledge Engineering. Eight Research Scholars are pursuing PhDs under his supervision.

Acknowledgments

I would like to especially acknowledge my Fellow Editors (G. Suseendran and R. Anandan) for all the hard work they did toward this book. Sadly, Dr. G. Suseendran passed away on May 1, 2021 from COVID-19 at the height of the coronavirus pandemic in India. We were in the middle of this book publication process, and it was a big shock to lose him, not only as a Fellow Editor of this book, but a research collaboration partner and a dear friend. He was instrumental in preparing the proposal for this edited book, revisions, and all the other work involved to get it approved for publication. His initial involvement in proposing and getting this book off the ground is much appreciated as were his words of encouragement and support. For this reason and to pay our tribute, we have included a separate "dedication page" in the front matter of this book.

We are proud to present the book on the *Convergence of Artificial Intelligence and Blockchains: Challenges and Opportunities*. We would like to thank all the reviewers that peer reviewed all the chapters in this book. We also would like to thank the admin and editorial support staff of World Scientific Publishing that have ably supported us in getting this book to press and publication. And finally, we would like to humbly thank all the authors that submitted their chapters to this book. Without your submission, your tireless efforts, and contribution, we would not have this book.

For any new book, it takes a lot of time and effort in getting the Editorial Team together. Everyone on the Editorial Team, including the Editor in Chief is a volunteer and holds an honorary position. No one is paid. Getting people with expertise and specialist knowledge to volunteer is difficult, especially when they have their full-time jobs. Next was selecting the right people with appropriate skills and specialist expertise in different areas of AI, blockchains, big data, IoT, technological convergence, and other technologies converging with AI and blockchain.

Every book and publisher have its own chapter acceptance, review, and publishing process. World Scientific Publishing gave us the flexibility to use our own rigorous process and we are grateful for that. Authors submitted their chapters directly to us. The Editor-in-Chief then does his own review and selects reviewers based on their area of expertise and the research topic of the chapter. After one round of peer review by more than three reviewers, a number of revisions and reviews, a chapter and subsequently all the chapters are ready to be submitted to World Scientific Publishing. All the chapters then go through the publisher's editing, reviewing, proof reading process before being typeset and published.

I hope everyone will enjoy reading the chapters in this book and will learn much from it. I hope it will inspire and encourage readers to start their own research on convergence of AI and blockchains, as well as convergence of other technologies. Once again, I congratulate everyone involved in the writing, review, editorial, and publication of this book.

Any comments or questions can be emailed to sam.goundar@gmail.com.

Professor Dr. Sam Goundar
Editor-in-Chief

Contents

Dedication   v

About the Editors   vii

Acknowledgments   ix

Introduction to the Convergence of Artificial Intelligence
with Blockchains: Challenges and Opportunities   xv

Chapter 1   An Overview of Blockchain Technology:
Fundamental Theories and Concepts   1
R. Ananadan and B. S. Deepak

Chapter 2   Blockchain and Artificial Intelligent for Internet
of Things in e-Health   23
*Geetha Velliyangiri, Vijaya Krishnamoorthy,
Chandra Inbaraj, Anbumani Venkatachalam,
Robbi Rahim, and Manikandan Ramachandran*

Chapter 3   Data Management and Industries Automatization
Using Blockchain, AI, and IoT   43
Krishna Kumar Vaithinathan and Latha Parthiban

Chapter 4   Using Frost Filterative Fuzzified Gravitational
Search-Based Shift Invariant Deep Feature Learning
with Blockchain for Distributed Pattern Recognition   69
S. Ilavazhagi Bala, Golda Dilip, and Latha Parthiban

Chapter 5   The Impact of Blockchain on Cloud and AI   93
             S. Karthik, K. Priyadarsini, and Trishant Baid

Chapter 6   Blockchain-Based Secure Authentication for an
             Intelligent e-Learning Framework with Optimized
             Learning Objects   115
             *Maithili Devi Reddy, Latha Parthiban, and
             Kavitha Chandrakanth*

Chapter 7   Indian Corporate Governance with Relation to
             Sarbanes Oxley (SOX) Act: Proposing Business
             Intelligence (BI) and Blockchain as an Integrated
             Key Strategy   145
             *Kuldeep Singh, Madhvendra Misra, and
             Jitendra Yadav*

Chapter 8   Efficient Secure Image Encryption Using RFID
             with Blockchain Technology in IIoT   159
             *V. R. Elangovan, R. Nirmala, R. Jayakarthik,
             P. Tamilarasi, and R. Kiruthiga*

Chapter 9   The Data Consensus Algorithm for Smart City
             Applications Using Blockchain Technology in
             Industrial IoT   181
             *S. Lavanya, D. Akila, Hannah Vijaykumar,
             P. Calista Bebe, and C. Sudha*

Chapter 10   Industrial IoT with Light-Weighted Supporting
             Hierarchical Storage in Distributed Co-operative
             Network for Blockchain Technology   201
             *K. Rohini, R. Kala, C. Kavitha, R. Hema, and
             P. Praveen Kumar*

Chapter 11   Blockchain-Based Internet of Things (IoT) Security
             for Data Sharing in Smart City Environment   221
             *Padmavathy Thirunavukarasu Velayudham,
             Vimal Kumar Maanuguru Nagaraju,
             Shakunthala Masi, Shobana Nageswari
             Chandrasekaran, Rajkumar Kulandaivel,
             and Manikandan Ramachandran*

Chapter 12 Security Issues in Blockchain from Networking
and Programming Perspective 243
Pranav Vyas and Sam Goundar

Chapter 13 Enhancing Security and Privacy in Pharmacovigilance
with Blockchain 271
Maithili Devi Reddy and Latha Parthiban

Chapter 14 Identity Management Using Blockchain in
IoT Applications 303
Pooja Tripathi and Aman Pradhan

Chapter 15 Digital Anonymity in Decentralized Environment 325
Ashish Seth and Kirti Seth

Chapter 16 Block Edge Computing: Blockchain-Edge Platform
for Industrial IoT Networking 353
T. Nathiya, B. Mahalakshmi, K. Kavitha,
Jabeen T. Nusrat, and K. Maheswari

Chapter 17 Strengthening Omnichannel Retail Supply Chain
with Blockchain Technology 373
Rahul Gupta

Chapter 18 Unmasking Counterfeit Readymade Garments
in India Using Blockchain Technology 393
Jitendra Yadav, Madhvendra Misra, Kuldeep Singh,
and Sam Goundar

Index 411

Introduction to the Convergence of Artificial Intelligence with Blockchains: Challenges and Opportunities

Sam Goundar

RMIT University, Vietnam

sam.goundar@gmail.com

Introduction

Artificial Intelligence (AI) is going to influence the way we work and live in the future. Innovative applications created with the use of AI determine our quality of life, health, longevity, and the way we work, where we work, and how we work. Blockchain with its immutability, transparency, consensus, decentralized distributed ledgers, enhanced security, and peer-to-peer network nodes grow and get embedded in technologies and applications of the future. After the success of blockchain technology with bitcoins and other cryptocurrencies, a number of blockchain platforms have been developed each improving and getting more efficient and innovative than the previous ones. Blockchain uses "smart contracts" to ensure trust and transparency and to verify and validate a record of transactions (block) that it is going to add to other (chain) records in the database (distributed ledger). The smart contract is a set of codes (a program) that automatically and autonomously executes when a transaction has satisfied predetermined conditions. This is where (in the smart contract) AI can be used to make the smart contracts more intuitive, adaptive, and intelligence by adjusting the smart contracts accordingly when faced with transactions that it has not encountered before.

We have already seen major improvements in healthcare, medical research, climate change, cyber security, smart homes, self-driving cars, smart cities, robotics, finance, economic forecasts, prediction models, and the list goes on. These hundreds of innovations have led us to become more efficient and productive in our work, and AI now augments most of the work we do. Not only work, but AI is also entrenched in our social life as well. There is extensive use of AI in Facebook, YouTube, Google search, and all other social media that we use and the games that we play. Because of the properties of blockchains mentioned in the earlier paragraph, they have been used for digital identities, asset management, land ownership records, insurance, peer-to-peer payments (remittances), finance (FinTech), cryptocurrencies, supply chain management, voting/elections, and the list goes on. By itself, AI has capabilities like deep learning, self-awareness, self-learning, facial recognition, and when these capabilities are converged with the capabilities of blockchain (immutability, transparency, consensus, decentralized distributed ledgers, enhanced security), what we get is a super technology with endless capabilities, and power comparable to no other.

The proposition of this book is to see AI and blockchain as supplementing each other, not competing. The intention is to use them to augment the weaknesses of the other and exploit each other strength to promote innovative opportunities. The whole idea of the convergence of AI and blockchain is to do whatever was not possible with each in isolation. To be the future driving force of the industry (4th Industrial Revolution), creativity, and innovative applications as well as the challenges of these converged technologies. AI is a powerful tool that can be used for malicious activities as well. For example, hackers when launching a cyberattack can use AI to learn the cyber security mitigation techniques being used. Then, they can program their AI to write malicious codes based on what it has learnt to bypass the mitigation strategies and breach cyber security. And as the AI learns more, it becomes better and will need some extraordinary countermeasures. These are some of the challenges of converged technologies. Then there are challenges of many of our jobs being replaced with AI.

According to Goertzel (2021), there are three types of AI: (1) Artificial narrow intelligence (AI), (2) artificial general intelligence (AGI), and artificial super intelligence (ASI). Artificial narrow intelligence (AI), the

AI that we mostly refer to and use can solve only a particular domain-specific problem like image recognition, speech recognition, text mining, etc. AGI, which we are working toward (and might be realized in the next 5–10 years) can generalize like human beings, transfer knowledge to domains, and adapt to new problems. ASI can self-program itself and do things beyond human comprehension. To move toward AGI and ASI, we need decentralized AI. Blockchain at the moment has the best decentralized network based on the peer-to-peer protocol that provides immutability, trust, transparency, consensus, and security. The power and capabilities of decentralized AI running on blockchain networks enable AI providers all over the Internet to converge, cooperate, and combine their resources toward new, creative, and emerging artificial super intelligence. "AI technology is transforming the world right now, in remarkable and practical ways. And these are still early days for AI — experts foresee that the coming years and decades will bring dramatic new AI advances such as artificial general intelligence, human-like robots walking the streets, and emergent Internet-scale intelligence" (DAIA, 2021).

A blockchain network of AI (decentralized AI) will be able to do almost anything. They will be able to outsource their capabilities, expertise, and intelligence to others and at the same time get from others what they are lacking. It will be possible for the future generations of AI to do computer science, engineering, write algorithms, smart contracts, share data with each other, and we will have AI that will start improving, enhancing, and refining other AIs. There exists many research and development initiatives at the country level (government funded) and other top organizations like IBM, Google, Facebook, and many others attempting to realize AGI and ASI. Many examples already exist with Deep Neural Networks and Convolutional Neural Networks. Organizations like SingularityNET <https://singularitynet.io/>, DeepBrain Chain <https://www.deepbrainchain.org/>, TODA network <https://www.toda.network/>, and Decentralized ML <https://decentralizedml.com/> are a few. The Decentralized Artificial Alliance (DAIA) <https://daia.foundation/> exists for the sole purpose of promoting decentralized AI (convergence of AI and blockchains). They have many partners working on the same concept at: https://daia.foundation/partners/. According to the DAIA (2021), "DAIA brings together diverse organizations working on decentralized AI — creating an ecosystem of ecosystems that advances decentralized AI faster with higher quality and impact than could be done by various entities acting in relative isolation."

The future is uncertain. This uncertainty will create new problems. We are already facing problems like climate change, the COVID-19 pandemic, economic uncertainty, food shortages, refugees, etc. We will need to converge technologies like AI and blockchains to solve these problems that we do not know about with solutions that do not exist. Cyber security is becoming a major issue for many organizations. All their assets are now within their database. Data is the currency in the age of technology. Blockchain with its immutability and security can be used with AI to come up with mitigation strategies to secure organizations and their assets. AI's ability to learn and predict are useful in countering real-time cyberattacks and warning others of impending exploits. With thousands of attacks taking place per day and thousands of devices to protect, the realm of cyber security is getting beyond human mitigation techniques. Cyber criminals are using sophisticated attacks with an arsenal of malicious code derived with AI. To mitigate these attacks, we need better AI, for example, artificial super intelligence that can understand what is happening in real time, modify its antivirus codes, change its firewall configurations, renew its access control lists, and provide defense in depth. These are the challenges of converged technologies of the future.

Technological Convergence

Information Communications Technology (ICT) is the simplest example of technological convergence. Before information technology, information was either disseminated via print media (newspapers), audio media (radios), or audio and video (TV). To consume this information, an individual was required to pay for and access three different technologies on three different mediums or devices. Now, via the Internet, on a webpage, a consumer can access all three media at once with a single technology. Therefore, the print, audio, and voice and audio technologies have all converged on a single web page and accessed via a single device (Goundar, 2021). With this convergence, the user has control in terms of when, for how long, and how many times, the user can access this information, with the option of archiving it for future retrieval and reference. With this simple example, we can say that the integration of different technologies into one and the provision of them as a single service is technological convergence. Likewise, it is expected that the convergence of AI and blockchain technologies result in super technologies for creativity and innovations.

Similar statements were echoed in an essay written by Papadakis (2007) for the International Telecommunications Union. He defines the term technological convergence as "a process by which telecommunications, information technology and the media, sectors that originally operated largely independent of one another, are growing together". He adds "technological convergence has both a technical and a functional side. The technical side refers to the ability of any infrastructure to transport any type of data, while functional side means the consumers may be able to integrate in a seamless way the functions of computation, entertainment, and voice in a unique device able to execute a multiplicity of tasks." Technological convergence if appropriately managed can play an important role in national economic and social development of every nation. "Governments can capitalize on the opportunity to stimulate market development and meet previous unmet society communication needs" (Papadakis, 2007).

In an organization, analog phone lines, fax machines, duplicating machines, and other stand-alone office equipment have converged into a computer network connected via digital data lines. Now, from one device, a number of different services on different technologies can be accessed. VoIP has replaced phone line communications and email attachments have replaced faxes and postal mails. Technological convergence results in greater benefits from increased diversity in products and services in an organization. Using networking technology that connects all information and communications services with a single network, companies can add services to their previous ones, without new investments in infrastructure. The ability to integrate different technologies (technological convergence) seamlessly has resulted in disruptive technologies like Uber, Netflix, 3D Printing, Self-driving cars, drone deliveries, and the list is not exhaustive. Technological convergence emerged as a saviour for all of us during the time of the COVID-19 pandemic.

Already converged technologies like AI, Blockchains, Robotics, Bioinformatics, and Data Science are converging again to provide totally automated and intelligent services that did not exist before. The article "The Technological Convergence Innovation" authored by Adams *et al.* (2018) discusses the acceleration and Integration of Everything (AIE), i.e., of all forms of electronic devices into a distributed communications grid that will, inexorably, ubiquitously change the way we exist toward a convergent singularity of robotics, informatics, genetics, and nanotechnology. The changes may be more than the collective or individual human psyche is prepared to engage and will require that societies get used to these changes and incorporate them. The use of communication and information technology is also as important for sociology as it is for any other subject as it influences and is influenced by different kinds of policy about citizenship (Adams *et al.*, 2018). This research article indicates that technological convergence still has a long way to go and there will be further disruptions.

Artificial Intelligence

Artificial narrow intelligence, AI as we know it and the type of AI referred to commonly by everyone is the ability of the machine to learn from human beings and gain intelligence. Intelligence as possessed by us enables us to generalize and deal with situations that we have not encountered before. We are able to reason, solve problems, analyze, perceive, understand relationships, learn, and understand language. At the moment with artificial narrow intelligence (AI), we are able to program machines to learn (machine learning), derive meaningful information from digital images (computer vision), code the computer to understand and comprehend our language (natural language processing), design robots to perform repetitive tasks (robotics), recognize patterns, and manage knowledge. The way current AI works is by understanding how humans react to particular problems. Computers are programmed that given problem A, if the human being reacts 99% of the time with solution X, then AI would learn that it has to react with solution X. This is the limitation of the current AI, because when it is presented with the problem that it is not programmed for or does not have a solution for, it does not know how to react or reacts with the best possible solution, not the right one.

Artificial general intelligence (AGI), also categorized as strong AI is not in existence yet, but there are potentially hundreds of research and developments going on to realize its potential and get it working for us. Lead researchers and experts in the field of artificial general intelligence are now predicting that in the next 5–10 years, we will have specialized applications powered by AGI. Artificial general intelligence is expected to learn like human beings, reason, analyze, perceive, and learn how to learn because it will utilize emergent algorithms that will result in emergent behavior. This emergent behavior will enable AGI to react and provide learnt responses to tasks and problems that it has not encountered before and overcome the limitations of artificial narrow intelligence (AI). Like human beings, when faced with an unknown problem, AGI will generalize and build upon its range of learnt behaviors, either combine them or modify them accordingly to solve the unknown problem. And as we train artificial general intelligence, it will become better and better at doing this and surpass human intelligence within hours. For example, a robot that is not programmed to take a particular action, might take that particular action (emergent behavior) based on what it has learnt from the emergent algorithm. According to Pei *et al.* (2019), "there are two general approaches to developing artificial general intelligence (AGI): computer-science-oriented and neuroscience-oriented. Because of the fundamental differences in their formulations and coding schemes, these two approaches rely on distinct and incompatible platforms, retarding the development of AGI."

As we still have not realized artificial general intelligence (AGI), artificial super intelligence (ASI) seems far-fetched. But it might not be the case. As AGI comes into action and because of its ability to learn how to learn like or better than human beings, it will spur the development and availability of ASI in no time. This is the scary AGI that we have been watching in movies where cyborgs go berserk and wage war on us. This is when the stuff of science fiction of humans and robots at war, mind control, space war, and existence of others apart from human beings has been touted as becoming real by some speakers. Think of movies like iRobot, Matrix, Extinction, AI Rising, Super Intelligence, and Social Dilemma. As stated by Batin *et al.* (2017), "Artificial Super intelligence is the level at which AI will supersede humans in all aspects, overtaking the intelligence of the entirety of human civilization. It will be able to govern the world, make scientific discoveries, launch space exploration, and create accurate simulations of the human past." While Bradley (2020) talks about the risks ASI might pose in the future, "the likely near future creation of artificial super intelligence carries significant risks to humanity. These risks are difficult to conceptualize and quantify, but malicious use of existing artificial intelligence by criminals and state actors is already occurring and poses risks to digital security, physical security, and integrity of political systems. These risks will increase as artificial intelligence moves closer to super intelligence." He laments "there is little research on risk management tools used in artificial intelligence development."

Blockchains

Blockchains are now topics of substantial impact that academia, practitioners, and the IT industry need to contemplate, study, research, publish, innovate, exploit, and adopt (Goundar, 2020). Blockchain technologies are being claimed to be as disruptive as the Internet. A white paper titled "Bitcoin: A Peer-to-Peer Electronic Cash System" appeared in 2008 written by a Satoshi Nakamoto (a pseudonym) that set everything into motion. The white paper detailed how an electronic cash transaction can take place between peers without the need for a third party (financial institution). Since then, the paper has been cited 15,683 times at the time of writing this introduction. Digital signatures and cryptography would be used to secure the financial transaction, and peers on the bitcoin network running on the blockchain technology would verify, validate, and authorize the transaction to eliminate the "double spend problem."

According to Nakamoto (2008), this would make the system and transaction transparent, immutable and under the control of peers, thus eliminating control of a financial institution and their exorbitant fees. The bitcoin network would timestamp transactions by hashing them into an ongoing chain of hash-based proof of work, forming a record that cannot be changed without redoing the proof of work. The longest chain will not only serve as proof of the sequence of events witnessed, but proof that it came from the largest pool of CPU power. Messages are broadcast on a best effort basis, and nodes can leave and re-join the network at will, accepting the longest proof-of-work chain as proof of what happened while they were gone.

The website (BlockGeeks.Com, July 2021) defines "blockchain as a growing list of records, called blocks, which are linked using cryptography. Each block contains a cryptographic hash of the previous block a timestamp, and transaction data (generally represented as a Merkle tree). By design, a blockchain is resistant to modification of the data. It is "an open, distributed ledger that can record transactions between two parties efficiently and in a verifiable and permanent way." Blockchains use with peer-to-peer electronic cash transactions enabled a number of Financial Technology (FinTech) applications, Distributed Ledger Technology (DLT) applications, and introduction of more than thousand other Cryptocurrencies. Bitcoin still remains the most popular cryptocurrency.

Blockchains have now moved from electronic cash to other applications in government, supply chain management, healthcare, agriculture, real estate, international development, and almost any application that utilize databases can be replaced with a more secure, immutable, consensus-based, transparent, and trust-based database. Apart from FinTech applications, other applications based on blockchains are emerging in every sector and industry as everyone is intent on taking advantage of the special properties of blockchains mentioned in the earlier sentence. After bitcoin's success or failure (it depends), people are trying to apply it to procedures and processes beyond financial transactions. In effect, they are asking, what other agreements can a blockchain automate? What other middlemen can blockchain technology retire?

According to Goundar (2020), "blockchain technology has to be one of the biggest innovations of the 21st century given the ripple effect it is having on various sectors, from financial to manufacturing as well as education. Unknown to many, is that blockchain history dates back to the early 1990s. Since its popularity started growing a few years back, a number of applications have cropped up all but underlining the kind of impact it is destined to have as the race for digital economies heat up." Smart contracts powered by blockchain render transaction processes more effective, secure, and efficient as compared to conventional contacts. Smart contracts facilitate trustless process, time efficiency, cost effectiveness, and transparency without any intervention by third-party intermediaries like lawyers. In today's high technological era, organizations have accelerated on the use of blockchain technology to enhance their business processes.

Convergence of AI with Blockchains

As we have seen in many cases above, when these two technologies (AI and blockchains) converge, we end up with a super technology that can enable us to do the near impossible. And as research and developments in the two technologies: AI (from artificial narrow intelligence (AI) to artificial general intelligence (AGI) to artificial super intelligence (ASI)) and blockchain (Blockchain as a Service (BaaS) model, different platforms, Hyperledger Fabric, enhanced security, and analytics, etc.) continue, we can expect exciting innovations and applications being developed for better quality of life and innovative work practices. Internet of Things (IoT) are becoming pervasive with billions of devices collecting sensory data (Big Data) from everywhere, every second of the day.

Machines are creating data and with the amount of user-generated content from YouTube, Facebook, and everything else on World Wide Web through the Internet, we will need some tools to receive, analyze, and interpret this data to find out and make sense of what is happening (knowledge and intelligence) around us. This is where the convergence of the two technologies come in. Blockchain with its immutability, security, and distributed network will become the conduit for receiving the data and then AI will be applied to analyze and getting meaningful information from the data.

Technologies like blockchain ensure that the data does not get corrupted, remain immutable, is based on consensus, trustable, and transparent as well as certifying the data gets safely transported to the data center containing AI that is going to do the analysis. With the proliferation of the Internet of Things (IoT), most computing and data processing will take place at the edge of the networks (edge computing) and we have to deal with unstructured data, and thus we need a distributed network (blockchain) to either take this data to AI for analysis or bring AI to the edge with cloud technologies (Blockchain as a Service (BaaS). Such applications of convergence of AI and blockchains are already available with more to come. For example, take the automobile industry (autonomous cars/self-driving cars). These cars use data from Internet of Things (IoT) sensors from the many nodes on the road to navigate themselves. The AI algorithms of these cars will get data from IoT through the blockchain networks, which help the cars decide where to go and recharge itself, which routes to take, where to find the best price for charging and if there are any mechanical troubleshooting required. While recharging cars with electricity and going through roads that require toll payments, the blockchain technology in these cars will have smart contracts to make digital payments on the go.

The convergence of AI and blockchain technology assists in the operations of the smart city. According to Singh *et al.* (2020), "in the digital era, the smart city can become an intelligent society by utilizing advances in emerging technologies. Specifically, the rapid adoption of blockchain technology has led a paradigm shift to a new digital smart city ecosystem". A broad spectrum of blockchain applications promise solutions for problems in areas ranging from risk management and financial services to cryptocurrency, and from the Internet of Things (IoT) to public and social services. They elaborate "furthermore, the convergence of AI and blockchain technology is revolutionizing the smart city network architecture to build sustainable ecosystems. However, these advancements in technologies bring both opportunities and challenges when it comes to achieving the goals of creating a sustainable smart cities." While Lobo *et al.* (2020) looks at the convergence of these technologies for applications in healthcare. They state "owing to enlarged digital data obtainability and AI progressions, there are quite a few occasions that can be reconnoitred in healthcare. Deep learning (DL) and inductive transfer practices are turning healthcare data such as phantasmagorias and videotapes into powerful data sources for predictive analytics." They offer "a gestalt of AI and blockchain and exhibit a roadmap for a blockchain-assisted decentralized bionetwork of private healthcare data to expedite new methodologies to drug discovery and precautionary healthcare."

The Challenges of the Convergence of AI with Blockchains

Most of the challenges that we face in regard to the convergence of AI and blockchains are the challenges present in the individual technologies as well as challenges of regulating the applications derived from the convergence of these technologies. The regulatory frameworks in terms of data within the blockchain network and exchange of data across jurisdictions might become a major challenge as different countries have different regulations for the privacy, security, and sharing of data. For example, the regulations within the European Union (EU) are based on General Data Protection Regulation (GDPR), while North America might have its own, Asia and Africa. This is a challenge for the decentralized artificial general intelligence (AGI) based on the blockchain network that wants to tap into data, expertise, and knowledge from AGI based in different parts of the world. How can we realize artificial general intelligence if we cannot make use of decentralized AI is our major challenge toward achieving AGI? Artificial general intelligence and artificial super intelligence are already making people scared. Questions like what if the super intelligence machines take over the world, what if they go berserk and start killing us. Coming up with laws, legislations, and ethical use of AGI and ASI is another challenge that we need to think about. What can we do with artificial general intelligence and artificial super intelligence and what we cannot? Who is going to decide? Who is going to police? These are some of the challenges.

The other challenges are in moving these terabytes of big data across the decentralized network that are spread over large geographical boundaries and spaces. Do we have the infrastructure, do we have the bandwidth? What about the security of the data? Does blockchain itself provide adequate security? Funding is another challenge for these converged networks. As there are many stakeholders within the decentralized and distributed blockchain network, who is going to pay for what? And what about the profits of the converged enterprise, who is going to get what percentage of the profit? In many of these cases, the stakeholders would be autonomous machines. Another major challenge for the AI part of this convergence is the AI bias. AI makes decisions and takes action based on the data that it is trained on. For example, I recently saw a video where a facial recognition system based on AI was not able to recognize a human being as a person because he or she was of black complexion. The reason for this was because the AI was trained with datasets of people with white complexion. Another example of AI bias is based on AI that learns based on datasets obtained from an organization's transactions. For example, in a supply chain where orders are automatically made and fulfilled, customers that make large orders and suppliers that fulfill those large orders will be given preference (bias). This is because the machine has learnt from the many transactions and mostly knows the major suppliers similar to a salesperson.

Privacy and security remain the main challenges of both technologies individually and converged. Deebak and Fadi (2021) confirm this as follows: "the blockchain applications associate the key features such as self-verification, and self-integrity to eliminate the role of trusted third parties' access." For AI, they state "it evolves scientific and industrial progress to reform as Industry 4.0 that uses Artificial Intelligence (AI) to process and extract the significant information of the real-time systems." Moreover, it applies digital analytics to link the data with blockchain and cloud repositories to improve system efficiencies. However, they claim "the security and privacy issues are still challenging to investigate the AI techniques and tools." They propose "a privacy preserving in smart contracts using blockchain and artificial intelligence (PPSC-BCAI) framework that simplifies human interaction, system activities, service alerts, security risks, and fraudulent claims." Singh *et al.* (2020), explain that to analyze big data, AI plays a significant role, "however, the design and development of a useful big data analysis tool using AI have some challenges, such as centralized architecture, security, and privacy, resource constraints, lack of enough training data." Conversely, as an emerging technology, blockchain supports a decentralized architecture. Despite the challenges above, the opportunities greatly outweigh the use of converged AI and blockchains.

The Opportunities of the Convergence of AI with Blockchains

For us human beings, our health is a number one priority. We care about our health first before we care about anything else. The opportunities available for healthcare with the convergence of AI and blockchains are many. Starting individually with the use of AI in quickly diagnosing diseases based on symptoms, investigating tissue samples, and analysing X-rays to blockchains securing electronic health records, decentralizing them, medicine supply chain, and reducing costs. Decentralized AI running on blockchain networks can take advantage of the skills and expertise of other experts and other AI around the world for diagnosing unusual symptoms and diseases. Additionally, the health big data collected in a country can be incorporated with big data from the World Health Organisation or other countries to extrapolate infection trends during disease outbreaks and pandemics. Already we have seen the extensive use of AI and blockchains for the COVID-19 pandemic. Since the start of the pandemic in January 2020, AI has been identified as the technology that can seamlessly integrate, interoperate, and make sense between our physical, digital, and biological world. It can learn fast — teach itself, other AI and non AI (humans). For example, AI is now extensively used to X-ray chests of patients suspected of coronavirus infections to identify the amount of damage to the lungs.

Another example of the use AI during the COVID-19 pandemic is the use of robotics in hospitals for cleaning and other routine non-expert tasks in order to prevent the spread of infections. Use of AI modeling to predict the spread of the virus, identifying and isolating infected clusters and mitigating the spread of the coronavirus was aided by AI as well. AI has been a powerful tool in the search for COVID-19 treatments. In January 2020, BenevolentAI identified a drug for rheumatoid arthritis as a potential therapy for the novel coronavirus. AI models and algorithms can save time and money in the search for potential drug leads for emerging diseases. Supply chains can better manage the production and distribution of products.

For example, the decentralized nature of supply chains with blockchain smart contracts can run autonomously and does not come to halt because human beings were not able to open the factory because of a lockdown. The smart supply chain relies on the convergence of AI and blockchain to understand the demands of the customer and responds to a pull market where the products are manufactured and delivered based on actual customer demand. Customization, personalization, and tailor-made products to target niche markets and manufacturing products and providing services to individual requirements becomes a byproduct of this converged supply chain.

Manufacturers can use the converged supply chain to practice distributing manufacturing where components of a product are made efficiently and cost effectively in different geographic regions, especially those components that require proximity to scarce raw materials. They can then travel through the blockchain supply chain to the next manufacturing plant for assembly, and the next for testing and packing before shipping. Smart contracts in the meantime take care of logistics, costing, distribution, sales, and all other arrangements and different stakeholders are billed what they are due and paid what they have earned under the governance of the smart contract. Manufacturing plants that have excess capacity or cannot run every day because of not enough orders can outsource their plant and machinery to those that need extra capacity — a system similar to the use of computing resources with cloud computing. Such a system can be easily managed with the converged technologies. According to Bhat *et al.* (2020), such opportunities are possible because "the internet is progressing towards a new technology archetype grounded on smart systems, heavily relying on AI, machine learning (ML), blockchain platforms, edge computing, and the internet of things (IoT)." They continue "the merging of IoT, edge computing, and blockchain will be the most important factor of empowering new automatic service and commercial models with various desirable properties, such as self-verifying, self-executing, immutability, data reliability, and confidentiality provided by the advancement in blockchain smart contracts and containers."

Convergence of AI with Blockchains Research and Practice

Research on the "Convergence of AI with Blockchain" seems to be a hot and trending topic. A search of the keywords "convergence of AI with blockchain research and practice" on Google Scholar <https://scholar.google.com> produces about 16,500 results in 0.03 seconds, while Google <https://www.google.com> generates about 1,390,000 results in 0.50 seconds. When Google Scholar is further refined to show the published research on the topic of "convergence of AI with blockchain research and practice," in the last 18 months, there are still 7,830 results produced in 0.05 seconds. Seven thousand and eight hundred and thirty research papers published in the last 18 months is an indication that there are considerable research and practice going on in regard to this topic. It also indicates how important these topics are to academics, researchers, graduate students, and industry practitioners. News media web sites such as Pring (June, 2021) of Forbes indicate how research into these technologies can lead to sustainable business practices in future of work with a boon in green business, while Wood (2020) advises investors to position their portfolios and invest in innovations emanating from the converged technologies as they are going to transform the global economy. Computer Weekly, a digital magazine and website for IT professionals in the United Kingdom indicates that universities such as the Amsterdam University of Applied Sciences have launched a center of expertise that will put into practice the convergence of AI and blockchain technologies.

An initiative of the European Commission, called The European Union Blockchain Observatory & Forum produced a thematic report titled "Convergence of Blockchain, AI and IoT." The report by Lyons and Courcelas (2020) has a section on blockchain and AI with subsections on "How blockchain can support AI and How AI can support blockchain?" In the section, they "explain to understand how blockchain can support AI, we can look along what we might call an AI value chain involving raw materials (data), production (training AI models) and distribution (the use of AI analyses and decisions)." The problem they indicate is "as is well known, to be useful, AI models need to train on massive amounts of data. Unfortunately, accumulating and storing enormous data sets as well as finding and hiring qualified AI and data experts to work with them is a complex and extremely expensive endeavour." This where AI needs to be converged with blockchain, as "blockchain could help address many of these issues by supporting the development of decentralized, open markets for AI training data. Blockchains can be used to identify and permanently record individual data points and small data sets at their point of origin, making it possible for information owners or aggregators to package the data they generate." Blockchains could also be used to provide the wrapping around larger data sets, recording their provenance and securing them against tampering.

An article published last year (2020) by Pandl *et al.* (2020) appropriately addresses this section. The article titled "On the convergence of AI and distributed ledger technology: A scoping review and future research" published be IEEE Access reaffirms the claims made in the paragraphs above of the converged technologies topic being hot and trending. The authors start off the article by indicating "developments in artificial intelligence (AI) and distributed ledger technology (DLT) currently lead to lively debates in academia and practice." They add "AI processes data to perform tasks that were previously thought possible only for humans. DLT has the potential to create consensus over data among a group of participants in untrustworthy environments." They discuss that "in recent research, both technologies are used in similar and even the same systems. This can lead to a convergence of AI and DLT, which in the past, has paved the way for major innovations of other information technologies." In their published research article "they review and synthesize extant research on integrating AI with DLT and vice versa to rigorously develop a future research agenda on the convergence of both technologies. In terms of integrating AI with DLT, they identified research opportunities in the areas of secure DLT, automated referee and governance, and privacy-preserving personalization."

Future Trends of Convergence of AI with Blockchains

The information provided in the earlier sections indicate that the future looks optimistic for both the technologies individually and the prospects are endless with the convergence of AI and blockchain. For example, as we progress along from Artificial narrow intelligence (AI) to Artificial general intelligence (AGI), and then to Artificial super intelligence (ASI), the innovations coming out will be those similar to the ones we have seen in science fiction movies. As history would indicate, what we saw in movies twenty years ago are now very much part of our real life (think touch screen interfaces). Blockchains continuous research and development and advances in Blockchain-as-a-Service (BaaS) model, different blockchain platforms, Hyperledger Fabric, enhanced security, and analytics, would eventually see it being used in all database applications and information systems. The challenges mentioned earlier would be overcome as both the technologies mature and with the current developments with computer hardware, it will get better with creative enhancements. The opportunities are many and are waiting to be tried, tested, and deployed. Industry experts and pioneers of technologies like Nick Bostrom (Superintelligence expert at University of Oxford), Bill Gates (Microsoft cofounder, software developer), Elon Musk (SpaceX, Tesla, co-founder of Neuralink and OpenAI), Sundar Pichai (Alphabet-Google's Quantum AI), Ben Goertzel (AGI-SingularityNET), and many others see the rise of AI and the future of humanity in AI.

Convergence of AI and blockchain technologies can be seen as a double-edged sword. Depending on which side of the coin you look at or how and for what you use this converged technology. The opportunities are many and so are the threats that come from the misuse of these converged technologies. For example, there has been a number of TED talks <https://www.ted.com/talks> from experts on the topic. Ethical AI expert Genevieve Bell talked about the "6 Big Ethical Questions about the Future of AI" in one of the TED Talks in December 2020. She touched on "How can we ensure the AI systems we build are responsible, safe and sustainable? In October 2019, Janelle Shane talked about "The danger of AI is weirder than you think." According to her, AIs are not smart enough. Accidents caused by self-driving cars, Amazon's resume sorting algorithm discriminating against women applicants, and Facebook's algorithms promoting conspiracy theories and bigotry are some examples she uses to emphasize the danger of AIs. The Real Reason to be Afraid of AI by Peter Haas at TEDxDirigo in December 2017 are the type of talks that put people on the edge. Peter Haas is a robotics researcher who is afraid of robots. The reason he claims are not the robots, but the people that design and program the AI algorithms in the robots. The people that own these robots can program these robots to do the unthinkable. And the next talk does not sugar coat but puts it as bluntly as it can "Artificial Intelligence: it will kill us" by Jay Tuck was delivered at TEDxHamburgSalon in February 2017 and it has been viewed 3,934,447 million times on YouTube.

As scientists, researchers, and academics, we have faith in computer science and in the fields of AI, blockchains, and convergence of AI and blockchains. The opportunities of the converged technologies are waiting to be exploited. The ongoing research and practice are extensive and will result in enhancements and overcome challenges. Putting aside the scary sci-fi movies, we can design, develop, and code accordingly to take care of technology. According to ITU (2021), "with the continuous implementation of AI applications, AI is rapidly changing human life. At present, plenty of countries around the world have adopted AI as one of the key points of national competition. Blockchain technology, as a technology to enhance trust, is developing with AI. Blockchain can promote the rapid development of AI and help AI applications solve problems such as computing power, privacy, security, and authenticity. The convergence of them brings more changes to current Internet and human life. In summary, if an application scenario requires multi-party collaboration, has extremely high requirements for data security, and needs to achieve high-quality information sharing, then the convergence technology of AI and blockchain can be applied." This statement encourages us to embrace the future of the converged technologies.

About This Book

This book covers the growing convergence between blockchain and AI, Blockchain and AI for Big Data, blockchain and AI for multi-agent systems, blockchain and AI for the Internet of Things, and blockchain and AI in 5G. Using real case studies and project outcomes, the book illustrates the intricate details of blockchain in these real-life scenarios. The book aims to bring a state-of-the-art assessment of these rapidly evolving trends in a creative way and provide a key resource for all those involved in the study and practice of AI and blockchain.

AI is, simply put, the building of machines capable of activities and tasks that appear to need human intelligence. Recent technological advances are making this a reality with regard to machine learning, artificial neural networks, and deep learning. Meanwhile, blockchain can be defined as a replacement file system for digital data that stores information in an encrypted, distributed ledger format across many computers, enabling the creation of tamper-proof, extremely strong databases which may be browsed and updated solely by those with permission. The biggest reason for the revolution in AI is the huge proliferation of information. Blockchain and distributed ledgers will record all information and variables that go through a decision process using machine learning. In addition, AI can boost blockchain efficiency far more effectively than humans or standard computing.

Multi-agent systems (MAS) are composed of loosely coupled entities (agents) interconnected and organized in a network. Each agent has the flexibility to unravel issues and attain its goals by interacting with another through collaboration, negotiation, and competition patterns. MAS area units are progressively managing sensitive information. Therefore, enforcing the notion of reputation and ensuring trust and reliability is essential for modern multi-agent systems. Blockchain technologies (BCT) are P2P distributed ledger technologies providing shared, immutable, clear, and updatable (append-only) registers of given values characterizing a given network. However, employing the BCT "as-is" and as a stand-alone solution in dynamic and quickly evolving scenarios can be a bad option. The reasons span from the fundamental properties of BCT, to application/domain-specific constraints. Reaching consensus in distributed multi-stakeholder networks with possible unaligned interests can be extremely complex or unsustainable.

AI is often referred to as a technology that enable machines to find out and reason in ways that have until now only been possible by humans. Combining AI with the divergent powers of IoT can create a gradient system that is invariably more powerful than either one by itself. The huge numbers of information points captured and registered by IoT are often analyzed by computer science to recognize substantive and decisive patterns that are, at best, difficult for humans to obtain and use. Better yet, the algorithms should improve with time to improvise further on these new trends in technology. On the other hand, BCTs, beneficial in many more ways than in the essential field of bitcoin are often accustomed to creating unalterable, persistent, and searchable records or transactions, contracts, and official documents. By combining these systems together, we begin to understand a brand new potential future: a world wherever information is gathered by multiple systems, analyzed by computer science to make selections on our behalf, which are then recorded and time stamped on blockchain as a permanent record of decisions which are made and communicated on our behalf.

This book will be of significance to and will cater to an extensive cross-sectional and multi-disciplinary readership. Academics, researchers and their students in topics, such as AI, cyber-physical systems, ethics, robotics, safety engineering, safety-critical systems, standardization, and certification of digital forensics and application domain communities, such as aerospace, agriculture, automotive, critical infrastructures, healthcare, manufacturing, retail, smart transport systems, smart cities, and smart healthcare will all find the book of great value.

Organisation of the Book

This edited book is organized into eighteen chapters. The chapters have been organized to first introduce the readers to an overview of the blockchain technology, and then look at its application with AI in e-Health. Next, we look at automatization with blockchain, AI, and IoT and using blockchain for distributed pattern recognition with deep feature learning. The impact of blockchain on cloud and AI is covered next followed by blockchain-based secure authentication for an intelligent e-Learning framework. The next section of the book deals with using business intelligence and blockchain as an integrated key strategy and using blockchain technology in IIoT to efficiently secure image encryption with RFID. Data consensus algorithm for smart city applications using blockchain technology is covered next followed by IIoT with light-weighted supporting hierarchical storage in distributed co-operative network for blockchain technology.

Chapter 11 of the book is on blockchain-based IoT security for data sharing in smart city environment, followed by Chapter 12 on security issues in blockchain from networking and programming perspective. The third section of the book starts off by dealing with enhancing security and privacy in pharmacovigilance with blockchain, identity management using blockchain in IoT applications, and a review of medical data security using blockchain with soft computing techniques. Chapter 15 is about digital anonymity in decentralized environment, followed by Chapter 16 on block edge computing — blockchain-edge platform for industrial IoT networking. The second last chapter is about strengthening omnichannel retail supply chain with blockchain technology, and the last chapter is about unmasking counterfeit readymade garments in India using blockchain technology

A brief description of each of the chapters is as follows:

Chapter 1: An Overview of Blockchain Technology: Fundamental Theories and Concepts

A blockchain formerly known as blockchain is an interesting technology developed in 2008 to aid as the public transaction ledger for the cryptocurrency Bitcoin but then, the original effort on cryptographically protected chain of blocks implemented in blockchain was initially defined in Haber and Stornetta in 1991. A blockchain chain can be defined as a growing list of blocks (records) or simply a chain of blocks (records) that is resilient to alteration of the information. It is a Merkle tree representation of blocks, which contains cryptographic hash (timestamp, transaction data, etc.) of the former block such that the chain is resilient to alteration of the information. It is now an actively emerging technology platform for developing decentralized applications like data storage, crypto currencies, etc. in various fields like Digital Forensics, Business sectors, Biomedical engineering Smart contracts, and many more. Thus, the aim of this chapter is to provide an on overview on blockchain, Distributed Systems, basic concept behind blockchain, impact of blockchain on digitalization, hashing, private vs. public blockchain, and introduction to bitcoin blockchain.

Chapter 2: Blockchain and Artificial Intelligent for Internet of Things in e-Health

Blockchain technology has attained importance in the field of health as it overcomes the challenges in securing EHR (Electronic Health Records) as well as EMR (Electronic Medical Records) in e-Health systems. Distributed nature of the technology produces a single ecosystem of patient information that can be monitored more efficiently and quickly by doctors, pharmacists, and hospitals or anyone who diagnosis or gives treatment. Thus, blockchain provides faster diagnoses and plans to care personally. Blockchain technology is used to securely store digital health records and maintain the source record to protect and preserve the identity of patients. This work aims to integrate secure data from IoT devices to clearly understand the effects of blockchain in the real environment field. A novel blockchain approach is designed for e-Health and is employed to discover different ways of sharing decentralized view of health information and improve medical accuracy, health, and prevent health disorders.

Chapter 3: Data Management and Industries Automatization Using Blockchain, AI, and IoT

The key technologies of future digital transformation are blockchain, AI, and IoT. The importance of the value of data makes it inevitable to combine blockchain, AI, and IoT. The convergence of these technologies will create a unique path for new business design models. The IoT devices like sensors, machines, cars, trucks, cameras which are termed as autonomous agents will act as the future profit-making centers that (i) have the digital twin controlling IoT, (ii) use the blockchain technology to transfer money automatically, (iii) autonomously derive a conclusion like self-governing economic agents using data analytics and AI. It is further argued that the triple convergence will enable the creation of such independent decision-making business models, which will be the beginning of a revolution in industrial corporations. The transformation of the business models by using these emerging technologies is necessary to improve the quality of life of the people. In this chapter, we study the importance of the amalgamation of these key technologies that improve the privacy, scalability, security, authentication, and automatization of business data models. We also present various use cases of convergence of these three technologies for better understanding.

Chapter 4: Using Frost-Filterative Fuzzified Gravitational Search-Based Shift Invariant Deep Feature Learning with Blockchain for Distributed Pattern Recognition

Echocardiogram is the test, which uses ultrasound to visualize the various heart-related diseases. In order to improve the pattern recognition accuracy, the Frost-Filterative Fuzzified Gravitational Searchbased Shift Invariant Deep Structure Feature Learning (FFFGS-SIDSFL) technique is introduced. The FFFGS-SIDSFL technique takes the echocardiogram videos as input for pattern recognition. The input echocardiogram videos are partitioned into frames. At first, the enhanced frost filtering technique is applied to a frame for removing the speckle noise and increase the quality of image. Second, an optimal combination of the feature selection is performed by applying Stochastic Gradient Learning Fuzzified Gravitational Search algorithm. The fuzzy triangular membership function is applied to enhance the Gravitational Search algorithm. Followed by the different statistical features such as texture, shape, size, and intensity are extracted. Finally, the Gaussian activation function at the output unit is used for matching the learned feature vector with the training feature vector. The matching results provide the accurate pattern recognition. Experimental measurement is conducted for analyzing the performance of

FFFGS-SIDSFL technique against the two state-of-the-art methods with different metrics, such as Peak signal-to-noise ratio, pattern recognition accuracy, computational time, and complexity with respect to a diverse number of electrocardiogram images. Based on this observation, the FFFGS-SIDSFL technique provides the better performance in terms of higher accuracy results than the two other existing approaches. As a future work, a distributed pattern recognition scheme that uses IoT with blockchain as event monitoring is proposed.

Chapter 5: The Impact of Blockchain on Cloud and AI

Both blockchain and disseminated registering are expecting a basic part in changing endeavors' work environments and the way standard handling works. Their rise has not quite recently gained energy in the current business establishment yet has furthermore changed the way the universe of usage headway, storing, online trade, and various organizations limits. Regardless, challenges suffer in the wide execution of Blockchain in cloud. This book area plans to introduce the impact of blockchain on cloud and how to diminish.

Chapter 6: Blockchain-Based Secure Authentication for an Intelligent e-Learning Framework with Optimized Learning Objects

As education field has become online due to COVID in both schools and colleges, e-learning security has become an important issue. An e-Learning framework provides a collection of online services that are helpful for the learners, resource persons, and others who are involved in enhancing the management and delivery of education to all sections of people. The two most important aspects of an e-Learning system are better search of learning resources and the secure authentication between the learner and the trainer. This chapter introduces two novel methods: (i) optimization of Learning Object (LO) search based on learners' characteristics and (ii) secure authentication of trainers and learners using visual cryptography. Storage and delivery of optimal resources that are well suited for individual learner is always a challenging task. To find the best learning objects, an enhanced attribute-based Ant Colony Optimization algorithm that provides flexibility for the learners based on learner characteristics is proposed. A novel visual cryptography-based technique with kite-based partition technique is designed to perform file sharing and blockchain-based secure authentication and verification of valid learners is proposed for the framework. Several measures like match ratio, relevancy factor, and heuristic values show the efficiency of the proposed ACO search technique in the context of an e-Learning framework.

Chapter 7: Indian Corporate Governance with Relation to Sarbanes Oxley (SOX) Act: Proposing Business Intelligence (BI) and Blockchain as an Integrated Key Strategy

Among all business disciplines, corporate governance falls under the most significant regulatory fields related to business organizations, in such a way that it affects overall productivity, growth, and even market survival. Owing to changing business conditions, stakeholders' responsibilities, and the increasing demand for fair business practices, organizations currently focus on reversing traditional governance practices with new initiatives such as blockchain technology, and business intelligence (BI) governance. Internal stakeholders may have an influence on many organizational decisions in a microenvironment, such as compensation policy, recruitment policy, and dividend policy. For this purpose, the Securities and Exchange Committee of the United States has introduced the Sarbanes Oxley Law (SOX), while in India, the same law was introduced as "Clause 49," issued in line with corporate governance by the SEBI. In this study, we compare the Indian version of corporate governance with the U.S. SOX by proposing business intelligence as an essential strategy powered through blockchain technology.

Chapter 8: Efficient Secure Image Encryption Using RFID with Blockchain Technology in IIoT

In industrial methods, cameras and intelligent image sensors are widely used in process design and also in quality control of the resulting product. In the Industrial Internet of Things (IIoT), the sensors are used to generate images that are constantly at risk of reporting and infringement. Given that third-party intrusion occurs, the only way to secure data that fades into IIoT environments is through traditional methods. Currently, blockchain technology is the main solution to trust problems and also to eliminate intrusion from third parties. The objective of this chapter is really to explore the mutual effect on supply chain transparency on Radio Frequency Identification (RFID), the IIoT, and blockchain technologies. Depends on the Number of Pixels per Change Rate (NPCR), and analysis of entropy information, the data can be analyzed. In support of a variety of attacks, we determine the power of an algorithm that is encrypted for image encryption. RFID technology affects all IIoT and Blockchain systems strongly and significantly, which in fact will have a significant and positive impact on Supply Chain Transparency (SCT). Through each industrial and blockchain IoT technology, the RFID system has an indirect impact on SCT. This research was the first scientific test of SCT's influence on RFID, IIoT, and blockchain technologies. To facilitate the generalization of the results, observations from the first wave may be repeated. The most recent measures are designed and tested with precision and consistency for the use of industrial IoT systems, including blockchain technology. This is the first research to examine the cumulative effect on supply chain technology of RFID, IIoT, and blockchain systems. Edwards-curve Digital Signature Algorithm (EdDSA), public key encryption using a variant of the Schnorr signature based on Edwards' twisted curves. In an IIoT environment, images can be secured by providing an authorized solution based on a private blockchain when the images are encrypted. In this method, the image includes the cryptographic pixel values, which are stored in the blockchain, checking the confidentiality and security of the data. We obtained the value of entropy closer to an absolute value of 8, which is protected against the attack of brute force. Thus, the suggested method is very effective in preventing data leakage and the security that is described in the encrypted results.

Chapter 9: The Data Consensus Algorithm for Smart City Applications Using Blockchain Technology in Industrial IoT

Solid waste management that impacts the health and environment of our society is a key environmental concern. One of the key issues of the current era is waste detection, tracking, and management. The smart waste monitoring system based on the Internet of Things (IoT) is being developed by this project. Using the mobile phone and blynk apps, the level of waste inside the trash can be monitored, which plays a major role in the work. The level of waste inside the garbage can be monitored by smart trash and it notifies the cleaner once the trash is fully loaded. The status of the waste bin is displayed to the user using the Light Crystal Display (LCD) screen. The internal waste distance can be detected by the main sensor, such as the ultrasonic sensor. Status information can be sent to the smartphone with the help of ESP8266, which acts as a WiFi module. Finally, the Blynk application notifies the cleaner when the information comes from the bin. The mastermind of this task is the microcontroller, Arduino Uno. When blynk sends the notification to the smartphone, the waste status may be displayed on the LCD screen that displays the resulting output. The result is made up of three different ranges of measures such as 0%, 50%, and 100%. The 0% result indicates that the distance between the waste and the ultrasonic sensor has to be greater than 10 cm. The 50% result means that the distance between the waste and the ultrasonic sensor must be greater than 5 cm or equal to 5 cm but less than 10 cm. Thus, the 100% result indicates that the waste distance for the ultrasound sensor has to be less than 5 cm. To address this problematic situation industry, with the help of IoT and blockchain technology, the Garbage monitor system is designed and implemented in Industrial IoT (IIoT). The proposed system uses multiple dustbins that are located all over the city or the campus that is provided with low-budget devices that tracks the condition of the dustbin.

Chapter 10: Industrial IoT with Light-Weighted Supporting Hierarchical Storage in Distributed Co-operative Network for Blockchain Technology

An innovation in the Industrial Internet of Things (IIoT) gives a promising chance to incorporate huge scopes to interfere with various heterogeneous gadgets in the Web. Most existing IIoT frameworks rely on a unified architecture as a cooperative network, which is simpler for executives at the same time cannot adequately support undeniable and immutable administrations between various gatherings. The ideal strengths for a large-scale IIoT foundation like reliability, dispersed co-activity, identifiability, and permanence are given by blockChain innovation. This chapter proposed the concept of the IIoT that relies on a blockchain to assist immutable and indisputable administrations. The issue of capacity is trending in this chapter by offering a structure based on the hierarchical blockchain. Exceptionally, the proposed design consists of a graded storage structure where most of the blockchain is placed in mist. While the latest blocks are put away in the overlay organization of the people IoT networks. Consistently, the proposed design links the blockchain, IIoT, and cloud overlay organization. Together through the blockchain connector and the cloud connector, to develop the various blockchain capabilities graded. In layering organizations, blockchain connector constructs impede blockchain from information produced in IIoT organizations. And the cloud connectors fix blockchain synchronization issues between fogs and overlay organizations. In this chapter, the co-employable ownership and access control system is proposed for lightweight IoT devices and is hardware to countless situations.

Chapter 11: Blockchain-Based Internet of Things (IoT) Security for Data Sharing in Smart City Environment

Blockchain (BC) gained significant interest because of its undeniable nature and related advantages of security and privacy. BC has the power to solve drawback of IoT (Internet of Things) like data protection and privacy. Due to the IoT network's distributive nature and massive scale, the privacy and security of IoT have a major challenge. Blockchain has huge attention to improving audibility, IoT anonymity, security, and reliability in which billions of recently used devices are linked with internet to offer personalized services and everyday life. The most prominent issue is the scalability approach and is limited to high resource devices and must be within the wireless range of every IoT device. BC mechanism plays a vital role in safeguarding IoT-oriented applications by becoming part of a security mosaic, in the context of BC context realizes secure network over untrusted parties, which is desirable in IoT with several heterogeneous devices. The BC technology has various advantages and various challenging techniques are presented to resolve the same issues in IoT. The proposed blockchain-based IoT is designed to handle mainly privacy and security threats, though consider many IoT device's resource-constraints. A BC-based innovative structure is used for secure IoT data sharing and privacy preserving in a smart city environment.

A smart city data exchange scenario is developed to verify the security efficacy and predict the utility of the concept proposed.

Chapter 12: Security Issues in Blockchain from Networking and Programming Perspective

As the world adopts more and more of blockchain-based technologies, it will increasingly attract malicious users who will find and exploit their vulnerabilities. Therefore, the study of these vulnerabilities and how they are exploited becomes vital. In this chapter, we have reviewed a variety of vulnerabilities of blockchain. We have looked at these vulnerabilities from networking as well as programming perspective. We have also discussed various attacks on blockchain-based systems as a case study to understand how vulnerabilities are exploited in the real world. We have also provided some tools and techniques that can help in detecting vulnerabilities and enhance security of the blockchain system.

Chapter 13: Enhancing Security and Privacy in Pharmacovigilance with Blockchain

Blockchain provides privacy and security without centralized authority. This work analyzes cryptography applications in blockchain and analyzes efficient sharing of health records using Attribute-Based Encryption (ABE). Secure data sharing of sensitive information stored in cloud is very important as anybody can access it from anywhere in the world. This work aims to provide a secure sharing of medical records in cloud using enhanced Ciphertext Policy (CP-ABE) and Key Policy (KP-ABE) techniques along with data owner specifying the access control policies. In an open networked system, machine-learning algorithms are effectively used in pharmacovigilance to find the Adverse Drug Reaction (ADR). Securing this sensitive data in cloud is very important as PHRs privacy concern is very important.

Chapter 14: Identity Management Using Blockchain in IoT Applications

To evaluate the efficiency of any system, a smart work monitoring system is required to ensure the accountability and reliability of each user in the process. The ever-growing pool of Internet of Things (IoT) devices poses not only new prospects and solutions as well new set of challenges for businesses in terms of security and privacy. The widespread adoption of these smart IoT-based solutions totally depends on the availability of platforms that ensure adequate sensor data integrity while ensuring adequate user privacy in organization. In light of these challenges, previous research suggests that the integration of IoT and blockchain technology is a good way to reduce data security problems arising in IoT. In this chapter, we have designed and developed a Real-Time Work Monitoring System (RTWMS) for all RACI (Responsible, Accountable, Consultant, and Information) levels involved in the cleaning and maintenance process of Public Toilets and Community Toilet Complex (CTC). Evaluation results indicate that the proposed design will ensure tamper-resistant collection, processing, and conversion of IoT sensor data into a safe, scalable, and efficient manner.

Chapter 15: Digital Anonymity in Decentralized Environment

Privacy has become a huge point of contention in recent days with tech organizations such as Google and Facebook, which make a great deal of revenue from monetizing user data, coming into conflict with regulatory bodies such as The European Data Protection Board (EDPB). So, there may be two research questions that can be raised in terms of privacy and user experience. First, what are the trade-offs when using efficient and integrated centralized systems in exchange for giving up vast amounts of personal information? Second, how does this apply to cryptocurrencies and blockchains? In blockchains, each person has a set of identities with which they interact with the blockchain. This means that a user's privacy will be reduced if their virtual identities can be linked to their real one. Hence, one can increase their privacy through anonymity, masking their identity; can gain access to some service while minimizing how much information they reveal about their real identity. Any software system comprises of three basic entities: an application, data, and the infrastructure. In general, the centralized environment keep holds on the applications, the data that is used in the application and the infrastructure on which the entire application runs. It means all the components or entities of a system are governed or controlled by the central authority.

Chapter 16: Block-Edge Computing: Blockchain-Edge Platform for Industrial IoT Networking

The rapid growth of Industrial Internet of Things (IIoT) architecture presents a unique scope for developing a broad field of networking to connect multiple interconnected nodes to the Internet. The majority of current IIoT technologies are focused on unified architecture, which is easier to maintain but cannot leverage to facilitate immutable and verifiable networks between different groups. The blockchain framework is built on many desirable features for large-scale IIoT technologies, such as centralization, reliability, tracking ability, and immutability. This chapter proposes an IIoT blockchain-based infrastructure designed to encourage unchanging and empirical transactions. Nevertheless, while abandoning blockchain technology to the IIoT framework, the necessary storage space is subject to a subsidizing challenge to the cluster-based IIoT architecture. The proposed frame has a centralized storage structure where most of the blockchain settles into clouds such as Global, Fog, and Edge. Nearly all notable nodes are processed in the superimposed network of independent industrial IoT networks. The proposed framework constantly links low-level IIoT networks, blockchain overlay networks, and combined cloud architecture through two connectors. The blockchain interface and fog interface port are interconnected for continuous data transmission. The blockchain interface in the stacked network extends blockchain blocks from the information gathered in IIoT nodes. And the cloud interface reconciles the constraints of optimizing the blockchain between the overlay network and the clouds. This is a test case to be provided to demonstrate the efficiency of the Edge Central Network Repository proposed in a practical example of IIoT.

Chapter 17: Strengthening Omnichannel Retail Supply Chain with Blockchain Technology

The last few decades have seen the transformation of the modern supply chain from a simple (inflexible, linear, and reactive) to a complex (flexible, multi-echelon, and proactive) supply chain. The supply chain encompasses a global network of third-party service providers (Logistic, IT, Customer support, Warehousing), practicing numerous procedures and policies. The complex management of retailers, buyers', and suppliers' relations are susceptible to quite a few challenges (transparency, trust, and security). Blockchain is an advanced technology with features like distributed notes, storage mechanism, consensus algorithm, decentralized structure, smart contracting, and asymmetric encryption, which helps to ensures supply chain network prominence, security, trust, and transparency. Blockchain technology turbocharges the profitability and efficiency of the supply chain. The level of security like physical management is complemented by process enhancements and technological leverages. Blockchain provides shared ledgers with error-free decentralized digital records, while every participating member act as a catalyst, by maintaining his data set for the transaction. Digitalization eliminates the need for traditional third-party verification; participants may self-verify the transactions. The information once entered is inconvertible and can never be obliterated. Transacted data is stored in time-stamped blocks and serves as the data structure. Blockchain technology serves flawlessly with features like storage mechanism and storage nodes, smart contract, consensus algorithm, and asymmetric encryption. Blockchain technology is successfully implemented in various sectors like finance, banking, IoT, and forex transactions. Current research focuses on providing abridged details of blockchain and serves to introduce its innumerable applications emphasizing, the potential to transform supply chain provenance, business process reengineering, to security enhancement for the success of omnichannel retail supply chain.

Chapter 18: Unmasking Counterfeit Readymade Garments in India Using Blockchain Technology

Counterfeit products are the replicated goods of authentic and original brands having indistinguishable packaging, labels, and trademarks on them. It is a very serious threat to economies all over the world. These products are not only causing loss to the nations at great lengths but are also affecting the employment growth by shutting down the local industries. In the context of India, counterfeiting is no new concept even though, the apparel industry is one of the major contributors to employment and growth in the Indian economy. This chapter focuses on removing the practice of counterfeiting from the Indian apparel industry by examining the ways in which blockchain technology can be integrated with the supply chain management to provide a genuine solution for traceability along with other various contributing operational factors such as reduction in cost, damage and combating the practice of counterfeit products from the apparel industry. Counterfeit, the term refers to products that are the replicated goods infringing trademarks and patents of big and popular brands that are of substandard quality manufactured and sold by another local and regional brand name without the consent or the authority of the original brand. Counterfeit products exist both in the physical and virtual market, that is, online stores and this tends to be the prime counterfeit.

References

Adams, T. L., Taricani, E., & Pitasi, A. (2018). The technological convergence innovation. *International Review of Sociology, 28*(3), 403–418.

Batin, M., Turchin, A., Sergey, M., Zhila, A., & Denkenberger, D. (2017). Artificial intelligence in life extension: From deep learning to super intelligence. *Informatica, 41*(4).

Bhat, S. A., Sofi, I. B., & Chi, C. Y. (2020). Edge computing and its convergence with blockchain in 5G and beyond: Security, challenges, and opportunities. *IEEE Access, 8*, 205340–205373.

Blockgeeks. (2021). What is blockchain technology? A step-by-step guide for beginners. https://blockgeeks.com/guides/what-is-blockchain-technology/ [accessed: July 1, 2021].

Bradley, P. (2020). Risk management standards and the active management of malicious intent in artificial superintelligence. *AI & SOCIETY, 35*(2), 319–328.

DAIA. (2021). The decentralized artificial intelligence alliance. Creating the future of decentralized AI. https://daia.foundation/. Retrieved July 1, 2021.

Deebak, B. D., & Fadi, A. T. (2021). Privacy-preserving in smart contracts using blockchain and artificial intelligence for cyber risk measurements. *Journal of Information Security and Applications, 58*, 102749.

Goertzel, B. (2021). The general theory of general intelligence: A pragmatic patternist perspective. arXiv preprint arXiv:2103.15100.

Goundar, S. (2020). Introduction to blockchains and cryptocurrencies. In *Blockchain Technologies, Applications and Cryptocurrencies: Current Practice and Future Trends* (pp. ix–xix).

Goundar, S. (2021). Introduction to enterprise systems and technological convergence. In *Enterprise Systems and Technological Convergence: Research and Practice*, 1.

ITU. (2021). Overview of convergence of artificial intelligence and blockchain. Series F: Non-Telephone Telecommunication Services: Supplement 4 (04/2021).

Lobo, V. B., Analin, J., Laban, R. M., & More, S. S. (2020, March). Convergence of blockchain and artificial intelligence to decentralize healthcare systems. In *2020 Fourth International Conference on Computing Methodologies and Communication (ICCMC)* (pp. 925–931) IEEE.

Loohuis, K. (2021). Amsterdam University of Applied Sciences combines AI and practice. News. *Computer Weekly*. https://www.computerweekly.com/news/252498465/Amsterdam-University-of-Applied-Sciences-combines-AI-and-practice [accessed: July 4, 2021].

Lyons, T., & Courcelas, L. (2020). Convergence of blockchain, AI and IoT. Produced by ConsenSys AG on behalf of the European Union Blockchain Observatory & Forum. European Commission. https://www.eublockchainforum.eu/sites/default/files/report_convergence_v1.0.pdf [accessed: July 4, 2021].

Pandl, K. D., Thiebes, S., Schmidt-Kraepelin, M., & Sunyaev, A. (2020). On the convergence of artificial intelligence and distributed ledger technology: A scoping review and future research agenda. *IEEE Access, 8*, 57075–57095.

Papadakis, S. (2007). Technological convergence: Opportunities and challenges. Ensayos de la Unión Internacional de Telecomunicaciones.

Pei, J., Deng, L., Song, S., Zhao, M., Zhang, Y., Wu, S., ... & Shi, L. (2019). Towards artificial general intelligence with hybrid Tianjic chip architecture. *Nature, 572*(7767), 106–111.

Pring, B. (2021). Leading in the green business boon. Cognizant brandvoice, innovation. *Forbes*. https://www.forbes.com/sites/cognizant/2021/06/29/partaking-in-the-green-business-boon/?sh=4559bac71b6a [accessed: July 4, 2021].

Singh, S. K., Rathore, S., & Park, J. H. (2020). BlockIoTIntelligence: A blockchain-enabled intelligent IoT architecture with artificial intelligence. *Future Generation Computer Systems, 110*, 721–743.

Singh, S., Sharma, P. K., Yoon, B., Shojafar, M., Cho, G. H., & Ra, I. H. (2020). Convergence of blockchain and artificial intelligence in IoT network for the sustainable smart city. *Sustainable Cities and Society, 63*, 102364.

Wood, C. (2020). Stand ready for the big five technology convulsions reshaping markets. *Opinion Markets Insight*. https://www.ft.com/content/cbe2861c-06bf-4a9e-919a-f42687b260cc [accessed: July 4, 2021].

Chapter 1

An Overview of Blockchain Technology: Fundamental Theories and Concepts

R. Ananadan*,† and B. S. Deepak*,‡

*Department of Computer Science and Engineering,
Vels Institute of Science, Technology and Advanced Studies (VISTAS),
Pallavaram, Chennai 600117, Tamil Nadu, India

†anandan.se@velsuniv.ac.in

‡mr.arivaali@gmail.com

Abstract

A blockchain formerly known as blockchain is an interesting technology developed in 2008 to aid as the public transaction ledger for the cryptocurrency Bitcoin but then, the original effort on cryptographically protected chain of blocks implemented in blockchain was initially defined by Stuart Haber and W. Scott Stornetta in 1991. A blockchain chain can be defined as a growing list of blocks (records) or simply a chain of blocks (records) that is resilient to alteration of the information. It is a Merkle tree representation of blocks which contains cryptographic hash (timestamp, transaction data, etc.) of the former block such that the chain is resilient to alteration of the information. It is now an actively emerging technology platform for developing decentralized applications like data storage, crypto currencies, etc., in various fields like Digital Forensics, Business sectors, Biomedical engineering Smart contracts, and many more. Thus, the aim of this chapter is to provide an on overview on blockchain, distributed systems, basic concept behind blockchain, impact of blockchain on digitalization, hashing, private versus public blockchain, introduction to bitcoin blockchain, Bitcoin Mining, Ethereum and Smart Contracts, Applications of blockchain in Land Registration, E-Governance and Medical Information Systems, etc.

Keywords: Cryptocurrency, bitcoin, distributed systems, digitalization, hashing, ledger

1. Introduction

Just like every other day, you are enjoying your morning with a cup of coffee and news feeds. Somewhere, a financially motivated hacker is finding all of the possible ways to compromise millions of users' accounts from a popular social networking site. If the hacker is successful in gaining access to the database, he gains access to a large amount of credentials (Gupta, 2018).

Once a massive credential theft is revealed publicly, an individual finds out that he/she was also a victim. In this computer age or information age, millions of users have a good reason to be worried about their attached trust and privacy. The examples range from the latest Equifax 2017 Data Breach case (143 million credentials compromised) to the Adult Friend Finder 2016 case (413 million account thefts), the Anthem 2015 case (78 million accounts were hacked), and many more. None of the preventative solutions can be 100% secure, but finding out what the problem was at the right time could have saved the misuse of these credentials (Gupta, 2018).

What if we can dream about a technology can do the following? To prevent us from a situation described above. This is what a blockchain does. In a nutshell, it's nothing but a smart, safe, and constantly growing database (Kaneko & Asaka, 2018). The blockchain network provides the ability to transfer any type of value or asset among independent parties by means of a peer-to-peer network. The initial objective of the blockchain technology was to establish trusted financial transactions between two independent parties without any involvement of third parties, such as a bank; however, later, several industries adopted blockchain to streamline their supply chain process, KYC system, data management, and so on (Bitcoin Gets Second, 2020). With the growing use of online services and a growing number of online transactions, users have to trust and depend on third parties, such as banks and payment gateway providers (Mudliar *et al.*, 2018). This led to the birth of the blockchain technology (Gupta, 2018).

2. History

The first effort on a cryptographically secured sequence of blocks was conducted by W. Scott Stornetta and Stuart Haber in 1991 and they desired to implement a framework where record timestamps couldn't be messed with. In 1992, Stornetta, Bayer, and Haber combined Merkle trees to the structure, which enhanced its productivity by allowing a little archive testimonies to be assembled into one square. Later, the foremost blockchain was abstracted by an individual (or group of individuals) identified as Satoshi Nakamoto in 2008. He/They enhanced the plan in a substantial manner by using a Hashcash-like technique to timestamp obstructs without requiring a signature from a trustworthy party and introduced a troubling constraint to stabilize the ratio with which blocks are added to the sequence (Yang *et al.*, 2019). The structure was executed in the next year by Nakamoto as a core component of the cryptocurrency bitcoin, where it serves as the public ledger for all transactions on the network (Blockchain, n.d.).

In August 2014, the bit-coin blockchain document size containing records of all transactions have occurred on the system and attained at 20 GB. In January 2015, the size had expanded to right around 30 GB, and from January 2016 till 2017, the bitcoin blockchain expanded from 50 to 100 GB in size. The record size had surpassed 200 GB by mid-2020. The verses block and chain were used individually in Satoshi Nakamoto's distinct paper yet were in the end encouraged as a solitary word "block-chain" by 2016. As per Accenture, an application of the distribution of innovations concept advises that blockchains accomplished a 13.05% selection proportion inside financial services in 2016, along these lines received at the initial adopter's stage. Industry altercation bunches combined to make the Global Blockchain Forum by 2016, an initiative of the Chamber of Digital Commerce. By May 2018, Gartner established that lone 1% of CIOs validated any sort of blockchain reception inside their associations, and just 8% of CIOs were in the current instant "assembling or [observing at] vibrant experimentation with blockchain" (Blockchain, n.d.).

3. Fundamentals of the Blockchain

Blockchain is a distributed database that maintains ledger of all transactions protected and in an append-only technique. Blockchain rapidly became

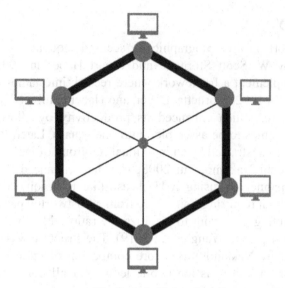

Blockchain Network

Figure 1.   Schematic Diagram of a Blockchain Network (Gupta, 2018)

prevalent among various industries because of its distributed nature in terms of its database. For an institute that cannot afford a single point of disappointment, the blockchain database makes it basically impossible for sensitive data or credentials to be compromised by cyber lawbreakers (in other words hackers). Moreover, blockchain isn't just achieved by trusted developers or administrators; it is well-achieved by someone who can be either trusted or known party (Gupta, 2018; Tonelli *et al.*, 2019). Figure 1 is a graphical representation of the blockchain network.

Each internet-connected computer needs to have blockchain node software and run an application specific to the blockchain ecosystem (Peck, 2018). Depending on the use cases, the participation of these computers can be restricted. For example, the blockchain-based ecosystem bankchain permits banks to run the bankchain node client application (Gupta, 2018).

4. Working Principle

In the current era of technology, blockchain has the capability to enter any industry as a disrupter. This could be to reduce operational expenditure, overcome cybersecurity-related issues, deliver identity and access management solutions, facilitate collaboration between private and public institutions, achieve a better data management system, enhance and simplify logistic and supply chain management, allow a seamless insurance sales and management system, or deploy a better health record database system to protect people against any data theft or espionage attempt (Gupta, 2018). To recognize the structure in its basic form, it is significant to use numerous states of blockchain and explore them further (Gupta, 2018):

1. **Record preparation:** In this phase, party X makes a payment that includes. Data with the public address of the receiver, a digital signature of the source, and a transaction message. Finally, this block is made accessible to all of the nodes in the blockchain network (Gupta, 2018).
2. **Record verification:** The blockchain node's work in a trust less model, where each and every node (the device running the blockchain customer software) accepts this transaction, and validates the e-signature with party X's public key. After successfully verifying, the legitimate transaction is packed as a block in the blockchain and waits till the maximum nodes effectively authenticate the same transaction (Gupta, 2018).
3. **Block generation:** The lined up records are organized together as a block by the nodes in the blockchain network. Now in the blockchain network, Bitcoins are compensated when a Bitcoin node, or a miner, creates a block by resolving arithmetically complex problems (Gupta, 2018).
4. **Block validation:** Upon successful generation of a block, nodules in the network process for an iterative authentication process where the majority of the nodules have to attain consensus. There are four prevalent ways to achieve consensus, Proof of Stack (PoS), Proof of Work (PoW), Practical Byzantine Fault Tolerance (PBFT), and Delegated Proof of Stack (DPoS). Bitcoin uses Proof of Work to achieve consensus; conversely, Ethereum uses Proof of Stack for consensus. This mechanism effects economic traits and ensures the security of all transaction procedures (Gupta, 2018).
5. **Blockchained:** After a efficacious consensus mechanism, the blocks are confirmed, and are added to the blockchain (Gupta, 2018).

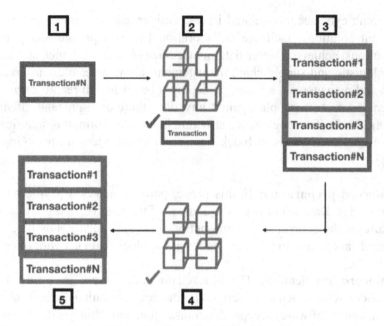

Figure 2.   Function of Blockchain

5. Ledger

Ledger can be defined as a record keeping book of all the economic transactions of an institute. In colleges and schools we call it as a register.

Since prehistoric periods, registers have been at the core of financial transactions to record payments, contracts, buy-sell deals, or movement of property or assets. The journey started with the recording on papyrus or clay tablets, made a big jump with the discovery of paper. Over the last few decades, computers have provided the practice of recording transactions and ledger maintenance at great expediency and rapidity (Yang *et al.*, 2019). Today, with the modernization of computers, the data stored on computers is heading toward much higher forms that are cryptographically fast, secure, and decentralized.

The blockchain ledger is a sort of databank where established transactions are recorded. Traditional centralized ledger systems work in a very similar way as the blockchain ledger system; however, there are few differences (Soze, 2019).

5.1 *Centralized ledger system*

An old way of doing a ledger system that is centralized by a bank. For example, it works like this: if you purchase from me, you pay me; really, you would only initiate a transfer from your bank account to my bank account (Hassan *et al.*, 2019). Then both of those banks, if they are not the same, would have all the details of the transaction registered. However, only those two banks would be able to access those transaction details, therefore, no other banks, nor anyone else, would have access to those details (Soze, 2019).

If someone wants to have access to see the details, they need to ask the bank for authorization first. Of course, it all depends on what is the reason for the access. But the point here is that this traditional ledger system is still working in the same way and is the backbone of any accounting system that holds non-financial and financial data for an institution. The collection of all transactions is known as a public ledger. In a non-computerized or manual system this may be a huge book. Each account in the public ledger contains two or more records.

5.2 *Distributed ledger system*

Imagine the ledger system as a family tree; but, instead of people's names, the huge ledger system holds information about payment value and addresses (transactions). In regards to the transactions, the ledger holds all the records of payments back to the first transaction that was ever made. In regard to the addresses, there are no URL's or location addresses. Instead, these are bitcoin, or any other cryptocurrency, addresses. The block diagram of a centralized ledger system is depicted in Figure 3 and the same of a distributed ledger system is depicted Figure 4. The ledger holds a series of transactions of all cryptocurrencies (Soze, 2019).

Additionally, the current values are continually computed of the previous transfers. One part of the ledger is representing the value that has been assigned, some other parts of the ledger represent the date and time of each transaction. This is very similar to any of the current Banking systems (Soze, 2019).

You can see who transferred to what account, what date and time, as well how much was each transaction; however, the ledger has no banker (Benčić & Žarko, 2018). Also, the addresses are not representing names of the individuals, neither who holds what amount; therefore, you can call

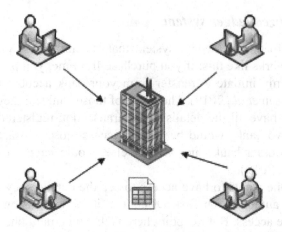

Figure 3.   Centralized Ledger System (Stackoverflow, 2020)

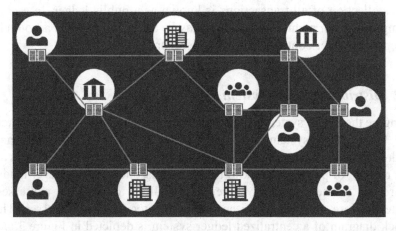

Figure 4.   Distributed Ledger System (Distributed Ledger System, 2020)

this an anonymous ledger system. What you have to understand is that when it comes to an individual's bank account who has no relatives, the bank could seize that account. In addition to banks, even the Police, FBI, or any government official can take any bank account if they find a possible reason for it. When it comes to a bitcoin account within the great ledger, the only person who can access it is the person who has the password to that account (Soze, 2019).

Of course, it's dangerous; if you accidentally lose the password to your bitcoin wallet that the ledger holds, whatever value it has will be lost forever (Kuhn *et al.*, 2019). With your bank account, if you lose your password, you call the bank, they ask security questions, and once you prove that you are the owner of that account, the bank will provide you access. On the other hand, having a bitcoin account, no bank will be able to help you to access your account. However, no one can tell that account is connected to you (Soze, 2019).

Due to the blockchain technology, every transaction is confirmed for its validity and goes into a block; then each block will join to the previously validated blocks, then eventually they all will form a chain of blocks, that we call blockchain. Every bitcoin citizen is required to keep a copy of the blockchain, after each block that gets created by the system; every blockchain member receives a finalized sealed block (Soze, 2019).

Then the system checks each block automatically and adds each block to each citizen. This is how blockchain holds every transaction and every value that was ever created. These methods ensure the legitimacy and correction of every transaction without any central authority. If all that sounds alien to you, just understand that is completely automated by the system, and you, as a bitcoin citizen, do not need to do any calculation, and it would probably take a very long time anyways (Soze, 2019).

Each transaction, once validated, is sealed into the ledger; this process is carried out by the miners. When a new validated block arrives, each new block must be added to every citizen's blockchain; however, before accepting the new block, everyone checks the logical continuation of all the values in the new block, to make sure that all the transfers of costs are legitimate (Siano *et al.*, 2019). This also prevents any replication of transfers or any counterfeiting done by hackers, or people with bad intentions, trying to steal bitcoin or any other cryptocurrency. This is a crucial step, as this validation will remain within the great ledger and within the blockchain forever. This process uses hashes for competition, to validate each block, and make sure that each citizen receives the same record (Soze, 2019).

This method is also known as a public ledger, or permission less ledger. If there is no central authority to manage the access for the ledger, such a ledger is termed as public ledger or, again, permission less ledger. So basically, you, or anyone, could join to the existing peer-to-peer network (for free of course) and receive a copy of the ledger of all existing transactions that have ever been recorded on the blockchain. This would date back to January 2009 when the great ledger began to work for the first time. As you can see, this is completely the opposite of what the current banking systems are providing (Soze, 2019).

5.3 *Private ledger*

If a central authority is there to manage access to the ledger, it's then called a private ledger, also known as a permissioned ledger. This is of course not a peer-to-peer network, and you would have to ask for permission from the central server to have access to a copy of the ledger (Soze, 2019).

The blockchain ledger is visualized as a series of blocks which are connected with each other. Each block is made of a header, containing metadata, such as its previous block hash, Merkle root hash, and nonce. Followed by a list of transactions. The blocks are connected with each other, by referencing each of its parents' block hash (Soze, 2019).

6. Private versus Public Blockchain

Many flavors of blockchain have evolved over the years, and several itera-tions have been undertaken to achieve business value. There are more than a thousand startups launching their products with distributed blockchain applications. When it is about business, it is important to know best-fit solutions. From its birth, blockchain has been permission less, open to the public without exception. You can download the node software and view the entire history of blockchain, initiate transactions, and store information. This makes life for end users easy; however, businesses interested in deploying blockchain may see this as a big challenge. Public blockchains do carry some critical disadvantages when it comes to business. Businesses are usually more interested in private blockchains to create blockchain solutions with better privacy and security (Gupta, 2018).

6.1 *Public blockchain*

With the public blockchain, the process of chaining a block is always with nodes that can be independent, untrusted, or even unknown, and can par-ticipate in the consensus process to validate a block. In a public block-chain, anyone can simply download the blockchain node client onto their system and transact with anyone, and anyone can read the transactions over the block explorer. Bitcoin and Ethereum are some of the major examples of public blockchains. Bitcoin was the first decentralized plat-form to transfer money safely and securely. However, Ethereum inno-vated with a different purpose — a purpose to provide a platform for anybody to develop their own decentralized application that won't be limited to the transfer of just currency, but any kind of value. Ethereum uses smart contracts to achieve a set of self-operating programs that execute when certain conditions are satisfied (Gupta, 2018).

6.2 *Private blockchain*

An organization that sets up a private blockchain configures it to work as a permissioned network. It is built to provide better privacy over transactions and is suited for banking and other financial institutions. Unlike a public blockchain, just connecting to the internet with a blockchain node client will not be enough to initiate transactions; however, a consortium blockchain allows only specific and pre-verified people to access and transfer any type of value over the network. In this system, the consensus mechanism is controlled and managed by pre-selected groups of nodes. This way, even though the blockchain works in a public network, it still remains restricted and can only be controlled and maintained by specific groups of nodes, or maybe even a single node. Private blockchains can also be called consortium blockchains based on their restrictions and control levels. One of the most popular implementations of this is Hyperledger Fabric. Figure 5 showcases the difference between public and private blockchains.

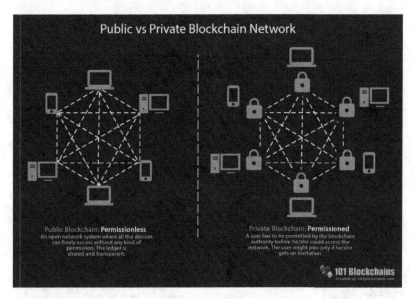

Figure 5. Private versus Public Blockchain Network (Private versus Public Blockchain, 2020)

7. Hashing

Hashing is referred to a fixed sized string of numbers, for example, 128, 256, 512, 1024, 2048 numbers. Hashing can be performed on various files, such as text, images, audio files, video files, or even software. It produces a unique hash based on that the particular file. An individual file goes through a hash on one end; then comes out scrambled on the other end. It doesn't matter what kind of file you try it out on; the result is always different. For example, you might try to put an MD5 hash in the word "blockchain." The hash would be completely different than the word "blockchain1" (Soze, 2019). A simple schematic representation of Hashing is shown in Figure 6.

Note: MD stands for Message Digest, and the number 5 is its version number. Basically, MD5 has taken over MD4 hashing. Let me show you how much of a difference there is between two very similar words. As I mentioned the word "blockchain," I will perform and generate an MD5 hash on it. Ok, so the MD5 hash value for "blockchain" is: 5510a843bc1b7acb9507a5f71de51b98.

However, now I will perform the same MD5 hashing on the word, "blockchain1." Let's see the result: 1150228f14788047028d774b7c83c5a6.

As you see, this is a completely different outcome; this is because the word is different, although very similar, it is still a different MD5 hashing

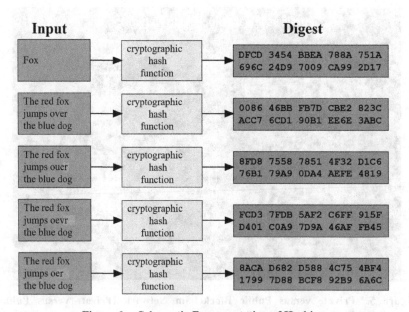

Figure 6.   Schematic Representation of Hashing

value. Let's try to do this now with a number, and for simplicity, I will use very few figures so you will see how powerful hashing can be. This time I will perform MD5 hashing on a number string of 123, and then 124, and see if there is any difference. Let's begin, shall we? Ok, so I have performed MD5 hashing on the number string: 123, and the hashing value is this: v202cb962ac59075b964b07152d234b70.

Now I will do the same MD5 hashing on the number string 124: c8ffe-9a587b126f152ed3d89a146b445. As you see, again, it's an entirely different outcome; therefore, hashing itself can provide excellent security. However, I will move on to more in-depth. In case you think I am some genius, or just making up the MD5 values, I would suggest you visit the link for md5hashgenerator and practice for yourself. Perhaps you can start with the same words and number strings I made examples of. The website to visit is: http://www.md5hashgenerator.com/MD5 is also case sensitive; therefore, using the very same letters, changing only one character to uppercase, the result of MD5 value would also be completely different. The closest example I can give you is fingerprints or DNS. Those are also unique, and there are no two people who have the same DNS or the same fingerprint. Hashing has been widely implemented, mainly used by software developers. One of the main reasons is making sure that the software is not modified or corrupted while downloading it personally, I had an issue before when I upgraded a Cisco Switch with a new code, which has gone into Rommon mode because I was too lazy to check the MD5 hash value of the software. Luckily, I was doing it within a test environment, and not in production network; however, it caused great pain and lost hours to recover the switch to its previous configuration. In my case I downloaded the code from the right source; but, it seemed to be that our Proxy server must have corrupted halfway. Still, if I would have checked the MD5 hashing value of the new code, I would have been more successful at the task. MD5 hashing is excellent; however, it is not called cryptography nor encoding. MD5 was implemented first in 1992, and if you think it's a little old, then you are right. MD5 has been compromised several times due to its vulnerabilities, alone it is not sufficient to provide the best security (Soze, 2019).

8. Ethereum

Ethereum is one of the oldest blockchain flavors and has provided platforms with a way to customize a system. Bitcoin aims to disrupt the current payment system and online banking with its own consensus mechanism, whereas Ethereum is in the midst of decentralizing the existing computer system since it works heavily on the client-server model (Gupta, 2018).

8.1 *History of Ethereum*

In 2013, Vitalik Buterin, a 22-year-old programmer involved in Bitcoin, first described Ethereum in a whitepaper. By 2014, a Swiss corporation called Ethereum Switzerland GmbH developed the first Ethereum software (Vujičić *et al.*, 2018). In June 2016, DAO (Decentralized Autonomous Organization) was compromised by an anonymous hackers group, sparking significant discussion in the crypto-community. This resulted the network to split into two groups: Ethereum Classic (ETC) and Ethereum (ETH) (Gupta, 2018). A simple visualization of Ethereum is shown in Figure 7.

8.2 *Principle of Ethereum*

Ethereum is a decentralized network that has the capability of running applications in a distributed environment. The idea is simply to avoid complete dependency on a single entity to store and manage a user's personal and business data. In the current database system, once data is stored online, the client has no information about how the data has been stored, what security prevention measures have been taken, who can read the data, and so on. Ethereum provides a platform to build distributed applications that connect each stock holder or party directly to achieve better transparency and zero dependency (Vujičić *et al.*, 2018). Even with the

Figure 7.   Visualization of Ethereum (Ethereum, 2020)

fundamental similarities between both Bitcoin and Ethereum, both notably differ in their purposes and capabilities. With Ethereum, any centralized services can be transformed into decentralized services with its unique programming capability (Maksutov *et al.*, 2019). There are basically three layers of Ethereum: the Ethereum Virtual Machine (EVM), the cryptocurrency ether, and gas (Gupta, 2018).

8.3 *Smart contract*

Smart contracts, in their simplest forms, are programs that are written to perform a specific execution by their creator. Although contracts can be encoded on any blockchain flavor, Ethereum is the most preferred option since it provides scalable processing capabilities. Ethereum lets software developers to code particular smart contracts (Gupta, 2018).

Smart contracts can be used to do the following:

- Streamline the procedure of claim settlement by spontaneously activating a claim when definite events occur.
- Manage agreements between users.
- Storing information about application such as health records and KYC information.

In Ethereum, each contract is given an address so that it can be uniquely identified. This address is calculated by hashing the creator's address and the number of transactions that have been performed (Gupta, 2018).

When we deploy a smart contract into a public blockchain environment, we get an address for our smart contract. We can now write code to interact with a specific instance in the smart contract. Contracts have standards such as ERC20 standards and it is also important to implement the required methods (Gupta, 2018).

Let's try and build our first smart contract. We will use Solidity to write the smart contract. The programming language Solidity is similar to JavaScript (Wang *et al.*, 2018). To start the process, we first have to set up the environment with the Ganache package, which will be used to create a private blockchain. Secondly, we need access to MyEtherWallet online, which can be found at https://github.com/kvhnuke/etherwallet/releases (Gupta, 2018).

Once the package has been installed, we can get started by going to the Ethereum IDE by using the link at https://remix.ethereum.org/ (Gupta, 2018).

8.3.1 *EVM*

EVM is a decentralized runtime environment for building and managing smart contracts. In Ethereum, with every program, a network of thousands of computers processes the data (Gupta, 2018). An outlook of an Electronic Voting Machine is shown in Figure 8.

Smart contracts are assembled into bytecode, which a feature termed EVM can understand and accomplish. All of the nodules perform this contract using their EVMs. As a fundamental definition, each node in the network stores a copy of the action and the smart contract's history of the network (Sathya *et al.*, 2019). EVM is responsible for executing a contract with the rules pre-programmed by the developer. EVM computes this data through stack-based bytecode, whereas a developer writes the smart contract in a high-level language, such as Solidity or Serpent (Gupta, 2018).

8.3.2 *Gas*

It costs a lot of energy when a smart contract is executed by every single node in the Ethereum network. Because consumption of more energy costs more money, it is also dependent on the level of smart contract programming. In other words, each low-level opcode in the

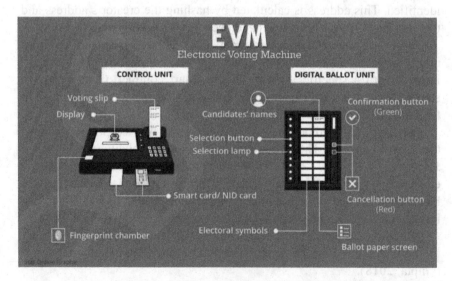

Figure 8.   Electronic Voting Machine (EVM)

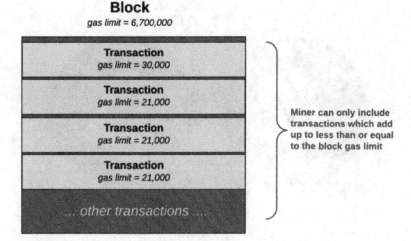

Figure 9.   GAS Unit Processed on the Ethereum Network (GAS)

EVM costs a specific amount of gas to produce its desired output (Gupta, 2018).

Gas just indicates the cost of performing a computation and helps developers understand energy consumption against their smart contract code. Like the Bitcoin market, the value of gas is determined by the market (Khoury *et al.*, 2018). If a higher gas price is paid, the node will prioritize the transactions for profit (Gupta, 2018).

8.3.3 *dApp*

dApp uses incentives such as crypto-tokens and inbuilt consensus mechanisms. A distributed application does not need to store all of its states; however, an Ethereum-based distributed application does store trusted states, and these results in an economical solution for end users (Gupta, 2018). Figure 9 represents a flowchart of GAS Unit processed on the Ethereum Network.

The dApp client is required to program the frontend, except the client interfaces with the Ethereum blockchain. The clients are often written in JavaScript because they can be run in a web browser, which most of us have (Gupta, 2018). A Schematic representation of Decentralized Application in showcased in Figure 9.

The dApp browser makes use of the dApp client, which is usually written in JavaScript, to interface with an Ethereum node that then

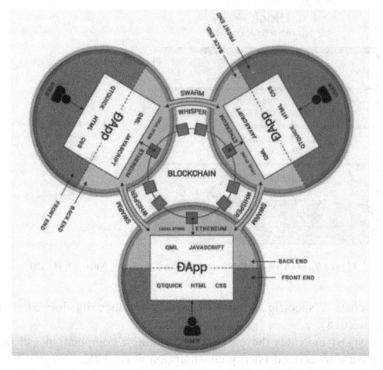

Figure 10.   Schematic Representation of Decentralizer Application (dApp, 2020)

communicates with a smart contract (Wessling *et al.*, 2018). dApp ensures a connection with the Ethereum node and provides an easy process to change the connection. It also provides an account interface for the user so that they can easily interface with these dApps (Gupta, 2018).

9. Bitcoin Mining

Bitcoin mining can be defined as a method of calculating the worth of cryptocurrency assets through a cryptographic procedure. These progressions mine Bitcoins in blocks, which are indeed simple ledger files which eternally record every latest cryptocurrency transaction. One should recognize that the magnitude of the block decreases with the increase in the number of coins. A block starts with 50 Bitcoin currency symbol (BTC), and as the quantity of blocks approaches 210,000, it halves. This results to a recurrent splitting of the bounties for a discrete block. This process is accomplished so that inflation proportion is planned. Otherwise, there could be an irrepressible number of paper money printing each and every second. This perception itself is evidence that mining is not an easy process. It requires investments in the form of time, computations and power. Also, with an increase in the time for mining these bitcoins, its comprehensive power requirements also increase. Another fact to note is that the speed of emerging Bitcoins drops exponentially (inversely proportional). Satoshi calculated the number to be roughly 21,000,000, which can never be surpassed. For example: If a block takes about 10 minutes to be mined, then a complete mining cycle halves every 4 years. So, it results in: 6 blocks for every 60 minutes. If we multiply it further by 1440 (minutes per day), 525,600 (minutes per year), and four (number of years in a blockchain cycle). So, we get: $6 \times (1440/60) \times (525,600/1440) \times 4 = 210,240 \sim 210,000$. After every 210,000 the block size is halved, and each block should have 50 Bitcoins. So, sum of all the sizes of block rewards becomes: $50 + 25 + 12.5 + 6.25 + 3.125 + \cdots = 100$.

So, the sum of coins that can be mined is equal to the product of 210,000 and 100. It is equal to 21,000,000. If we discuss about it in financial terms, the bit coin currency is dividable infinitely. Thus, a precise value for cryptocurrency coins can be disregarded until we can fix a limit, which is 21 million. There is no doubt that there can be a time when the number of bitcoins mined touches 21 million, and there is no more profit left until a way to redefine the calculations and new guidelines and regulations are identified. This process takes a while because; the yearly consumption of energy for mining cryptocurrencies (bitcoins) has been predicted to be around 30 TWh. This is equal to the steady energy of 114 MW for an entire year. Correspondingly, a discrete transaction of a Bitcoin can consume power used for supplying energy to at least 10 U.S. houses in one day. Certainly, it has been predicted that the power consumption expenditures for mining Bitcoins are high (Zhu *et al.*, 2017).

Also, the expenditures for the mined bitcoins surpass the charges of electricity and equipment consumed for mining. Less competent and cost-effective equipment will not be sufficient for the industry. This activity is financially reasonable, with increase in the mining activity. Figure 11 represents a visualization for Bitcoin. This indeed increases the investment required for developing challenging computation hardware's. In fact, the trouble in computations has increased to about 210,000,000,000 times correspondingly the overall mining capability for computations have reached to 1,500,000,000 hashes per second.

Figure 11.   Image of a Bitcoin (Bitcoin Gets Second, 2020)

References

Benčić, F. M., & Žarko, I. P. (2018). Distributed ledger technology: Blockchain compared to directed acyclic graph. In *IEEE 38th International Conference on Distributed Computing Systems (ICDCS)*. IEEE. Vienna, Austria.

Bitcoin gets second (or third, or fourth) wind by PYMNTS. May 14, 2019. Retrieved on April 19, 2020, from https://www.pymnts.com/cryptocurrency/2019/bitcoin-price-increase-digital-currency/.

Blockchain, (n.d.). Wikipedia. Retrieved April 18, 2020, from https://en.wikipedia.org/wiki/Blockchain.

Cryptographic hash function, (n.d.). Wikipedia. Retrieved April 18, 2020, from https://en.wikipedia.org/wiki/Cryptographic_hash_function#/media/File:Cryptographic_Hash_Function.svg.

dApp. blockchainhub.net. Retrieved April 18, 2020, from https://i.stack.imgur.com/jzm8y.png.

Distributed Ledger System. btxchange.io. Retrieved April 18, 2020, from https://btxchange.io/wp-content/uploads/2018/12/what-is-a-distributed-ledger-featured.png.

Ethereum. ethereumprice.org. Retrieved April 18, 2020, from https://ethereumprice.org/wp-content/uploads/2017/12/ethereum-price-fb.jpg.

EVM. artezio.com. Retrieved April 18, 2020, from https://artezio.com/wp-content/uploads/2020/02/evm-1024x576.jpg.

GAS. blockgeeks.com. Retrieved April 18, 2020, from https://blockgeeks.com/wp-content/uploads/2018/03/image7-3.png.

Gupta, R. (2018). *Hands-on Cybersecurity with Blockchain*. Packt Publishing Ltd. Birmingham, UK.

Hassan, N. U., Yuen, C., & Niyato D. (2019). Blockchain technologies for smart energy systems: Blockchain, challenges, and solutions. *IEEE Industrial Electronics Magazine, 13*(4), pp. 3.

Kaneko, Y., & Asaka, T. (2018). DHT clustering for load balancing considering Blockchain data size. In *Sixth International Symposium on Computing and Networking Workshops (CANDARW.)* IEEE. Takayama, Japan.

Khoury, D., Kfoury, E. F., Kassem, A., & Harb, H. (2018). Decentralized voting platform based on ethereum Blockchain. In *IEEE International Multidisciplinary Conference on Engineering Technology (IMCET)*. IEEE. Beirut, Lebanon.

Kuhn, R., Yaga, D., & Voas, J. (2019). Rethinking distributed ledger technology. *Computer, 52*(2), 2–4.

Maksutov, A. A., Alexeev, M. S., Fedorova, N. O., & Andreev, D. A. (2019). Detection of Blockchain transactions used in Blockchain mixer of coin join type. In *IEEE Conference of Russian Young Researchers in Electrical and Electronic Engineering (EIConRus)*. IEEE. Saint Petersburg and Moscow, Russia.

Marchesi, L., Marchesi, M., Destefanis, G., Barabino, G., & Tigano, D. (2020). Design patterns for gas optimization in ethereum. In *IEEE International Workshop on Blockchain Oriented Software Engineering (IWBOSE)*. IEEE. London, ON, Canada.

Mudliar, K., Parekh, H., & Bhavathankar, P. (2018). A comprehensive integration of national identity with blockchain technology. In *International Conference on Communication Information and Computing Technology (ICCICT)*. IEEE. Mumbai, India.

Peck, M. (2018). *Understanding Blockchain Technology: Abstracting the Blockchain*. IEEE.

Private versus Public Blockchain. 101blockchains.com. Retrieved April 18, 2020, from https://101blockchains.com/wp-content/uploads/2018/07/Public_vs_Private_Blockchain.jpg.

Sathya V., Arpan S., Aritra P., & Sanchay M. (2019). Block chain based cloud computing model on EVM transactions for secure voting. In *3rd International Conference on Computing Methodologies and Communication (ICCMC)*. Erode, India.

Siano, P., De Marco, G., Rolán, A., & Loia, V. (2019). A survey and evaluation of the potentials of distributed ledger technology for peer-to-peer transactive energy exchanges in local energy markets. *IEEE Systems Journal, 13*(3), 3.

Soze, K. (2019). *Blockchain: Novice to Expert*. Sabi Shepherd Ltd.

Stackoverflow. How permissioned private blockchain is differ from centralised system? Retrieved April 19, 2020 from https://stackoverflow.com/questions/53077649/how-permissioned-private-blockchain-is-differ-from-centralised-system.

Tonelli, R., Lunesu, M. I., Pinna, A., Taibi, D., & Marchesi, M. (2019). Implementing a microservices system with Blockchain smart contracts. In *IEEE International Workshop on Blockchain Oriented Software Engineering (IWBOSE)*. IEEE. Hangzhou, China.

Vujičić, D., Jagodić, D., & Ranđić, S. (2018). Blockchain technology, bitcoin, and Ethereum: A brief overview. In *17th International Symposium INFOTEH-JAHORINA (INFOTEH)*. IEEE. East Sarajevo, Bosnia and Herzegovina.

Wang, S., Yuan, Y., Wang, X., Li, J., Qin, R., & Wang, F-Y. (2018). An overview of smart contract: Architecture, applications, and future trends. In *IEEE Intelligent Vehicles Symposium (IV)*. IEEE. Changshu, China.

Wessling, F., Ehmke, C., Hesenius, M., & Gruhn, V. (2018). How much Blockchain do you need? Towards a concept for building hybrid DApp architectures. In *IEEE/ACM 1st International Workshop on Emerging Trends in Software Engineering for Blockchain (WETSEB)*. IEEE. Gothenburg, Sweden.

Yang, S., Chen, Z., Cui, L., Xu, M., Ming, Z., & Xu, K. (2019). CoDAG: An efficient and compacted DAG-based blockchain protocol, In *IEEE International Conference on Blockchain (Blockchain)*. Atlanta, GA, USA.

Yang, X., Chen, Y., & Chen, X. (2019). Effective scheme against 51% attack on proof-of-work Blockchain with history weighted information. In *IEEE International Conference on (Blockchian)*. Atlanta, GA, USA.

Zhu, J., Liu, P., & He, L. (2017). Mining information on Bitcoin network data. In *IEEE International Conference on Internet of Things (iThings) and IEEE Green Computing and Communications (GreenCom) and IEEE Cyber, Physical and Social Computing (CPSCom) and IEEE Smart Data (SmartData)*. IEEE. Exeter, UK.

© 2022 World Scientific Publishing Company
https://doi.org/10.1142/9789811225079_0002

Chapter 2

Blockchain and Artificial Intelligent for Internet of Things in e-Health

Geetha Velliyangiri[*,**], Vijaya Krishnamoorthy[†,††],
Chandra Inbaraj[‡,‡‡], Anbumani Venkatachalam[*,§§],
Robbi Rahim[§,||], and Manikandan Ramachandran[¶,¶¶]

[*]*Department of Electronics and Communication Engineering, Kongu Engineering College, Perundurai, India*

[†]*Department of CSE, Velalar College of Engineering and Technology, Thindal, Erode, India*

[‡]*Department of CCE, Rajalakshmi Institute of Technology, Chennai, India*

[§]*Department of Management, Sekolah Tinggi Ilmu Manajemen Sukma, Medan, Indonesia*

[¶]*School of Computing, SASTRA Deemed University, Thanjavur, India*

[**]*geethavelliyangiri@gmail.com*

[††]*Vijaya.krishnamoorthy@gmail.com*

[‡‡]*chandra.rajaguru@gmail.com*

[§§]*anbumanivenkat@gmail.com*

[||]*usurobbi85@zoho.com*

[¶¶]*srmanimt75@gmail.com*

Abstract

Blockchain technology has attained importance in the field of health as it overcomes the challenges in securing EHR (Electronic Health Records) as well as EMR (Electronic Medical Records) in eHealth systems. Distributed nature of the technology produces a single ecosystem of patient information that can be monitored more efficiently and quickly by doctors, pharmacists, and hospitals or anyone who diagnosis or gives treatment. Thus, blockchain provides faster diagnoses and plans to care personally. Blockchain technology is used to securely store digital health records and maintain the source record to protect and preserve the identity of patients. This chapter aims to integrate secure data from IoT devices to clearly understand the effects of blockchain in the real environment field. A novel blockchain approach is designed for eHealth and is employed to discover different ways of sharing decentralized view of health information and improve medical accuracy, health, and prevent health disorders.

Keywords: Blockchain, eHealth, Security, Electronic health records, Electronic medical records

1. Introduction

Blockchain technology is a peer-to-peer technology that provides a global consensus and assures that no one can alter or change previously validated transactions. Blockchain is a very good security solution but it still suffers from some problems especially when used by IoT devices. Blockchain is an IT system that allows a community of unreliable actors to validate transactions. It offers an unchanging, transparent, accurate, and auditable ledger (Reyna *et al.*, 2018). Once entered into the blockchain, information can never be modified or erased. It provides a transparent and verifiable record of each transaction (Crosby *et al.*, 2017). It is mainly a distributed archive containing all transactions or digital activities carried out and exchanged by the parties concerned. Blockchain technology has been the focus of many organizations and academics since it has offered numerous advantages over traditional solutions (Back *et al.*, 2014) as one of the most recent issues. In essence, a blockchain is a distributed, decentralized, and permanent ledger that preserves details of different transactions that have existed in P2P network (Khan & Salah, 2018). Any of the nodes should register their agreement to store a transaction in distributed ledger. This includes a system of consensus. Evidence of Stake (PoS) and Proof of Work are most basic and successful consensus processes (PoW). In the ledger, a set of transactions are compiled and block is assigned. For connecting block to previous block, a timestamp and hash function associated with each block is utilized. So, and given term blockchain, several blocks are chained together.

IoT is a new technology where, mostly without human interference, separate physical and virtual objects are linked and interact with each other over Internet. IoT systems are generally used to solve our daily challenges and to make our lives easier by detecting and capturing different forms of knowledge used to construct new digitized services about our local physical world. With billions of units sold and used internationally to date in many consumer markets, IoT has experienced tremendous popularity on an international scale (Atlam & Wills, 2019). The centralized IoT architecture, so that all IoT objects are connected, managed, and dominated by a central server, faces many challenges, considering the many advantages introduced by IoT systems in various areas. See obstacles stand in the face of future advances in IoT technologies as a hurdle.

There are several benefits of combining the IoT with the blockchain. For instance, the use of blockchain technology's decentralized and distributed characteristics will manage security problems and a single point of failure associated with centralized IoT structure. Also, blockchain has improved protection and anonymity, since blockchain uses advanced cryptographic methods, hash features and timestamps to offer a stable computing setting. Blockchain also gives a manipulative, yet immutable ledger which prevents data from malicious attacks, such that no change of data can be stored in blockchain only if it is verified by majority of contributing users (Karafiloski & Mishev, 2017). This in turn allows for a trustworthy scheme where only objects that approve or deny a contract based on their approval are the IoT devices participating (Reyna *et al.*, 2018).

About any realm of life is embedded in IoT. Intelligent healthcare is a crucial area in which IoT infrastructures and solutions are used widely. Through the use of wearable and mobile technologies, IoT-based smart healthcare solutions have enormously added value to the healthcare domain. This adds to a major use of the exchange of health data for strengthened, precise, and timely diagnosis. Smart health systems are nevertheless extremely vulnerable to numerous security violations and malignant attacks, such as privacy leakage, humidification, falsification, etc. The blockchain platform has recently emerged as a suitable solution to these abuses and obstacles.

Blockchain has been first used for financial transfers and cryptocurrencies where all nodes in blockchain network carry out transactions as well as store them. Blockchain is then incorporated into different fields because of the massive advantages it gives. The IoT scheme is one of these realms. Blockchain and IoT combination will offer numerous advantages for many IoT applications (Atlam & Wills, 2019). Meanwhile, since it is ideal for IoT implementations like hospitals, smart houses, smart communities, smart transportation, and others, the blockchain is decentralized and trustless. AI needs data and blockchain allows for encrypted data. Blockchain will help to determine the logic present in the algorithmic decision-making process.

The value of eHealth is its potential to provide patients, globally, with evolution of IoT and linked objects, access to their medical data and real-time health tracking. Therefore, enhancing coordination between patients and health providers means improving the efficacy of treatment and wellness surveillance, improving access to primary services and reducing the burden on budgets for public health (Liu *et al.*, 2017).

An eHealth framework should provide a method that can track any changes in medical data for patients. Blockchain is one of the most promising innovations that allow EHR credibility to be introduced. The actual reasons for using blockchain in eHealth services still need to be clarified. A program can provide transactional accountability to an individual's medical record (Rifi *et al.*, 2017) in broader eHealth networks composed of many separate systems operated by multiple providers.

2. Related Works

Tomasz Hyla (Hyla & Pejas, 2019): A blockchain-based eHealth integrity model was developed to ensure the integrity of information in eHealth networks using a licensed blockchain with off-chain storage of information. Unlike current solutions, the proposed model allows the elimination of details, which is a legal necessity in eHealth systems in many countries and is based on a blockchain using the Practical Byzantine Fault Tolerant Algorithm (PBFTA). The suggested blockchain paradigm is specifically utilized to incorporate a data-integrity service. Through other methods, this service is introduced, but a blockchain offers a solution that does not need trustworthy third parties, operates in a collaborative eHealth environment, and supports elimination of records.

***Kuo et al. (2017)*:** Traditional blockchain technology (bitcoin features) and its design are primarily addressed. Hence, the authors explain several blockchain technology aspects to the administration of patient history, insurance claims procedure, biomedical investigations, and medical evidence. Moreover, the authors have not clarified the technical implications of the structured dissemination of information.

***Stagnaro*:** Describe several examples of use of blockchain healthcare technologies. The usage cases are based in particular on interoperability claims, health records and supply chain management (SCM). Key drawback of report is restricting use cases and not tracking modern blockchain-based medical technologies in a restricted manner.

***Radanovic & Likic (2018)*:** The blockchain medicine technology, including medical care, HRDs, medication delivery, health science, acquisition and medical education has been reviewed. Similar to other surveys, several big blockchain-based healthcare technologies such as intelligent contracts, data sharing, interoperability, and cloud storage were not discussed in the paper.

***Chen et al. (2018)*:** Built a decentralized blockchain data sharing system through the design of secure cloud storage to the confidential medical records of patients. Medical records management is accomplished in this sense using a public archive and access to information ownership privileges for its owners. This is stored in the chain by the use of cloud encryption.

***Thein Than Thwin and Sangsuree Vasupongayya (2019)*:** Goal to handle these infringements and propose a Personal Healthcare Record (PHR) platform based on blockchain. The model proposed is designed to promote a tamper resistance function using blockchain technologies. To maintain anonymity, proxy re-encryption and other encryption methods are used. Fine-grain and versatile entry management, consent revocability, audibility, and tamper resistance are characteristics of the proposed model. A thorough security review reveals the proven anonymity of the proposed model and its deceptive resistance. The performance review reveals that in contrast with the current methodology the proposed model produces a higher cumulative performance. The suggested model is thus more fitting for the application of the PHR method.

Youssef Wehbe et al. (2018): present an EHR management system coupling AI-blockchain. The purpose is a forum for (i) stable EHR management, (ii) successful data integration, and (iii) accurate computer-based diagnostics, using both blockchain and (AI) artificial intelligence. The framework specifications are elicited by a target-oriented modeling approach with the Constrained Goal Model (CGM). Results of questionnaire for Abu Dhabi, UAE case study used for evaluation and perfection of the model to optimize number of device users.

Mettler (2016): Provides a quick overview of blockchain-based healthcare technologies. The research only covers three areas: public health, medicinal use, and drug counterfeiting. While report was first to provide a high-level analysis of new healthcare technologies of blockchain, it focused largely on the practical dimensions and advantages of such technology.

Genestier et al. (2017): A new concept was applied to reshaping health care consent management, which primarily allows users with the use of blockchain to monitor the whole health record.

Junaid Gul et al. (2021): Propose a smart healthcare business model focused on a blockchain that keeps patients in the business core. Our proposed business model of smart health will forecast the status of consumers and compensation under the company's regulations. However, corporations still demand something, and we are worried about data in wild in our case. Internet of Medical Things is our model that collects "data in the wild." This model will however be seen in any market environment in which there is a consumer award scheme. Our approach is more consumer and market oriented by leveraging technologies to promote consumers and other business members. As the business will decide the course of operation and make choices accordingly, this fusion makes business more successful. It is easy for organizations to modernize by integrating innovations into established market models, such as the "consumer-centered model."

***Sudeep Tanwar et al. (2020)*:** To increase data accessibility between healthcare facilities, an Access Management Policy Algorithm is proposed to assist in modeling of environments to incorporate Hyperledger-based EHR distribution mechanism that uses chain code principle. To produce better results, performance metrics in blockchain networks, such as latency, throughput, round trip time (RTT), are refined. The proposed framework uses blockchain to boost performance and security compared to conventional EHR systems, which use the client-server structure.

***Badr et al. (2018)*:** The blockchain has been used to boost patient data protection. They introduced a standard with various authorities to secure the privacy of eHealth data (EHRs) based on pseudonym-based encryption (PBE-DA). Also, blockchain was used as a step between IoT medical devices and healthcare systems.

***Zhang and Lin (2018)*:** Suggest a safe and privacy-preserving personal health information (PHI) exchange (BSPP) blockchain-based infrastructure for diagnostic upgrades in e-Health systems. Private blockchain as well as consortium blockchain are utilized in this instance. Private blockchain is responsible for PHI storage, while blockchain consortium maintains track of secure indexes of PHI. To connect new blocks to the blockchain, block producers must have a conformance test, which ensures device availability.

***Castaldo & Cinque (2018)*:** The study proposes a new solution to disruptive logging implementation: an audit framework for cross-border sharing of OpenNCP eHealth data, offering protection for traceability and responsibility within OpenNCP structure. Related parties may be legitimately obligated to maintain a list of all OpenNCP users' privacy-critical activities.

***Efendi et al. (2018)*:** Introducing an explanation of encryption using an asymmetrical key for protecting data from sensors to data lakes before being migrated to a shared, integrated blockchain system.

3. System Model

The proposed method is to integrate secure data from IoT devices to clearly understand the effects of blockchain in the real environment field.

A blockchain approach is designed for eHealth and is employed to discover different ways of sharing decentralized view of health information and improve medical accuracy, health, and prevent health disorders. Physical aspects of the human body, using modern devices to provide data for medical professionals, can only be utilized to verify patients' health issues. Blockchain is a type of data system utilized to build and exchange a digital transaction log between a distributed computer network. Blockchain's promise for healthcare relies on its readiness to help develop the technological infrastructure required by hospitals, clinics, and other organizations. Healthcare blockchain requires a way to persuade someone who needs it, everywhere, to find a patient's identity.

The dilemma is that health status information is extremely sensitive, and can only be reviewed by the patient, patient's family as well as medical officer. Interconnection with blockchain technologies of remote health networks is extremely probable. But the wellbeing of its customers should still be taken into consideration behind the ease of the advantages of this breakthrough of IT. A strategy of information protection is necessary to avoid leakage of patient data gathered by sensors connected to patient's

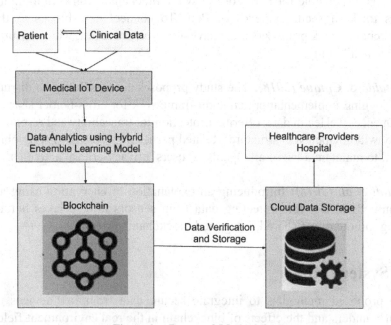

Figure 1.   Proposed Methodology

body, which are seen in Figure 1. One of them is to encrypt stored data of patients and is sent through public sources such as the Internet.

3.1 *Data analytics using hybrid ensemble learning model (DA-HELM)*

The hybrid setup approach can be described as the method of mixing multiple algorithms and techniques so that it can take advantage of the strengths and disadvantages of each technique. The method is multi-level. The proposed methodology consists of three distinct methods, including the self-organization map (SOM), the k-means and MLP, which are seen in Figure 2. This multi-layered method consists of three different techniques. First, soft clusters should be formed by intelligent clustering technique called SOM and secondly, the soft cluster is generated by the statistical clustering technique k-means.

Any new concepts such as soft clusters and parallel neural fusion are integrated into the solution suggested and these ideas are discussed below.

Soft clusters are classified as clusters with different faith in a class (e.g. disease). Soft clusters are generated based on the assumption that each class will have over one category called soft clusters in a classification problem. The integration of soft cluster effects into neural weight learning could boost the learning process and precision of the overall classification. Soft clustering concept is exactly the reverse of hard clustering. Both data in several clusters within a disease and within no disease groups would be clustered, though, for soft clusters.

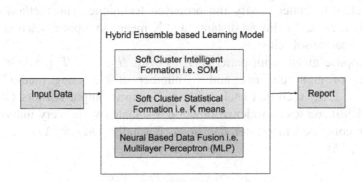

Figure 2. Multilayer Process

Neural fusion parallels mean that cluster output values are fed into MLP simultaneously from various clustering algorithms. The product is fused/merged into a single vector by feeding to MLP for data. Let $\{c_{11}, c_{12}, c_{13}\}$ be output values from 1st clustering method and $\{c_{21}, c_{22}, c_{23}\}$ be output values from 2nd clustering method. This is parallel combination to create an input to MLP.

$$\{c_{11}, c_{12}, c_{13}, c_{21}, c_{22}, c_{23}\}$$

The proposed solution, which consists of a merger of self-organizing diagrams, k-means, and multi-layered perceptron (MLP), builds features from a medical library into softened clusters utilizing non-supervised learning methods. Idea is to observe correlations in characteristics and merge decisions (by learning method) to classify strong clusters that can affect overall machine efficiency. In particular, the proposed methodology integrates several smart and statistical cluster algorithms which differ in searching and depicting methods to ensure diversity in errors of models studied. Based on a clustering principle, the suggested clustering method is formed: data (features) that are related to the same definition can be clustered. This theory explicitly implies the isolation of relevant data from non-relevant data with accurate algorithms of clustering. In fusion theorem it assumes that more like data a cluster contains more dependable cluster is in decision-making. This is understandable from the notion of neural cluster fusion.

In particular, each group algorithm presented in the ensemble introduces the whole amount of data. Each Algorithm logs combines and fuses soft clusters in MLP in parallel. An unsupervised clustering simulator is developed by utilizing the self-organization map and k-means clustering parameters to better clarify the proposed technique. The method suggested measures Euclidean distance and K-means in input cases and produces separate soft clusters.

Suppose given input patterns: $IP = \{IP_1, IP_2, \ldots, IP_n\}$, where n is number of input patterns, and c_n number of clustering methods Ai ($i = 1, \ldots, c_n$) such that each method A_i returns output clusters OC_i of IP which increases confidence function associated with every individual cluster contained in cluster decisions. Formally, $OC_i = \{X1, \ldots, Xk, X1, \ldots, Xk\}$.

$$f_c(OC_i(IP)) = \max\{OC_i(IP)\}$$

where OC_i indicates collective output clusters or soft clusters produced by A_i clustering algorithms. X_k indicates value of kth cluster. Soft clusters produced by Algorithm 1

$$OC_1 = \{X_1^1, \ldots, X_k^1\}$$

Soft clusters generated by nth algorithm

$$OC_n = \{X_1^n, \ldots, X_k^n\}$$

$f_c\{OC_i(IP)\}$ provides optimum dependency on the nearest similitude of the clusters with input attributes in each method to actual cluster. This study indicated that trust should be based on two grouping criteria: Euclidean Distance and k mean, as seen.

$$f_c(OC_i(IP)) = \max(\|IP = W\|)$$

where W is weight values of output units. Above Equation can be further refined as

$$f_c(OC_i(IP)) = \max\left((IP_1 - W_1)^1 + (IP_2 - W_2)^2 + \cdots + (IP_n - W_n)^n\right)$$

Input pattern is known to be the output unit with the least Euclidean distance. The confidence function is also known as for the k-mean criterion

$$f_c(OC_i(IP)) = \max\left(\sum_{i=1}^{k} IP - \mu_i\right)$$

where IP is vector space with k clusters of OC_i, $i = 1, 2, \ldots, k$ and μ_i is centroid or mean point of IP.

If $T = \{Ti, \ldots, T_k\}$ is target class (desired output) coupled with input patterns, then confidence function are distinct as

$$f_c(OC_i(IP), T_{i-k})$$

The output units are built almost twice as wide as input characteristics spaces for taking decisions from variety of soft clusters utilizing the SOM criterion. SOM consists of 16 neurons, separated into a 2-D grid of 4×4 neurons, in a single layer. Each partition is constructed and allocated to random input vectors (neuron weights). The Euclidean distance from each input was determined for each input. The minimal distance reference vector is calculated. Since the most related condition is found, all neurons in the neighborhood, linked to the same link, change their weight to a two-dimensional group about the reference vector. Whole procedure is repeated several times, lowering learning rate so that reference vector is increased before convergence takes place.

Input data is arbitrarily divided into k-cluster centers with all the nearest features in the k-means criteria. It determines the mean point of each function for each input function and creates a new partition by associating data entities to one of k clusters. The characteristics of the cluster are iteratively transferred between clusters of k and intra-country similarities.

At every step, distances are determined. Features stay in the same cluster until they move to a different cluster closer to it. After each step, the centers for each cluster are recalculated. When moving objects, the integration obtained increases inherent distance and dissimilarity decreases.

Let us have $x_1, \ldots, x_m$ are soft clusters created through the application of the proposed grouping criteria as shown. The decision-making by SOM and k-Means are seen utilizing the decision matrix: $X_1 \ldots X_m$

$$Decision\,Matrix = \begin{bmatrix} Y_{11} & \cdots & Y_{1m} \\ \vdots & \ddots & \vdots \\ Z_{n1} & \cdots & Z_{nm} \end{bmatrix}$$

where $Y_{11}-Y_{1m}$ represents number of class 1 clusters and $Z_{n1}-Z_{nm}$ represents number of class m clusters. In other words, the decision matrix is co-relation of classified patterns with actual soft clusters. $Y_{11}-Y_{1m}$ is output clusters that showcase that is classified as a Class 1, whereas $Z_{n1}-Z_{nm}$ clusters show cases that may belong to Class m. In decision matrix which is produced by individual cluster algorithms (e.g., SOM), every column (e.g., distinguishes strong clusters Y_{11}, Z_{1m}) of the matrix and the maximum value is evaluated and the respective class labeled depending on the majority vote. The evaluated column cluster is regarded as an efficient cluster for the related class. For both columns in decision matrix, procedure is repeated.

The results for individual clustering methods are then produced and transferred to the neural network for fusion after strong clusters have been established. Let C_{in} be output of i clusters from n algorithms and it is represented as.

$C_{i1} = \{x_{i1}, x_{i1}, \ldots, x_{i1}\}$ strong clusters output produced by Algorithm 1.

$C_{in} = \{x_{in}, x_{in}, \ldots, x_{in}\}$ strong clusters output produced by Algorithm n.

Neural network input is $I = (C_{i1}, \ldots, C_{in})$ and output is target value.

A single multi-layer perceptron-neural system has been developed and used for the Cluster Fusion with a backpropagation training method. For both groups, the device creates trust value. If there is data for 2 types, such as disease and no disease, so the outputs for disease and no classes of disease are determined after feeding input, and the method predicts the existence of disease depending on the output confidence value or not.

3.2 *Blockchain*

The blockchain private is a blockchain certificate where people are known to join. They are trusted in their industrial group or group of companies, for example, and certain authorization processes are not required. In certain cases, civil contracts replace them. Official regulators (MHRA, FDA, CROs) and conventional clinical data management systems will retain Blockchain's networks, that are private and approved such as Ethereum (Wood, 2014) and use these networks (CDMS). Cryptography and smart contracts enable data transparency and enable doctors to make safer decisions and have the ability to minimize the risk of patients on one hand and attempts to reduce the amount of data abuse accessible to financial health providers. Ethereum technology also shares networking between peer and peer that distributes it. This site even utilizes its Ether (Gupta & Sadoghi, 2019) cryptocurrency. You can exchange this cryptocurrency between Ethereum blockchain account (Chohan, 2017). Ethereum also offers programmers a language, which is known as solidity, to personalize their blockchain. It has been designed for smart contracts which are Ethereum's key feature.

The intelligent contract is known as the code feature which is used in blockchain tasks. This is the code when the transfers are submitted by the recipient (Atzei *et al.*, 2018). They run directly on the blockchain so that they are protected from both abuse and modification. Intelligent contracts typically use a vocabulary of solidity which can be used to program some form of operation on the blockchain by a programmer.

The use of massive databases is part of almost every transaction in health care. There are the drawbacks of files like imaging scans (PDF, TIFF, etc.). Where to keep files, how to pass and prevent third-party modifications or other changes. Through using the distributed infrastructure, blockchain solves this. It does not need data to be stored completely on the chain.

3.3 *Data verification and storage*

```
Contract between user and cloud = S_UC;
Contract between layers = S (UC layer);
Send data packet P contract S_UC;
Sink node receive and check P for S_UC;
if S_UC==true then Forward it to oracle;
  else Goto end;
end Oracle check and validate S_UC again;
if S_UC is validated then Forward packet to blockchain
and cloud;
else Goto end;
end End();
```

3.4 *Cloud data storage*

Master patient index (MPI) is a medical database (https://www.colleaga. org/article/implementing-master-patient-index). It comprises electronic records of each registered patient and offers information such as a patient's name, DOB, race, race, gender, security number, place of residence or other material in the history of the patient. Data on doctors and/ or other medical products can also be included. MPI means that only once each patient is represented. It also ensures that hospital data structures are continuously demographically classified. The organization that maintains the data will provide quality treatment for its patients if the MPI is structured properly.

4. Results and Discussion

This section discusses performance of proposed and existing methods. The existing method is PBFTA (Hyla & Pejas, 2019).

Figure 3 shows number of transactions for each of these cases and their association patient waiting list as estimated by our system is plotted. The X axis and Y axis indicate that the Specialty/Department and Number of patients on Waiting List, respectively. The Pro_DAHELM and Exi_ PBFTA indicates Proposed Data analytics using Hybrid Ensemble-based Learning Model (DAHELM) and Existing Practical Byzantine Fault Tolerant algorithm (PBFTA) methods.

4.1 *Accuracy*

It is most common evaluation technique to measure performance of Hybrid ensemble learning model. In the proposed method, it was calculated by using following formula.

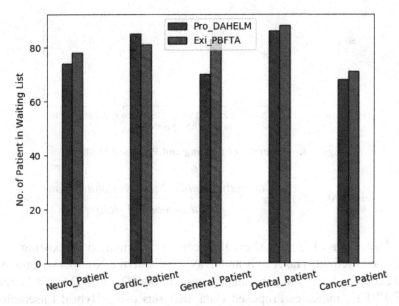

Figure 3.   Inpatients and Day Cases Across Different Departments/Specialty for Smart Contract Deployment

Table 1. **Accuracy of Existing and Proposed Methods**

Number of Patients	Existing PBFTA	Proposed DAHELM
50	39	42
100	48	56
150	55.7	68.2
200	69.1	74.3
250	74.8	80.8

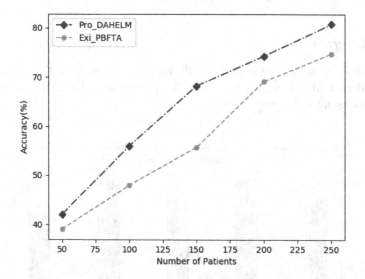

Figure 4. **Accuracy of Existing and Proposed Methods**

$$Accuracy(\%) = \frac{Correctly\ identified\ the\ availability\ data}{Total\ number\ of\ data}$$

Table 1 and Figure 4 show the accuracy calculation of existing and proposed method. The X axis and Y axis indicate the Number of patients and accuracy values in percentage, respectively. The Pro_DAHELM and Exi_PBFTA indicates Proposed Data analytics using Hybrid Ensemble-based Learning Model (DAHELM) and Existing Practical Byzantine Fault Tolerant algorithm (PBFTA) methods. When compared to existing method, proposed method shows better results.

4.2 *Root mean-squared error (RMSE)*

RMSE shows the error rate by variance and means between the predicted and the real one.

$$RMSE = \sqrt{\frac{\sum_{i=1}^{N}(PR - RR)^2}{N - 1}}$$

where, *PR* is the predicted rate, *RR* is the real rate, *N* is total number of Patients.

Table 2 indicates RMSE values calculation for existing and proposed method.

Table 2.   RMSE of Existing and Proposed Methods

Number of Patients	Existing PBFTA	Proposed DAHELM
50	21	18
100	34	22
150	56	43
200	69	58
250	81	66

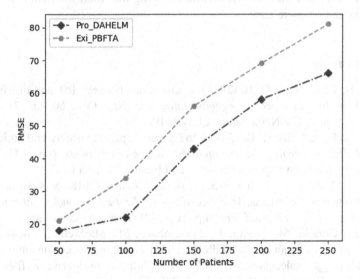

Figure 5.   RMSE of Existing and Proposed Methods

Figure 5 shows the RMSE calculation of existing and proposed method. The X axis and Y axis indicate the Number of patients and RMSE values, respectively. The Pro_DAHELM and Exi_PBFTA lines in the graph indicates Proposed Data analytics using Hybrid Ensemble-based Learning Model (DAHELM) and Existing Practical Byzantine Fault Tolerant algorithm (PBFTA) methods. When compared to existing method, proposed method shows better results.

5. Conclusion

In this chapter, proposed work addressed the existing needs of healthcare sector, shortcomings of current method, and proposed blockchain and AI-related IoT in eHealth. The proposed method is to integrate secure data from IoT devices so as to clearly understand the effects of blockchain in the real environment field. A blockchain approach is designed for eHealth and is employed to discover different ways of sharing decentralized view of health information and improve medical accuracy, health, and prevent health disorders using Hybrid ensemble-based learning model. For the proposed framework to build an iterative, distributed, open, and decentralized environment, uses blockchain technology. Patients can then openly and safely share their medical records with physicians, hospitals, research institutions, and other partners while ensuring that their medical history is kept under complete care.

References

Atlam, H. F., & Wills, G. B. (2019). Intersections between IoT and distributed ledger. In *Advances in organometallic chemistry* (Vol. 60, pp. 73–113). Amsterdam, The Netherlands: Elsevier BV.

Atlam, H. F., & Wills, G. B. (2019). IoT security, privacy, safety and ethics. In *Intelligent sensing, instrumentation and measurements* (pp. 123–149). Berlin, Germany: Springer Science and Business Media LLC.

Atzei, N., M. Bartoletti, T. Cimoli, S. Lande, & R. Zunino (2018). SoK: Unraveling bitcoin smart contracts. In *Proceedings of the International Conference of Principles, Security, and Trust* (pp. 217–242). Thessaloniki, Greece.

Back, A., Corallo, M., Dashjr, L., Friedenbach, M., Maxwell, G., Miller, A., Poelstra, A., Timón, J., & Wuille, P. (2014). Enabling blockchain innovations with pegged sidechains. Available online: http://kevinriggen.com/files/sidechains.pdf [accessed: October 13, 2020].

Badr, S., Gomaa, I., & Abd-Elrahman, E. (2018). Multi-tier blockchain framework for IoT-EHRs systems. *Procedia Computer Science, 141,* 159–166.

Castaldo L., & Cinque V. (2018) Blockchain-based logging for the cross-border exchange of ehealth data in Europe. In Gelenbe, E. *et al.* (Eds.), *Security in Computer and Information Sciences.* Euro-CYBERSEC 2018. Communications in Computer and Information Science, Vol. 821. Springer, Cham. https://doi.org/10.1007/978-3-319-95189-8_5.

Chen, Y., Ding, S., Xu, Z., Zheng, H., & Yang, S. (2018). Blockchain-based medical records secure storage and medical service framework. *Journal of Medical Systems, 43,* 5.

Chohan, U. W. (2017). Cryptocurrencies: A brief thematic review. *SSRN Electronic Journal.*

Efendi, S., Siregar, B., & Pranoto, H. (2018). Concept designs of patient information security using e-Health sensor shield platform on Blockchain infrastructure. In *Proceedings of MICoMS 2017 (Emerald Reach Proceedings Series,* Vol. 1, pp. 641–646). Emerald Publishing Limited.

Genestier, P., Zouarhi, S., Limeux, P., Excoffier, D., Prola, A., Sandon, S., & Temerson, J. M. (2017). Blockchain for consent management in the eHealth environment: A nugget for privacy and security challenges. *The Journal of the International Society for Telemedicine and eHealth, 5,* GKR-e24.

Gupta, S., & M. Sadoghi, (2019). Blockchain transaction processing. *Encyclopedia of big data technologies,* 366–376.

https://www.colleaga.org/article/implementing-master-patient-index [accessed: May 5, 2021].

Hyla, T. & Pejas, J. (2019). eHealth integrity model based on permissioned blockchain. *Future Internet, 11,* 76, 1–14.

Junaid Gul, M., Subramanian, B., Paul, A., & Kim, J. (2021). Blockchain for public health care in smart society. *Microprocessors and Microsystems, 80,* 103524.

Karafiloski, E., & Mishev, A. (July 6–8, 2017). Blockchain solutions for big data challenges: A literature review. In *Proceedings of the IEEE EUROCON 2017 — 17th International Conference on Smart Technologies,* Ohrid, Macedonia, 763–768.

Khan, M. A., & Salah, K. (2018). IoT security: Review, blockchain solutions, and open challenges. *Future Generation Computer Systems, 82,* 395–411.

Kuo, T. T., Kim, H. E., & Ohno-Machado, L. (2017). Blockchain distributed ledger technologies for biomedical and health care applications. *Journal of the American Medical Informatics Association, 24,* 1211–1220.

Liu, W., Zhu, S. S., Mundie, T., & Krieger, U. (2017). Advanced blockchain architecture for e-Health systems. In *2017 IEEE 19th International Conference of e-Health Networking,* Appl Serv. 1–3.

Mettler, M. (September 14–16, 2016). Blockchain technology in healthcare: The revolution starts here. In *Proceedings of the 2016 IEEE 18th international conference on e-health networking, applications and services (Healthcom)*, Munich, Germany, pp. 1–3.

Michael Crosby, N., Pattanayak, P., Verma, S., & Kalyanaraman, V. (2017). Blockchain technology. Sutardja Center for Entrepreneurship and Technology.

Radanovic, I., & Likic, R. (2018). Opportunities for use of blockchain technology in medicine. *Applied Health Economics and Health Policy, 16,* 583–590.

Reyna, A., Martín, C., Chen, J., Soler, E., & Díaz, M. (2018). On blockchain and its integration with IoT. Challenges and opportunities. *Future Generation Computer Systems, 88,* 173–190.

Rifi, N., Rachkidi, E., Agoulmine, N., & Taher, N. C. (2017). Towards using blockchain technology for eHealth data access management. In *2017 Fourth International Conference Adv Biomed Engineering*, pp. 1–4.

Stagnaro, C. White Paper: Innovative blockchain uses in health care. Available online at: https://www.freedassociates.com/ [accessed: April 24, 2019].

Tanwar, S., Parekh, K., & Evans, R. (2020). Blockchain-based electronic health-care record system for healthcare 4.0 applications. *Journal of Information Security and Applications, 50,* 102407.

Thwin, T. T., & Vasupongayya, S. (2019). Blockchain-based access control model to preserve privacy for personal health record systems. Hindawi, Security and Communication Networks, Article ID 8315614, pp. 1–15.

Wehbe, Y., Zaabi, M. A., & Svetinovic, D. (2018). Blockchain AI framework for healthcare records management: Constrained goal model. In *26th Telecommunications forum TELFOR 2018*.

Wood, G. (2014). Ethereum: A secure decentralised generalised transaction ledger. Ethereum Project, Yellow Paper.

Zhang, A., & Lin, X. (2018). Towards secure and privacy-preserving data sharing in e-health systems via consortium Blockchain. *The Journal of Medical Systems, 42*(8), 140.

Chapter 3

Data Management and Industries Automatization Using Blockchain, AI, and IoT

Krishna Kumar Vaithinathan[*,‡] and Latha Parthiban[†,§]

[*]*Department of Computer Engineering,
Karaikal Polytechnic College, Varichikudy, Karaikal,
Puducherry, India*

[†]*Department of Computer Science,
Pondicherry University Community College, Puducherry, India*

[‡]*vkichu77@gmail.com*

[§]*lathaparthiban@yahoo.com*

Abstract

The key technologies of future digital transformation are blockchain, artificial intelligence (AI), and internet of things (IoT). The importance of the value of data makes it inevitable to combine blockchain, AI, and IoT. The convergence of these technologies will create a unique path for new business design models. The IoT devices like sensors, machines, cars, trucks, cameras which are termed as autonomous agents will act as the future profit-making centers that (i) have the digital twin controlling IoT, (ii) use the blockchain technology to transfer money automatically, (iii) autonomously derive a conclusion like self-governing economic agents using data analytics and AI. It is further argued that the triple convergence will enable the creation of such independent decision-making business models, which will be the beginning of a revolution in industrial corporations. The transformation of the business models by using these emerging technologies is necessary to improve the quality of life of the people. In this chapter, we study the importance of the amalgamation of these key technologies that improve the privacy, scalability, security, authentication, and automatization of business data models. We also present various use cases of convergence of these three technologies for better understanding.

Keywords: Blockchain, Artificial Intelligence, Internet of Things, Tokenization, Supply chain, Agriculture

1. Introduction

Nowadays, Artificial Intelligence (AI), internet of things (IoT), and blockchain are identified as vital innovations that have the potential to enhance present business processes, develop unique business models that interrupt whole industries. For example, a blockchain can improve transparency, trust, privacy, and security of business model processes by giving them a decentralized distributed ledger that can be safely shared among trusted entities. The blockchain is a distributed ledger (Diedrich, 2016) that can save different kinds of digital resources/assets like the ordered data in a register. Predominantly, these assets can be associated with trusted identities and money. IoT enhances the industries automatization, and the ease of use in business model processes that is important for any industries all around the globe. Furthermore, the detection of unique patterns and business processes (Salah *et al.*, 2019) outcome optimization are the main tasks that are efficiently handled by AI.

Up until now, the integration of these three technologies is well implemented in few applications. However, these technologies can be combined efficiently and will be an important one in the future. One possible interrelation between these innovations could be that the IoT is the source of data, blockchain delivers the engagement rules and infrastructure, while the optimization of processes (Salah *et al.*, 2019; Zheng *et al.*, 2020), and data is done by AI. These technologies are complementary to one another and can reach their full efficiency if combined. The amalgamation of these innovations is very for the automatization of business processes and data management.

1.1 *IoT, blockchain, and AI*

For the past decade, blockchain technology is purely discussed in the payment perspective, i.e., bitcoin (Nakamoto, 2018), and ether. Recently, more non-financial applications like digital identities and supply chain management are developed using blockchain (Treleaven *et al.*, 2017). Now, the value of merging blockchain with IoT and AI is realized by new applications (Roeck *et al.*, 2020). For example, the IoT devices' infrastructure is improved using blockchain, The authors of (Huh *et al.*, 2017) outline that there is a significant improvement in the transaction speed by using blockchain in the infrastructure of IoT devices. Other studies combine AI with blockchain (Dorri *et al.*, 2017). Currently, the primary focus is on integrating blockchain with IoT or AI and not applying all the three simultaneously. Also, their true potential can only be realized when these technologies are combined. (Park, 2020) shows an infrastructure using blockchain with IoT and AI is very efficient and gives a non-technical summary of all the benefits of each technology and how they interact with each other.

A stable use case is very important to realize the power of the combination of IoT, blockchain, and AI. The ideas explained in this chapter apply to both private and public blockchains. The vital difference between public and private blockchains is that every user can access the public blockchain data, and only trusted entities can access the private blockchain data. In the view of the concepts explained in this chapter, the applications can be implemented irrespective of both blockchain data accesses.

1.2 *Data management*

Enhancing the standardization, security, scalability, and privacy of the data is very important in managing relevant databases of the industries business models. A vast amount of data is gathered by IoT devices like smart buildings, smart cars, grids, and sensors. The format of these data is not often standardized and saved in a centralized server. Multiple legacy systems which are commonly used in companies make it difficult to extract and identify cross-platform data. A trusted multi-party IoT data access is possible using blockchain technology by creating a harmonized platform of digital assets. The universal data format is the main outcome of the above-said combination. This is possible because of the blockchain hash functions. Furthermore, the interoperability (Karafiloski & Mishev, 2017) of the saved data is also significantly improved.

On-chain and off-chain data storages are the two main storage options for blockchain technologies. In on-chain storage, data is always present and can be extracted from any system. Here, the memory requirements are very high and it leads to blockchain bloating Which affects the scalability and throughput of the network. In the off-chain option, only cumulative metadata is saved on-chain which significantly improves the scalability of the blockchains. But the transparency of the data is decreased in off-chain storage.

Another important function of blockchain is the high degree of privacy provided by advanced cryptography algorithms (Zyskind *et al.*, 2015). The transactions are mainly carried out using pseudonyms. Also, some blockchains allow the transactions to be completely anonymous. The asymmetric cryptosystem (Leroy, 2017) used the blockchain architecture allows only the device itself to read/write the data. IoT devices and machines involve handling a large amount of sensitive information. Today, the cloud directly saves the collected IoT data. But, the privacy of the data is affected, as the data is unencrypted. The blockchain data is always privacy protected and is inherently secure by its design itself.

Furthermore, low hack risks are also an important feature of blockchain. The consensus protocol and the cryptography algorithms lead to a high level of data security. But there is a trade-off between the hacking activities control and level of privacy. The full anonymous setup of blockchain (Steger, 2017) leads to a situation where it is impossible to relate transactions to any specific party. Terrorist financing, money laundering are some of the common applications of anonymous blockchains. AI is efficiently used to identify prohibited activities and thereby increases data security. Yin *et al.* (2019) show that AI with data analytics can be used to reduce the threat of anonymity in data transactions. The IoT devices give a sufficient amount of data to the AI algorithm to train itself in reaching better decisions.

High data management is a major limitation of IoT. The scalability of the data is greatly improved by the combination of blockchain and AI easily. The alternatives of blockchain technology complain about the energy-consuming transaction validation mechanisms like proof of work (Li *et al.*, 2019) to affect the scalability of the blockchain networks. This issue is solved using other energy-efficient transaction validation schemes like proof or authority or proof of stake (Narayanan *et al.*, 2016).

The consumption of high energy is one of the issues in bitcoin networks. Also, AI can further enhance scalability when used along with the blockchain. A blockchain-based IoT network shows better optimization in scaling the networks. Higher throughput can be achieved by using deep learning/machine learning algorithms (Liu *et al.*, 2019). Dynamic selection of block producers, size, interval, consensus algorithm by deep reinforcement learning algorithm shows a good increase in optimization performance.

In summary, the inherent features of blockchain-like trustability, transparency, immutability, privacy/security improve the IoT data management capabilities when used alongside AI.

2. Identity Authentication Using Blockchain

The management of IoT network users is an important aspect of security and blockchain can be applied to verify them. Here, authentication applies to both IoT devices and machines. The blockchain provides a digital identity to every transaction for each user that is related to their physical identity. This helps improve the efficiency of the transactions between a user and the machine or between two entities, i.e., transactions with low cost and high speed (Zhu & Badr, 2018).

In the future, money transactions will happen between machines, devices, users, and companies. A 2020 IoT analytics (IoT Analytics, 2021) survey indicates that there will be 20 billion machines/devices connected to the internet. The payment system will also be partly integrated by these machines. Hence, a novel decentralized immutable infrastructure specifically is needed. The blockchain registers the digital identities of the users, companies, and devices. The vital role will be played by the identity management processing system of the blockchain.

The data protection policies have to comply when digital identities are issued on the blockchain. But the criticism indicating that the blockchain cannot inherently protects data by design is not valid. This is mainly because the blockchain innovation is integrated with access systems and encryption algorthims (Suliman *et al.*, 2018) which can provide data security, authenticate the data ownership, and effectively monetize the data.

An additional benefit is the immutable property of blockchain which makes it extremely difficult to forge the digital identity. For the independent interaction for devices and machines, the identity of these devices is very important and it is improved by blockchain technology.

2.1 *Automatization using smart contracts*

Apart from the advantage of managing data and identity, the amalgamation of three technologies by joining IoT, blockchain, and AI can help improve the automatization of business processes. Smart contracts can be efficiently used in connecting these three technologies.

Smart contracts are automatically executed and are defined by a set of rules (Szabo, 1996). These contracts are equal to "if-then" statements that execute particular actions if a specific event takes place. For example, consider the situation if in the case of sending of an item is successful, then the payment is directed automatically. Alternatively, these contracts can be used as an important connector for the three building blocks like blockchain, AI, and IoT technology.

Even though smart contracts have high potential, industrial companies are not using them effectively. Here, the main problem is the requirement of digital crypto-assets like Ether or EOS. However, due to economic and regulatory issues, industries are reluctant to use crypto assets.

One vital restriction is the high fluctuation in the value of crypto assets. If a smart contract is applied in Ether, then the exchange rate risk is higher at the receiving end. Also, the ether value may fluctuate by more than ten percent within a day. Although the high volatility issue can be reduced by the use of stable digital coins, industries or companies will not use them due to the following reasons:

- Regulatory issues of stablecoins. So unregulated coins will not be used by risk-averse companies.
- Industries/companies/accounting firms are mainly using regular currencies like Euro. Therefore, the conversion of stablecoins to their current currency will be seen as an operational burden for these companies. The conversion costs include both personnel and financial investments.

The only way to exploit the potential of smart contracts is to develop a blockchain-based cryptocurrency that is applied through the smart contract. The Euro smart contracts are only enabled by a blockchain-based crypto Euro. These contracts can be applied on a pay-per-demand basis for cars, sensors, and other devices. This blockchain-based crypto Euro enables the creation of new business process models like devices with autonomous decision-making capabilities using their own AI and doing financial payments using their blockchain and developing a profit-based logic at the device level.

The advantages of such a device-level-transaction-based crypto Euro are diverse.

- IoT devices-based micro-payments could be done with low transaction fees which will further evolve the IoT Technology.
- Each transaction done in crypto Euros will be added to the ERP (Enterprise Resource Planning) systems which are directly used by proprietary accounting and invoicing systems.
- Valuable assets can be saved, as there is no need to convert to system currencies (CashOnLedger, 2021; Monerium).
- Regulatory policies can be easily applied to these crypto assets.

As the uncertainty (Sander, 2020) in the regulatory policies is not applicable for blockchain-based crypto Euro systems, companies/industries can smoothly switch over to the blockchain solutions without any fear.

Central banks, e-money institutes can issue blockchain-based crypto Euros which are easily used for secure financial purposes. According to a survey of Bank of International Settlements (Barontini & Holden, 2019), it is noted that more than seventy central banks around the globe currently checking the feasibility of having their own CBDC (central bank digital currency). At present, no bank has yet announced its own digital currency. However, the Chinese and Swedish central banks are pioneering in this field and might introduced their own first central bank digital currency. Currently, the Chinese CBDC project is being tested in multiple Chinese cities, and also in a few Chinese subsidiary companies. To date, the CBDC has not been yet launched by EBC (European Central Bank). Nevertheless, European industries require a European blockchain-based CBDC to apply smart contracts with central bank-backed crypto Euro.

Here, the main question is why there is a need for the central bank-issued crypto Euro if the digital money issuers have a blockchain-based crypto Euro already? The detailed answer is as follows:

- The money provided by the central bank is more authenticated and secure than the money issued by other digital money issuers/commercial banks.

- Even if both banks represent the currency Euro, during bankruptcy, the money issued by the central banks is the claim of the central bank and therefore not go bankrupt, whereas the money of the commercial banks would go default.
- This difference is important to note at the time of crisis and it is non-relevant in times of economic stability.

3. Characteristics of Tokenization

The tokenization of sustainable infrastructure will help to solve some of the asset class's biggest problems, such as a lack of liquidity, high transaction costs, and minimal transparency.

3.1 *Lower transaction costs*

According to the Organization for Economic Co-activity and Development (2017), the normal guaranteeing charge for the first sale of stock (IPO) with a size of not exactly USD 100 million can be 9–11% in the United States. PricewaterhouseCoopers (2012) gauges that the endorsing expenses can run somewhere in the range of 49% and 60% of the general posting costs for this arrangement size. At the end of the day, the expense of opening up to the world can be somewhere in the range of 15% and 22% of the exchange esteem. This number may shift to some degree for recorded framework; notwithstanding, it is an unpleasant sign of the expenses related to getting to fluid public business sectors. As tokenization disposes of the vast majority of the monetary, lawful, and administrative go-betweens, the exchange costs are essentially lower. In light of the current arrangements accessible, the specialists talked with a gauge that the general charge for tokenization ought to be under 5% as the blockchain area develops.

Non-recorded land venture trusts (REITs) normally have a front-end heap of somewhere in the range of 10% and 15% of the exchange (Tokenestate, 2021). It is a one-time commission charged when financial backers buy the asset. This sort of charge isn't pertinent for tokenized resources, as financial backers can without much of a stretch purchase the tokens on a fluid auxiliary market. For recorded land speculation believes, financial backers need to pay the business commission for value exchanges. For bigger institutional financial backers, it tends to be pretty much as low as 0.20%; for retail investors, fees can arrive at 2% for the buy and 2% for the offer of the protections (UBS Switzerland, 2021). Exchange charges of token trades typically range somewhere in the range of nothing and 0.25%. For instance, the biggest crypto trade by volume, Binance, is charging 0.10% to retail customers (Binance, 2021).

Conventionally recorded protections need to go through a scope of mediators, some of which have a manual part associated with how exchanges are handled. This clarifies why our present monetary measures can't encourage limited scope exchanges in a frictionless way, barring retail financial backers from large numbers of the resource classes. Likewise, by taking out mediators, token exchanges additionally have a fundamentally lower counterparty hazard.

3.2 *Better transparency*

Smart Contracts can automatize foundation store the board far past the current arrangements accessible. They can convey productivity gains in tasks both at the level of the undertaking and the substance dealing with the resource. Smart Contracts can encourage customer revealing, gathering, and sharing information from the IoT gadgets, while improving straightforwardness, as examined further underneath. Brilliant agreements can likewise automatize monetary exchanges, including new approaching assets from financial backers, drawdowns, capital calls from financial backers, and reclamations.

Blockchain's fundamental guarantee of being a "trust machine" is that it can improve transparency and responsibility for framework projects by significant degrees. It can encourage and improve the observing of monetary, operational, social, and natural execution. The information created by the IoT gadgets, like brilliant sensors, can diminish the expenses related to the arranging and readiness of undertakings. It will make key presumptions utilized in project account demonstrating significantly more precise, including determining future incomes and expenses. This will permit supporters to diminish the possible costs that they need to save for development. Too, the size of liquidity and working capital offices can be lower if income and cost examples can estimate all the more precisely. These variables will add to a lower cost of financing and better generally speaking bankability of the undertaking.

By improving the amount and nature of data accessible, the resource will likewise have a higher valuation during its working life.

Financial backers anticipate that assets should sell for a markdown in 10 years if they are not on a blockchain. As for this situation, the purchaser would have to perform due ingenuity the conventional way, which isn't just expensive, it probably won't be pretty much as exact as what might be the situation for a tokenized project.

3.3 *Enhanced liquidity*

A framework is an illiquid resource class. Exchanges in elective resources are moderate and include an enormous number of mediators. Executing parties are needed to lead a long due persistence measure and go through a lot of desk work. In customary private gives, it can require a very long time to sell a position and cost about USD 10,000–20,000 to re-paper the exchange. Through tokenization, the liquidity of the resource class can be improved by significant degrees. It can empower the making of optional business sectors and dispose of the requirement for the lofty liquidity expenses as of now estimated by banks and different financial backers in the space. As indicated by Josh Stein, CEO of Harbor, the illiquidity markdown to the net resource esteem (NAV) of the asset is assessed to be 20–30 for each penny dependent on scholastic examination, however, actually, it can arrive at 40–60%.

3.4 *Access to alternative sources of capital*

Tokenization can swarm in the scope of non-conventional capital suppliers into a framework, including retail and other more limited size financial backers. The resource class is presently not open to noninstitutional financial backers because of the high least venture sizes, high relative exchange costs, and severe customer appropriateness prerequisites because of the illiquid idea of these speculations.

Tokenization empowers fragmentary responsibility for resource's worth and mechanizes numerous parts of the customer onboarding measure. This declines exchange expenses and makes more modest speculation estimates monetarily feasible for foundation reserves and different substances giving tokens. Tokenization in this manner improves financial backer admittance to framework projects both at the hour of issuance and on the auxiliary market.

3.5 *Less counterparty risk through decentralization*

Decentralization is one of the keys offers for most blockchain-based arrangements. The advantage of decentralized frameworks is that there is no essential issue of disappointment. In a monetary setting, this implies that there is less counterparty hazard, as frameworks can work without the need to confide in an outsider. Counterparty hazard is ostensibly the most noticeable danger in monetary exchanges. This can be seen by the business' dependence using loan appraisals. Through tokenization of framework, one has counterparty hazard as, on account of obligation, for instance, the borrower can in any case default on its obligation commitments. In any case, tokenization kills the counterparty hazard related to monetary go-betweens that executing parties ordinarily need to depend on account of conventional monetary exchanges.

3.6 *Increased transaction efficiency*

Optional market exchange of privacy protections can require weeks or even a long time to finish. For recorded protections, settlement times are typically three business days (T + 3), expecting that the exchange is coordinated and protections are conveyed with no postponements. As activities staff in banks can affirm, this isn't generally the situation, as it can require a few days of manual intercession from various gatherings to settle a solitary exchange.

The majority of the tokenization activities assessed for this paper depend on the Ethereum blockchain. At the hour of composing, the exchange season of the Ethereum blockchain is practically immediate, with a middle holding up to 27 seconds (ETH Gas Station, n.d.). As exchanges are executed on a peer-to-peer premise without a brought together clearing house, exchanges are constantly coordinated, and in this way, it is difficult to have delays in conveying the fundamental security token. Moreover, crypto trades work 24 hours per day and seven days every week, giving liquidity and empowering value revelation nonstop.

3.7 *Overcoming the limitation of small project size*

Admittance to modest financing is one of the fundamental boundaries of financing limited scope framework. Private wellsprings of financing are frequently not affordable under a specific task size because of the great exchange costs included. This is one reason why little framework projects need to depend on open financing and battle to draw in private capital at scale. Current activities to package these undertakings to expand the general ticket size for financial backers have had blended success. Small-scale projects frequently convey the most monetary and social effect per dollar spent.

By tokenizing limited scope foundation, due ingenuity and exchange expenses can be altogether diminished, as laid out prior. This empowers cost-productive packaging through tokenizing an arrangement of resources or even individual ventures.

If there is no base venture size, financial backers would have the option to develop portfolios with a quite certain sort of foundation openness. For instance, a financial backer should fabricate a portfolio, purchasing framework in city A, benefiting from a cost increment, and short selling foundation in city B, benefiting from a value decline. Tokenization can empower a new degree of portfolio development with the capacity to acquire quite a certain venture openness.

4. Challenges of Tokenization

Tokenization can be understood in its maximum capacity in financing economical foundation if the primary administrative and specialized difficulties are adequately tended to.

4.1 *Regulatory challenges*

The absence of administrative lucidity for tokenized resources is turning into a significant impediment for the more extensive execution of this new resource class. While a few purviews are moving quicker than others (Hassans, 2021), there is still a ton of vulnerability around key inquiries, for example, how security tokens can be agreeable with important monetary guidelines. This represents an issue for the entire monetary worth chain of computerized resources, including guarantors, caretakers, trades, and financial backers.

The test is to discover a system where the key incentive of tokenized resources isn't altogether decreased or lost during the time spent following guidelines intended for customary monetary instruments.

4.2 *Technical challenges*

There must be a confided approach to guarantee consistency between the on-chain tokens and the hidden off-chain resources. While shrewd agreements and programming consistently execute in an anticipated way, in our off-chain world there could be a scope of unforeseen occasions that should be observed and reflected on the blockchain as needs are.

As of now, most security tokens depend on the Ethereum blockchain, which has had some eminent accomplishments, yet also a couple of disappointments. There is still some reluctance among institutional financial backers about its unwavering quality, as by the day's end it is a work-in-progress item with a three-year history.

5. The Joint Perspective of IoT, Blockchain, and AI

From the previous discussion, it is noted that the combination of IoT technology with blockchain and AI can unravel novel business process models for the commercialization of IoT devices. An application to understand the discussed concepts is given below:

- Let us consider a street light that has its own blockchain-based crypto identity and uses blockchain-based crypto Euro to execute smart contracts. Here, the street light can be referred to as an autonomous entity working on its own. Micro-payments/transactions are made directly to the street light to switch it on for a specific period. The street light will be turned on when the entities like company/individual/public administration pay in crypto Euro. In this environment, pay-per-demand schemes can be easily implemented. A unique digital wallet is associated with the street light and it can be termed as its center for making profits. As all the street lights are interconnected in blockchain, they will save many details like usage, on-time, downtime, and performance. Optimization of network maintenance can be done using AI algorithms using the street-lights data stored in the blockchain. For example, AI could identify the street-lights that are often turned on and inform and dispatch the maintenance department in case of faults. Furthermore, AI can enhance the maintenance process by initiating the ordering process for replacing defective parts of the system or it can also predict the number of defective old parts for periodic replacement which will increase the efficiency of the overall system. This AI-based blockchain would reduce the down time of the street lights. These street lights are labeled as assets (IISD, 2019) which will be made available to the investors. The investors might be interested in a full-scale revamp of the street lights networks. These investors will receive the returns in terms of their share in street-lights profits. This use-case can be viewed as a potential gamechanger when compared with other conventional systems. This type of asset labeling might increase the investments, as the investor will get the money directly with a share for returning street lights digital assets. The advantage of this kind of labeling is applicable for all types of IoT devices and can be extended to multiple industrial applications. For example, interconnected devices such as cars, cameras, machines, and sensors are connected online with a blockchain network.

5.1 *Smart cities application*

5.1.1 *Infrastructure*

On a foundation level blockchain could be joined with AI and IoT to deal with the basic frameworks that urban communities rely on, just as mechanize measures and, where conceivable, make it feasible for these frameworks to all more effectively work working together with one another.

Take, for instance, energy and waste the executives. Here the blockchain layer could assist with secure information assortment from sensors took care of into an AI that decides about squander pickup and control, keen or environmentally friendly power energy, supporting the force lattice and the like. Blockchain could likewise help encourage P2P energy markets inside the city, in which people could purchase and sell their overabundance energy locally, assisting with making the city more independent. Such use cases are as of now live.

On account of new companies like GridPlus (GridPlus); occupants in Texas can purchase their energy utilizing a blockchain furthermore, an AI-controlled arrangement that purchases and sells energy locally at the best second and rate. Sensors, AI, and blockchain could likewise work together in improving public vehicles.

Through individuals counters or potentially blockchain-based online installment frameworks, just as different methods, the city would have a lot of ongoing information on open vehicle designs. This could be utilized by an AI to deal with the framework progressively just as to help organizers in planning upgrades and extensions.

We can likewise envision shrewd city upkeep frameworks depending on blockchain, AI, and IoT to robotize upkeep assignments just as plan and timetable preventive support work through shrewd machines. Since blockchains are by their tendency exchange stages, they could likewise be utilized to organize upkeep activities performed by people as well, giving a stage to approving the qualifications of sub-workers for hire, allocating assignments, offering for contracts, and paying for work done.

These three advances could assist urban communities with imaginative new methodologies. For example, they could help savvy urban communities "help themselves" by supporting self-streamlining frameworks through market-based learning draws near. Consider the accompanying situation. Soon, we accept that one element of keen urban areas will be armadas of self-governing, self-driving cabs (with the end goal of this model viewed as IoT gadgets). The individual vehicles could be furnished with a specific AI model advanced to boost incomes and limit costs. Yet to do so effectively, they should have information about fruitful systems on which to prepare themselves. We further accept that the best techniques will be those that streamline for the best quality help at the most minimal cost.

A blockchain-based information market would permit the vehicles in the armada to execute with each other, buying and selling their ride information utilizing tokens. The more effective vehicles could likewise sell their prepared calculations — their insight — to the others by means of the stage, and those fruitful models would then probably proliferate themselves through the organization. This thus could bring about a consistently improving taxi administration for inhabitants as the vehicles become more astute and more adjust to their customers' requirements and wishes.

5.1.2 *Quality of life*

For occupants, blockchain could cooperate with AI and IoT to add to personal satisfaction through, in addition to other things, more secure and all the more very much planned metropolitan conditions. For instance, they could help urban communities better get ready for and manage crises, like fire or outrageous climate, by consolidating AI-based observing and prescient displaying with self-governing crisis reaction through associated gadgets. Human specialists on call for health-related crises could be equipped with gadgets that entrance singular clinical records of casualties in a protection-saving way through a blockchain, improving the quality of first aid (Kamel Boulos *et al.*, 2015). A united framework could assist with metropolitan arranging also, with IoT sensors and different gadgets gathering on individuals and traffic designs, populace densities, foundation use, and so forth, and taking care of that through the blockchain to the AI which breaks down and make expectations for some time later.

Blockchain-based e-casting a ballot and resident interest platforms could make it simpler to include nearby networks and neighborhoods in metropolitan arranging too, giving a stage to social occasion input and maybe in any event, deciding on proposed projects. Blockchain-based stages could likewise be utilized to boost occupants to carry on desirably, for instance by offering compensations for utilizing public transportation or clearing up litter.

Public medical care and social administrations are another zone that could profit colossally from applying blockchain, AI, and IoT. This could be everything from more intelligent, more effective frameworks for privileges however utilizing information examination and man-made consciousness to improve the two administrations and medical services strategies (OpenLedger Insights, 2021). Such concurrent savvy city stages could likewise be utilized to improve personal satisfaction for inhabitants. To take only one model, we can envision a keen city-stopping framework. In this situation, IoT sensors convey data on free parking spaces. Computer-based intelligence investigates this data and consolidates it with current traffic designs and conceivably other significant data, similar to an occasion in the city that day that could prompt expanded interest for stopping and uses this to project accessibility. Utilizing a cell phone, an occupant inquiry the framework and gets a proposal on the best spot to stop at a given time and area. The blockchain would be utilized, as on the whole our situations, as the correspondences layer, yet could likewise be utilized to deal with a stopping reservation, "open" a parking space through a savvy lock and conceivably handle installment.

6. Agriculture

Figure 1 outlines the overall picture of blockchain, IoT, and AI in agriculture. While improving profitability under unfavorable environmental conditions, the agriculture sector has many challenges to overcome, such as:

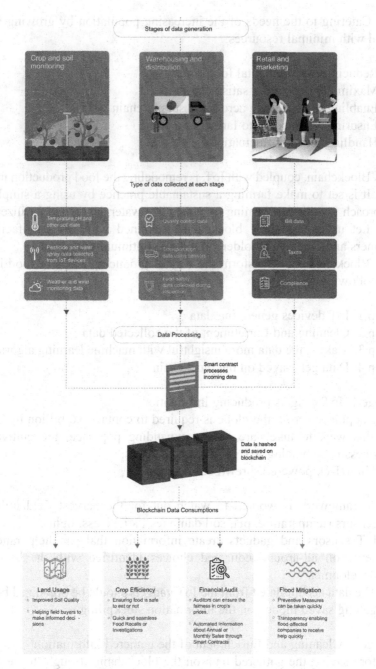

Figure 1. An Overall Diagram of Blockchain, IoT, and AI in Agriculture (LeewayHertz, 2021)

Catering to the needs of the increasing population by growing more food with minimal resources:

- Reducing environmental footprint
- Maximizing customer satisfaction
- Enabling transparency across the supply chain
- Ensuring fair income to farmers
- Handling weather fluctuations

Blockchain, coupled with IoT, is remodeling the food production industry. It is set to make farming a sustainable practice by using a simplified approach to optimize farming resources like water, labor, and fertilizers.

Let us explore how blockchain combined with IoT can facilitate farmers and other stakeholders in making optimum decisions.

Blockchain can transform the way of producing crops or food items by following four steps:

Step 1: IoT devices generating data
Step 2: Cleaning and Enrichment of the collected data
Step 3: Making the data more insightful with machine learning algorithms
Step 4: Data gets saved on the blockchain

Stage 1: IoT gadgets producing information
The populace across the globe is required to contact 9.6 billion by 2050. In this way, to take care of the expanding populace, the cultivating business is embracing IoT gadgets and sensors.

In IoT-empowered shrewd cultivating:

- A framework is worked to watch out for the harvest field utilizing sensors (temperature, pH, soil dampness, stickiness, light).
- IoT sensors and gadgets create information that can help ranchers settle on all-around educated choices identified with the harvests' development.
- The data accumulated from the IoT gadgets should be organized before getting saved money on the information stockpiling.

Stage 2: Cleaning and Enrichment of the gathered information
Before saving the gathered data on the blockchain, it ought to be organized and justifiable. Information Enrichment is done to enhance the

caught data to improve its quality. The accompanying two stages guarantee that the information is cleaned before it gets put away on the dispersed stockpiling stage:

- Adding Meta Information
  - To structure information proficiently, data identified with the accompanying ought to be added: timestamp, demography, and type
- Preparing information for consistence
  - Saving information on the blockchain makes consistent implementation more consistent.
  - Meeting consistency guarantees that the recognizable data related to the information gathered from IoT gadgets is ensured and follows safety efforts.

When the information is advanced, it is placed into the AI-prepared arrangement.

Stage 3: Making the information more astute with AI calculations
AI is applied to the information created from the sensors to give valuable bits of knowledge. Prescient models can drive a few high-esteem use-cases, including Harvest Quality Recommendations, Harvest Identification, Harvest Yield Prediction, GrowScore (Automated harvest development factor), Harvest Demand Prediction.

Ranchers and different partners will want to improve the water system framework now and then with the data caught through AI calculations.

The canny information ought to be put away on the blockchain to empower agribusiness market members like cultivators, trend-setters, makers, specialist co-ops, and retailers to get to it straightforwardly.

Stage 4: Data gets saved money on the blockchain
The high-esteem information assembled by applying AI is put away in IPFS (Interplanetary File System), an appropriated stockpiling stage with addresses hashed and put away on the blockchain.

The current technique for putting away fundamental data in the unified worker has a danger of a solitary mark of disappointment. Be that as it may, with blockchain, the information is circulated across each hub in the organization. Consequently, it forestalls a focal power to control the framework.

The data caught in the blockchain will trigger savvy agreements to handle rules characterized inside them. Savvy contracts encourage the trading of information put away on the blockchain with the particular partners in the framework. Since data will be noticeable to each agribusiness market member, it will get consistent to acquire productivity harvest or food creation.

After seeing how blockchain can improve harvest and food creation, we should examine what it can mean for the food store network.

7. Food Supply Chain

Food Supply Chain following is basic to investigate the food's source. It guarantees that the provided eatables are protected to eat. Yet, with regards to how the food inventory network is overseen as of now, it gets trying for the food makers and retailers to affirm its starting point. With the rise of the blockchain, it has gotten conceivable to acquire trust and straightforwardness in the food store network biological system, guaranteeing sanitation for everybody. Figure 2 represents the Bidding Platform for farming with Blockchain.

Blockchain food store network can decrease food fakes with the assistance of the accompanying advances:

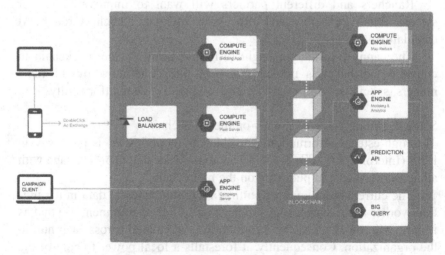

Figure 2.   Bidding Platform for Farming with Blockchain (LeewayHertz, 2021)

Stage 1: IoT sensors creating information or Farmers putting away information
Stage 2: Distribution of developed yields to the food handling organizations
Stage 3: Supply of Processed Food to Wholesalers and Retailers
Stage 4: Consumers can backtrace the store network

Stage 1: IoT sensors producing information or Farmers putting away information
As examined in the above use-case, keen cultivating permits sensors to create vital data identified with the yields planted in the fields.

Assume the rancher isn't utilizing innovation-driven techniques. All things considered, they can store fundamental data by utilizing their versatile application, for example, crop quality, sort of seed, climate conditions under which the harvests were planted. The information caught either by utilizing IoT sensors or physically by ranchers is saved in the circulated stockpiling stage, i.e., IPFS with addresses put away in the blockchain.

Stage 2: Distribution of developed yields to the food handling organizations
When the harvests are developed, the food handling organizations begin offering on the offering stage. The yields can be moved to the treatment facilities through IoT-empowered vehicles, catching temperature conditions under which they are kept and conveyed. After the bid is approved through keen agreements, the yields go through handling, and organizations store data caught at each progression of the interaction on the blockchain. The data assembled from treatment facilities can help wholesalers or retailers to affirm if the conveyed food is of acceptable quality or not. Putting away information on the blockchain can likewise guarantee if the consistency has been met at each progression of the food store network.

Stage 3: Supply of processed food to wholesalers and retailers
After the food things or harvests are prepared, wholesalers and retailers can offer the items they need through the offering stage. Like the transportation of harvests to the treatment facilities, food things are additionally dispersed to wholesalers and retailers in IoT-empowered vehicles.

The blockchain inventory network offers recognizability by aiding food organizations to lead food reviews or examinations rapidly and flawlessly.

Stage 4: Consumers can backtrace the inventory network
As subtleties are carefully connected to the food things inside the blockchain, buyers can investigate everything by backtracing the inventory network, for example,

- Ranch beginning subtleties
- Transportation subtleties
- Bunch numbers
- Food handling
- Plant information
- Termination subtleties
- Capacity temperature

The blockchain-based food inventory network can help various partners access data about the food's quality at each stage.

As blockchain acquires straightforwardness in the food production network environment, it will be simpler to sort out when and how food has been defiled.

8. Conclusion

The technologies AI, IoT, and blockchain can be connected in multiple dimensions. It is noted that a combination of these technologies will be applied to business process models and will help enhance their services. Multiple autonomous agents like cars, cameras, machines, and sensors can be applied with such business models. These devices can send/receive money automatically and train data analytics with AI to develop independent decision-making economic agents. This convergence will improve the creation of such business process models and the digitization of industrial corporations. To obtain significant profits, the executives should use these technologies. A novel digitization era can be forged with the combination of blockchain with AI and IoT. For the past decade, blockchain technology experiences tremendous improvement. The main criticism of blockchain technology is its restricted scalability and speed. This problem can now be resolved with crypto assets like EOS that can beat the present real-time transaction system in terms of executed transactions per second. However, other limitations have to be resolved. The integration of industrial legacy systems, data security with General Data

Protection Regulation (GDPR) policies are some examples of such problems. It is concluded that blockchain technology will evolve and address these limitations/shortcomings soon like resolving the scalability and efficiency problems.

The principal incentive of tokenization lies in its capability to diminish the expense of financing of foundation/infrastructure projects. Better terms of long-haul financing can influence the equilibrium toward monetary feasibility for projects that either needed to stay on the planning phase or depended on some type of derisking arrangements, regularly utilizing public assets, to get bankable. Despite the scope of potential benefits, the inquiry remains whether tokenization will have a broad appropriation for the framework in the coming years. Market members need to have total trust in the fundamental innovation furthermore, sureness about the administrative and lawful consistency of these new monetary instruments. Building this trust will require some serious energy and require numerous effective pilot projects. Blockchain has a few use cases for framework past financing that could be investigated in more detail. For instance, one zone to be probed further is how blockchain could bring straightforwardness to the resource class and how might affect the various partners included. Undoubtedly, having a huge measure of solid information opens up a scope of opportunities for all partners, including project supports, financial backers, and governments furthermore, neighborhood networks. Another squeezing question is the way the advantages and difficulties of tokenization would contrast in the non-industrial nation setting. While the utilization case for blockchain-based arrangements is the most obvious in these nations, they likewise will in general be the most prohibitive with regards to directing the space. One of the vital dangers of putting resources into the framework in agricultural nations is political danger. For instance, on account of capital limitations, benefits designated in nearby cash may be difficult to localize for worldwide financial backers.

Regardless of whether blockchain will follow through on every one of the normal advantages advocates guarantees, and undoubtedly will play a part in making a more comprehensive monetary framework, is yet to be seen. Nonetheless, this innovation is setting down deep roots, and it will be problematic. Similarly as with the Internet during the 1990s, how quickly market members incorporate this "trust machine" into the financing and activity of the blockchain foundation will influence their intensity for quite a long time to come.

References

Barontini, C., & Holden, H. (January 8, 2019). Proceeding with caution — A survey on central bank digital currency. [Online]. Available: https://papers. ssrn.com/abstract=3331590 [accessed: April 3, 2021].

Binance. (2021). Fee Structure on Binance — Binance. https://binance.zendesk. com/hc/en-us/articles/115000429332-Fee-Structure-on-Binance [accessed: April 4, 2021].

CashOnLedger. (2021). The payment engine for the machine economy. https:// cash-on-ledger.com/ [accessed: April 3, 2021].

Diedrich, H. (2016). *Ethereum — Blockchains, digital assets, smart contracts, decentralized autonomous organizations*. Washington, DC: Wildfire Publishing.

Dorri, A., Kanhere, S. S., & Jurdak, R. (2017). Towards an optimized blockchain for IoT. In *2017 IEEE/ACM Second International Conference on Internet-of-things Design and Implementation (IoTDI)*, Pittsburgh, PA, USA, pp. 173–178.

Es-Samaali, H., Outchakoucht, A., & Leroy, J.P., 2017. A blockchain-based access control for big data. *International Journal of Computer Networks and Communications Security*, 5(7), p. 137.

GridPlus. https://web.gridplus.io/energy [accessed: April 4, 2021].

Hassans. (2021). Regulation of blockchain business — A jurisdiction comparison. https://www.gibraltarlaw.com/insights/blockchain-regulation/ [accessed: April 4, 2021].

Huh, S., Cho, S., & Kim, S. (2017). Managing IoT devices using blockchain platform. In *2017 19th International Conference on Advanced Communication Technology (ICACT)*, PyeongChang, Korea (South), pp. 464–467.

IISD. (2019). Tokenization of infrastructure — A blockchain-based solution to financing sustainable infrastructure. Available online at: https://www.iisd. org/sites/default/files/publications/tokenization-infrastructure-blockchain-solution.pdf [accessed: August 5, 2019].

IoT Analytics. (2021). Industrial AI Market Report 2020–2025. https://iot-analytics.com/product/industrial-ai-market-report-2020--2025/ [accessed: April 3, 2021].

Kamel Boulos, M. N., Tsouros, A. D., & Holopainen, A. (January 14, 2015). Social, innovative and smart cities are happy and resilient': Insights from the WHO EURO 2014 International healthy cities conference. *International Journal of Health Geographics*, 14(1). BioMed Central Ltd. doi: 10.1186/1476-072X-14-3.

Karafiloski, E., & Mishev, A. (2017). Blockchain solutions for big data challenges: A literature review. In *IEEE EUROCON 2017-17th International Conference on Smart Technologies*, Ohrid, Macedonia, pp. 763–768.

LeewayHertz. (2021). Blockchain in agriculture — Improving agricultural techniques. https://www.leewayhertz.com/blockchain-in-agriculture/ [accessed: April 4, 2021].

Li, J., Li, N., Peng, J., Cui, H., & Wu, Z. (2019). Energy consumption of cryptocurrency mining: A study of electricity consumption in mining cryptocurrencies. *Energy, 168*, 160–168.

Liu, M., Yu, F. R., Teng, Y., Leung, V. C. M., & Song, M. (2019). Performance optimization for blockchain-enabled industrial Internet of Things (IIoT) systems: A deep reinforcement learning approach. *IEEE Transactions on Industrial Informatics, 15*(6), 3559–3570.

Monerium. Available online at: https://monerium.com/ [accessed: August 5, 2021].

Nakamoto, S. (2008). Bitcoin: A peer-to-peer electronic cash system. Available online at: https://git.dhimmel.com/bitcoin-whitepaper/ [accessed: August 3, 2008].

Narayanan, A., Bonneau, J., Felten, E., Miller, A., & Goldfeder, S. (2016). *Bitcoin and Cryptocurrency Technologies: A Comprehensive Introduction.* Princeton University Press, Princeton, New Jersey, USA.

OpenLedger Insights. (2021). The blockchain revolution in the governance of nations and cities. https://openledger.info/insights/blockchain-public-governance/#Blockchain_in_Networks_for_Public_Services [accessed: April 4, 2021].

Park, J. H. (2020). BlockIoTIntelligence: A blockchain-enabled intelligent IoT architecture with artificial intelligence. *Future Generation Computer Systems, 110*, 721–743.

Roeck, D., Schöneseiffen, F., Greger, M., & Hofmann, E. (2020). Analyzing the Potential of DLT-based Applications in Smart Factories. In Treiblmaier H. & Clohessy T. (Eds.), *Blockchain and Distributed Ledger Technology Use Cases*, pp. 245–266.

Salah, K., Habib Ur Rehman, M., Nizamuddin, N., & Al-Fuqaha, A. (2019). Blockchain for AI: Review and open research challenges. *IEEE Access, 7*, 10127–10149. doi: 10.1109/ACCESS.2018.2890507.

Sander, P. (2020). How will blockchain technology transform the current monetary system? Medium, Online. Available online at: https://medium.com/the-capital/how-will-blockchain-technology-transformthe-current-monetary-system-c729dfe8a82a [accessed: August 5].

Steger, P. (2017). *Blockchain — Die revolutionäre Technologie erklärt. Das System, ihre Anwendungen und Gefahren.* Amazon Fulfillment, Wrocław.

Suliman, A., Husain, Z., Abououf, M., Alblooshi, M., & Salah, K. (2018). Monetization of IoT data using smart contracts, *IET Networks, 8*(1), 32–37.

Szabo, N. (1996). Smart contracts: Building blocks for digital markets. *EXTROPY: The Journal of Transhumanist Thought*, (16), *18*(2), 28.

Tokenestate. (2021). Investing made simple — Tokenestate.io. https://www. tokenestate.io/ [accessed: April 4, 2021].

Treleaven, P., Brown, R. G., & Yang, D. (2017). Blockchain technology in finance. *Computer*, *50*(9), 14–17.

UBS Switzerland. (2021). The foundation for your investments. https://www.ubs. com/ch/en/private/investments/custody-account.html [accessed: April 4, 2021].

Yin, H. H. Sun, Langenheldt, K., Harlev, M., Mukkamala, R. R., & Vatrapu, R. (2019). Regulating cryptocurrencies: A supervised machine learning approach to de-anonymizing the bitcoin blockchain. *Journal of Management Information Systems*, *36*(1), 37–73.

Zheng, P., Zheng, Z., Wu, J., & Dai, H. N. (2020). Xblock-ETH: Extracting and exploring blockchain data from Ethereum. *IEEE Open Journal of the Computer Society*. 1:95–106 [accessed: May 5, 2021].

Zhu, X. & Badr, Y. (2018). Identity management systems for the internet of things: A survey towards blockchain solutions. *Sensors*, *18*, 4215. doi: 10.3390/s18124215.

Zyskind, G., Nathan, O. *et al.* (2015). Decentralizing privacy: Using blockchain to protect personal data. *2015 IEEE Security and Privacy Workshops*, 180–184.

Chapter 4

Using Frost Filterative Fuzzified Gravitational Search-Based Shift Invariant Deep Feature Learning with Blockchain for Distributed Pattern Recognition

S. Ilavazhagi Bala[*,§], Golda Dilip[†,¶], and Latha Parthiban[‡,∥]

*Research scholar, Department of Computer Science,
Bharathiar University, Coimbatore, India*

†*Department of Computer Science and Engineering,
Vadapalani Campus, SRM Institute of Science and Technology, India*

‡*Department of Computer Science,
Pondicherry University Community College, Pondicherry, India*

§*ilavazhagibala@gmail.com*

¶*goldad@srmist.edu.in*

∥*lathaparthiban@pondiuni.ac.in*

Abstract

Echocardiogram is the test which uses ultrasound to visualize the various heart-related diseases. In order to improve the pattern recognition accuracy, the Frost-Filterative Fuzzified Gravitational Search-based Shift Invariant Deep Structure Feature Learning (FFFGS-SIDSFL) technique is introduced. The FFFGS-SIDSFL technique takes the echocardiogram videos as input for pattern recognition. The input echocardiogram videos are partitioned into frames. At first, the enhanced frost filtering technique is applied to a frame for removing the speckle noise and increase the quality of image. Second, an optimal combination of the feature selection is performed by applying Stochastic Gradient Learning Fuzzified Gravitational Search algorithm. The fuzzy triangular membership function is applied to enhance the Gravitational Search algorithm. Followed by, the different statistical features such as texture, shape, size and intensity are extracted. Finally, the Gaussian activation function at the output unit is used for matching the learned feature vector with the training feature vector. The matching results provide the accurate pattern recognition. Experimental measurement is conducted for analyzing the performance of FFFGS-SIDSFL technique against the two state-of-the-art methods with different metrics, such as Peak signal to noise ratio, pattern recognition accuracy, computational time, and complexity with respect to a diverse number of electrocardiogram images. Based on this observation, the FFFGS-SIDSFL technique provides the better performance in terms of higher accuracy results than the two other existing approaches. As a future work, a distributed pattern recognition scheme that uses IoT with blockchain as event monitoring is proposed.

Keywords: Echocardiogram videos, Preprocessing, Enhanced frost filtering, Stochastic gradient learning fuzzified gravitational search, Gaussian activation function, IoT, Blockchain

1. Introduction

Human beings are suffered from the dangerous diseases such as cancer, heart blockage, kidney failure, and so on. Detection of such kinds of diseases at early stage is essential. Image is as critical part of medical diagnosis. Here, the heart related diseases are identified using the Echocardiogram. The echoes are transferred into video. The visualization of images captured from the heart varied for different patients. Precision recognition plays a major role in clinical diagnosis and decision making for providing the perfect remedy for tumor affected person. Echocardiogram is a highly developed system used to find the heart related diseases. In this work, pattern recognition is done to identify presence or absence of heart disease with the help of optimized deep learning classification technique.

A paired-views LV network (PV-LVNet) was introduced in Ge *et al.* (2019) using CNN and frame level feature extraction. However, the

PV- LVNet failed to achieve higher accuracy for clinical cardiac function estimation with lesser complexity. Neuro-Fuzzy GA was proposed in Kaur *et al.* (2019) for measurement of fetal growth using ultrasounds images. But the designed optimization algorithm was not considered the computational cost in terms of time and complexity involved in pattern recognition.

An artificial neural networks was proposed in Ghosh *et al.* (2019) for finding cardiovascular diseases based on the evaluation of echocardiogram parameters. But the optimal feature selection and extraction was not concentrated to minimize the time for pattern recognition. A CNN architecture was proposed in Madani *et al.* (2018) to concurrently categorize the echocardiograms images taken from the videos. But the filtering technique was not applied for accurate classification performance and minimizes the noise rate.

A mid-level image representation was presented in Penatti *et al.* (2015) for the classification of echocardiogram images. The Gaussian filtering technique was applied for the classification process to minimize the feature extraction time but the computational complexity was not minimized. A fully convolutional networks (FCN) was developed in Dong *et al.* (2018) to increase the segmentation accuracy based on feature fusion. But it failed to consider the end-to-end deep learning framework for achieving the higher accuracy.

A dynamic CNN was introduced in Yu *et al.* (2017) depends on multiscale information for increasing the segmentation accuracy. However, the CNN failed to perform the quantitative analysis of the performance metrics. Artificial intelligence (AI) technology was introduced in Alsharqi *et al.* (2018) to perform accurate diagnosis of heart disease by performing the feature reduction. The speckle noise removal was not performed to increase the performance of the disease diagnosis.

An automatically detect and diagnose system was presented in Balaji *et al.* (2016). The designed system performs the denoising to identify and diagnose the hearts affected disease. But it failed to use the larger dataset for increasing the efficiency of the system. A standardized evaluation approach was developed in Bernard *et al.* (2016) to enhance the segmentation accuracy with lesser mean square error. But the various performance discussions were not performed. An Echo state network (ESN) was introduced in Wootton *et al.* (2017) for performing the static pattern recognition task. The designed framework failed to perform the feature extraction for increasing the performance of classification.

In González *et al.* (2015), a Fuzzy based on Genetic algorithm (Fuzzy GSA) was designed to recognize neural networks. CNNs was developed in Ghorbani *et al.* (2020) using echocardiograms images to identify local features for detecting the local cardiac structures. But the designed CNN failed to offer accurate predictions. An adaptive group dictionary learning was introduced in Guo *et al.* (2017) for segmenting the fetal echocardiogram images. The designed algorithm failed to make a more accurate classification and segmentation.

A data-efficient deep learning models were developed in Madani *et al.* (2018) for classification of echocardiogram images. Though the model increases the accuracy, the time complexity analysis remained unsolved. An automated 3D echocardiography analysis of Left Ventricular mass using machine learning algorithm was designed in Volpato *et al.* (2019). The noise removal and feature selection process were not performed.

A Fuzzy-ANN was developed in Shakeel *et al.* (2019) to perform the echocardiography image segmentation. Though the network obtains maximum PSNR and lesser error rate, the accuracy was not improved. new method was introduced in Balajia *et al.* (2015) for identifying the heart muscle scratch from an images. But the designed method was not performed the feature extraction as well as filtering for detecting the normal or abnormal patterns. A two-step transfer learning method was introduced in Teng *et al.* (2020) using filtering technique with more images. The method failed to consider more training images. Encoder-decoder networks was introduced in Leclerc *et al.* (2019) for accurate segmentation of 2D echocardiography images. But the designed network failed to perform the segmentation with lesser computational complexity.

1.1 *Contribution of the work*

The contribution of the work is explained in the following lines,

- A novel FFFGS-SIDSFL technique is introduced to achieve accurate pattern recognition which includes different processing steps.
- In preprocessing, enhanced frost filtering technique is applied in FFFGS-SIDSFL technique to remove the speckle noise from the video frames. The noise filtering process increases the performance.
- In feature selection and extraction, Stochastic Gradient Learning Fuzzified Gravitational Search algorithm is employed to find the optimal feature combination and also extract the different statistical

features. The Stochastic Gradient Learning concept is used to find the best fit and worst fit feature combination for pattern recognition.

- The pattern recognition is done at the output unit of the deep structure network by matching the learned feature vector with training feature vector with the help of Gaussian activation function. Based on the matching results, the patterns are correctly recognized with minimum time as well as computational complexity.
- Finally, a number of experimental tests are carried out with the various related algorithms to discover the performance improvement of FFFGS-SIDSFL technique with the estimation of various performance metrics.

1.2 *Outline of the chapter*

The remaining chapter explains this method. In Section 2, the brief description of proposed FFFGS-SIDSFL technique is presented. In Section 3, experimental evaluation using electrocardiogram dataset and the parameter description are presented. Followed by, the parameter description and analysis are carried out. Section 4 provides the conclusions.

2. Frost Filterative Fuzzified Gravitational Search-Based Shift Invariant Deep Structure Feature Learning for Pattern Recognition

The proposed Frost Filterative Fuzzified Gravitational Search based Shift Invariant Deep Structure Feature Learning (FFFGS-SIDSFL) technique and feature matching is implemented in the shift invariant deep structure learning concept for pattern recognition. The proposed method initially performs preprocessing to remove the speckle noise which improves the PSNR and recognition accuracy. Then the fuzzy implemented gravitational search algorithm is employed in FFFGS-SIDSFL technique to perform the feature selection and extraction. This process minimizes the pattern recognition time. Finally, recognition is performed with higher accuracy with minimum time.

Figure 1 shows flow process of the proposed FFFGS-SIDSFL technique to improve the pattern recognition with higher accuracy. The input Electrocardiogram videos are taken from the database to perform pattern recognition. The construction of shift invariant deep structure learning

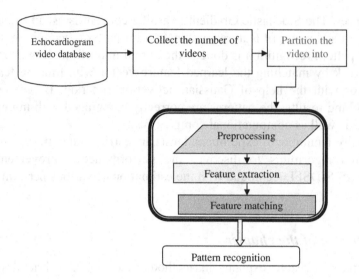

Figure 1.   FFFGS-SIDSFL Technique

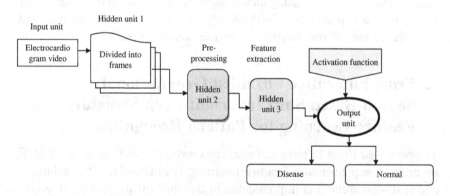

Figure 2.   Construction of Deep Structure Learning

framework is illustrated in Figure 2. Deep structure learning comprises the neurons like nodes. The shift invariant deep structure learning framework includes the cascade of several processing units such as input, one or more hidden unit and output unit. Each successive unit receives the input from the previous unit. The input is transferred from input unit to output unit by the means of multiple hidden units.

The construction of shift invariant deep structure learning framework is illustrated in Figure 2. The deep structure learning comprises the neurons like nodes. The shift invariant deep structure learning framework includes the cascade of several processing units such as input, one or more hidden unit and output unit. Each successive unit receives the input from the previous unit. The input is transferred from input unit to output unit by the means of multiple hidden units.

The Electrocardiogram video is the taken from the database and it given to the input unit. The Electrocardiogram video is partitioned into different video frames $f_1, f_2, f_3,..., f_m$ in the first hidden unit. The shift invariant system of the deep structure network is expressed as follows:

$$Z(t) = F(B(t)) \tag{1}$$

where, $Z(t)$ indicates a time-dependent output function of the deep neural network, $B(t)$ represents time-dependent input function, F signifies the transfer function. the input of the first hidden unit is transformed into the next hidden unit.

2.1 *Enhanced frost filter-based preprocessing*

The proposed FFFGS-SIDSFL technique starts to perform the image pre-processing using enhanced frost filter for increasing the peak signal to noise ratio. There are different types of noises appeared in images and it may cause the inaccurate pattern recognition. Therefore the proposed technique FFFGS-SIDSFL technique uses the enhanced frost filter to obtain the contrast enhanced image.

Let us consider the input video frames (i.e., images) $f_1, f_2, f_3,..., f_m$. The pixels $v_1, v_2, v_3,..., v_r$ in the input frames are arranged in the filter window.

As shown in Figure 3, the pixels are ordered in the form of row and columns v_{ij}. middle value of the kernel is taken by sorting the pixels in an

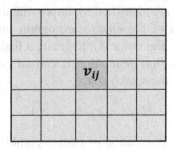

Figure 3.   5 × 5 Filter Window

increasing order. After arranging the pixels, the middle value is selected. In case of any even number of in the kernel, the averages of these two neighboring pixels are considered as the middle value of the filter window. Within the kernel size of 5 x 5, then the center pixel is replaced by adding neighborhood values in kernel. The enhanced frost filter is applied to eliminate the noise from an image.

$$D = \sum_{wXw} z \vartheta \exp(-\vartheta\, T) \tag{2}$$

where, D indicates the filter output, z designates a normalized constant, indicates the size of the filter window (i.e. kernel), is the coefficient of variation $T = (x - x_0) + (y - y_0)$ is the center pixel coordinates in the kernel. The coefficient of variation is referred as

$$\vartheta = \frac{\sigma^2}{\mu^2} \tag{3}$$

where, σ^2 denotes a local deviation, μ^2 refers to the square of mean. Finally, the noisy pixels in the filter window are replaced by weighted sum of values of neighborhood. As a result, speckle in electrocardiogram are eliminated to obtain noise free images.

2.2 *Stochastic gradient learning fuzzified gravitational search*

After performing the speckle noise removal, the feature selection and extraction process is carried out to improve the pattern recognition with minimum time consumption. applying the stochastic gradient learning Fuzzified Gravitational Search (SGLFGS), the best combination of the features from the input are identified for improving the pattern recognition accuracy. The features of the electrocardiogram image are texture (T), intensity (I), shape (S), and color (C) to create a feature vector.

Initially, the population generation is carried out with the combinations of the features in the search space.

$$C_i = (c_1, c_2, c_3, \ldots, c_m) \tag{4}$$

where, C_i indicates the population of feature combination. The combination is formed as follows $c_1 = (T, I, S, C)$, $c_2 = (T, S, C)$, $c_3 = (T, I, C)$ and so on. Among these combinations, optimal one is selected for accurate pattern recognition with minimum time. By applying the gravitational search algorithm, agents are considered as feature combination and their performance is determined by their masses. The mass of each agent is computed as follows

$$M_i(t) = G(t) * \frac{m_i(t)}{\sum_{j=1}^{n} m_j(t)} \tag{5}$$

$$m_i(t) = \frac{fit_i(t) * fit_{worst}(t)}{fit_{best}(t) * fit_{worst}(t)} \tag{6}$$

From (5), $M_i(t)$ refers to the mass of the agent "i" at a time "t," "$G(t)$" indicates the gravitation constant. From (6), "$fit_i(t)$" indicates the fitness of agent "i" at time "t," "$fit_{worst}(t)$," represent the worst fitness in an iteration at time "t" and "$fit_{best}(t)$" signifies the best fitness in an iteration at time "t." fitness of each individual is computed based on the how the feature combination is more suitable to perform accurate pattern recognition

By applying the fuzzy triangular membership function to the optimization, the best fit and worst fit is identified. By applying the fuzzy membership, each agent is associated with a membership vector μ which returns the value in the range from 0 to 1, representing how much an agent is fit for pattern recognition. The proposed technique uses triangular fuzzy membership function as shown in Figure 4.

Based on the triangular fuzzy membership function, best fit and worst fit are obtained using stochastic gradient learning as follows:

$$fit_{worst}(t) = \arg min\left(fit_j(t) \right), j \in 1, 2, \ldots, n \tag{7}$$

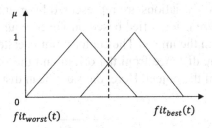

Figure 4.   Triangular Fuzzy Membership Functions

$$fit_{best}(t) = \arg max\left(fit_j(t)\right), j \in 1, 2, \ldots, n \qquad (8)$$

From (7), (8), arg *min* and arg *max* denotes a stochastic gradient descent and ascent function to find the minimum and maximum of a function. In order to obtain the better recognition accuracy, the best fitness $fit_{best}(t)$ is selected as optimal from the population. on the obtained results, the position "$p_i^d(t+1)$" and velocity "$V_i^d(t+1)$" of agent "i" in "d" dimension at time "t" is updated as given below.

$$V_i^d(t+1) = V_i^d(t) + \frac{F_i^d(t)}{M_{ii}(t)} \qquad (9)$$

where, $V_i^d(t)$ indicates the current velocity of the agent "i," $F_i^d(t)$ refers to the total forces that acts on agent "i" in a dimension "d" at time "t" and "$M_{ii}(t)$" represents the inertial mass of agent "i" at time "t."

$$p_i^d(t+1) = p_i^d(t) + V_i^d(t+1) \qquad (10)$$

From (10), $p_i^d(t+1)$ indicates the updated position of the agent, $p_i^d(t)$ denotes a current position of the agent at time "t," $V_i^d(t+1)$ is the updated velocity of the agent "i." this way, the optimal best features combinations are selected for creating the feature vector.

The texture feature provides the spatial representation of color or intensities which is evaluated as follows,

$$T = \frac{\sum_i \sum_j (v_i - \mu_i)(v_j - \mu_j)}{\sigma_i * \sigma_j} \qquad (11)$$

From (11), T indicates the texture feature, μ_i and μ_j are the mean of the pixels v_i, v_j and their deviations are represented by σ_i and σ_j.

The shape feature is identified based on the contour in which the center point is located in the image. The center point is called as origin of the image i.e. (0,0). The distance from the origin and the edge is determined to find the outline of the object. Here, the Euclidean distance is calculated to find the shape.

$$D = \sqrt{\sum_{i=1}^{n} [a_i - b_i]^2} \qquad (12)$$

From (12), the Euclidean distance between the point "a_i" and "b_i" are measured. Similarly, the exact shape boundary is identified and it extracted for pattern recognition. The intensity of the image is identified based on the difference between one pixel and their neighboring pixels in an image. Therefore, the pixel intensity is estimated as follows,

$$I = \sum_i \sum_j \left\| v_i - v_j \right\|^2 \tag{13}$$

From (13), I indicates the intensity of the pixels (v_i) in an image and their neighboring pixels v_j. Finally, the color feature is determined by converting the RGB color into the HSV (hue, saturation, value). Then calculate mean, variance and skewness of HSV is denoted as follows:

$$\mu_{HSV} = \frac{1}{m} I \tag{14}$$

where, μ_{HSV} indicates the mean of image block, I denotes pixel intensity, m indicates a total number of pixels in an image. With the mean value, the variance is estimated as follows:

$$\sigma^2_{(HSV)} = \frac{1}{m} \sum \left(I - \mu_{HSV} \right)^2 \tag{15}$$

From (15), $\sigma^2_{(HSV)}$ indicates the variance, I indicates the pixel intensity, μ_{HSV} denotes a mean of HSV. At last, the skewness is estimated as follows:

$$\gamma = \frac{\frac{1}{m} \sum \left(I - \mu_{HSV} \right)^3}{\left(\frac{1}{m} \sum \left(I - \mu_{HSV} \right)^2 \right)^{3/2}} \tag{16}$$

where, γ indicates the skewness. Based on the above said mean, variance and skewness, the color feature are extracted. With the extracted feature, the feature vector is created.

$$S(t) = \omega_1 * B(t) + \omega_2 * K(t-1) \tag{17}$$

From (17), $S(t)$ represents output unit at time "t," ω_1 represents weight ω_2 represents` weight of hidden unit, $B(t)$ represents the input, $K(t-1)$

denotes a output of previous hidden unit. At output, the pattern recognition is done by applying the activation function. The generated feature vector is compared with testing feature vector to identify the presence and absence of the disease from the electrocardiogram image. The output of the deep structure learning is expressed as follows:

$$Z(t) = \delta_F * \left[\omega_3 * S(t) \right] \tag{18}$$

where, $Z(t)$ indicates the output, δ_F is the activation function used to perform the pattern recognition, ω_3 indicates an adjustable weights between the hidden and an output units, $S(t)$ refers to the output of hidden unit. The Gaussian activation function is applied for feature vector matching at the output layer.

$$\delta_F = e^{\left[-0.5 * \frac{\|F_v - F_t\|^2}{d^2} \right]} \tag{19}$$

From (19), e indicates the exponential function, F_v indicates the feature vector generated from the image, F_t indicates the testing feature vector (disease or normal), "d" denotes a deviation. The Gaussian activation returns two binary results "0" and "1" as follows,

$$\delta_F = \begin{cases} 1, & F_v = F_t \\ 0, & F_v \neq F_t \end{cases} \tag{20}$$

The extracted features F_v are correctly matched with the testing feature vector F_t, then the δ_F returns "1" as an output. If these two features are not correctly matched and then it returns "0." Based on the matching results, the disease patterns or normal patterns are correctly recognized from the electrocardiogram image. For each output results, the error is determined to obtain the final predicted results,

$$R = \left[Z_a(t) - Z(t) \right]^2 \tag{21}$$

where, R denotes a error, $Z_a(t)$ refers to actual output of pattern recognition, $Z(t)$ indicates the predicted output of the pattern recognition. The adjustable weights between the input, hidden and output units are regulated and the process is iterated till the proposed technique finds the lesser training error in the pattern recognition with the electrocardiogram images. This in turn minimizes the inaccurate pattern recognition and increases the accurate recognition. The algorithmic description of the pattern recognition is illustrated as follows.

Algorithm 1: Frost Filterative Fuzzified Gravitational Search based Shift Invariant Deep Structure Feature Learning

Input: Electrocardiogram database, Electrocardiogram videos,
Output: Improve pattern recognition accuracy

Begin
    Given the Electrocardiogram videos into **the** input unit
      For each video
        Divide the frames $f_1, f_2, f_3, \ldots, f_n$
        For each f_i
          Apply filtering technique D
          Remove the speckle noise
      end for
    end for
    for each preprocessed f_i
      Find optimal combination of feature vector
      Initialize the population of the agents
      for each agent "i"
        Measure mass $M_i(t)$ and fitness $fit_i(t)$
        Apply fuzzy membership
        Find best fit and worst fit
        Select best fit arg $max \, (fit_j(t))$
        Update the velocity $V_i^d(t+1)$ and position $P_i^d(t+1)$ of agent "i"
in "d" dimension at time "t"
        Repeat process until convergence is met
      End for
      Return (optimal combination of feature)
End for
Extract the features T, I, S, and C to create a feature vector "F_v"
    If $(F_v = F_t)$ **then**
      δ_F returns "1"
      Learned features vector matched with the testing feature
vector

Else

δ_F returns "0"

Learned features vector not matched with the testing feature vector

End if

Calculate the error R

Update the weights $\Delta\omega_1$, $\Delta\omega_2$, $\Delta\omega_3$

Process is repeated until find minimum error

End

The above algorithmic process describes the effective pattern recognition. First the proposed technique starts to perform the image preprocessing for removing the speckle noise and enhancing the quality of image. After that, the optimal combination of the features is identified for pattern recognition. Then different features are extracted from input image. Then feature matching is done at output unit. Based on the activation function results, the normal patterns and disease patterns are correctly recognized.

3. Experimental Settings and Results Discussion

In order to estimate the performance of FFFGS-SIDSFL technique and the two existing classification methods namely PV-LVNet (Ge *et al.*, 2019), Neuro-Fuzzy based on Genetic algorithm (Kaur *et al.*, 2019) are implemented in the MATLAB using echocardiogram videos taken from the https://e-echocardiography.com/page/page.php?UID=1429484681. The echocardiogram images are used for conducting the experimentation taken from the Cardiac Motion and Imaging Planes. Initially, the input images are divided into number of frames with various sizes for accurate pattern recognition. There are four quantitative parameters are employed for analyzing the performance of proposed technique than the existing methods. The description of the various parameters are listed below,

- Peak signal to noise ratio P_{SNR}
- Pattern recognition accuracy
- Computation time
- Computation complexity

3.1 P_{SNR}

It is measured as ratio of the maximum pixel value to the mean square error. The error is determined based the squared difference between the size of original image before preprocessing and sizes of the image after pre-processing. The noise ratio is mathematically estimated using given formula,

$$P_{SNR} = 10 * \log_{10} \left[\frac{R^2}{E_q} \right] \tag{22}$$

$$E_q = \left[S_{AP} - S_{BP} \right]^2 \tag{23}$$

From (22), R^2 represents a Maximum possible pixel rate (i.e. 255). From (23), E_q is the mean square error, S_{AP} indicates the image size after preprocessing, S_{BP} refers to the image size before preprocessing.

3.2 *Pattern recognition accuracy*

The second performance parameter is the pattern recognition accuracy measured as ratio of correctly recognized patterns (i.e. disease presence or absence) from echocardiogram images to the total number of echocardiogram images taken as input for experimentation. The accuracy of pattern recognition is computed as follows:

$$PRecAcc = \left[\frac{CRecPatterns}{I_n} \right] * 100 \tag{24}$$

where, *PRecAcc* refers to the pattern recognition accuracy, *CRecPatterns* indicates the number of correctly recognized patterns from the images and the total number of images "I_n" provided as input. The accuracy measurement is done by the means of percentage (%).

3.3 *Computational time (CT)*

The significant metric in the results discussion is the computation time consumed for pattern recognition. The computational time of the three different algorithms are calculated as follows:

$$CT = I_n * Time \left[Pattern \, Recognition \right] \tag{25}$$

where, I_n represents the number of echocardiogram images and pattern recognition time is ms.

3.4 *Computational complexity (CC)*

The final metrics for the experimental evaluation is the computational complexity which helps to measure the amount of memory space consumed by the algorithm. The mathematical formula for measuring the computational complexity is expressed as follows,

$$CC = I_n * MEM \left[Pattern\, Recognition \right] \tag{26}$$

where, I_n represents the number of images considered for experimentation, MEM denotes memory consumption for pattern recognition. The computational complexity is estimated in terms of kilo bytes (kB).

Table 1 illustrates the simulation results of the peak signal to noise ratio versus size of the echocardiogram images with different sizes. The above comparison results demonstrate that the noise ratio is said to be higher using FFFGS-SIDSFL technique when compared to other two approaches. In addition, the FFFGS-SIDSFL technique decreases the

Table 1.   PSNR Comparison

Echocardiogram image sizes	PSNR (dB)		
	PV-LVNet	Neuro-Fuzzy based on GA	FFFGS-SIDSFL
5.7 kB	50.06	48.13	52.56
20.7 kB	47.30	45.85	50.06
18.6 kB	48.13	46.54	51.22
7.80 kB	50.06	48.13	52.56
8.10 kB	51.22	49.04	54.15
6.77 kB	51.60	50.40	53.01
13.4 kB	52.56	49.04	56.08
12.6 kB	51.22	48.13	54.15
11.8 kB	50.06	47.30	52.56
10.3 kB	48.13	46.54	50.06

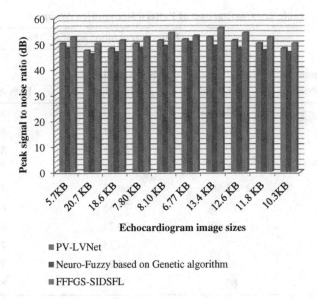

Echocardiogram image sizes

■ PV-LVNet

■ Neuro-Fuzzy based on Genetic algorithm

■ FFFGS-SIDSFL

Figure 5. Peak Signals-to-Noise Ratio Comparisons Using Three Methods

mean square error while preprocessing the input images. The various results are illustrated in the Figure 5.

Figure 5 illustrates the PSNR comparison versus various sizes of the electrocardiogram images. The input is given to the horizontal axis of the graph and the output is obtained at the vertical axis. The graphical illustration depicts the FFFGS-SIDSFL technique achieves higher PSNR. Therefore, to obtain the best performance of the proposed FFFGS-SIDSFL technique from the Cardiac Motion and Imaging Planes, the size of population, and the number of iterations were set to 10, respectively. The FFFGS-SIDSFL technique uses the enhanced frost filter remove the speckle noise from the input images using kernel approach. The noisy center pixel in the filtering window are replaced and removing the noisy pixels. These processes of FFFGS-SIDSFL technique enhance the image quality and improve peak SNR. The comparison of three methods proves that the average PSNR is significantly increased by 5% than the PV-LVNet (Ge *et al.*, 2019) and also improved by 10% when compared to Neuro-Fuzzy based on Genetic algorithm (Kaur *et al.*, 2019) respectively.

The comparison of three different methods PV-LVNet (Ge *et al.*, 2019), Neuro-Fuzzy based on Genetic algorithm (Kaur *et al.*, 2019) and

Table 2. Comparison of Pattern Recognition Accuracy

Echocardiogram images (numbers)	Pattern recognition accuracy (%)		
	PV-LVNet	Neuro-Fuzzy based on Genetic algorithm	FFFGS-SIDSFL
15	80	73.33	86.66
30	76.66	75.35	83.33
45	77.77	74.25	84.44
60	73.33	70.15	76.66
75	74.66	68.55	80
90	77.77	71.35	82.22
105	76.19	70.25	80
120	75	69.55	78.33
135	72.59	65.25	77.03
150	80	70.15	85.33

FFFGS-SIDSFL technique is illustrated in Table 2. For the better comparison, the various counts of echocardiogram images are taken as input in the ranges from 15, 30, 45, ..., 150. For the similar counts of input images, three various accuracy results are obtained as shown in Table 2. Let us consider the 15 images for conducting the experimentation. Among the 15 images, 13 images are correctly recognized as a disease presence or absence by applying a FFFGS-SIDSFL technique and their accuracy is obtained as 86.66%. The accuracy of PV-LVNet (Ge *et al.*, 2019), Neuro-Fuzzy based on Genetic algorithm (Kaur *et al.*, 2019) are 73.33% and 80% respectively. The above statistical discussion accurately confirms that the proposed technique obtain higher accuracy of pattern recognition. This improvement is achieved by applying the shift invariant deep structure learning concept. The activation function used in the output unit of the deep neural network for matching the learned feature vector with the testing feature. The matching results used to accurately determine the disease patterns or normal patterns from the echocardiogram images. The proposed FFFGS-SIDSFL technique outperforms the existing method, with the average pattern recognition accuracy increased by 7% and 15%. The proposed method uses the deep feature learning concept and deeply learns the features. The graphical illustration of the pattern recognition accuracy of three methods is shown in Figure 6.

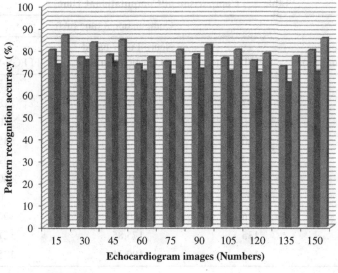

PV-LVNet
Neuro-Fuzzy based on Genetic algorithm
FFFGS-SIDSFL

Figure 6. Pattern Recognition Accuracy Comparisons

Figure 6 demonstrates the pattern recognition accuracy comparison versus various input images. From the above graphical representation, the accuracy of three methods is illustrated in three colors. It is observed from the Figure 6 that the FFFGS-SIDSFL technique achieves the highest performance among the other two methods.

Table 3 and Figure 7 depict the performance comparison of the computational time using three different methods namely PV-LVNet (Ge *et al.*, 2019), Neuro-Fuzzy based on Genetic algorithm (Kaur *et al.*, 2019) and FFFGS-SIDSFL technique. As shown in Table 3 and Figure 7, the computational time of all the methods gets increased while increasing the number of input images. But comparatively, the proposed FFFGS-SIDSFL technique outperforms the pattern recognition, with estimating 150 more images. FFFGS-SIDSFL technique significantly decreases the computational time by means of applying the stochastic gradient learnt fuzzified gravitational search to select the optimal combination of the feature and perform feature extraction. The fuzzy triangular membership function is applied to find best fittest feature combination and also

Table 3.　Comparison of Computational Time

Echocardiogram image (Numbers)	Computational time (ms)		
	PV-LVNet	Neuro-Fuzzy based on Genetic algorithm	FFFGS-SIDSFL
15	16.5	20.25	13.5
30	27	45.55	18
45	40.5	68.35	30.6
60	60	75.55	45
75	67.5	95.25	52.5
90	85.5	105.35	60.3
105	93.45	135.55	70.35
120	116.4	150.55	96
135	135	175.85	121.5
150	162	190.35	135

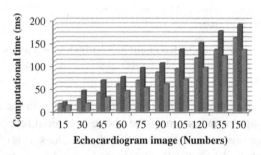

Figure 7.　Performance Comparison of Computational Time

extracts the texture, pixel intensity, color and shape. With the extracted features, the feature vector is created for accurate pattern recognition with lesser time consumption. Besides, the image preprocessing also minimizes the pattern recognition time. As a result, the comparison of three methods illustrates that the computational time is said to be minimized by 22% when compared to the PV-LVNet (Ge *et al.*, 2019) and also reduced by 42% than the Neuro-Fuzzy based on Genetic algorithm (Kaur *et al.*, 2019).

The comparison results of computational complexity of three methods are reported in Table 4. It shows that, among the three methods, the FFFGS-SIDSFL technique performs the best with the number of echocardiogram images. The computational complexities of the three methods are illustrated in Figure 8.

Figure 8 shows the computational complexity of the algorithms including PV-LVNet (Ge *et al.*, 2019), Neuro-Fuzzy based on Genetic

Table 4. Comparison of Computational Complexity

Echocardiogram image (Numbers)	Computational Complexity (KB)		
	PV-LVNet	Neuro-Fuzzy based on Genetic algorithm	FFFGS-SIDSFL
15	255	375	225
30	480	730	390
45	765	855	630
60	1020	1135	840
75	1125	1450	975
90	1260	1580	1080
105	1365	1735	1155
120	1680	1955	1320
135	2160	2535	1755
150	2700	3015	1950

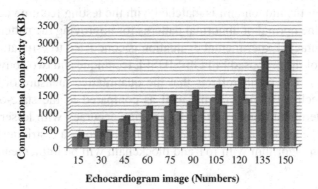

■ PV-LVNet
■ Neuro-Fuzzy based on Genetic algorithm
■ FFFGS-SIDSFL

Figure 8.   Performance Comparison of Computational Complexity

algorithm (Kaur *et al.*, 2019) and FFFGS-SIDSFL technique. Figure 7 graphically depict comparisons among FFFGS-SIDSFL technique versus the other two methods in terms of computational complexity. This significant improvement of FFFGS-SIDSFL technique is achieved by removing the speckle noise from the input image. The noisy pixels in an image have more space for pattern recognition. The proposed technique uses the frames for pattern recognition instead of using the whole videos taken from the echocardiogram database. The memory consumed for pattern recognition includes measuring the best fit and worst fit with the help of the fuzzy triangular membership function. The average of ten results for each method indicates that the computational complexity is found to be minimized using FFFGS-SIDSFL technique by 18% and 34% when compared to PV-LVNet (Ge *et al.*, 2019), Neuro-Fuzzy based on Genetic algorithm (Kaur *et al.*, 2019), respectively.

4. Conclusion

In this chapter, a novel FFFGS-SIDSFL technique is introduced for the capable of providing accurate pattern recognition and higher PSNR with lesser time as well as complexity using echocardiogram image. First, in this FFFGS-SIDSFL technique, eliminate the speckle noises from the input video frames based on the filtering window concept. Next, with the preprocessed image, optimal feature combination is selected and perform the feature extraction for better recognition. Finally, with the learned feature vector from the hidden unit is matched with the testing feature vectors and identifies the normal or abnormal patterns for improving the pattern recognition accuracy. Experimental evaluation is conducted to estimate the performance of the proposed FFFGS-SIDSFL technique and two conventional approaches. The result reflects that the quantitative measure of FFFGS-SIDSFL technique outperforms well as compared to the state-of-the-art works in terms of higher pattern recognition accuracy with lesser computational time as well as complexity. As a future work, a distributed pattern recognition algorithm with IoT and blockchain will be implemented.

References

Alsharqi, M., Woodward, W. J., Mumith, J. A., Markham, D. C., Upton, R., & Leeson, P. (2018). Artificial intelligence and echocardiography. *Echo Research and Practice*, 5(4), 115–125.

Balaji, G. N., Subashini, T. S., & Chidambaram, N. (2015). Detection of heart muscle damage from automated analysis of echocardiogram video. *IETE Journal of Research, 61*(3), 1–8.

Balaji, G. N., Subashini, T. S., & Chidambaram, N. (2016). Detection and diagnosis of dilated cardiomyopathy and hypertrophic cardiomyopathy using image processing techniques. *Engineering Science and Technology, An International Journal, 19,* 1871–1880.

Bernard, O., Bosch, J. G., Heyde, B., Alessandrini, M., Barbosa, D., Camarasu-Pop, S., Cervenansky, F., Valette, S., Mirea, O., Bernier, M., Jodoin, P. M., Domingos, J. S., Stebbing, R. V., Keraudren, K., Oktay, O., Caballero, J., Shi, W., Rueckert, D., Milletari, F., Ahmadi, S. A., Smistad, E., Lindseth, F., van Stralen, M., Wang, C., Smedby, O., Donal, E., Monaghan, M., Papachristidis, A., Geleijnse, M. L., Galli, E., & D'hooge, J. (2016). Standardized evaluation system for left ventricular segmentation algorithms in 3D echocardiography. *IEEE Transactions on Medical Imaging, 35*(4), 967–977.

Dong, S., Luo, G., Wang, K., Cao, S., Li, Q., & Zhang, H. (2018, September). A combined fully convolutional networks and deformable model for automatic left ventricle segmentation based on 3D echocardiography. *BioMed Research International, 2018,* 1–16.

Ge, R., Yang, G., Chen, Y., Luo, L., Feng, C., Zhang, H., & Li, S. (2019). PV-LVNet: Direct left ventricle multitype indices estimation from 2D echocardiograms of paired apical views with deep neural networks. *Medical Image Analysis, 58,* 1–12.

Ghorbani, A., Ouyang, D., Abid, A., He, B., Chen, J. H., Harrington, R. A., Liang, D. H., Ashley, E. A., & Zou, J. Y. (2020). Deep learning interpretation of echocardiograms. *NPJ Digital Medicine, 3,* 1–10.

Ghosh, S., Chattopadhyay, B. P., Roy, R. M., Mukherjee, J., & Mahadevappa, M. (2019). Estimation of echocardiogram parameters with the aid of impedance cardiography and artificial neural networks. *Artificial Intelligence in Medicine, 96,* 45–58.

González, B., Valdez, F., Melin, P., & Prado-Arechiga, G. (2015). Fuzzy logic in the gravitational search algorithm for the optimization of modular neural networks in pattern recognition. *Expert Systems with Applications, 42,* 5839–5847.

Guo, Y., Yu, L., Wang, Y., Yu, J., Zhou, G., & Chen, P. (2017). Adaptive group sparse representation in fetal echocardiogram segmentation. *Neurocomputing, 240,* 59–69.

Kaur, P., Singh, G., & Kaur, P. (March 2019). An intelligent validation system for diagnostic and prognosis of ultrasound fetal growth analysis using Neuro-Fuzzy based on genetic Algorithm. *Egyptian Informatics Journal, 20*(1), 55–87.

Leclerc, S., Smistad, E., Pedrosa, J., Østvik, A., Cervenansky, F., Espinosa, F., Espeland, T., Berg, E. A. R., Jodoin, P.-M., Grenier, T., Lartizien, C., D'hooge, J., Lovstakken, L., & Bernard, O. (2019). Deep learning for segmentation using an open large-scale dataset in 2D echocardiography. *IEEE Transactions on Medical Imaging, 38*(9), 2198–2210.

Madani, A., Arnaout, R., Mofrad, M., & Arnaout, R. (2018). Fast and accurate view classification of echocardiograms using deep learning. *NPJ Digital Medicine, 1*, 1–8.

Madani, A., Ong, J. R., Tibrewal, A., & Mofrad, M. R. K. (2018). Deep echocardiography: Data-efficient supervised and semi-supervised deep learning towards automated diagnosis of cardiac disease. *NPJ Digital Medicine, 1*, 1–11.

Penatti, O. A. B., Werneck, R. de O., Almeida, W. R. de, Stein, B. V., Pazinato, D. V., Mendes J., Pedro R., Torres, R. da S. & Rocha, A. (2015). Mid-level image representations for real-time heart view plane classification of echocardiograms. *Computers in Biology and Medicine, 66*, 66–81.

Shakeel, P. M., Baskar, S., Sampath, R., Jaber, M. M. (2019). Echocardiography image segmentation using feed forward artificial neural network (FFANN) with fuzzy multi-scale edge detection (FMED). *International Journal of Signal and Imaging Systems Engineering, 11*(5), 270–278.

Teng, L., Fu, Z., Ma, Q., Yao, Y., Zhang, B., Zhu, K., & Li, P. (March 2020). Interactive echocardiography translation using few-shot GAN transfer learning. *Computational and Mathematical Methods in Medicine, 2020*, 1–9.

Volpato, V., Mor-Avi, V., Narang, A., Prater, D., Gonçalves, A., Tamborini, G., Fusini, L., Pepi, M., Patel, A. R., & Lang, R. M. (2019). Automated, machine learning-based, 3D echocardiographic quantification of left ventricular mass. *Echocardiography, 36*(2), 312–319.

Wootton, A. J., Taylor, S. L., Day, C. R., & Haycoc, P. W. (2017). Optimizing echo state networks for static pattern recognition. *Cognitive Computation, 9*, 391–399.

Yu, L., Guo, Y., Wang, Y., Yu, J., & Chen, P. (2017). Segmentation of fetal left ventricle in echocardiographic sequences based on dynamic convolutional neural networks. *IEEE Transactions on Biomedical Engineering, 64*(8), 1886–1895.

Chapter 5

The Impact of Blockchain on Cloud and AI

S. Karthik[*,‡], K. Priyadarsini[†,§], and Trishant Baid[†,¶]

*Department of ECE, College of Engineering and Technology,
SRM IST, Vadapalani, Chennai, India*

†*Department of Data Science and Business Systems,
College of Engineering and Technology, SRM IST, Chennai, India*

‡*karthiks1@srmist.edu.in*

§*drkpriyadarsini@gmail.com*

¶*baidtrishant@gmail.com*

Abstract

Both blockchain and disseminated registering are expecting a basic part in changing endeavors' work environments and the way standard handling works. Their rise has not quite recently gained energy in the current business establishment yet has furthermore changed the way the universe of usage headway, storing, online trade, and various organizations limits. Regardless, challenges suffer in the wide execution of blockchain in cloud. This book area plans to introduce the impact of blockchain on cloud and how to diminish.

Keywords: Blockchain, Cloud, Artificial intelligence

1. Introduction

1.1 *The uses of blockchain and cloud computing*

Conveyed registering and blockchain development are the two on-demand progresses that are impacting in the bleeding edge market and are being used by adventures all throughout the planet (Gai *et al.*, 2020). One essential difference between the two is that the records of the record data bases in blockchain development are invariable, while data set aside in the cloud is variable (Dhaliwal, 2016).

The ascent and improvement of cloud development and blockchain has moved the universe of programming headway, amassing, organizations, and online trades (Agbo *et al.*, 2019).

Conveyed processing offers diverse online kinds of help like system as a Service, Platform as a Service, and Software as a Service. This development conveys a particularly oiled model for beneficially getting to various mechanical parts and organizations for application improvement and compromise (Bonneau *et al.*, 2014).

Blockchain advancement gives a fundamental record data base to taking care of significant worth-based records known as squares, and associations them with different informational collections known as the chain. These lasting records are then checked cryptographically using a circled arrangement or endorsement show (Sumitha *et al.*, 2020; Wang *et al.*, 2020).

This component of blockchain secures the popularity of incredible trade execution in multi-essential business conditions.

1.2 *Working of blockchain*

Blockchain is a plan of recording information with the end goal that makes it irksome or hard to change, hack, or cheat the system. A blockchain is essentially a modernized record of trades that is replicated and appropriated across the entire association of PC structures on the blockchain (Bore *et al.*, 2019).

A blockchain is a high level record of trades. The name comes from its plan, in which individual records, called blocks, are associated together in single summary, called a chain. ... Each trade added to a blockchain is affirmed by various PCs on the Internet (Christidis & Devetsikiotis, 2016).

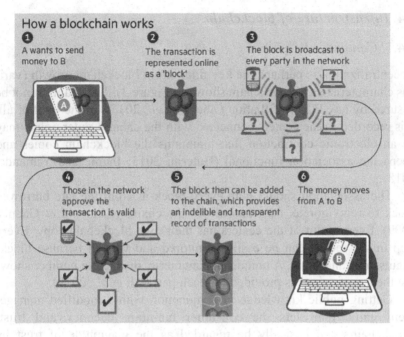

Figure 1. How Blockchain Works

Blockchain, widely suggested as distributed lined technology (DLT), allows decentralization and cryptographic hacking unalterable and guide the registered scenery of any modernized assets (Aletheia, 2018).

A basic analogy (as shown in Figure 1) is a Google Doc to understand blockchain growth. The documents are appropriated instead of copied or transmitted right when we record and sell them with a social event for people. This makes the chain of dispersion decentralized and allows anyone to report. No one is rushing out anticipating changes from another, as all changes to the document are continually tracked and changes are made perfectly clear (Ante *et al.*, 2018).

1.3 *Overall explanation of square chain*

Progressed assets are distributed instead of copied or moved. The asset is decentralized, allowing full progressing access (as shown in Figure 2). A clear record of changes jam dependability of the report, which makes trust in the asset.

1.4 *Infrastructure of blockchain*

1.4.1 *Centers*

Decentralization is perhaps the key thinking in blockchain growth (various characteristics of blockchain shown in Figure 3). The chain cannot be ensured by any PC or affiliation (Zheng *et al.*, 2017). In the light of all, it is recorded in the centers connected with the chain. Center points may be an electronic contraction that maintains the blockchain copies and keeps the association functional (Buterin, 2013; Ingole and Yamande, 2018).

The association should help every block as from the late burrowed block to reinvigorate, trust and affirm the chains (Khurshid & Gadnis, 2009). Every point of the centers has their own blockchain copy. Every step in the record can be easily monitored and viewed because blockchains are transparent. A unique alphanumeric, distinctive number showing their professions is provided for each part (Ali *et al.*, 2019).

Getting public knowledge in conjunction with a modified management game plan lets the consumer maintain decency and trust. Blockchains can basically be regarded as the magnitude of trust by growth (Wood, 2014).

1.4.2 *Tractors*

Via a loop called a mining, earthmovers render new squares on the chain (Böhme *et al.*, 2015).

Each square in one block has its own novel nonce and hash, but also the hash of the past block in the chain is a matter of reference, so mining a square is not fundamental, particularly in huge chains (Crosby *et al.*, 2016).

Diggers use excellent programming to tackle the impossible multifaceted numerical query to find an unknown hash (Cochrane, 2018; Nugent *et al.*, 2016). As the nonce is 32 pieces and the hash is 256, the possible nonce-hash blends are approximately 4 billion which should be mined before the correct one is identified. Just as the diggers occur, the "splendid nobility" is said to have found and their square is attached to the chain (Almenberg *et al.*, 2009).

If we alter a barrier earlier on in the chain, we need to reminisce the square, however, by the aggregate of the following squares. This is the reason why blockchain progress is hard to manage. Consider it as "prosperity in math," because it takes a monster share of time and computational power to find splendid notes (Tasatanattakool & Techapanupreeda, 2018).

If a block is successfully mined, the shift is recognized by the sum of the association's centers and the digger is financially compensated.

1.5 *Role of blockchain*

- Secure Control in Smart Buildings and Cities
- Coordinations
- In and Between Vehicles
- Mechanical IoT

Nearly endless applications across almost all industries are available in blockchain. To track fraud in finance securely share medical records between medical professionals and even acts in order to better track intellectual property in enterprise and music rights for artists, Ledger technology can be used.

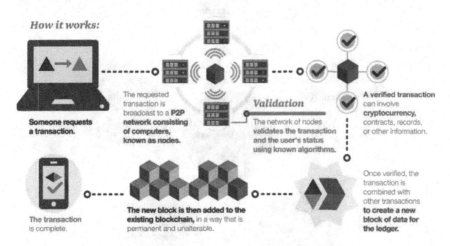

Figure 2.   Role of a Blockchain

1.6 *Cloud enlisting*

It is the movement of enrolling organizations that joins programming, storing, laborers, informational collection, arranging, examination, information, etc. outrageous. These figuring organizations give versatile utilization of resources, speedy headway, and economies of scale. In this way, attempts and affiliations are moving from standard enrolling configuration to cloud-based designing.

Here, customers pay for the cloud benefits that they are using. We can run more structure through this approach without stressing over organization, upkeep, and security (Bonneau *et al.*, 2014).

1.7 *Blockchain vs cloud figuring*

Circulated figuring for the most part runs on a standard informational index plan where the set aside data resides in the machines including individuals. On the other hand, blockchain is an ethically stable and strong online data base vault of various electronic trades where individuals can adjust the data by taking the support of each social event included.

Figure 3.   Characteristics of Blockchain

1. Associations like Amazon Web Services (AWS), Alibaba Cloud, Google, IBM, and Microsoft give circulated processing organizations while projects like Ethereum, Bitcoin, Hyperledger Fabric, and Quorum use blockchain development.

Both blockchain and circulated processing are accepting a basic part in changing undertakings' work environments and the way in which standard figuring works.

Their ascent has not quite recently gained energy in the current business establishment yet has moreover changed the way the universe of utilization headway, amassing, online trade, and various organizations limits. Disregarding the way that cloud is an especially oiled model that can accelerate blockchain projects, their union and blockchain cloud organizations are at this point in beginning phases.

2. Simulated Intelligence Artificial Intelligence with Block Registering

Enormous data just continues moving more noteworthy with no signs of maneuvering down. Engaging it is mechanized thinking (AI) stages. Table 1 shows blockchain comparison table. Computerized reasoning is used in banking, retail, clinical benefits, and basically some other

Table 1.   Blockchain Comparison Table

	æternity	◆	Ⓑ
Operational	2018	2014	2009
On-Chain Governance	☑	✗	✗
Block Time	3sec on-chain & instant in state channels	15sec	10min
Transaction Per Second (measured) [1]	116 / unlimited	15	7
Consensus Algorithm	Proof of Work	Proof of Work	Proof of Work
Smart Contract Language	Sophia	Solidity	Forth (Script)
Permissionless, public	☑	☑	☑
Mining Algorithm	Cuckoo Cycle	Ethash	SHA256
Decentralized Apps Live	☑	☑	✗
Node Language	Erlang	C/C++	C/C++
Native token	☑	☑	☑
Software Development Kit	☑	☑	☑

industry. It's used in gaming and online media networks. Thusly, fundamentally, it is everywhere, and it reaches us no matter how you look at it structure or another. Computerized reasoning is used for our potential benefit in various respects in light of the fact that the data acquired through AI instructs substances (associations, organizations, etc.) on our own tendencies, which hence impacts the idea of the experience, organization, or thing (Nakamoto, 2008).

Nonetheless, huge data is interesting, also, in that an unnecessary measure of information is being gained. A segment of this information we probably won't want to be uncovered. A part of this information may be unreasonably up close and personal (Dubovitskaya *et al.*, 2017).

The fix to the above issue is fundamental: blockchain development. Blockchain grants customers of AI to make trades furtively, which suggests less unequivocal information about the customer is assembled for enormous data purposes. Blockchain transports data through encryption. Joining AI with blockchain, consequently, produces three express advantages (Altunay *et al.*, 2011).

2.1 *Advantage no. 1: Improving security and creating trust*

Figure 4 shows various advantages of blockchain. PC based knowledge isn't altogether trusted by clients. Things like the Internet of Things (IoT) has been shown to be hackable. That cautions people. Nevertheless, getting AI together with blockchain development — where information is encoded and secure — security can be upgraded express AI organizes, and improved security will assemble customer trust (Da, 2017).

2.2 *Advantage no. 2: Identifying decisions and enabling understanding*

Man-made knowledge is complicated. It takes in a lot of components and assesses those variables before making a decision about whatever the AI is connected with, whether or not it's a financial decision (e.g., perceiving blackmail), a retail one (e.g., what thing to sell), or a clinical benefits one (e.g., what treatment is ideal). Now and again that "decision" may not be clear or helpfully understood on the beginning, and accepting not fathom, it isn't trusted. Blockchain advancement can be executed to record how decisions are made. Straightforwardness is, accordingly, made, and through straightforwardness there is trust (Anwar, 2019).

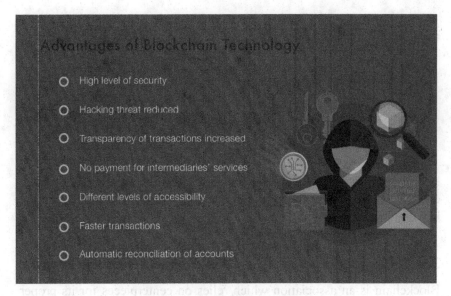

Figure 4.   Advantages of Blockchain

2.3 *Advantage no. 3: Efficiency is always a benefit*

Viability is reliably critical, paying little heed to if you are a business or an individual. Computers have made our lives more compelling. However, we have reliably expected to enter the rules into the PC to make them do what we need them to do. Along these lines, it really takes a lot of energy (Seth, 2019). Blockchain development in like manner takes a huge load of energy — it isn't splendid and powerful. PC based insight, of course, is. Recreated knowledge makes wise advancement — it can even be seen as wise. Getting AI together with blockchain can use blockchain advancement more compelling, and that accordingly makes us more capable all things considered.

Both AI and blockchain propels are at this point making. Joining the two is fundamental for this normal progression measure. As it grows autonomously and together, so too will more benefits show up.

3. Advantages and Demerits of Blockchain

Table 2 shows merits and emerits of Blockchain. Decentralized association, simplicity, trustful chain, inalterable and unbreakable infrastructure are the

Table 2.   Merits and Demerits

Advantages of blockchain	Disadvantages of blockchain
Trust	Can't edit data in a block
Decentralized database	It is not for everyone
Secure	Data is visible to all
Faster transaction	Lower performance
True trackability	It is costly to host

key advantages of the blockchain technology. In the same direction, high energy dependency, irritating joining patterns and enormous costs are the key drawbacks of the blockchain.

3.1 *Blockchain is positively not a distributed computing system*

Blockchain is an association which relies on centerpieces for its proper function. The notion of the center points chooses the blockchain concept. Bitcoin's blockchain, for example, is strong and makes the center points examine the connection. However, for a blockchain network which does not help centers the identical cannot be valid.

It does not, however, rely on the connection and the support of the center points. It is certainly not a dispersed figural structure. A suited management framework would ensure that the transaction is affirmed in accordance with the directives, that it registers trade and, in addition, that the trading history of any business is restrictive. These exercises are all like blockchain, but there is a lack of concerted action, mutual support and follow-up with each of them.

Clearly, blockchain could be an adequate network but the features that make a running registration system so essential for businesses are missed (Adhami *et al.*, 2018).

3.2 *Versatility is an issue*

As an accomplice of their consolidated structure, Blockchains are not scalable. You will have to realize that you have used the Bitcoin association, depending on the blockage of the business. This problem concerns flexibility problems with blockchain networks. The more persons or center points join the association, the more likely it is to go down! (ASCB, 2015).

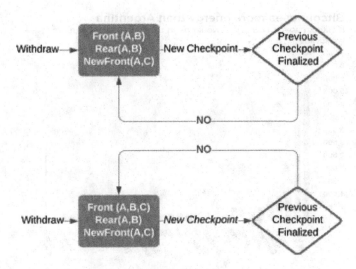

Figure 5. Versatility of Blockchain

In any case, the blockchain capacity for production has changed more and more. With the correct change of progress, the Bitcoin network combines flexibility decisions. The way to work is for off-blockchain businesses and simply for storing and accessing information using blockchain. Versatility of blockchain is shown in Figure 5.

Besides, there are also better ways to tend towards versatility, such as the use of approved partnerships and a blockchain strategy for substitutes such as Corda.

3.3 *Energy consumption*

Energy consumption of blockchain is shown in Figure 6. However, at this point all these game plans with concentrated structures are not normal. You'll find a monster comparison between them if you take a trading speed Bitcoin and VISA gander. Bitcoin can only make 4.6 trades per second right now. VISA can do 1700 trades per second in relation. It says that 150 million trades can be done every second in one day.

Altogether, we may assume that blockchain will probably not yet be available for real applications. It will be very huge, until it is generally regularly improved. Some blockchain solutions consume too much energy.

The creation of blockchain has been granted Bitcoin. It uses the computer for proof of work understanding which relied on earthmovers to accomplish difficult work. The earthquakes are assisted by complicated

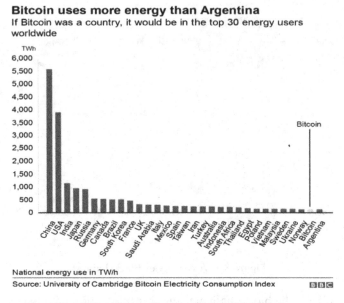

Bitcoin uses more energy than Argentina
If Bitcoin was a country, it would be in the top 30 energy users worldwide

National energy use in TW/h
Source: University of Cambridge Bitcoin Electricity Consumption Index   BBC

Figure 6.   Energy Consumption of Blockchain

mathematical problems. High energy consumption is what not so perfect for this current reality are these complex mathematical problems (Ashta & Biot-Paquerot, 2018).

Whenever the record with other trades is re-enacted, the backhoes have to deal with problems that need a lot of effort. All blockchain proposals, however, do not function in the same way. There are other computations of understanding that handle the problem. For example, approved or private organizations, when the number of center points within the association is restricted, do not have these issues. In addition, they use competent understanding structures to be arranged so there is no need for overall arrangement (Felin & Lakhani, 2018).

However, if you take Bitcoin, the most remarkable blockchain network, the problem persists.

To put it straightforward, permitted networks can use resources but open associations can use a great deal of energy in order to stay operational (Bonneau *et al.*, 2014).

3.4 *No switching*

The perpetual data quality was maybe the best blockchain weight. It clearly benefits many systems, including the establishment, money-related structure, etc. In any event, you should appreciate how organizations operate if the association centers are nicely dispersed and the perpetual standard should be available.

What I plan to say is that a blockchain association will be compelled by a substance if it affirms the center points to be half or more popular, rendering them vulnerable.

The data once rendered cannot be wiped out as another problem that you experience. All on earth has the safety advantage. However, if a comparative person uses a high level stage which has abrupt spikes for blockchain creation he would not be willing to destroy his system followers if he does not have to worry about it. In plain terms, he is extremely far-fetched, will scrub his follow-up and break down security rights (Aune *et al.*, 2017).

3.5 *Blockchains are sometimes inefficient*

From now on, there are various blockchain inventions. You will find a huge amount of disappointments inside the system if you get the most notable ones like blockchain growth. This is one of blockchain's huge weaknesses (Almenberg *et al.*, 2009).

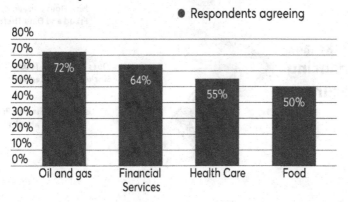

Will blockchain disrupt your industry?

Source: Deloitte, 2018 survey of 1,053 senior executives in seven countries

Figure 7. Inefficiency of Blockchain

I quickly found that the record would cross 100 GBs without an extremely remarkable distance when I tried to install the bitcoin tractor on my machine. Data storage was not viable, which can cause problems for many center points that have to become relevant to the association.

Obviously, a better technique should be available than managed as centers need to repeat it every time the data is relived. In addition, with more exchange and centers, the blockchain scale makes. In the event that it happens, the whole association will be passed down. This is not ideal for business blockchains where the association is always fast and stable (Fisch, 2019). Figure 7 shows inefficiency of blockchain.

With the support of other blockchain plans, gradual vulnerabilities are being strengthened. Bitcoin also partners with lightning networks to address inadequacies (Böhme *et al.*, 2015).

3.6 *Not completely secure*

The implementation of blockchain is safer than different levels. It doesn't in any case mean it's not completely secure as shown in Figure 8. The blockchain relation can be subverted in various ways. What about us going through them separately to look good.

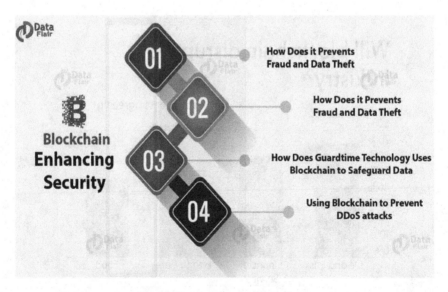

Figure 8.   Security in Blockchain

Percent Attack: if a substance accepts the 51% attack, the association centers may take up 51% or the more prominent measure. They may then adjust record data and double expenditure. This can be done on networks where it is possible to monitor diggers or centers. That implies that private associations would certainly be protected from attacks of 51%, but open organizations are much more vulnerable.

Double spending: Double spend is another problem with the new growth of the blockchain. To prevent duplication of the blockchain network, various understandings such as proof-of-stake, proof-of-work and so forth are passed on only networks with a 51% attack shortfall have double expenditure necessary.

DDoS's attack: In the event of a DDoS attack, the middle points are blasted by relative demands, preventing and cutting them down.

Cryptographic breaking: Another way blockchain progress is not safe is by using the cryptographic solution. Quantum calculations or enlists are more than good for cryptographic breakage. In all events, blockchain plans currently perform cryptographic quantitative calculations (Engelhardt, 2017).

4. Customers are Their Own Bank: Private Keys

It is essential to allow individuals to become their own bank, to decentralize blockchain. In either case, this causes another problem in the same way.

You need private keys to reach the goods or the details that the customer sets down in the blockchain. It is delivered during the production of the wallet and the customer is obliged to take care of it properly. You must also ensure that you do not give it to another person. If you do not think doing it, your wallet is in danger. In addition, they will lose their wallet permission for ever if they lose their private key. Customer reliance makes it one of blockchain's downsides (Chen, 2004).

So, if, as a client, you don't remember your personal key, you are logged out of your pocket and nobody will recover it. This is a genuine disadvantage because not everyone is instructed to make mistakes and has more flexibility to make them. It denies the position of decentralization if there is a concentrated power that manages it. Cost and Implementation Struggle.

The cost of carrying out blockchain progress is huge. While the majority of blockchain game plans like Hyperledger are open source by far, they require a huge amount of hypothesis from the members who are looking for them (Abeyratne & Monfared, 2016).

There are costs related to using developers, managing a meeting that governs various development blockchain components, authorizing costs when selecting a paid blockchain plan, etc.

In addition, you must control the maintenance costs of the plan. More than $1,000,000 can also be spent on large business blockchain ventures.

For associations that like a blockchain opportunity but have no money or spending to do so, they can need to stay in addition until they can bounce into the momentary blockchain mode.

5. Expertise Knowledge

It is difficult to do and manage a project blockchain. Cautious business data are required for the entire period.

You need to use various experts in the field of blockchain to cause the issue, and it is then seen as one of the blockchain injuries.

Not simply that they must also develop their present experts on the best technology to use blockchain, so that the administrative collection will understand the nuances and consequences of a blockchain-powered enterprise (Chen *et al.*, 2017).

They will thus understand their basic elements to make use of blockchain, and help transform their business cycles.

Likewise, when you encounter blockchain designs and prepared experts, they will find and will cost more because of their advantages and scale of supply.

5.1 *Advancement*

Progress from blockchain is just 10 years old. This implies that there is another progress that is expected to build that period. When you look, you can see many players who are trying with their wonderful course of action to deal with the decentralized issue.

Corda, Hyperledger, Ethereum, Ripple, for example, etc. We have it! In all respects, there is still an enormous amount of time left until the blockchain innovation develops and associations would have less to embrace blockchain growth (Dutra *et al.*, 2018).

As with any more progress, improvement is another problem that blockchain needs to solve, which means blockchain is one of the obstacles.

Similarly, blockchains are not built for the present in a long time. There's always a tone left for us to see improvements in blockchain normalization. Right now, there are too different approaches to deal with the intermediate questions, so they do not coordinate to standardize them.

5.2 *Interoperability*

Interoperability is another weakness that blockchain development meetings have. There are various types of blockchain networks in the last item that function suddenly, trying to deal with the DLT problem in a novel way. This leads to interoperability problems when the chains cannot be properly conferred.

The interoperability problem also involves the use of blockchain architecture for regular frameworks and systems (Dierksmeier & Seele, 2018).

5.3 *Legacy systems*

Not all organizations have moved from their heritage structures. Due to heritage systems, there are different affiliates at this stage. However, if you have to build blockchain, you have to thoroughly throw away your systems and move to blockchain progress, which is not possible for any business. (Cruz *et al.*, 2018).

6. Conclusion

As of now a days blockchain advancement is in inescapable access. It expects a basic part in our step by step plan applications similarly as in endeavors. In this chapter, we inspected about the blockchain and that impacts on the cloud and AI comparing to cloud, blockchain has a principal part in light of its decentralized plan. At the disadvantage it needs package of energy for the same. Cloud can be subverted this. While using AI with blockchain, the capability of the blockchain will be extended in various ways. Anyway the mix of three will be more comfort in general aspects. In future, merged cloud features with AI–blockchain.

References

Abeyratne, S., & Monfared, R. (2016). Blockchain ready manufacturing supply chain using distributed ledger. *International Journal of Research in Engineering and Technology, 5*, 1–10.

Abraham, I., & Mahlkhi, D. (2017). The blockchain consensus layer and BFT. *Bull. EATCS, 123*, 1–22. Available online at: https://dahliamalkhi.files.wordpress.com/2016/08/blockchainbft-beatcs2017.pdf.

Adhami, S., Giudici, G., & Martinazzi, S. (2018). Why do businesses go crypto? An empirical analysis of initial coin offerings. *Journal of Economics and Business, 100*, 64–75.

Agbo, C. C., Mahmoud, Q. H., & Eklund, J. M. (2019). Blockchain technology in healthcare: A systematic review. *Healthcare, 7*(2), E56.

Aletheia. (2018). Aletheia Foundation — Github Repository. Available online at: https://github.com/aletheia-foundation.

Ali, M., Nelson, J., Blankstein, A., Shea, R., & Freedman, M. J. (2019). The Blockstack Decentralized Computing Network.

Almenberg, J., Kittlitz, K., & Pfeiffer, T. (2009). An experiment on prediction markets in science. *PLoS ONE, 4*, e8500. doi: 10.1371/journal.pone.0008500.

Altunay, M., Avery, P., Blackburn, K., Bockelman, B., Ernst, M., Fraser, D., *et al.* (2011). A science driven production cyberinfrastructure — The open science grid. *Journal of Grid Computing, 9*, 201–218. doi: 10.1007/s10723-010-9176-6.

Androulaki, E., Barger, A., Bortnikov, V., Cachin, C., Christidis, K., De Caro, A., *et al.* (2018). Hyperledger fabric: A distributed operating system for permissioned blockchains. In *EuroSys '18 — Proceedings of the thirteenth EuroSys conference (Porto: ACM), 30*, 1–30, 15. doi: 10.1145/3190508.3190538.

Anonymous (2016). Towards open science: The case for a decentralized autonomous academic endorsement system. *Zenodo*. doi: 10.5281/zenodo.60054.

Ante, L., Sandner, P., & Fiedler, I. (2018) Blockchain-based ICOs: Pure hype or the Dawn of a new era of startup financing? *Journal of Risk and Financial Management, 11*(4), 80.

Anwar, H. (2019). Blockchain vs. distributed ledger technology.

ASCB (2015). ASCB member survey on reproducibility. Technical report, American Society for Cell Biology.

Ashta, A., & Biot-Paquerot, G. (2018). FinTech evolution: Strategic value management issues in a fast changing industry. *Strategic Change-Briefings in Entrepreneurial Finance, 27*(4), 301–311.

Aune, R. T., Krellenstein, A., O'Hara, M., & Slama, O. (2017). Footprints on a Blockchain: Trading and information leakage in distributed ledgers. *Journal of Trading, 12*(3), 5–13.

Böhme, R., Christin, N., Edelman, B., & Moore, T. (2015). Bitcoin: Economics, technology, and governance. *Journal of Economic Perspectives, 29*(2), 213–238.

Bonneau, J., Narayanan, A., Miller, A., Clark, J., Kroll, J. A., & Felten, E. W. (2014). Mixcoin: Anonymity for bitcoin with accountable mixes. Cryptology ePrint Archive, Report 2014/077.

Bore, N., Karumba, S., Mutahi, J., Darnell, S. S., Wayua, C., & Weldemariam, K. (2017). Towards blockchain-enabled school information hub. In *Proceedings of the Ninth International Conference on Information and Communication Technologies and Development*, pp. 1–4.

Boucher, P. (2016). What if blockchain technology revolutionised voting? Scientific Foresight Unit (STOA), European Parliamentary Research Service.

Buterin, V. (2013). Ethereum white paper: A next-generation smart contract and decentralized application platform [Internet]. GitHub. Available from: https://github.com/ethereum/wiki/wiki/White-Paper [Cited: November 23, 2019].

Chen, C. (2004) Searching for intellectual turning points: Progressive knowledge domain visualization. *Proceedings of the National Academy of Sciences of the United States of America, 101*(suppl), 5303–5310.

Chen, Z., Li, Y., Wu, Y., & Luo, J. (2017). The transition from traditional banking to mobile internet finance: An organizational innovation perspective — A comparative study of Citibank and ICBC. *Financial Innovation, 3*(1), 12.

Christidis, K., & Devetsikiotis, M. (2016). Blockchains and smart contracts for the internet of things. *IEEE Access, 4*, 2292–2303.

Cochrane, M. (2018). The History of Bitcoin [Internet]. *The Motley Fool*. Available from: https://www. fool.com/investing/2018/04/02/ the-history-of-bitcoin.aspx [Cited: November 24, 2019].

Crosby, M., Pattanayak, P., & Verma, S. (2016). Blockchain technology: Beyond bitcoin. *Applied System Innovation, 2*, 6–19.

Cruz, J. P., Kaji, Y., & Yanai, N. (2018). RBAC-SC: Role-based access control using smart contract. *IEEE Access, 6*, 12240–12251.

Da, H. (2017). NEO White Paper [Internet]. Neo. Available from: https://docs.neo.org/docs/en-us/basic/whitepaper.html [Cited: November 23, 2019].

Dai, J., & Vasarhelyi, M. A. (2017). Toward Blockchain-based accounting and assurance. *Information Systems Journal, 31*(3), 5–21.

Deng, H., Huang, R. H., & Wu, Q. (2018). The regulation of initial coin offerings in China: Problems, prognoses and prospects. *The European Business Organization Law Review, 19*(3), 465–502.

Dhaliwal, S. (2016). Blockchain-Based Smart Identity Will Free World of Paper ID's [Internet]. Cointelegraph. Available from: https://cointelegraph.com/news/blockchain-based-smartidentity-will-free-world-of-paper-ids [Cited: November 24, 2019].

Dierksmeier, C., & Seele, P. (2018). Cryptocurrencies and business ethics. *Journal of Business Ethics, 152*(1), 1–14.

Dubovitskaya, A., Xu, Z., Ryu, S., Schumacher, M., & Wang, F. (2017). Secure and trustable electronic medical records sharing using blockchain. *AMIA Annual Symposium Proceedings, 2017,* 650–659.

Dutra, A., Tumasjan, A., & Welpe, I. M. (2018). Blockchain is changing how media and entertainment companies compete. *MIT Sloan Management Review, 60*(1), 39–3+.

Eich, B., & Bondy, B. (2018). Basic Attention Token White Paper [Internet]. *Basic Attention Token.* Available from: https://basicattentiontoken.org/BasicAttentionTokenWhitePaper-4.pdf [Cited: November 23, 2019].

Engelhardt, M. A. (2017). Hitching healthcare to the chain: An introduction to Blockchain Technology in the Healthcare Sector. *The Technology Innovation Management Review, 7*(10), 22–34.

Fanning, K., & Centers, D. P. (2016). Blockchain and its coming impact on financial services. *The Journal of Corporate Accounting and Finance, 27*(5), 53–57.

Felin, T., & Lakhani, K. (2018). What problems will you solve with Blockchain? *MIT Sloan Management Review, 60*(1), 32–3+.

Fisch, C. (2019). Initial coin offerings (ICOs) to finance new ventures. *The Journal of Business Venturing, 34*(1), 1–22.

Gai, K., Guo, J., Zhu, L., & Yu, S. (2020). Blockchain meets cloud computing: A survey. *IEEE Communications Surveys and Tutorials, 220*(3), 2009–2030.

Ingole, K. R., Yamde, S. (2018, April). Blockchain technology in cloud computing: A systematic review. *International Research Journal of Engineering and Technology (IRJET)* e-ISSN: 2395-0056, *05*(04). www.irjet.net p-ISSN: 2395-0072.

Khurshid, A., & Gadnis, A. (2009). Using blockchain to create transaction identity for persons experiencing homelessness in America: Policy proposal. *JMIR Research Protocols, 8*(3), e10654.

Nakamoto, S. Bitcoin codebase: First implementation v0.1.0 [Internet]. Satoshi Nakamoto Institute. 2009. Available from: https://satoshi.nakamotoinstitute.org/code/ [Cited: November 24, 2019].

Nakamoto, S. (2008). Bitcoin: A peer-to-peer electronic cash system [Internet]. Bitcoin.org. Available from: https://bitcoin.org/bitcoin.pdf [Cited: June 7, 2018].

Nugent, T., Upton, D., & Cimpoesu, M. (2016). Improving data transparency in clinical trials using blockchain smart contracts. [version 1; peer review: 3 approved]. F1000Res. *5,* 2541.

Review on biometric technologies in cloud computing.

Seth, S. (2019). Why NEO can do what no other cryptocurrency can do [Internet]. Investopedia. Available from: https://www.investopedia.com/tech/china-neo-cryptocurrency/ [Cited: November 24, 2019].

Sumitha, J., Arish, V. M. B., & Saranath, J. (February 2020). *International Research Journal of Engineering and Technology (IRJET)* e-issn: 2395-0056, *07*(02). www.irjet.net p-issn: 2395-0072

Tasatanattakool, P., & Techapanupreeda, C. (2018). Blockchain: Challenges and applications, *2018 International Conference on Information Networking (ICOIN)*, Chiang Mai, Thailand, pp. 473–475, doi: 10.1109/ICOIN.2018.8343163.

Wang, S., Wang, X., & Zhang, Y. (2020). A secure cloud storage framework with access control based on blockchain. *IEEE Access*, 7, 112713–112725.

Wood, D. D. (2014). Ethereum: A secure decentralised generalised transaction ledger. Ethereum Project Yellow Paper [Internet]. Semantic Scholar. Available from: https://www.semanticscholar.org/paper/.

Zheng, Z., Xie, S., Dai, H., Chen, X., & Wang, H. (2017). An overview of blockchain technology: Architecture, consensus, and future trends. In *6th IEEE International Conference on Big Data*, Honolulu, HI. doi: 10.1109/BigDataCongress.2017.85.

Chapter 6

Blockchain-Based Secure Authentication for an Intelligent e-Learning Framework with Optimized Learning Objects

Maithili Devi Reddy[*,§], Latha Parthiban[†,¶],
and Kavitha Chandrakanth[‡,||]

[*]*Bharath Institute of Higher Education and Research, Chennai, India*

[†]*Department of Computer Science, Pondicherry University Community College, Pondicherry, India*

[‡]*Department of Computer Science, Pondicherry University Community College, Pondicherry, India*

[§]*maithilidumpa@gmail.com*

[¶]*lathaparthiban@yahoo.com*

[||]*kavitha.ck13@gmail.com*

Abstract

As education field has become online due to covid in both schools and colleges, e-learning security has become an important issue. An e-Learning framework provides a collection of online services that are helpful for the learners, resource persons and others who are involved in enhancing the management and delivery of education to all sections of people. The two most important aspects of an e-Learning system are better search of learning resources and the secure authentication between the learner and the trainer. This chapter introduces two novel methods: (i) optimization of Learning Object (LO) search based on learners' characteristics, (ii) secure authentication of trainers and learners using visual cryptography. Storage and delivery of optimal resources that are well suited for individual learner is always a challenging task. To find the best learning objects, an enhanced attribute-based Ant Colony Optimization (ACO) algorithm that provides flexibility for the learners based on learner characteristics is proposed. A novel visual cryptography-based technique with kite-based partition technique is designed to perform file sharing and blockchain-based secure authentication and verification of valid learners is proposed for the framework. Several measures like match ratio, relevancy factor, and heuristic values show the efficiency of the proposed ACO search technique in the context of an e-Learning framework.

Keywords: E-learning, ACO, Learning objects, Adaptive learning, Visual cryptography

1. Introduction

The internet has revolutionized the society, economy, and technological systems. Most Learning Management Systems (LMS) do not offer personalized services where all the students are provided access to same resources. As Morrison stated, "Just as people differ in many respects, so do ways in which they learn differ. Some of these differences are evident in the kinds of experiences each person requires to learn and, if competence in a skill is to be acquired, in the amount of time and practice each person needs. It is essential, therefore, early in the planning process, to give attention to the characteristics, abilities, and experiences of the learners — both as a group and as individuals." This give rise to two basic questions in Adapting E-learning Systems (AES) as follows:

- "What can we adapt to," which can be learner characteristics.
- "What can be adapted" which can be the way of presentation and navigation.

Learner modeling is the identification of characteristics of learner (Brusilovsky, 2001). Using this information, adaptation actions are taken as in Figure 1. The growth of searching technology helped in fast access to information but gives: the "one size fits all" strategy that offer the same

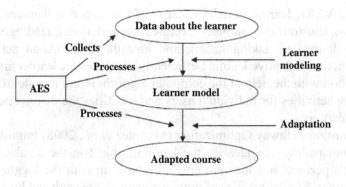

Figure 1.   Adaptive E-Learning Systems

learning materials to each learner (Semet *et al.*, 2003). To overcome this problem, the population-based heuristic ACO algorithm for adapting the learner characteristics is proposed. Establishing the best LO for the learners is not totally a new approach but when done based on the paths followed by the earlier learners, the learner characteristics have resulted in the expansion of adaptive learning.

The existing approaches towards adaptive learning path deals with the learner attributes only. More over only static characteristics like learning style and knowledge level, etc. are taken in to account in most of the approaches. The dynamic characteristics of the learners are not taken into account. Each learner will be having some dynamic characteristic which will be changing over time during a session, and which uniquely identify the learner needs.

2. Literature Survey

Over the years, different approaches are used to find the best learning object in an e-learning system. Some of the highly used methods are Learning Profile of Previous Users, Adaptive learning based on style, Adaptable Learning Pathway Generation, Adaptive learning based on pattern graph model.

Fulcher (2006) builds new learning profiles based on the history of previous users. Learning paths are important factors in searching the learning objects data. Many machine learning methods are explored to learn the common patterns of the preceding user information which are used to improve the efficiency to discover the closest learning objects.

The VARK learning model consists of four types of learners: visual (pictures, illustrations), auditory (lectures, consultations), reading/writing (textbook reading, taking notes), and kinesthetic (hands-on activities, experiments). Adaptive learning efficiently combines the learner and tutor interaction with the help of the computer algorithms and it customizes the learning activities for individual users and identifies the distinct needs of every learners.

Learning Pathway Optimization (Marquez *et al.*, 2008) improves the minimum pathway to identify the learning object in the database. The learner's performance logs are gradually built up with the logging in of new learner. Similar profiles of previous learners are analyzed by ACO to create the new learner path. Swarm intelligence, neural networks, and ACO are also used to create an enhanced algorithm for the representation and the search of the learning object. Performance logs and various activities of the learner initiated by the tutor are used to improve the quality of the data search.

Graph-based learning models are also efficiently used in finding out the optimized pathway for the adaptive learning models. (Back *et al.*, 1997) generates several learning path graphs for the system and tries to locate the best pathway for the search model. Here adaptive learning based on FP model is used to arrive at the learning path.

Van Merrienboer & Ayres (2005) proposes an attribute based adaptive learning style which identifies several key fields to improve the overall performance of the system. Attributes of the learner are used to represent the learning object. Kolb's learning style was modeled as in Figure 2. The learning activities of each learner in e-learning are recorded into learner object repository and based on the learner attributes, the learning object is provided.

Recently, hypermedia based adaptive learning with Kolb's style is also one of the frequently used models. A non-linear mode of instruction tools like graphics, video, audio, text, and hyperlinks are collectively called as hypermedia. Learner control is high in these type of environments. Also this can improve the motivation and interest of the students/learners and provide constructive information processing between various learners of the system.

Hyperlinks-based adaptive learning includes the usage of the online materials in education (Harasim, 1990). The learner forms the vertex of the graph leaving pheromones in the arc, referred as man-hill. Success is

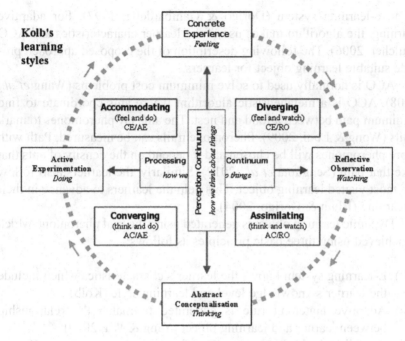

Figure 2. Kolb's Learning Styles

represented by positive pheromones and failure by negative pheromone (Bonabeau *et al.*, 1999). Table 1 provides the different learner context considered by different learners. Data securing in cloud is done with multiagent systems effectively (Latchoumi *et al.*, 2016).

3. Proposed Methodology

3.1 *ACO based learning object discovery*

An adaptive learning system is a system that understand the student behavior, where the behavioral patterns of an individual learner can be followed and understand their performance at the end of that behavior pattern or learning path and provide the learner that immediate path (James Kennedy, 2006). That is the system adapts to the individual preferences, provide continuous feedback so that the learners can improve their performance. ACO for adaptive learning provide the best learning object in an e-learning system (Dorigo & Gambardella, 1997). For adaptive learning, the algorithm makes use of the learner characteristics and ACO (Fulcher, 2006). The following description of the proposed approach provide suitable learning object for learners.

ACO is normally used to solve minimum cost problems (Wang *et al.*, 2008). ACO is a metaheuristic algorithm where ants coordinate to find minimum path between a food and nest. The ants lay pheromones to mark trails (Wong & Looi, 2009). Pheromone trails can be measured. Path with more pheromones will be chosen and it depend on the density of ants that take that path (Sengupta *et al.*, 2012). Similarly, the learners also follow the most visited learning object. This help the learners to advance in their e-learning (Blum & Dorigo, 2004).

Dynamic learning object is generated using the trial pheromone which is achieved using three basic principles as follows:

(i) E-learning system knows the learner's characteristics which include the learner's knowledge level and learning style (Kolb).

(ii) Adaptive matching rule is generated to match the relationship between learner and learning object (Yang & Wu, 2009).

(iii) Providing the best learning object for the learner based on ACO.

    (a) The e-learning system should have complete knowledge about the learner characteristics and desires (Dahbi *et al.*, 2006). Advanced e-learning provide more suitable LO to the learners. The following table created for differentiating the learner's and LO's characteristics (Gutiérrez *et al.*, 2007).

    (b) Adaptive matching rule is generated to match the relationship between learner and LO's.

        Adaptive matching rule is illustrated using an example. As shown in Figure 3, the learner has the characteristics of learning style as converging and knowledge level as Intermediate, the adaptive matching rule provide the best LO to the learners, Converging style learner use the LO in the format of text (doc, ppt, etc.) and the Intermediate level use the LO as advance level. Final alone is the complete contest to learner characteristics.

    (c) Providing the best learning object for the learner set on characteristics based ACO.

    ACO Algorithm for adaptive learning is as follows:

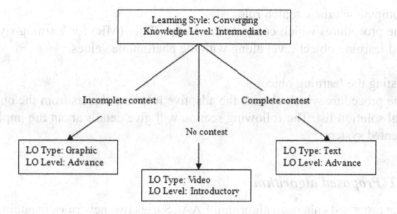

Figure 3. Matching Circumstances

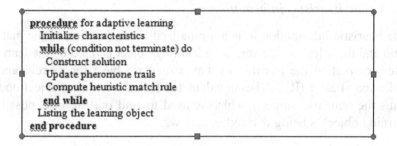

Initialize characteristics

The procedure which initializes the learning style, knowledge level, LO type and LO level. Learner characteristics are the inputs from the learner and learning objects are the output provided by the system.

Construct solution

The procedure which construct the solution, the learner visit the learning object based on the paths of previous learner and put into optimal solution list.

Update pheromone trails

The procedure which updates the most visited paths of the learner. Considering learning characteristics of the learner, dynamically it adds the learning object has the same characteristic each time.

Compute heuristic match rule
The procedures which compute the Match Ratio (MR) for learning style and learning object level along with the pheromone values.

Listing the learning object
The procedure which obtains the adaptive learning objects from the optimal solution list. The following section will give details about the implemented system.

3.2 *Proposed algorithm*

The proposed enhanced algorithm EAACS uses two new rules in addition to existing for pheromone update and heuristic information.

3.2.1 *The heuristic information*

The heuristic information η_{ij} is a normalized value function of the match ratio and the relevancy factor. Each learning object is rated by the learner after completing the learning of that particular object for its relevancy. Relevancy Factor (RF) is being calculated for each learning object node. Thus the heuristic value η_{ij} which is used to find out the next possible learning object is being derived as follows:

$$\eta_{ij} = 1 - \left(\frac{(RF_{ij} * MR_{ij})}{\sum_{k=1}^{N_i} RF_{ik}} \right) \tag{1}$$

η_{ij} gives the quantitative measure associated with the node relevancy factor rated by the previous learners and the match ratio. The higher the η-value then there is higher probability of the node to be chosen according to learner preference and relevancy.

3.2.2 *Pheromone trail update*

Pheromone trail intensity τ_{ij}. Measures the intensity between nodes and its increment $\Delta\tau_{ij}(t)$ is:

$$\tau_{ij}(t) = \rho\tau_{ij}(t-1) + \Delta\tau_{ij}(t) \tag{2}$$

ρ is evaporate ratio. The amounts of pheromone laid by the ants is given by,

$$T_{ij}(t) = \rho T_{ij}(t-1) + x * \Delta T_{ij}{}^{Style}(t) + \Delta T_{ij}{}^{Preference}(t) + \Delta T_{ij}{}^{Level}(t) \quad (3)$$

where $\Delta T_{ij}{}^{Style}(t)$, $\Delta T_{ij}{}^{Level}(t)$ and $\Delta T_{ij}{}^{Preference}(t)$ are variable amounts of pheromone deposited and the adaptive solution is:

$$\Delta T_{ij}^{k,Style}(t) = \sum_{n=0}^{m}(m-n) * Q * MR_{ij}^{Style}(t) \quad (4)$$

where m is the number of $MR_{ij}^{k,style}$ on the arc (i, j)

$$\Delta T_{ij}^{k,Level}(t) = \sum_{n=0}^{m}(m-n) * Q * MR_{ij}^{Level}(t) \quad (5)$$

$$\Delta T_{ij}^{k,Preference}(t) = \sum_{n=0}^{m}(m-n) * Q * MR_{ij}^{Preference}(t) \quad (6)$$

Match ratio is given by:

$$\sum_{\forall j \in Ni} MR_{ij} = \sum_{\forall j \in Ni} MR_{ij}^{Style} + \sum_{\forall j \in Ni} MR_{ij}^{Level} + \sum_{\forall j \in Ni} MR_{ij}^{Preference} \quad (7)$$

where

$$MR\_Style_{ij} = \left(\frac{(S_i - T_j)}{\sum_{\forall r \in Ni}(S_i - T_r)} + 1 \right)$$

$$MR\_Level_{ij} = \left(\frac{(K_i - L_j)}{\sum_{\forall r \in Ni}(K_i - L_r)} + 1 \right)$$

$$MR\_Preference_{ij} = \left(\frac{(P_i - O_j)}{\sum_{\forall r \in Ni}(P_i - O_r)} + 1 \right)$$

$$MR_{ij}^{Style} = e^{-MR\_Style} \quad (8)$$

$$MR_{ij}^{Level} = e^{-MR\_level} ij \tag{9}$$

$$MR_{ij}^{Preference} = e^{-MR\_Preference} ij \tag{10}$$

where S is learner style, T is LO type, K is learner knowledge level, L is LO level, P is learner preference, and O is LO orientation.

3.3 *Educator and learner sharing with visual cryptography*

Visual cryptography techniques involve secure sharing and storage of data in the form of image between the sender and the receiver (Vinodhini *et al.*, 2012). Many methods are proposed in the literature for secure sharing using visual cryptography (Sah *et al.*, 2018) with comparison on the various access based control methodologies available in literature. (Priyanka, 2016) proposed a methodology for secure biometric-based document search and retrieval. (Brindha & Jeyanthi, 2017) designed a technique using VC to protect data storage in cloud. Many Pharmacy related data concerning adverse drug reactions (ADR) must be transmitted very securely and the proposed algorithm can be used.

To secure the data stored in cloud, many secure authentication methods are proposed in literature. In this research, a novel algorithm that uses biometric authentication (fingerprint/any picture) is proposed. A kite based split is designed as shown in Figure 4(a).

The kite shape partition is split to seven subsets as in Figure 4(b). The generated subset images are shown in Figure 5.

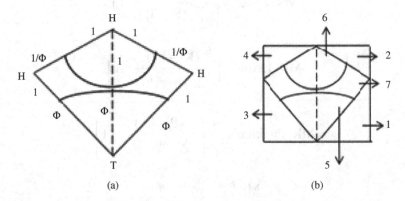

(a)   (b)

Figure 4.   (a) Kite Based Split (b) Applying Kite Method to Secret Image

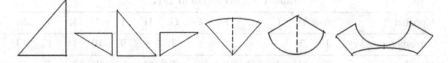

Figure 5. Generated Subset Images

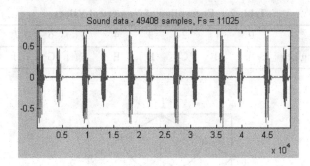

Figure 6. Secret Image

Figure 7. Partitioned Subsets

A secret image used for key exchange/authentication is shown in Figure 6. The generated subsets are shown in Figure 7.

By using stegano algorithm, stegano tile is generated to carry the information to reconstruct the secret image at the receiver side. The generated stegano tile is encrypted using attribute based encryption technique and then transmitted along with generated subset (considered as tile). The steps for stegano algorithm is given by

- Introduce Lamps in secret figure.
- Label edges as H_{ik}, i = 1 to L and k = 1 to number of edges in ith tile connection among subsets is specified in stegano tile.
- Encryption of stegano tile.

Table 1.   Encryption of Text

Alphabet	A	B	C	D	E	F	G	H	I	J	K	L	M
Corresponding key	1	2	3	4	5	6	7	8	9	10	11	12	13
Alphabet	N	O	P	Q	R	S	T	U	V	W	X	Y	Z
Corresponding key	14	15	16	17	18	19	20	21	22	23	24	25	26

Table 2.   Encryption of Numerical Values

Number	0	1	2	3	4	5	6	7	8	9
Corresponding key	A	B	C	D	E	F	G	H	I	J

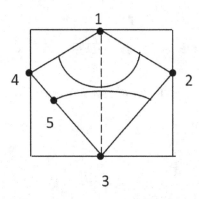

Figure 8.   Lamps for the Proposed Method

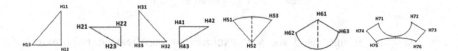

Figure 9.   Labeled Tiles for the Proposed Method

Encryption methodology followed is simple, such that for characters, numbers are used as in Table 1 and for numbers, alphabets are used as in Table 2.

The lamps generated (five lamps) are shown in Figure 8. The labeling process is shown in Figure 9. The generated stegano tile is shown in Figure 10.

ABE is applied to Figure 10 and encrypted stegano tile is shown in Figure 11.

1 | H21 H42 H61

2 | H23 H73 H11

3 | H32 H13 H52

4 | H43 H74 H31

5 | H51 H75

Figure 10.   Generated Stegano Tile

B | 8CB 8DC 8FB

C | 8CC 8HC 8BB

D | 8CC 8BC 8EC

E | 8DC 8HD 8CB

F | 8EB 8HE

Figure 11.   Encrypted Stegano Tile

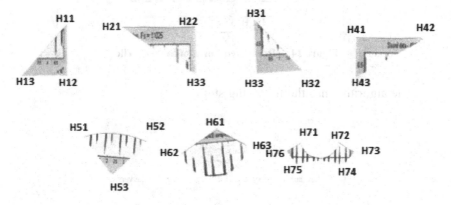

Figure 12.   Labeled Tiles

Figure 12 shows the labeled tiles and Figure 13 shows the received stegano tiles. Figure 14 shows the decrypted stegano tiles.

The reconstruction process is done for the proposed approach and the received labeled tiles are shown in Figure 15.

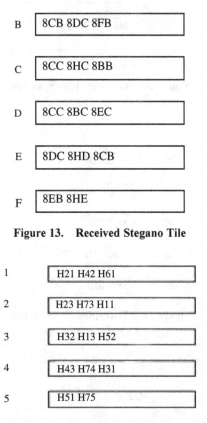

B | 8CB 8DC 8FB |

C | 8CC 8HC 8BB |

D | 8CC 8BC 8EC |

E | 8DC 8HD 8CB |

F | 8EB 8HE |

Figure 13.   Received Stegano Tile

1 | H21 H42 H61 |

2 | H23 H73 H11 |

3 | H32 H13 H52 |

4 | H43 H74 H31 |

5 | H51 H75 |

Figure 14.   Decrypted Form of Stegano Tile

The algorithm has the following steps

- Retrieving the RSA public key of the verifier

- Encrypting the blockchain address of the requester

- Sending the encrypted blockchain address to the verifier

- Decrypting the encrypted blockchain address

Figure 15.　Reconstructed Secret Image

- Retrieving the RSA public key of the requester

- Generating a random string and timestamp and hash

- Sending the hash to the requester

- Decryption of the hash

- Signing of the hash by the requester

- Creating the encrypted envelope

- Sending the encrypted envelope to the verifier

- Decrypting of the encrypted envelope by the verifier

- Verification of the digital signature

An user uses "post /api/v1/onboard_user" and passes the required parameters with

{ "user identifier": "23792387", "user description": "E learner1's Noodle Bank app on her iPad"}:

The output is the user's primechain address, private key, public key, transaction id, RSA public key and private key

{"status": 200,
"response": {"primechain_address": "16g8d8U3K3PbcvY6LYafgZ23JrnxRXwZqBP8sA",
"primechain_private_key": "VECSuwoYmF8LHpBy67eaE7435xUcS9FGQ48WdXfjc",

"primechain_public_key": "021c2d2e89d68a7cd4505f33f57ac619a9c52fc907042309",
"tx_id": "ef3f1cde044f0a16382230d4e700143da3ef5138a2bfb60791c05461a0ff1de2",
"rsa_public_key": "-----BEGIN PUBLIC KEY-----
MIIBIjANBgkqhkiG9w0BAQEFAAOCAQ8AMIIBCgKCAQEAiB49uO +CWPYqiYS/
+pYrUjoCe3owwn395o68IPmYDm2NCYk17Dwx2bDW5/B4OFgznw+eSe
Hg1K2RrCQbwArKssjez04VtVBODowv/h8usq6R/g1zsA/YtZTLHMR0tdr9Ton0Op
GBbc/qsgAo76OJvGcy7dwCXcbzVkscjURiVQ8Grn+yvpS5DQW0fskdUoX6UO8esT
IF1u+TFDaizMu5i1bl/CibiRzc5iT/E907ynBc2PZApcices8Eera8Ye8kGG2cz5
Lluf49OfTlF5Tg4cVmxOH4XU3sbfPNxnvTVCBONq59LYvGsNBXuDH hQIDAQAB
-----END PUBLIC KEY-----","rsa_private_key": "-----BEGIN PRIVATE KEY-----
MIIEvAIBADANBgkqhkiG9w0BAQEFAASCBKYwggSiAgEAAoIBAQCIHj244Ah/Daca
y55uhUv4JY9iqJhL/6litSOgJ7ejDCff3mjrwg+ZgObY0JiTXsPDHZsNbn8Hg4WD
OfD55J4eDUrZGsJBvACsqyyN7PThW1UE4OjC/+Hy6yrpH+DXOwD9i1lMscxHS12v
1OifQ6kYFtz+qyACjvo4m8ZzLt3AJdxvNWSxyNRGJVDwauf7K+ILkNBbR+ySVShf
pQ7x6xOUXW75MUNqLMy7mLVuX8KJuJHNzmJP8T3TvKcFzY9kClyJx6zwR6trxh7y
QYbZzPksi5/j059OWrnNFBAvOsdIXlODhxWbE4fhdText883Ge9NUIE42rn0ti8a
w0Fe4MeFAgMBAAECggEAJvWw6OeGxwbbW3oIYM3aTq5BehWTcb09eDksdzym/Q4P
mVkDxoBhXCi/6QyLLB8WJGwaewKBgQCi/1zwo/9z3CCKEn8baQkReUDmifaG4PVs
ZEAsz0WQ/bphRBQIlwoL6xXTTuGAczfoEonSyH+jfm2sLcysMRpyAAPI2Q//d+b2
AFm+eBH/45TGKvfD7kdYj830sSzYaA6i/Z2DziG7fmC/auJmgtT1wQ5UMjD3Oghk
lCxzn6oF/wKBgGyR/Gz6wQJG/xMVhd8MD2r8i6a5IbBOnwgRa69FVbVGF4G/cOBl
pCcRfRn03gyPj87MFwqa5scgjdGXdAdNv/WKdLNPdHMYGbXIS5E+49ww/ulBEj4w
8G50HjDsbVrUHyUf+4D1248YNIWt+aTtEBLkxZ8sUZmc/nzTjHoPR0NvAoGAFSKr
ulBrdWiLx5uSY8mA5YUlhz9IekDdUgrFz4mo6Z4c9tPPEPi+0sDO+bF2yCMokq0k
tfJNqrOQIQ1nRsSvOJUJfk3Sl9B1UQTgRfwSCPgAq+SeeyFwu+lwYKXJ1RmIzu
SdMGyLsgbHG9nbFFUACSjRRdCRG7WN9lzDBd6Z0CgYAeg3Be/Kox+anF2pRulDa3
Ro9UiVPrsJQv/0qKO8vLsJyDyCFmaut2v1XPQm1c50gaQ5Crn/a1IavgVyoU5Kl8
RQJsaS/5ZgA5Hm1XIdv6edCNn8bvFw6927aC5BsRuwFzPzplplfJ2fQRQpBtpJN+
E4ZylXnYyCN1ar3WSp6/eQ== -----END PRIVATE KEY-----"}}

AUTH_USERS_MASTERLIST datastream: has new user's identifier, description, address, public key, new user's RSA public key. No private key published anywhere. The algorithm for authentication is explained below in steps. The user to be authenticated is called 'requester (Elearner1)' and the user who does authentication is called 'verifier (Noodle Bank)'. with prime-chain addresses

- 17SEyDKEwvA46U1FTUVVZWYgnR4X4L576vVAbp (Noodle Bank) and
- 16g8d8U3K3PbcvY6LYafgZ23JrnxRXwZqBP8sA (Elearner1)

Step 1: Elearner1 retrieves 'RSA public key' using post /api/v1/get_rsa_key

{ "primechain_address": "17SEyDKEwvA46U1FTUVVZWYgnR4X4L576vVAbp"}

Noodle Bank's 'RSA public key' is the output.

{"status": 200,
"rsa_public_key": "-----BEGIN PUBLIC KEY-----
MIIBIjANBgkqhkiG9w0BAQEFAAOCAQ8AMIIBCgKCAQEAkydbbI+
68zjRmp0n7Yss
NwKbUl1IzBEqgm0Rp/utue8VNPfZaW7YrnwmEO7jO939C0/xAgayE6vR5VT7sItX
uMKwvP0DozxWtUGGcoHEZgImzSXJGomZpr2+M6TdW+kbisUUKbjIApQvnGlh93Zv
XiRTsvMkxC1Lf8Wkj52V7Xdn7O2p1tGg/j4wv78kT9wJ67xEnBmsGpGUZZYPAMZr
j0WrsakvT5vqwtkGum2OI9eRNIB7qgDsuOrxAm3jyx17s+tOi2Sasn1GywHQmU6n
YpCSsVv6ywGCMH5xLGAWT3glGCx2mwjAi+/QbpSXIWorlzzlZOR2xI+844dyDxbW
MQIDAQAB -----END PUBLIC KEY-----"}

Step 2 — Blockchain address of requester is encrypted using post /api/v1/ encrypt_data_rsa

{"data": "16g8d8U3K3PbcvY6LYafgZ23JrnxRXwZqBP8sA",
 "rsa_public_key": "-----BEGIN PUBLIC KEY-----
MIIBIjANBgkqhkiG9w0BAQEFAAOCAQ8AMIIBCgKCAQEAkydbbI+
68zjRmp0n7Yss
NwKbUl1IzBEqgm0Rp/utue8VNPfZaW7YrnwmEO7jO939C0/xAgayE6vR5VT7sItX
uMKwvP0DozxWtUGGcoHEZgImzSXJGomZpr2
+M6TdW+kbisUUKbjIApQvnGlh93Zv
XiRTsvMkxC1Lf8Wkj52V7Xdn7O2p1tGg/j4wv78kT9wJ67xEnBmsGpGUZZYPAM
Zr
j0WrsakvT5vqwtkGum2OI9eRNIB7qgDsuOrxAm3jyx17s+tOi2Sasn1GywHQmU6n
YpCSsVv6ywGCMH5xLGAWT3glGCx2mwjAi+/QbpSXIWorlzzlZOR2xI+
844dyDxbW MQIDAQAB -----END PUBLIC KEY-----"}

Encrypted RSA output is:

{"status": 200,
"encrypted_data_rsa":
"acN4z1AbYKHbuK5Tixi+AgYwg/3XMqVxU3UJmZrXcRuSXYSPyDLrB7
+BQeiazfcFk9WxpnvT8nXHkQ6Hz2rTUF1K1Lv5XM33iQMqdRUa9WzQ
GJS9IakS5TSw+OpxhCR0KWa1kJ4XIa6QHwCGqUQrUo7WXTV9k/Lb5
5eLZh9bINy6LAAeYQfQX7LZMVCuC7lmJcUAkDTYuccgZdtAc1BCHl0
ODq7rcMSLpr/M0h+tjKE6fuGP9AuB7NznoAy+
7yf9toy67DNIWAeQXptTq8ukBJ6AzBTerUbTrbwOWIBWOyVcnsyPkXRt
PUNryu5Jvqlw6//w0Fc9FG3dM+lmuzWQ5A"}

Step 3 — Encrypted blockchain address is sent to the verifier
Step 4 — Decryption of the encrypted blockchain address using

{ "rsa_private_key": "-----BEGIN PRIVATE KEY-----
MIIEvQIBADANBgkqhkiG9w0BAQEFAASCBKcwggSjAgEAAoIBAQCTJ1tsj7rzONGa
nSftiyw3AptSXUjMESqCbRGn+6257xU099lpbtiufCYQ7uM73f0LT/ECBrITq9Hl
Quk8SOH4Ame9TcBrP95bpxUzBKapBj/ncW8lJKDD7zLYTQalWUG+KX/17i6NPgD6
YS93Qj3Pw6ZSTqGTW4FYM9f4tawEWaGFGBL2CBYEp9nUTUBEAq8HJes0bimeScGn
Tawewg84U4oiHuyTbtwli5PkB+XIKfGaXU3SMaHYHiORRe7BhQwWKHpLdob4JJtm

CdNBuN+I1w9yaWG1TeWVjk8= -----END PRIVATE KEY-----",
 "encrypted_data_rsa":
"acN4z1AbYKHbuK5Tixi+AgYwg/3XMqVxU3UJmZrXcRuSXYSPyDLrB7
+BQeiazfcFk9WxpnvT8nXHkQ6Hz2rTUF1K1Lv5XM33iQMqdRUa9WzQGJS9IakS5TSw
+OpxhCR0KWa1kJ4XIa6QHwCGqUQrUo7WXTV9k/Lb55eLZh9bINy6LAAeYQfQX7LZ
MVCuC7lmJcUAkDTYuccgZdtAc1BCHI0ODq7rcMSLpr/M0h+tjKE6fuGP9AuB7NznoAy+
7yf9toy67DNIWAeQXptTq8ukBJ6AzBTerUbTrbwOWIBWOyVcnsyPkXRtPUNryu5Jvqlw6
//w0Fc9FG3dM+lmuzWQ5A=="}

Decrypted data is obtained as output

{"status": 200,"decrypted_data": "16g8d8U3K3PbcvY6LYafgZ23JrnxRXwZqBP8sA"}

Step 5 — RSA public key is retrieved from the requester using post /api/v1/get_rsa_

{ "primechain_address": "16g8d8U3K3PbcvY6LYafgZ23JrnxRXwZqBP8sA"}

RSA public key' of the requester is obtained as output

{"status": 200,"rsa_public_key": "-----BEGIN PUBLIC KEY-----
MIIBIjANBgkqhkiG9w0BAQEFAAOCAQ8AMIIBCgKCAQEAiB49uOAIfw2nGsu
eboVL +CWPYqiYS/
+pYrUjoCe3owwn395o68IPmYDm2NCYk17Dwx2bDW5/B4OFgznw+eSe
Lluf49OfTlq5zRQQLzrHSF5Tg4cVmxOH4XU3sbfPNxnvTVCBONq59LYvGsNBX
uDH hQIDAQAB -----END PUBLIC KEY-----"}

Step 6 — Generation of a random string with timestamp and hash using get/api/v1/create_string_timestamp

{"status": 200,"response": {"string":
"mroHlYTyC5gtYD3NcvS0vKG0rIrQOOF1DmdfMl5NCFBg7Xi0Yf9xsKS
N987OUwcnSKfoGn6q"timestamp": 1544601150,"hash":
"e7d0265f614a53dada9ecbe2555930cb4cfc3fc1accf6afb18b35a3619baff59f0
dce692edcd51e2284fb8f72cecaf75a6ab5e6cdbfabafcbc1020f606d6fd82"}}

The hash is encrypted with E-Learner1's RSA public key using post /api/v1/encrypt_data_rsa

{"status": 200,"response": {"string":
"mroHlYTyC5gtYD3NcvS0vKG0rIrQOOF1DmdfMl5NCFBg7Xi0Yf9xsKS
N987OUwcnSKfoGn6q"timestamp": 1544601150,"hash":
"e7d0265f614a53dada9ecbe2555930cb4cfc3fc1accf6afb18b35a3619baff59f0
dce692edcd51e2284fb8f72cecaf75a6ab5e6cdbfabafcbc1020f606d6fd82"}}

The hash is encrypted with E-Learner1's RSA public key using post /api/v1/encrypt_data_rsa
{

{   "data":
"e7d0265f614a53dada9ecbe2555930cb4cfc3fc1accf6afb18b35a3619baff59f0dce692edcd51
e2284fb8f72cecaf75a6ab5e6cdbfabafcbc1020f606d6fd82",
        "rsa_public_key": "-----BEGIN PUBLIC KEY-----
MIIBIjANBgkqhkiG9w0BAQEFAAOCAQ8AMIIBCgKCAQEAjAcsDs6uRwW2EpqRwm
Ot ZYXPID+rWvcV3ZKmGUr4mUictf/RVk0/o8Q/pGbeeKqfNXTBfvAh4ZcaFmXP3p98
56XowLHpYrutlYr9ZaOgZKWaA6NR8ThVVdyhTpU3FhigwdR5UGtAjVU08Ot14H9F
6rUyqtHINjfTQyMxDYiwVmfcAW0UJ1Nsp/ZkBOAUG+FOymHtYTsNbtacMkPi2O16
WwIDAQAB -----END PUBLIC KEY-----"}

The output is the encrypted data_rsa:

{"status": 200,"encrypted_data_rsa":
"HuQ6xjyEN9nayNAHg34enp89It2e10iew0mh3zyc7ZSMtz/i6weuai+PrLdR+LL3KbIT
QSJZHA1XDkKNvz7GmV6eDSX7meZWMXQJDVpBYeQYV+v38bGlAFOTmGos
CeaK+CeLFYPkC6J1SKulHU07hSNdO4BGkek0/au87ztK2RLo5E7qUjGOtxbfu5zM
QEYBghNhXVxfD2jO+Jr8zzkoRPeq7yfKtYtjtR68u6emlkRJIh08KHXZarplHFeDnaJ1
onqZMWYB0BbBSJDVt06S4PFzceMk5pdF5MwUe9y8OSzdeD0jsmGfG/YLEtpNSc
2IxCO0OtYgw3XbWbnbZvVntA=="}

Step 7 — Hash is sent to the requester.

Step 8 — Hash is decrypted using 'post /api/v1/decrypt_data_rsato"

{ "rsa_private_key": "-----BEGIN PRIVATE KEY-----
MIIEvgIBADANBgkqhkiG9w0BAQEFAASCBKgwggSkAgEAAoIBAQCMBywOzq5HBbYS
mpHCY61lhc8gP6ta9xXdkqYZSviZSJy1/9FWTT+jxD+kZt54qp81dMF+8CHhixoW
nq67jX6qPMKSemwvDBuXtk1EJVLnk3jyC86dgvTDH3m4Z4tOdtZ2lt2yIHBI6bNb
DV4bdXtbYmjn37AX+HdUiaI2lZmt5ep2SbW8TH+gpQKBgG3j7+t5N9wsCMv0JuS3
k1Kx2gY2tJfn3+JWd5FNPh5HUwD+gkJyuX2sJSKk8o3xHvxcM/2SCHoqLHUdXbQ9
q0AEVEwy6XV1wsJ+6ASoA+CbcL3mlllbB1E+fYiA4km9RabHwTbh82rogsOUMPXm
9qVefyQneafYs+zz1RuX0ya3 -----END PRIVATE KEY-----",
 "encrypted_data_rsa":
"HuQ6xjyEN9nayNAHg34enp89It2e10iew0mh3zyc7ZSMtz/i6weuai+PrLdR+LL3KbITQSJZHA1
XDkKNvz7GmV6eDSX7meZWMXQJDVpBYeQYV+v38bGlAFOTmGosCeaK+CeLFYPkC6J
1SKulHU07hSNdO4BGkek0/au87ztK2RLo5E7qUjGOtxbfu5zMQEYBghNhXVxfD2jO+Jr8zzko
RPeq7yfKtYtjtR68u6emlkRJIh08KHXZarplHFeDnaJ1onqZMWYB0BbBSJDVt06S4PFzceMk5p
dF5MwUe9y8OSzdeD0jsmGfG/YLEtpNSc2IxCO0OtYgw3XbWbnbZvVntA=="}

Hash is now obtained.

{"status": 200,"decrypted_data":
"e7d0265f614a53dada9ecbe2555930cb4cfc3fc1accf6afb18b35a3619baff59f0dce692ed
cd51e2284fb8f72cecaf75a6ab5e6cdbfabafcbc1020f606d6fd82

Step 9 — Requester signs the hash using post /api/v1/create_signature

{ "data":
"e7d0265f614a53dada9ecbe2555930cb4cfc3fc1accf6afb18b35a3619b
aff59f0dce692edcd51e2284fb8f72cecaf75a6ab5e6cdbfabafcbc1020f60
6d6fd82", "primechain_private_key":
"VEjwBWC6mgp8CNFPguZwt997rB5JCExQzB7wavwgKSZimBmae
KwPWdKH"}

The output is the digital signature.

{"status": 200,
"signature":
"H60blR7quU3GD5S3Apdh1uqM7ydEzMNRiQNAtKi6uOkdMhO14bjZpo
pURvbCoRKCsXusBRL7Yx03QiW0lvHO554="}

Step 10 — Encrypted envelope is created

{ "data":
{"signature":"H60blR7quU3GD5S3Apdh1uqM7ydEzMNRiQNAtKi6uOkd
MhO14bjZpopURvbCoRKCsXusBRL7Yx03QiW0lvHO554
=","primechain_address":"16g8d8U3K3PbcvY6LYafgZ23JrnxRXwZqBP8s
A",
"data":"e7d0265f614a53dada9ecbe2555930cb4cfc3fc1accf6afb18b35a3619
baff59f0dce692edcd51e2284fb8f72cecaf75a6ab5e6cdbfabafcbc1020f606d
6fd82" },
 "rsa_public_key": "-----BEGIN PUBLIC KEY-----
MIIBIjANBgkqhkiG9w0BAQEFAAOCAQ8AMIIBCgKCAQEAkydbbI+
68zjRmp0n7Yss
YpCSsVv6ywGCMH5xLGAWT3glGCx2mwjAi+/QbpSXIWorlzzlZOR2xI
+844dyDxbW MQIDAQAB -----END PUBLIC KEY-----"}

The output is encrypted_data_rsa:

{"status": 200,
"encrypted_data_rsa":
"R15SEiQtvY2QpxAY5MMXq2ar51ByO2y8TQcQtG9cge7SDPxT2cx8pQ8JcC89DV
ZuifLv4n6BGPtl/iIJDRtbyW+lEci+iVIGkOo5wM+Qz4PxIUUWGYRMGDPv2/K7tOHf
ElnNw+fjM5oS1NJRsq+
+UR1cQayteJiYTuea0XLOhNjerFCDJlG6tcinHIsNw+CSLKFrjjWo97v5U7llb+bUpAP
1xYRmS3EPVzP1Eu00ymhNlyUdIVZbI48si2p0ePhorE2S8bSOnOOBt6QW9rOSG4V
XAVBjUrHOw/nNIwWoYXXs6oSvOCykcelRNjMF0="}

Step 11 — Send the encrypted envelope to the verifier
Step 12 — Decrypting of the encrypted envelope using "post /api/v1/ decrypt_data_rsa" by verifier

{ "rsa_private_key": "-----BEGIN PRIVATE KEY-----
MIIEvQIBADANBgkqhkiG9w0BAQEFAASCBKcwggSjAgEAAoIBAQCTJ1tsj
7rzONGa nSftiyw3AptSXUjMESqCbRGn+
6257xU099lpbtiufCYQ7uM73f0LT/ECBrlTq9Hl

YS93Qj3Pw6ZSTqGTW4FYM9f4tawEWaGFGBL2CBYEp9nUTUBEAq8HJes
0bimeScGn
Tawewg84U4oiHuyTbtwli5PkB+XIKfGaXU3SMaHYHiORRe7BhQwWKHpLd
ob4JJtm CdNBuN+I1w9yaWG1TeWVjk8= -----END PRIVATE KEY-----",
"encrypted_data_rsa":
"R15SEiQtvY2QpxAY5MMXq2ar51ByO2y8TQcQtG9cge7SDPxT2cx8pQ8JcC
89DVZuifLv4n6BGPtl/iIJDRtbyW+lEci+iVIGkOo5wM+Qz4PxIUUWGYRMGD
Pv2/K7tOHffEInNw+fjM5oS1NJRsq+
TszlMb1cttdaG6wsJykqcSjW0NDD6wh2/4h3g7u45TzcgPpw8Ixmf6HFUtB1VP
+P5EQuA2kR/ZbQSFgo1CUw0LhMzQ3
+xnbDnZkS/TWbuwKtd9RcUQ9HEFdn3xFzrvlBQ3bqwfMXMzC4Y6NVhtV+
UR1cQayteJiYTuea0XLOhNjerFCDJIG6tcinHIsNw+CSLKFrjjWo97v5U7llb+b
UpAP1xYRmS3EPVzP1Eu00ymhNlyUdIVZbI48si2p0ePhorE2S8bSOnOOBt6Q
W9rOSG4VXAVBjUrHOw/nNIwWoYXXs6oSvOCykcelRNjMF0="}

Decrypted_data is seen as output

{"status": 200,
"decrypted_data": "
{ "signature":"H60blR7quU3GD5S3Apdh1uqM7ydEzMNRiQNAtKi6uOkdMhO14
bjZpopURvbCoRKCsXusBRL7Yx03QiW0lvHO554=",
"primechain_address":"16g8d8U3K3PbcvY6LYafgZ23JrnxRXwZqBP8sA",
"data":"e7d0265f614a53dada9ecbe2555930cb4cfc3fc1accf6afb18b35a3619baff59f
0dce692edcd51e2284fb8f72cecaf75a6ab5e6cdbfabafcbc1020f606d6fd82" }"}

Step 13 — Digital signature is verified

{"data":"e7d0265f614a53dada9ecbe2555930cb4cfc3fc1accf6afb18b35a3619baff59
f0dce692edcd51e2284fb8f72cecaf75a6ab5e6cdbfabafcbc1020f606d6fd82",
"primechain_address":"16g8d8U3K3PbcvY6LYafgZ23JrnxRXwZqBP8sA",
"signature":"H60blR7quU3GD5S3Apdh1uqM7ydEzMNRiQNAtKi6uOkdMhO14bj
ZpopURvbCoRKCsXusBRL7Yx03QiW0lvHO554="}

The obtained output is

{"status": 200,"response": true
}{"status": 200,"response": false

Signature is verified if the output is true, if false output is false.

4. Experimental Results

Figure 16 illustrates the overall block diagram of the proposed system. It consists of two components: first, the design and optimization of ACO training and search of the learning database; second, the design of kite-based partition authentication technique for the verification of a valid learner. The architecture of the ACO algorithm is as shown in Figure 17.

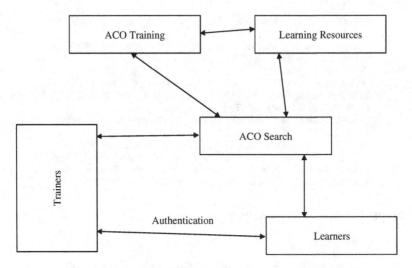

Figure 16.   Overall Block Diagram of the Proposed System

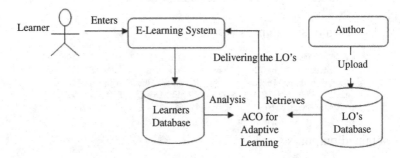

Figure 17.   The Architecture of ACO Search

The system includes learner, e-learning system, learner database, learning object database, author and algorithm of ACO based adaptive learning. Initially the learner enters into the e-learning system. The learner details are automatically updated in the learners database. Learner details consist of learning styles, knowledge level and keyword to search. This will be analyzed by the algorithm of ACO-based adaptive learning. This provides heuristic match rule, which is responsible for ranking learning objects and matching ratio is calculated. The author upload the new learning object into the LO database in a commonly accessible format, so that the learner can efficiently search and retrieve the suitable learning object.

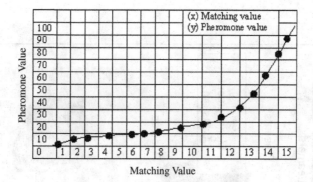

Matching Value

Figure 18. Heuristic Match Ratio

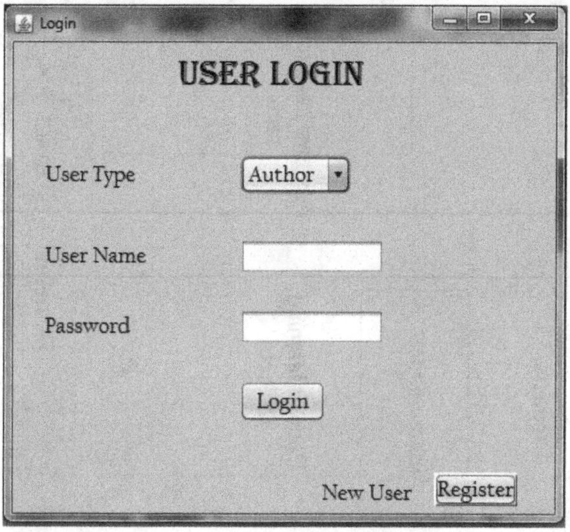

Figure 19. The User Interface of E-Learning System for Registration

Figure 18 shows the match ratio efficiency with pheromone updation. Figure 19 shows the graphical user interface of e-learning system where learners can register and enters the details. The learner should mention his/her style of learning. The learner has to mention the knowledge level and keyword to search SQL learning objects. Using learner characteristics the adaptive LOs are created. Also it presents the LO represented by paths. Figure 20 shows the detailed layout of the system from designing of the learning resources from authoring tools to the generation of the individual path for multiple LOs.

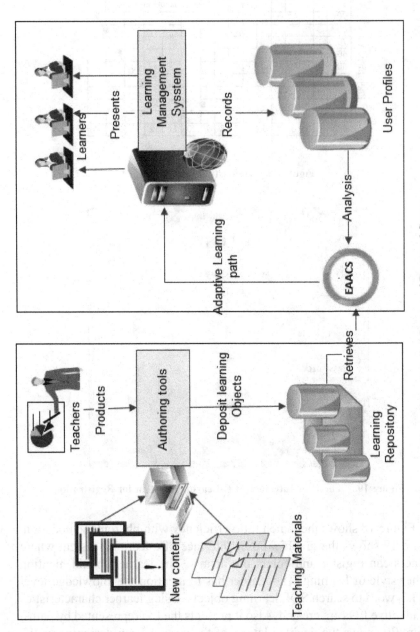

Figure 20.   Detailed Layout of Proposed System

Enhanced attribute based ant colony system (EAACS) is provided for generating adaptive learning path. It considers the static learner attributes such as learner learning style, knowledge level, preference and these attributes are matched with the LO attributes such as LO level, LO type, LO orientation. Three adaptive rules to reinforce pheromone update is also presented. More over a new parameter called node relevancy rating (RF) given by the learner for each LO along with match ratio of corresponding node is taken as the heuristic decision factor.

Section 3.3 explains the secure encryption process for the valid identification of the learner. The authentication process between the trainer and the learner is as follows:

1. A secret image is sent to the learner through a secure channel.
2. Kite based labeled tiles are used as key and are combined with the image for verifying the learner.
3. The key in the Step 2 is sent in the public channel which are itself encrypted by ABE for improved security.

This process provides two level security for the e-Learning system.

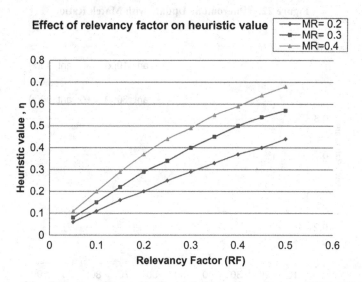

Figure 21.   Relevancy Factor Vs Heuristic Value for a Constant Match Ratio

4.1 *Heuristic value analysis*

The heuristic value η_{ij} is defined as $\eta_{ij} = 1 - e^{-(RFij * MRij)/\sum k=1 \text{ to } Ni (RFik)}$. As the relevancy factor (RF) is increasing the heuristic value also need to be increased. The effect of RF value on the heuristic value is shown in Figure 21.

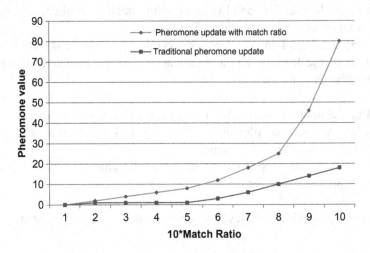

Figure 22.　Pheromone Update with Match Ratio

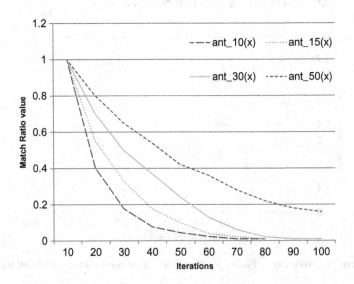

Figure 23.　Match Ratio Values Deviation

4.2 *Evaluation of trail intensities*

The variation of the intensity of two trails (Figure 22), i.e., traditional pheromone update and EAACS-based pheromone update after considering the match ratio is shown in Figure 23.

5. Discussion and Conclusions

The important aspects of this research are: (a) understandable learner's characteristics and learning style (Kolb), (b) Adaptive matching rule is generated to match the relationship between learner and learning object, and (c) Providing the best learning object for the learner based on ACO is defined.

The learning object can be generated using Ant Colony Optimization. This is because the various learner's characteristics are measured for adaptive learning. The heuristic matching ratio values deviation learner's from knowledge level and style are calculated. In this work, the kite tiling concept is embedded in secret image and then the image is partitioned into frames according to the concept of kite which is encrypted and transmitted. The reconstruction of transmitted secret image is done without complicated calculations. This method can be utilized for sharing of file between sender and receiver. Blockchain with cryptography provides secure authentication for valid users.

References

Back, T., Hammel, U., & Schwefel, H. P. (1997). Evolutionary computation: Comments on the history and current state. *IEEE Transactions on Evolutionary Computation, 1*(1), 3–17.

Blum, C., & Dorigo, M. (2004). The hyper-cube framework for ant colony optimization. *IEEE Transactions on Systems, Man, and Cybernetics, Part B (Cybernetics), 34*(2), 1161–1172.

Bonabeau, E., Dorigo, M., Directeur de Recherches Du Fnrs Marco, Theraulaz, G., Théraulaz, G., *et al.* (1999). *Swarm Intelligence: From Natural to Artificial Systems.* Oxford University Press, United Kingdom.

Brindha, K., & Jeyanthi, N. (2017). Securing portable document format file using extended visual cryptography to protect cloud data storage. *IJ Network Security, 19*(5), 684–693.

Brusilovsky, P. (2001). Adaptive hypermedia. *User Modeling and User-Adapted Interaction, 11*(1–2), 87–110.

Dahbi, A., Elkamoun, N., & Berraissoul, A. (2006). Adaptation and optimisation of pedagogical paths by ants's algorithm. In *2006 2nd International Conference on Information & Communication Technologies*, Vol. 1, pp. 546–551.

Dorigo, M., & Gambardella, L. M. (1997). Ant colony system: A cooperative learning approach to the traveling salesman problem. *IEEE Transactions on Evolutionary Computation, 1*(1), 53–66.

Fulcher, J. (2006). *Advances in Applied Artificial Intelligence*. IGI Global.

Gutiérrez, S., Valigiani, G., Collet, P., & Kloos, C. D. (2007). Adaptation of the ACO heuristic for sequencing learning activities. In *Proceedings of the EC-TEL*, pp. 17–20.

Harasim, L. M. (1990). Online education: An environment for collaboration and intellectual amplification. In L. M. Harasim (Ed.), *Online education: Perspectives on a New Environment* (pp. 39–66). New York: Praeger Publishers.

Latchoumi, T. P., & Parthiban, L. (2019). Secure data storage in cloud environment using MAS. *Indian Journal of Science and Technology, 9*(24). doi: 10.17485/ijst/2016/v9i24/95280.

Marquez, J. M., Ortega, J. O., Gonzalez-Abril, L., & Velasco, F. (2008). Creating adaptive learning paths using ant colony optimization and Bayesian networks. In *2008 IEEE International Joint Conference on Neural Networks (IEEE World Congress on Computational Intelligence)*, pp. 3834–3839.

Priyanka, K, Merc, V., & Rajaselvi M. E. (2016). Secure document search and retrieval using visual cryptography scheme in cloud environment. *International Journal of Computer Technology and Applications, 7*(3), 458–464.

Sah, H. R., Gunasekaran, G., & Parthiban, L. (2018). A novel privacy preserving visual cryptography based scheme for telemedicine applications. *Biomedical Research, Special Issue*, S145–S149.

Semet, Y., Lutton, E. & Collet, P. (2003). Ant colony optimisation for e-learning: Observing the emergence of pedagogic suggestions. In *Proceedings of the 2003 IEEE Swarm Intelligence Symposium. SIS'03 (Cat. No. 03EX706)*, pp. 46–52.

Sengupta, S., Sahu, S., & Dasgupta, R. (2012). Construction of learning path using ant colony optimization from a frequent pattern graph. *ArXiv Preprint ArXiv:1201.3976*.

Van Merrienboer, Jeroen J. G., & Ayres, A. (2005). Research on cognitive load theory and its design implications for e-learning. *Educational Technology Research and Development, 53*(3), 5–13.

Vinodhini, A., Premanand, M., & Natarajan, M. (2012). Visual cryptography using two factor biometric system for trust worthy authentication. *International Journal of Scientific and Research Publications, 2*(3), 1–50.

Wang, T-I., Wang, K-T., & Huang, Y-M. (2008). Using a style-based ant colony system for adaptive learning. *Expert Systems with Applications, 34*(4), 2449–2464.

Wong, L-H., & Looi, C-K. (2009). Adaptable learning pathway generation with ant colony optimization. *Journal of Educational Technology and Society, 12*(3), 309–326.

Yang, Y. J., & Wu, C. (2009). An attribute-based ant colony system for adaptive learning object recommendation. *Expert Systems with Applications, 36*(2), 3034–3047.

Chapter 7

Indian Corporate Governance with Relation to Sarbanes Oxley (SOX) Act: Proposing Business Intelligence (BI) and Blockchain as an Integrated Key Strategy

Kuldeep Singh*,‡, Madhvendra Misra†,§, and Jitendra Yadav†,¶

*Department of Commerce, Koneru Lakshmaiah
Education Foundation, Guntur, India

†Department of Management Studies, Indian Institute
of Information Technology, Allahabad, India

‡kuldeepsinghcsr@gmail.com

§madhvendra@iiita.ac.in

¶yadavjitendra.phd@gmail.com

Abstract

Among all business disciplines, corporate governance falls under the most significant regulatory fields related to business organizations, in such a way that it affects overall productivity, growth, and even market survival. Owing to changing business conditions, stakeholders' responsibilities, and the increasing demand for fair business practices, organizations currently focus on reversing traditional governance practices with new initiatives such as blockchain technology, and business intelligence (BI) governance. Internal stakeholders may have an influence on many organizational decisions in a microenvironment, such as compensation policy, recruitment policy, and dividend policy. For this purpose, the Securities and Exchange Committee of the United States has introduced the Sarbanes Oxley Law (SOX), while in India, the same law was introduced as "Clause 49," issued in line with corporate governance by the Securities and Exchange Board of India. In this study, we compare the Indian version of corporate governance with the U.S. SOX by proposing BI as an essential strategy powered through blockchain technology.

Keywords: Corporate governance, Business intelligence (BI), Blockchain, Clause 49, Sarbanes Oxley Law (SOX)

1. Introduction

A corporation consists of a community of stakeholders such as staff, customers, creditors, sponsors, government, and society (Ferrell, 2004; Singh *et al.*, 2019, 2021; Singh & Misra, 2020a, 2020b, 2021; Yadav *et al.*, 2021). Contradictions have been found in business and management literature in the ties between stakeholders due to the difference between their goals, a lack of information, ownership structure, and division of control (Itzik *et al.*, 2016; Welford *et al.*, 2008). From developed to developing nations, it is apparent that corporate fraud is both a significant problem and a growing concern (Hass *et al.*, 2016; Yadav *et al.*, 2020a). As fraud and scandals have occurred increasingly in the corporate world, laws and regulations have emerged as a necessarily required step for any country to take (Pontell, 2005; Yadav *et al.*, 2020a, 2020b).

On one hand, as new technologies are discovered, the complexity of commercial activities increases with complex business transactions that are not easy to address and organizations find that solutions are difficult to identify. On the other hand, shareholders assume that managers can always increase their gains at the expense of shareholders (Ben-Amar & Andre, 2006). The concept of corporate governance therefore came into existence to mitigate these disputes. In order to deal with the changing work environment, companies need to have access to information about their ongoing performances and for this, business intelligence (BI) could play an important role in supporting such processes at different organizational levels (Chugh & Grandhi, 2013).

Corporate governance in the corporate world has received considerable attention after the high-profile controversies in the United States, such as Adelphia and WorldCom which were exposed, as well as in India after Ketan Parekh, Harshad Mehta, Satyam and the Indian industry 2G were exposed (Rezaee *et al.*, 2003; Sehgal & Mulraj, 2008). Because of this, the most significant corporate governance law in the United States, the Sarbanes Oxley Law (SOX), emerged in 2002 (Aguilera, 2005; Ghosh *et al.*, 2010), and the same was introduced in India in the form of "Clause 49" as an Indian version of corporate governance law issued by Securities and Exchange Board of India (SEBI) in 2005 (Balasubramanian *et al.*, 2010; Col & Sen, 2019). Initially, the goal of these laws was to ensure the elimination of corporate theft and malpractice. According to these governance laws, it has been stated that independent auditors and heads of finance should provide financial statements. Proponents of the Rules discuss how they are necessary because corporate crises result in a requirement to strengthen current oversight processes for public corporations.

As can be seen in emerging literature, the concept of BI governance provides crucial support to business organizations to adequately develop and sustain governance for a longer time (Chugh & Grandhi, 2013). BI governance provides business organizations with a framework according to which required resources can be channeled toward business policies. Basically, BI is able to provide a more significant opportunity to organizations as they become equipped to observe data from a number of different viewpoints. When BI is successfully executed, it can contribute to achieving competitive advantages; simultaneously, it enables organizational learning to manage undesirable consequences which may include loss of reputation and investors' confidence (Chugh & Grandhi, 2013). The datacenters contributing to information ingestion in the BI framework can be secured through the integration of the blockchain technology, thus offering a fool-proof infrastructure of governance.

2. Historical Perspective

The term "corporate governance" was initially used as early as 1963 to ensure fair returns on investment to shareholders who invest their money in a business, as well as to provide protection from unethical management practices and to prevent them from misusing their investment (Zengul *et al.*, 2019). Several critical developments have subsequently taken place over the last two decades which have brought about a radical change in the management of corporations (Nheri, 2014).

The corporate governance system in the United States has changed continuously over the last few decades (Gillan & Starks, 2003; Singh *et al.*, 2019) and strong management and weak investors could be seen during this period. Until Enron, there were many organizations in the United States which applied a corporate governance model that was in operation (Mizrach, 2006), but there was also a concurrent surge of conjecture and as a result, there was an increase of many possibilities of initial public offering (IPO) profit-making in the short term. With the collapse of Enron in 2001, a comprehensive review of corporate governance practices was undertaken around the globe (Mallin *et al.*, 2005). Enron announced that there were very many reasons why the system did not work according to standard as well as many other factors. The WorldCom controversy attacked corporate governance of the United States again in 2002, leading to the commencement of SOX which was generally considered a "progressive" piece of administrative legislation (Unerman & O'Dwyer, 2004).

In the Indian context, this was around the time when a few business organizations conducted speculation-based activities and sought to make short-term profits through IPOs. The Harshad Mehta scandal was the first time that it came under the spotlight in 1992 (Sehgal & Mulraj, 2008). Mehta was illegally conducting stock-processing practices funded by worthless bank receipts. When Harshad Mehta declared as "Dalal Street Sultan," his tricks were blindly followed. Harshad Mehta misused his reputation for its financial advantage by exploiting share prices for certain shares. SEBI had, at the time, no such power for controlling investor and stockbroker transactions. The Central Bureau of Investigation was the only authoritative entity with the jurisdiction to investigate the matter. However, in view of this, the Indian Legislative system approved the Securities Exchange Board of India Act, 1992 (Manna *et al.*, 2019). The SEBI Act consisted of mainly three functions: a protection function, development function, and a regulation function.

Harshad Mehta's methods came back into business again in 1997, by employing stockbrokers who bought and sold shares in his name for a charge (Goel, 2017). However, the Securities Exchange Board of India was able to catch his tricks on this occasion, as it had grown and become a regulator of the market. The consequence of all this led to the emergence of Clause 49 which was adopted by the end of 2002 (Balasubramanian *et al.*, 2010). Nevertheless, after the emergence of Clause 49, similar fraudulent behavior and scams continued, as can be seen in the case of the Ketan Parekh fraud exposed in 2001, followed by the 2008 2G scam, and the 2013 coal scam (Agarwal, 2014). This indicates that the Securities Exchange Board of India alone was still unable to detect such scams, although somehow it managed to firmly react to deal with these types of illegal practices so that they would never occur again.

3. Reporting Structure of Corporate Fraud in India and the United States

Corporate scamming is a global phenomenon affecting all countries and economic sectors. Such fraud concerns a large number of illegal activities and unethical practices which include intentional deception and misrepresentation of facts.

In this regard, the U.S. government's first move was the implementation of the 1977 Foreign Corrupt Practices Act, initiated to ensure good governance (Weismann *et al.*, 2014). The primary purpose of implementing such an initiative was to deal with such illegal practices and unethical systems. As reputed organizational scams emerged, the U.S. Treadway Commission was established in 1985 by stressing essential conditions for the constitution of Independent Boards and Committees (Singleton, 2008). The Commission was designed to ensure clarity regarding a company's financial position and other related issues. After Enron collapsed in 2002, the United States legislature passed the SOX Act to protect investors from any possibility of corporate fraud (Wintoki, 2007). Basically, the SOX Act deals with the independence of the auditor and the financial disclosures in particular.

While governance efforts were acknowledged around the developed nations, India was lagging in the adoption of such practices. However, corporate governance became popular in India in the wake of liberalization through the 1990s. In 1992, the reform of the SEBI was a primary mover (Mishra & Mohanty, 2014). At that time the Indian Securities Exchange Board played the primary role in regulating and monitoring stock market activities, as well as creating other rules and regulations on corporate governance. In 1996, the Confederation of Indian Industry also adopted it as a voluntary initiative (Khanna & Palepu, 2004). At that point, it forged a series of laws which included rules and procedures for companies in India to promote corporate governance. To deal with corruption and insider trading and to design a code for better corporate governance, the Indian Securities and Exchange Board formed two committees on May 7, 1999, Narayan Murthy and Kumar Mangalam Birla (Sharma, 2015). These committees provided their recommendations to introduce

Clause 49 to improve and encourage corporate governance practices. At that time, Clause 49 was updated to consider the challenges and address them through all rules and requirements.

4. The United States and India Corporate Governance Legal Framework

A comparative study was carried out between the United States and India to gain factual information about the term corporate governance legal framework. Such a study provides the detail of various factors which are similar in both legal frameworks and where they are different.

While both regulations have the same purpose, they vary in terms of their structure and provisions.

- The SOX Act was issued in line with the internal controls for financial reporting (Rikhardsson *et al.*, 2008). In compliance with section 404 (b) of the SOX Act, an independent auditor is required to certify management assessment (Lenard *et al.*, 2016). In compliance with the Act, an organization has to take the financial information and consistency which has occurred throughout the whole organization into consideration. From the Indian perspective, the principles for the corporate governance of the entire company are based on Clause 49 which encompasses all the procedures and not only the corporation's financial operation.
- As per the SOX Act, the boards are responsible for internal control. The boards consist of the principal financial officers having certifying authority for similar functions. However, in India, Clause 49 was found to provide no guidelines for such committees and mentioned similarities for the Chief Executive Officer (CEO) and Chief Financial Officer (CFO) of a business organization. The CEO and the CFO have the authority to certify that the implementation of internal controls is active in the firm. Where any wrongdoing occurs in the company, the CEO and the CFO will be held responsible.
- The SOX Act tells companies to set up a commission to supervise the financial and accounting procedures established by the issuer's board of directors. If there is no committee then all the directors of the company who are serving as board members would be declared to be members of the audit committee. The duration for audit committee meetings

and the number of audit committee directors is not specified under the SOX Act. However, as per Clause 49:

(a) There have to be at least three directors on the audit committee.
(b) Two-thirds of the members of the audit committee have to be independent directors.
(c) All members of the audit committee have to be financially capable and at least one of them must have experience in financial management and accounting.

- Provision for an independent director mentioned above, to act as an audit committee member is the same for the SOX Act as well as Clause 49, however, information about this differs in each law. In terms of an independent person, the SOX Act specifies that that person cannot charge any consultancy fees or receive any form of payment from the business organization. In Clause 49, the person is an independent director if:

(a) Only the salary of the director is considered and they receive no other additional advantages except their pay.
(b) The person has no relationship with any other individual holding the managerial spot in the firm and also has no ties to the development of the company.
(c) The person hasn't been a director, nor been a partner in any of the laws and consulting firms or audit firms in the company during the preceding three years.
(d) The person should not be a business service provider or a firm supplier.
(e) The person holds no more than two percent of voting shares.

The description of the independent directors can be seen clearly in the above points. In Clause 49, the independent director's exclusion scope is much broader than the SOX Act.

- Section 301 of the SOX Act outlines the Audit Committee's responsibilities, including the retaining and resolution of complaints, as well as the establishment of procedures for receiving complaints (Ribstein, 2003). The claims may apply to the supervision, funding, and controls which are internal to the company. Under Clause 49 on the other hand, there is a disclosure provision, stating that a Committee for Investors' Grievances has to be created which involves no receipts of declared dividends or balance sheets and shares transfers. Hence, it can be noticed that the SOX Act takes accounting-related issues very seriously, unlike Clause 49.

Organizations should reveal the accepted code of conduct in compliance with the SOX Act and explanations should be given by the committee if there is no agreed-upon code of conduct. However, it is stated in Clause 49 that the code of conduct must be published on a company's official website and that all senior management and members of the company's board of directors must follow said code. For each organization, the code of conduct is required as per the Indian legal framework. The code of conduct also applies to all stakeholders; although, as mentioned in the SOX Act, the code of conduct applies only to the CFO(s).

5. Limitations

From this study's analysis, the system of rules and regulations for corporate governance seems to be appropriate in both countries. Nevertheless, it is believed that the rules-based approach alone may not be enough to improve corporate governance. As both countries have clearly specified in their legislation that it is necessary to keep a board, including a non-Executive Director, and describing some directors as being independent. It shows that they are regarded as being independent because they have appropriate skills, expertise, and are not in conflict with any provisions. Nonetheless, other concerns about such directors that matter to stakeholders are as follows:

- Their interest seems to have artificial desires.
- They have a more conservative approach.
- They use financial resources for spending.
- There is a moderator of independence for timely service.

Independent directors cannot ensure completely perfect corporate governance, but the independent decision could be of significant importance and hold considerable potential benefit.

Should there be a rigorous law or mandate structure, then enforcement is again uncertain, since it is not necessarily true that fear of a fine for non-compliance would influence the firms. Some organizations may simply ignore and be non-compliant with the laws and regulations. If a successful business has satisfied stakeholders, it follows that corporate governance may be a subordinate need for them. Fines are somehow flexible in India and regulations also do not translate as a criminal offense, as U.S. businesses are more concerned with non-compliance under SOX.

6. Proposing BI and Blockchain as an Integrated Key Strategy

Chugh and Grandhi (2013) suggested a process for developing BI as a governance strategy in four steps, based on the features which BI tools provide and which guarantee value and sustain good governance. These steps are helpful in supporting business corporations in their understanding and actual utilization of BI tools for designing their own governance framework (Chugh & Grandhi, 2013). The first step is the *identification and conceptualizing* of the need for BI in the business context which supports organizational objectives through BI, in line with corporate governance and, most importantly, stakeholders' recognition. The next step is to focus on *action plans* to align BI at all organizational levels. This will help to strategize stakeholders' authority, accountability, and roles and responsibilities. The third step is *execution*, through which several issues and causes relating to data accessibility and issues of standards can be addressed. BI tool enables the decision makers to gather data from various sources and through analysis obtain meaningful insights. However, since the data for the corporates is being generated by organizational and non-organizational entities, the probability of data corruption increases due to the factors of self-fulfillment and greed (as discussed above). For the effective utilization of the BI tools, proper enforcement of the governance laws and inculcate the practice of fair trade the authors suggest the integration of the blockchain technology in the existing infrastructure. Blockchain technology offers a streamlined peer-peer transfer of data following a feed-forward flow. Entities (stakeholders) can input the data at various levels that are stored in the individual blocks and are progressed forwards for others to view the data in the network and also enter the data at their levels. Yadav *et al.* (2020a) have proposed a scheme for the granular data traceability and security through the blockchain technology where the data is being generated by the entities (both human and IoT devices) at various levels of operations. The infrastructure of IoT and human integrated data generation and dissemination powered by the blockchain technology has been tested in a more formal infrastructures where the government laws have also been included through the use of smart contracts (Yadav *et al.*, 2020b). Organizations through the use of blockchain technology provide a unique identifier to every stakeholder and can effectively enforce the corporate governance laws through the use of smart contracts. The blockchain adoption will not only bring fairness in the trade practices, operations, and auditing but will also enable the organizations to meet the economies of scale by restricting mal-practices and frauds.

7. Conclusion

Acts such as the SOX Act 2002 and Indian Clause 49, which are identical in many ways, have been brought forward for the security of creditors and other firms' stakeholders with certain specific provisions. These laws have been passed and revised periodically to closely track a company's operations. While Corporate Governance laws in India are addressed in the 2013 Companies Act, some stringent characteristics similar to the SOX Act are included, although, a few provisions are still missing in the Indian Government's Clause 49. Indian Acts need to be transparent, effective, and efficient in the form of internal control measures taken by corporations within their organizations. These provisions will undoubtedly increase the trust of investors and provide them with a perception of security against misinterpretation. The SOX has several of these types of provisions which deal with non-compliant white-collar workers and their offenses.

Overall, after a systematic review of both laws on the same approach toward corporate governance, it is recommended that the provisions of the Indian Act and the Indian Law have a much larger scope for implementation; however, timely reforms and refinement could be used to cope with changes so that an effective sense of governance practices in India can be provided. Based on this, BI powered through blockchain technology for better corporate governance is proposed in this study. From this study, it can be concluded that BI and blockchain based corporate governance not only for the organization but also for stakeholders, can offer multiple benefits, such as competitive advantages, ROI, the ability to deal with uncertainty, data security, authenticity, transparency, etc.

References

Agarwal, A. K. (2014). Corporate governance: Changing trends in interpreting fiduciary duty. *Vikalpa: The Journal for Decision Makers, 39*(3), 1–12. https://doi.org/10.1177/0256090920140301.

Aguilera, R. V. (2005). Corporate governance and director accountability: An institutional comparative perspective. *British Journal of Management, 16*(s1), S39–S53. https://doi.org/10.1111/j.1467-8551.2005.00446.x.

Balasubramanian, N., Black, B. S., & Khanna, V. (2010). The relation between firm-level corporate governance and market value: A case study of India. *Emerging Markets Review, 11*(4), 319–340. https://doi.org/10.1016/j.ememar.2010.05.001.

Ben-Amar, W., & Andre, P. (2006). Separation of ownership from control and acquiring firm performance: The case of family ownership in Canada. *Journal of Business Finance, 33*(3–4), 517–543. https://doi.org/10.1111/j.1468-5957.2006.00613.x.

Chugh, R., & Grandhi, S. (2013). Why business intelligence? *International Journal of E-Entrepreneurship and Innovation, 4*(2), 1–14. https://doi.org/10.4018/ijeei.2013040101.

Col, B., & Sen, K. (2019). The role of corporate governance for acquisitions by the emerging market multinationals: Evidence from India. *Journal of Corporate Finance, 59*, 239–254. https://doi.org/10.1016/j.jcorpfin.2017.09.014.

Ferrell, O. C. (2004). Business ethics and customer stakeholders. *Academy of Management Perspectives, 18*(2), 126–129. https://doi.org/10.5465/ame.2004.13836176.

Ghosh, A., Marra, A., & Moon, D. (2010). Corporate boards, audit committees, and earnings management: Pre- and post-SOX evidence. *Journal of Business Finance and Accounting, 37*(9–10), 1145–1176. https://doi.org/10.1111/j.1468-5957.2010.02218.x.

Gillan, S. L., & Starks, L. T. (2003). Institutional investors, corporate ownership and corporate governance: Global perspectives. In L. Sun (Ed.), *Ownership and Governance of Enterprises* (pp. 36–68). Palgrave Macmillan, London. https://doi.org/10.1057/9781403943903_2.

Goel, U., Kumar, S., Singh, K., & Manrai, R. (2017, October). Corporate Governance: Indian perspective with relation to Sarbanes Oxley Act. In *Proceedings of the International Conference on Economics and Development* (Vol. 1, No. 1, pp. 60–72).

Hass, L. H., Tarsalewska, M., & Zhan, F. (2016). Equity incentives and corporate fraud in China. *Journal of Business Ethics, 138*(4), 723–742. https://doi.org/10.1007/s10551-015-2774-2.

Itzik, N., Reinhartz-Berger, I., & Wand, Y. (2016). Variability analysis of requirements: Considering behavioral differences and reflecting stakeholders' perspectives. *IEEE Transactions on Software Engineering, 42*(7), 687–706. https://doi.org/10.1109/TSE.2015.2512599.

Khanna, T., & Palepu, K. G. (2004). Globalization and convergence in corporate governance: Evidence from Infosys and the Indian software industry. *Journal of International Business Studies, 35*(6), 484–507. https://doi.org/10.1057/palgrave.jibs.8400103.

Lenard, M. J., Petruska, K. A., Alam, P., & Yu, B. (2016). Internal control weaknesses and evidence of real activities manipulation. *Advances in Accounting, 33*, 47–58. https://doi.org/10.1016/j.adiac.2016.04.008.

Mallin, C., Mullineux, A., & Wihlborg, C. (2005). The financial sector and corporate governance: The UK case. *Corporate Governance: An International Review, 13*(4), 532–541. https://doi.org/10.1111/j.1467-8683.2005.00447.x.

Manna, A., Sahu, T. N., & Gupta, A. (2019). Corporate governance in India. In *Governance-Led Corporate Performance: Theory and Practice* (pp. 13–32). Emerald Publishing Limited. https://doi.org/10.1108/978-1-78973-847-620191003.

Mishra, S., & Mohanty, P. (2014). Corporate governance as a value driver for firm performance: Evidence from India. *Corporate Governance, 14*(2), 265–280. https://doi.org/10.1108/CG-12-2012-0089.

Mizrach, B. (2006). The Enron Bankruptcy: When did the options market in Enron lose it's smirk? *Review of Quantitative Finance and Accounting, 27*(4), 365–382. https://doi.org/10.1007/s11156-006-0043-2.

Nheri, O. (2014). Economic reforms, corporate governance and privatization method as determinants in performance changes of new privatized firms: The case of MENA countries. *Journal of Management and Governance, 18*(1), 95–127. https://doi.org/10.1007/s10997-012-9222-9.

Pontell, H. N. (2005). White-collar crime or just risky business? The role of fraud in major financial debacles. *Crime, Law and Social Change.* https://doi.org/10.1007/s10611-005-1934-1.

Rezaee, Z., Olibe, K. O., & Minmier, G. (2003). Improving corporate governance: The role of audit committee disclosures. *Managerial Auditing Journal, 18*(6/7), 530–537. https://doi.org/10.1108/02686900310482669.

Ribstein, L. E. (2003). International implications of Sarbanes-Oxley: Raising the rent on US law. *Journal of Corporate Law Studies, 3*(2), 299–327. https://doi.org/10.1080/14735970.2003.11419905.

Rikhardsson, P., Best, P., & Juhl-Christensen, C. (2008). Sarbanes-Oxley compliance, internal control, and ERP systems. In *Enterprise Resource Planning for Global Economies* (pp. 208–226). IGI Global. https://doi.org/10.4018/978-1-59904-531-3.ch012.

Sehgal, A., & Mulraj, J. (2008). Corporate governance in India: Moving gradually from a regulatory model to a market-driven model — A survey. *International Journal of Disclosure and Governance, 5*(3), 205–235. https://doi.org/10.1057/jdg.2008.9.

Sharma, P. K. (2015). Codes and standards of corporate governance. In *Corporate Governance Practices in India* (pp. 28–42). Palgrave Macmillan UK. https://doi.org/10.1057/9781137519368_3.

Singh, K., & Misra, M. (2020a). Developing an agricultural entrepreneur inclination model for sustainable agriculture by integrating expert mining and ISM–MICMAC. *Environment, Development and Sustainability.* https://doi.org/10.1007/s10668-020-00806-x.

Singh, K., & Misra, M. (2020b). Linking harmonious CSR and financial inclusion: The moderating effects of financial literacy and income. *The Singapore Economic Review*, 1–22. https://doi.org/10.1142/S0217590820500629.

Singh, K., & Misra, M. (2021). Linking corporate social responsibility (CSR) and organizational performance: The moderating effect of corporate reputation. *European Research on Management and Business Economics*, *27*(1), 100139. https://doi.org/10.1016/j.iedeen.2020.100139.

Singh, K., Misra, M., Kumar, M., & Tiwari, V. (2019). A study on the determinants of financial performance of U.S. agricultural cooperatives. *Journal of Business Economics and Management*, *20*(4), 633–647. https://doi.org/10.3846/jbem.2019.9858.

Singh, K., Misra, M., & Yadav, J. (2021). Corporate social responsibility and financial inclusion: Evaluating the moderating effect of income. *Managerial and Decision Economics*, mde.3306. https://doi.org/10.1002/mde.3306.

Singleton, T. (2008). Internal controls: Strategies for smaller companies. *Journal of Corporate Accounting & Finance*, *19*(4), 37–40. https://doi.org/10.1002/jcaf.20400.

Unerman, J., & O'Dwyer, B. (2004). Enron, WorldCom, Andersen *et al.*: A challenge to modernity. *Critical Perspectives on Accounting*, *15*(6–7), 971–993. https://doi.org/10.1016/j.cpa.2003.04.002.

Weismann, M. F., Buscaglia, C. A., & Peterson, J. (2014). The foreign corrupt practices act: Why it fails to deter bribery as a global market entry strategy. *Journal of Business Ethics*, *123*(4), 591–619. https://doi.org/10.1007/s10551-013-2012-8.

Welford, R., Chan, C., & Man, M. (2008). Priorities for corporate social responsibility: A survey of businesses and their stakeholders. *Corporate Social Responsibility and Environmental Management*, *15*(1), 52–62. https://doi.org/10.1002/csr.166.

Wintoki, M. B. (2007). Corporate boards and regulation: The effect of the Sarbanes–Oxley Act and the exchange listing requirements on firm value. *Journal of Corporate Finance*, *13*(2–3), 229–250. https://doi.org/10.1016/j.jcorpfin.2007.03.001.

Yadav, J., Misra, M., & Goundar, S. (2020a). An overview of food supply chain virtualisation and granular traceability using blockchain technology. *International Journal of Blockchains and Cryptocurrencies*, *1*(2), 154. https://doi.org/10.1504/IJBC.2020.108997.

Yadav, J., Misra, M., & Goundar, S. (2020b). Autonomous Agriculture marketing information system through blockchain: A case study of e-NAM adoption in India. In *Blockchain Technologies, Applications and Cryptocurrencies* (pp. 115–138). World Scientific. https://doi.org/10.1142/9789811205279_0005.

Yadav, J., Misra, M., & Singh, K. (2021). Sensitizing Netizen's behavior through influencer intervention enabled by crowdsourcing — A case of reddit. *Behaviour and Information Technology*, 1–12. https://doi.org/10.1080/01449 29X.2021.1872705.

Zengul, F. D., Byrd, J. D., Oner, N., Edmonds, M., & Savage, A. (2019). Exploring corporate governance research in accounting journals through latent semantic and topic analyses. *Intelligent Systems in Accounting, Finance and Management, 26*(4), 175–192. https://doi.org/10.1002/isaf.1461.

Chapter 8

Efficient Secure Image Encryption Using RFID with Blockchain Technology in IIoT

V. R. Elangovan*,‖, R. Nirmala†,**, R. Jayakarthik‡,††,
P. Tamilarasi§,‡‡, and R. Kiruthiga¶,§§

*Department of Computer Applications,
Agurchand Manmull Jain College,
Meenambakkam, Chennai, India

†Department of B.Com (Computer Applications),
Shri Krishnaswamy College for Women, India

‡Department of Computer Science, Vels Institute of Science,
Technology and Advanced Studies, Chennai, India

§Department of Computer Science,
R. B. Gothi Jain College for Women, Chennai, India

¶Department of Computer Applications,
St Anne's Art's and Science College,
Madhavaram, Chennai, India

‖elangotesting@gmail.com

**nimmi_kala@yahoo.com

††drrjayakarthik@gmail.com

‡‡tamilmalu@yahoo.com

§§Chennaikirthimrk238@gmail.com

159

Abstract

In industrial methods, cameras and intelligent image sensors are widely used in process design and also in quality control of the resulting product. In the Industrial Internet of Things (IIoT), the sensors are used to generate images that are constantly at risk of reporting and infringement. Given that third-party intrusion occurs, the only way to secure data that fades into IIoT environments is through traditional methods. Currently, blockchain technology is the main solution to trust problems and also to eliminate intrusion from third parties. The objective of this chapter is really to explore the mutual effect on supply chain transparency on Radio Frequency Identification (RFID), the IIoT, and blockchain technologies. Depends on the Number of Pixels per Change Rate (NPCR), and analysis of entropy information, the data can be analyzed. In support of a variety of attacks, we determine the power of an algorithm that is encrypted for image encryption. RFID technology affects all IIoT & blockchain systems strongly and significantly, which in fact will have a significant and positive impact on Supply Chain Transparency (SCT). Through each industrial & blockchain IoT technology, the RFID system has an indirect impact on SCT. This research was the first scientific test of SCT's influence on RFID, IIoT, and blockchain technologies. To facilitate the generalization of the results, observations from the first wave may be repeated. The most recent measures are designed and tested with precision and consistency for the use of industrial IoT systems, including blockchain technology. This is the first research to examine the cumulative effect on supply chain technology of RFID, IIoT, and blockchain systems, Edwards-curve Digital Signature Algorithm (EdDSA), public key encryption using a variant of the Schnorr signature based on Edwards' twisted curves. In an IIoT environment, images can be secured by providing an authorized solution based on a private blockchain when the images are encrypted. In this method, the image includes the cryptographic pixel values which are stored in the blockchain, checking the confidentiality and security of the data. We obtained the value of entropy closer to an absolute value of 8, which is protected against the attack of brute force. Thus, the suggested method is very effective in preventing data leakage and the security that is described in the encrypted results.

Keywords: Radio frequency identification, Industrial IoT, Supply chain technology, EdDSA, Blockchain technology

1. Introduction

By employing state-of-the-art and revolutionary technology, the beginning of a fourth industrial revolution is rapidly developing (Kasapoğlu, 2018). Techniques such as RFID enable instantaneous communication to warn users and prevent cataclysmic events. By ensuring that the data obtained is accurate and secure, blockchain has the potential to boost confidence. It is then clear from the analysis of the sequence leading to the 4th Industrial Revolution that this is a progressive development, as shown in Figure 1. The system hackers to permit such a new dimension of networking are the 4th revolutionary industrial technology. The new era of networking is called the Internet of Things (IoT) (Ottonicar *et al.*, 2018). It will have an evolving network called IIoT. The use of RFID services has increased the potential to collect data close enough to make a better assessment. Such a subsystem is an adequate adjustment. Fortunately, to use the information, pairing RFID with technologies such as IoT and IIoT can lead to improved and quicker details. The use of blockchain adds depth to the framework that, the use of a seamless distributed database, can theoretically improve SCT. To create synergies that can't even occur, Networks Model focuses on inter-employment-dependencies but has grown to cover almost all areas.

To explore the synergistic activity of IIoT and blockchain against SCT, theory systems are used in this research. The study of the convergence of 3 techniques to create a device that theoretically improves SCT has been its specificity.

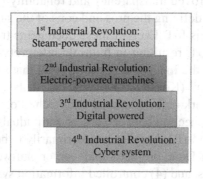

Figure 1.   Sequencing of the Industrial Revolution

IoT is an innovation having broad extension and can turn into a significant piece of our day by day experience what's to come. In the new years, the development in the field of IoT and its applications have been persevering. Despite the fact that it is as yet in its early stages, it has acquired a gigantic interest of even the huge players like IBM and Amazon. Various things that are utilized each second are fitted with electronic gadgets and conventions to tie them to the Internet. Regardless, the IoT has a couple of significant security gives that should be routed to guarantee its consistent and splendid future. In IoT, as things cycle and trade data without human impedance, human support is negligible. This total self-sufficiency clearly makes the malignant designers focus on these associations obviously. It carries an intense need to recognize and validate the substances and assurance the uprightness of their data traded. Due to IoT's complete degree and different attributes, making a productive incorporated encryption plot is practically improbable. Presently, another promising innovation that may very well purpose the security issues in IoT is blockchain. In this methodology, an underlying decentralized framework is recommended to determine this limitation, which ensures strong gadget distinguishing proof and confirmation. It likewise protects the uprightness and openness of data. This methodology depends on the security components conceded by the blockchains to accomplish a particularly level headed and assists with producing safe virtual zones where things can characterize and confide in one another. Significant security gives that have been experienced in the IoT have been tended to and settled utilizing blockchain.

A study looked at the connection between each of these innovations separately, and improved transparency and reliability in the supply chain. For example, when defining the pros and cons of the supply chain, several articles deal with this IoT. Each of these documents tries to describe and then describe the IoT, resulting in multiple interpretations that are complex. Among them, the IoT is the network of all that identifies this as the "last major problem" (Kocsi & Ola'h, 2017). It describes this IoT as a wide range of network objects infused with technological tools. It identifies the IoT as a connection between assets, individuals, and devices. The same IIoT is also an IoT subset designed primarily to be used in manufacturing sectors. (1) Data protocol and server software, (2) detectors, (3) electrical motors, and (4) controlled information systems were significant elements of IIoT. The use of a subsystem consisting of IIoT, one of its IIoT detection devices being RFID, would monitor the transmitted information. Blockchain technology allows information accessible within the IIoT framework to be equally secure and open, culminating in the availability of information exchanged between providers and customers (Ehret & Wirtz, 2017). Evidence suggests that SCT has been influenced by RFID, IIoT & blockchain. The influence has not yet been examined in-depth and in a factual manner. However, the development of IoT leads to an improvement in SCT, which allows members of the supply chain to make an informed decision. IIoT is indeed an essential element of the IoT concept. The IIoT remains encapsulated and then regulated inside the IoT, where the accessibility of communication is limited to something like clients and providers exclusively. IIoT task would be to "control processes, assess production that speeds up productivity gains." The use of RFID and blockchain must result in verifiable decisions depending on the proximity of the information in real-time (Zhu *et al.*, 2018).

It will have an IIoT network that will evolve over time. The usage of RFID services has enhanced the ability to gather data at a close enough distance to produce a more accurate evaluation. A subsystem like this is a good compromise. Fortunately, combining RFID with technologies like IoT and IIoT can enhance and speed up the information's utilization. The integration of blockchain provides depth to the framework, which might possibly improve SCT by using a seamless distributed database. Networks Model focuses on inter-employment — interdependence to produce synergies that would otherwise be impossible to achieve. However, it has expanded to encompass practically all fields.

RFID tags possess special attributes that increase the potential to recognize objects at such an interpersonal level and link those stuff back to several other data that can be used, leading to improved SCT. Using a central database with all vendors, blockchain can help ensure that the data has not been compromised. The rise in the incorporation of RFID into IIoT, the growing need for blockchain as well as the effect of enhanced SCT on such innovations imply that discovery and study in the field are imperative. To determine the relation between new technologies, it will explore RFID, blockchain as well as IIoT as an integrated edition of IoT systems. A conceptual framework is theorized in which all RFID, IIoT, and blockchain frames are integrated as SCT antecedent factors.

Our ultimate premise would be that relevant data capabilities underpin end-to-end access to a supply chain (Casado-Vara *et al.*, 2018). The rest of the chapter consists of a literature review that introduces the theoretical framework which promotes the underlying theories, a summary of the data collection methodology as well as the statistical techniques adopted, a presentation of Covariance-Based Structural Equation Modelling (CB-SEM) CB-SEM study findings, administrative conse-quences, research findings, and a generalized study.

The remainder of this chapter is comprised of the following: Section 2 provides a related work of Industrial automation and IoT used in RFID. Section 3 describes the proposed methodology. The performance evalua-tion is explained in the Section 4. Section 4 presents experimental results and performance evaluations of the Industrial Internet of Things (IIoT) with blockchain technology, while Section 5 concludes the chapter.

2. Related Works

A lot of research seems to have been done on RFID with SCT. As well, one of the three methods presented in this analysis was tested. For instance, it suggests a tool to make supply chains transparent. On a com-parable basis, the correlation between blockchain & SCT technology has been explored through some experiments. The effect of IIoT in the supply chain has been studied.

Blockchain is a decentralized record created to empower the trade in the digitized money, execute exchanges and arrangements while guaran-teeing the security. The blockchain includes interest of individuals and each member in the organization has the admittance to most recent variant of encoded record. The blockchain has a remarkable property where just the partaking individuals can approve another exchange. Fundamentally, it's a disseminated information base set up so as to keep a constantly devel-oping information structure blocks while adjusting its legitimacy and holds volumes of individual exchanges. Blockchain involves an unchanging arrangement of blocks actually like any ordinary public record which holds a whole rundown of records of exchange. Figure 1 shows the construction of a blockchain. A regular square has an interesting guardian block and in its square header it contains the past block hash. The Ethereum blockchain additionally have the uncle blocks for example offspring of the precursors of the square and their hashes are likewise put away. The principal square of a blockchain having no parent block is called beginning blocks.

At each point in the supply chain, this study also clearly addresses RFID as a means of monitoring assets. In particular, though, some studies see every innovation in contrast. Research in the theory of common systems can serve as a framework for a variety of topics.

The use of Generalized Theoretical Framework serves as a bridge to recognize real-time systems that can provide synergies leading to developments that develop our specialized areas via application and system. General Systems Theory provides a holistic framework to remain successful at responding to transitions, including such technologies (Helo & Shamsuzzoha, 2020).

IoT devices can be ordered into numerous levels yet they vary generally as far as security levels. Some associate utilizing GPS, 4G, or are hardwired while others use closeness-based conventions like Bluetooth, RFID, or Wi-Fi. It is generally simple to interface them basically by checking for close by gadgets, by taking care of a little code that could be changed from a default or by applying a type of verification to affirm gadget and recipient authorizations. Web of things applications are pretty much as different as the IoT administrations they are utilizing, yet present advancements show that change is required, despite the fact that it could require some investment for all producers to go through. A practically identical methodology to IoT frameworks is PKI where virtual declarations exhibit the legitimacy of the IoT protests in the present circumstance. Computerized testaments would ensure a degree of trust in an IoT framework that in any case may be missing and could perceive and debilitate admittance to unapproved frameworks with helpless wellbeing when combined with IoT frameworks to manage the establishments.

Common Working Systems Theory (another expansion in General Systems Theory) enables organizations and subcomponents like supply chains which develop by altering and enhancing tools like RFID, IIoT & blockchain to change or confirm (Fournaris *et al.*, 2019). The use of technologies such as these in the sub-components of an organization can improve access to information. It also provides the basis for interactions within the supply chain which may be described as pathological or symbiotic. In the sense of the supply chain, a parasite arrangement may be characterized as just an entity with the primary purpose of supply (Mazzei *et al.*, 2020). A single entity with a product, component, or operation becomes dependent on a single organization. The loss of income in a parasitic society can be devastating. Some organizations may have close relationships within the system that are communal.

Such interactions within such a supply chain will be mandatory or optional. Use systems theory to describe how the use of RFID is associated with operational effectiveness. The outcome contributes to the overall impact on the development of both the (internal) organization and the efficiency of the supply chain (Alladi *et al.*, 2019).

Many authors state that systems theory provides a basis for specifying which other participants in the supply chain may be influenced by the behavior adopted by an organization. This means that, in a required partnership, success with one or more supply chain partners depends on the other participants. While there are benefits for all participants in a voluntary partnership, in the absence of a partnership, supply chain partners will continue.

RFID is a critical relationship technology for improving supply chain efficiency (Latchoumi *et al.*, 2010). As it forms the foundation for the aggregation process across the framework, RFID is essential. RFID was amongst the most important IoT technologies. RFID functions as a production gateway for IoT and IIoT. Although RFID is a resource to lower prices and raise revenues connecting the physical and digital worlds, allowing almost anything to be connected to the Internet. In this context, one of its greatest RFID potentials is for artifacts that do not need sensors (Kumari *et al.*, 2020).

The overall efficiency of the supply chain is improved while using an RFID system combined with such a supply chain information framework. By increasing performance and competitiveness by providing SCT, the use of RFID influences operational performance (Seok *et al.*, 2019). Assigning all these results should lead to an SCT improvement once RFID is used with various systems, like IIoT & blockchain. To enhance supply chain transparency notes that the future may be bright for RFID and IoT. RFID technology allows us to monitor the movements of products, such as raw materials, fabrication work, including final products (Loganathan *et al.*, 2017).

IoT is an important factor in designing a real-time understanding of supply chain management. Provided that perhaps the IIoT is indeed an industry-oriented variant of the IoT, we suggest that now the IIoT will be a dominant problem that would boost SCT for the production of reliable details. The use of detectors, including labels, is important to IIoT since it facilitates communication and data flow by objects and devices throughout the process. RFID is a key issue for IIoT. The integration of communications can be encapsulated into different IIoT environments.

Blockchain can be considered to provide chain management transparency, integrity validation, and approval and protection details. Blockchain is a distributed ledger in storage registering transactions that are immutable. Supply chains would also get a public database using blockchain. Through the transaction made by members of the supply chain is put in a kind of framework. For the supply chain members, the blocks with the transactions were tied up and taken together because the inputs are permanent throughout the chain. When content is changed one way or the other, it would be clear to something like supply chain partners that the data may be corrupted. The IIoT-integrated RFID enables relatively close data to be injected into blocks instantaneously, while manual input normally suggests a pause in the insertion of information into blocks (Khan & Salah, 2018). RFID is a strategic effort to strengthen supply chain management and should have a beneficial impact on the application of blockchain technology.

3. Proposed Methodology

3.1 *Blockchain technology*

Blockchain is the form of data structure created by connected blocks in a sequenced order. Block metadata is incorporated into a block header. Timestamp, block hash value, an ID of a block, parent block ID are all important elements of blocks. It will have an IIoT network that will evolve over time. The usage of RFID services has enhanced the ability to gather data at a close enough distance to produce a more accurate evaluation. A subsystem like this is a good compromise. Fortunately, combining RFID with technologies like IoT and IIoT can enhance and speed up the information's utilization. The integration of blockchain provides depth to the framework, which might possibly improve SCT by using a seamless distributed database. Networks Model focuses on inter-employment — interdependence to produce synergies that would otherwise be impossible to achieve. However, it has expanded to encompass practically all fields.

Before blockchain arrangements were carried out, the improvement of computerized supply chains has passed far. Toward the beginning, huge sending specialists utilized ERP-frameworks to react to conveyance demands quicker. At that point the Internet age started, different Internet destinations and gatherings began showing up, which were utilized for publicizing their administrations, looking for clients or a project worker for transportation orders. At long last, payload administrations like the UBER traveler transportation stage showed up. The issue with these administrations is that the client is offered to lease an entire truck for a little distance, while the transportation of little products or the multimodal transportation with utilizing a few unique vehicles isn't accessible at the hour of composing the article. Likewise, present day unified stages can't totally oversee calculations that are impervious to harm of products; wipe out the issue of trust between members.

A chain structure that is made by all blocks is created by the existence of an identifier of the parent block as indicated in Figure 2. The existing blocks are unchanged, which is a key rule of the blockchain, but the addition of new blocks can only be performed in the queue.

3.2 *The layout of blockchain technology and its features*

In the distributed shared ledger in which the database is distributed, all-digital information is stored using this blockchain technology. The cryptographic algorithm checks the cache information before the blocks are formed and enters the distributed database. Many nodes are involved in the blockchain network that is spread geographically throughout the world and the mode of communication is said to be peer-to-peer mode. With the help of these peer-to-peer synchronization protocols, identical blockchain data that is embedded in all nodes of the network is automatically downloaded. It leads to useless central supremacy. Instead of central supremacy, each member of the blockchain network depends on the interconnection of all nodes within that network.

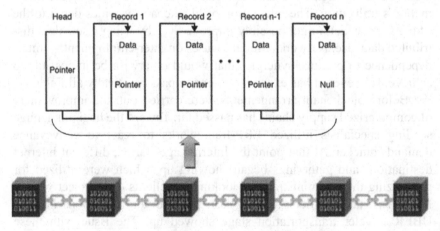

Figure 2.   Typical Structure of Blockchain

3.3 *Supply chain technology on blockchain*

Behind cryptocurrencies, blockchain technology discovers its implementation in various fields mainly in the supply chain management process and logistics. Numerous existing technologies would be disrupted by new technologies. Managing the supply chain is one of these emerging technologies. IBM's Sawtooth Lake is a great example of supply chain management.

3.4 *Principal characteristics of blockchain technology*

Since blockchain technology emerges from cryptocurrency, it has a major blow across many industries. It was originally intended for budget purposes. Complete registration of transactions carried out on the network is maintained by a blockchain which is a large digital book. By developing a trusted digital currency, their main characteristics in silver transactions eliminated third parties. Related blocks that are aggregated are connected through block hash values for some time. The blockchain contains all information that is permanent and not tampered with.

The former integer block is defined as the genesis block. All the information is transported by each node and then it is connected with the address of the hashed value of its previous node.

A hashed address is unique as a human fingerprint recognizing the block and its contents. Its hash is computed while creating the node. The hash changes whenever something in the block is changed. The hash from the previous block is ported by each block and therefore the blockchain is created. There is not central supremacy since blockchain is a peer-to-peer network.

Each node can check that each process is still in order by receiving the entire copy of the blockchain. Each block is incorporated with the time-stamp, so you cannot interfere with other data. Each node in the chain is intimately bound up with the creation of a new block. Each node creates a concordance after it verifies that this block has not been interfered with. The structure is decentralized since there is no central supremacy. Blockchain classifies into two types. Primary is said to be public, e.g., Bitcoin and Ethereum, and then secondary are said to be private, particularly developed for different organizations. Smart contracts are scripts that are executed by individuals. The benefits of such smart contracts help prevent fraud.

3.4.1 *A secure frame encryption scheme based on blockchain*

In an IIoT-based network system, image sensors are essential. Depending on the requirement, the information is obtained through various tools as well as in different formats. A sensor's internal memory stores data received or occasionally discharged to the cloud. In low real-time conditions, image processing can be performed on clouds, and also subsequent processing is performed. Industries could face different problems due to several attacks, which leads to data loss, the loss of device disturbance control of the service providers, delinquent activity, and also the cost of recovering data that is lost. A lot of data is exchanged by IoT devices with servers for scanning and processing at the edge and also in the cloud. The devices collect a large amount of data like environmental data and send them to the device for processing after the data is encrypted. The data collected can be minced. Development of a human fingerprint known as hashing. The entire fingerprint will be modified once the information is changed. Blockchain stores the entire fingerprint and compares it with the entry fingerprint to verify that the data is interfered with. It helps the data get protected from intruders before the destination. When checking data quality, the blockchain is used. The authorities for many decentralized devices are designed by the BCT that allows peer-to-peer communication. For all self-contained systems, the BCT ensures governance and compliance while defining the complexity of security in the emerging new landscape as shown in Figure 3.

In public-key cryptography, the EdDSA is a digital signature scheme using a variant of the Schnorr signature based on crooked Edwards's

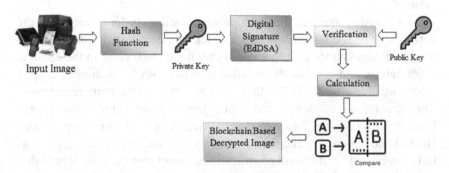

Figure 3.   Proposed Hybrid Method (EdDSA with Blockchain Technology)

curves. It is intended to be faster than existing computerized signature plans without forfeiting the warranty.

3.5 *Assumptions*

Sensors play an important part in IIoT image decision-making. Therefore, it posits that images are data sensitive and therefore we propose our method for data security. To check our method, we are going to make sure that the data is encrypted and that the hash value is stored on the ledger. In consideration, we have assumed that the decrypted picture is the resulting output, which is a simple picture under ideal conditions. We postulate that the original size of the image is m _ n, and thus we may divide the resulting output by 16. By preserving all pixels to be randomly assigned variables, an additional image of 256 _ 256 pixels could be generated effectively which is mentioned in our empirical research. Since the encryption of the images must be supplied with the security system, the encrypted images are made to check the robustness using various tests determined in the results.

3.6 *Encryption of an image*

A sequence of bytes is created from an image, so the initial shape cannot be approached in the image encryption process. Content in digital images can be protected with this useful technique. The encryption process can be carried out by various cryptographical algorithms. To modify the encrypted data to obtain the original values, the bytes which are encrypted can be converted into another system for the decryption process. We make use of algorithms depends on certain key functions for the encryption process and the deciphering process.

$$Eckey(A) = B \tag{1}$$

$$Dckey(B) = A \tag{2}$$

Encrypted data is plain text and its decryption process is explained in Equations (1) and (2). Where Eckey(A) describes the encrypting process which is executed on image A and its output image is said to be image B. We execute Dckey(B) that decrypts the image that is encrypted to retrieve the exact image X.

3.7 *Proposed algorithm for encryption*

An authorized ledger or blockchain that is private can be readily deployed in industrial areas. All IIoT platform requirements are met mainly by the hyper ledger platform which is based on the blockchain. Under the guidance of Linux foundations, it is an open-source platform. In several fields such as medical, chain supply, logistics, and IoT data that are used at a large scale, hyper ledger tissue is used. In various problems such as security measures, confidence, and decentralization, the IIoT is supported by the blockchain which is easily connected to multiple devices. It is said that these devices are terminal nodes or supercomputers for data processing. Secure data can be transferred by nodes to other peers so that no intruder can hack into the middle or pierce through it. By connecting to other devices, data may be sent to a central location or distributed devices.

Algorithm for the process of Image Encryption using Blockchain Technology

```
Input: IoT device using web service and Blockchain
Output: Blockchain-based Decrypted image
if n=true then
if req =true then
the response is processed (res)
hash(image)
revise the chain
else
res -> node (req)
end if
else
req is denied
end if
revise and a new block is added in the chain
end if
```

3.8 *Supply chain architecture*

Architecture describes the process within the blockchain-based supply chain. It includes the product processing process which begins with the producer and ends with the consumer. Each process can be visualized by anyone from the blockchain makes the method to be transparent. As a result, changes cannot be made within this process. Supply chain management is integrated into the design and plan, as well as the various processes carried out. This includes the hardware stream and the data in addition to the money stream. A summary of supply chain methods is as follows:

Production of goods: In the built application for the supply chain, the details of the goods that are produced are recorded by the producer. In this step, the RFID is planted and the details of the good are stored in this ID. In real-time, goods are tracked using a GPS sensor. Without any physical work, sensor data can be stored separately in the cloud as smart contracts are used.

Manufacturing Process: The web application can be used to track the position of commodities at any time. It also updates schedules in the database when the manufacturer receives the goods and terminates their work in the goods.

Distribution of goods: After the manufacturing process, the goods are received by the distributor and given to the retailer. The web application updates the schedule once the process is complete. It will have an IIoT network that will evolve over time. The usage of RFID services has enhanced the ability to gather data at a close enough distance to produce a more accurate evaluation. A subsystem like this is a good compromise. Fortunately, combining RFID with technologies like IoT and IIoT can enhance and speed up the information's utilization. The integration of blockchain provides depth to the framework, which might possibly improve SCT by using a seamless distributed database. Networks Model focuses on inter-employment — interdependence to produce synergies that would otherwise be impossible to achieve. However, it has expanded to encompass practically all fields.

Sale of goods: The goods received would apply to trade in the store with the respective identification number of the product when received by the retailer.

Purchase of the goods: In the web application, the respective ID is entered by the customer when he goes to the retailer's store. Thus, all the details of the product are delivered to the customer and make them happy. The confidence between them strengthens the reputation of the merchant.

4. Experimental Results

Suggested plot simulation is to produce excellent results. To investigate, MATLAB 2015a is used on Microsoft Windows 10 and 8GB RAM frame is equipped with a Core i7 processor. Correlation Coefficient Analysis is the encryption method is completed by examining the relationship coefficient for testing purposes and utilizing the IoT product image.

The Image histogram is taken first for getting the contiguous pixels in the first image. At this time, it contrasted with the rearranged histogram image with the contiguous pixels of the encoded image. Figure 4 illustrate the correlated the original input image of the IoT product for encoded image based on the blockchain.

In several fields such as medical, chain supply, logistics, and IoT data that are used at a large scale, hyper ledger tissue is used. In various problems such as security measures, confidence, and decentralization, the IIoT is supported by the blockchain which is easily connected to multiple devices. It is said that these devices are terminal nodes or supercomputers for data processing. Secure data can be transferred by nodes to other peers so that no intruder can hack into the middle or pierce through it.

The correlation coefficient is extremely high in the image, even though the connection coefficient zero is filled in encrypted image. It shows a close relationship between the pixels in the corner to corner, flat and vertical landing of the first picture as shown.

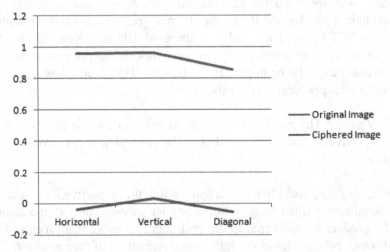

Figure 4.   Correlation Coefficient Analysis

Figures 5 (a–f) shows that the input image of IoT Product image with their histogram values, this image is shuffled by an algorithm and encrypted using Edwards-curve Digital Signature Algorithm (EdDSA). Finally, the image decrypted using Hash functionality and blockchain technology.

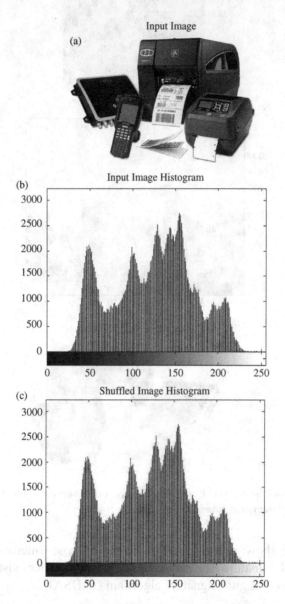

Figure 5. (a) Input Image (b) Input Image Histogram (c) Shuffled Image Histogram

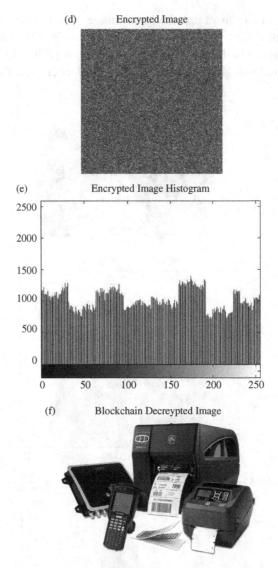

Figure 5. (*Continued*)   (d) **Encrypted Image** (e) **Encrypted Image Histogram** (f) **Blockchain Decrypted Image**

Figure 6 shows the comparison of the proposed method Edwards-curve Digital Signature Algorithm (EdDSA) with another existing method of Elliptic curve digital signature algorithm (EcDSA).

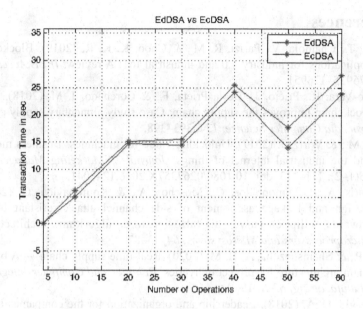

Figure 6.   Comparison between EdDSA versus EcDSA

5. Conclusion

In an IIoT environment, the security risk can be eliminated by block-chain Hack proof cryptography. Each node or sensor may be followed by this technology. Data can be offloaded from devices by a system that secures image encryption for the IIoT blockchain-based network system. We perform numerous tests to guarantee the solidity of the security by an algorithm that is proposed. However, it has a few limitations such as limited transaction speed and computer resources. Performing as nodes in the blockchain can be prevented by multiple IIoT devices such as sensors that are connected that has a memory deficit and resource processing. This issue can be addressed by web services, but it remains to be addressed. Edwards-curve Digital Signature Algorithm (EdDSA), public key encryption using a variant of the Schnorr signature based on Edwards' twisted curves. In future technology, image security may be reviewed in the cloud after the data has been unloaded. To achieve high efficiency and adaptability, further work is required.

References

Alladi, T., Chamola, V., Parizi, R. M., & Choo, K. K. R. (2019). Blockchain applications for industry 4.0 and industrial IoT: A review. *IEEE Access, 7,* 176935–176951.

Casado-Vara, R., Prieto, J., De la Prieta, F., & Corchado, J. M. (2018). How blockchain improves the supply chain: Case study alimentary supply chain. *Procedia Computer Science, 134,* 393–398.

Ehret, M., & Wirtz, J. (2017). Unlocking value for machines: Business models and the industrial internet of things. *Journal of Marketing Management, 33*(1–2), 111–113. doi: 10.1080/0267257X.2016.1248041.

Fournaris, A. P., Dimopoulos, C., Moschos, A., & Koufopavlou, O. (2019). Design and leakage assessment of side channel attack resistant binary edwards elliptic curve digital signature algorithm architectures. *Microprocessors and Microsystems, 64,* 73–87.

Helo, P., & Shamsuzzoha, A. H. M. (2020). Real-time supply chain — A blockchain architecture for project deliveries. *Robotics and Computer-Integrated Manufacturing, 63,* 101909.

Kasapoğlu, O. A. (2018). Leadership and organization for the companies in the process of industry 4.0 transformation. *International Journal of Organizational Leadership, 7*(3), 300–308.

Khan, M. A., & Salah, K. (2018). IoT security: Review, blockchain solutions, and open challenges. *Future Generation Computer Systems, 82,* 395–411.

Kocsi, B., & Olàh, J. (2017). Potential connections of unique manufacturing and Industry 4.0. *LogForum, 13*(4), 389–400.

Kumari, A., Tanwar, S., Tyagi, S., & Kumar, N. (2020). Blockchain-based massive data dissemination handling in IIoT environment. *IEEE Network.*

Latchoumi, T. P., & Sunitha, R. (2010, September). Multi-agent systems in distributed datawarehousing. In *2010 International Conference on Computer and Communication Technology (ICCCT),* (442–447).

Loganathan, J., Janakiraman, S., & Latchoumi, T. P. (2017). A novel architecture for next generation cellular network using opportunistic spectrum access scheme. *Journal of Advanced Research in Dynamical and Control Systems,* (12), 1388–1400.

Mazzei, D., Baldi, G., Fantoni, G., Montelisciani, G., Pitasi, A., Ricci, L., & Rizzello, L. (2020). A blockchain tokenizer for industrial IOT trustless applications. *Future Generation Computer Systems, 105,* 432–445.

Ottonicar, A. L. C., Valentim, M. L. P., & Mosconi, E. (2018). A competitive intelligence model based on information literacy: Organizational competitiveness in the context of the 4th industrial revolution. *Journal of Intelligence Studies in Business, 8*(3), pp. 55–65.

Seok, B., Park, J., & Park, J. H. (2019). A lightweight hash-based blockchain architecture for industrial IoT. *Applied Sciences*, *9*(18), 3740.

Zhu, S., Song, J., Hazen, B. T., Lee, K., & Cegielski, C. (2018). How supply chain analytics enables operation supply chain transparency: An organizational information processing theory perspective. *International Journal of Physical Distribution and Logistics Management*, *48*(1), 47–68. doi: 10.1108/IJPDLM-11-2017-0341.

Chapter 9

The Data Consensus Algorithm for Smart City Applications Using Blockchain Technology in Industrial IoT

S. Lavanya[*,||], D. Akila[†,**], Hannah Vijaykumar[‡,††],
P. Calista Bebe[§,‡‡], and C. Sudha[¶,§§]

[*]*Thiruthangal Nadar College, Selavsyal, Chennai, India*

[†]*Department of Information Technology,
Vels Institute of Science, Technology and Advanced Studies,
Chennai, India*

[‡]*Department of Computer Science,
Anna Adarsh College for Women, Chennai, India*

[§]*New Prince Shri Bhavani Arts and Science College,
Chennai, India*

[¶] *Department of Computer Science, Pattammal Alagesan
College of Arts & Science, Chengalpattu,
Chennai, India*

[||]*lavanya3002@yahoo.co.in*

[**]*akiindia@yahoo.com*

[††]*hannahvijaykumar@annaadarsh.edu.in*

[‡‡]*calismail@gmail.com*

[§§]*srisudhasri.kpm@gmail.com*

181

Abstract

Solid waste management that impacts the health and environment of our society is a key environmental concern. One of the key issues of the current era is waste detection, tracking, and management. The smart waste monitoring system based on the Internet of Things (IoT) is being developed by this project. Using the mobile phone and blynk apps, the level of waste inside the trash can be monitored, which plays a major role in the work. The level of waste inside the garbage can be monitored by smart trash and it notifies the cleaner once the trash is fully loaded. The status of the waste bin is displayed to the user using the light crystal display (LCD) screen. The internal waste distance can be detected by the main sensor such as the ultrasonic sensor. Status information can be sent to the smartphone with the help of ESP8266 which acts as a Wi-Fi module. Finally, the Blynk application notifies the cleaner when the information comes from the bin. The mastermind of this task is the microcontroller, Arduino Uno. When blynk sends the notification to the smartphone, the waste status may be displayed on the LCD screen that displays the resulting output. The result is made up of three different ranges of measures such as 0%, 50%, and 100%. The 0% result indicates that the distance between the waste and the ultrasonic sensor has to be greater than 10 cm. The 50% result means that the distance between the waste and the ultrasonic sensor must be greater than 5 cm or equal to 5 cm but less than 10 cm. Thus, the 100% result indicates that the waste distance for the ultrasound sensor has to be less than 5 cm.

To address this problematic situation industry, with the help of IoT and blockchain technology, the Garbage monitor system is designed and implemented in Industrial IoT (IIoT). The proposed system uses multiple dustbins that are located all over the city or the campus that is provided with low-budget devices that tracks the condition of the dustbin. To identify the bin that is fully loaded and requires clearing immediately, each bin is provided with a unique identification. The details are sent to the administrator when the tray is full. The proposed system helps to minimize route collection and fuel rate by the ability to answer and update the status of a specific bin in real-time. As a result, we can build a healthy and clean environment.

Keywords: Arduino Uno, Wi-Fi module, GPS module, GSM, Blockchain

1. Introduction

Waste management in farming countries has become huge. Flood images of waste containers are regularly seen in our everyday lives, causing contamination. That garbage containers in public places flood well in advance before the start of the next clean-up action is the primary focus of inadequate waste administration. IoT plays an important role in today's environment. IoT is used in family units, horticulture, banks, health care, and thriving urban communities. The ideas used in IoT are to make urban zones smart. This commitment will be extremely useful to the metropolitan office for the clean-up of urban areas with IoT control authorities (Khan & Salah, 2018).

In this way, management needs may reduce the problem to some extent. Innovation makes it possible to find solutions to such problems. The smart bin is the only response for waste management. This task also incorporates the idea of blockchain innovation that will help affected clients and help the administration to clean up waste in a specific area. The ultrasonic sensor that recognizes the level of waste and stores information in a data set worker via a Wi-Fi module is used for this purpose. The information identified with the situation of the filled dustbin is sent utilizing GPS and GSM modules to the administrator which teaches the transporter to gather the trash from the predefined container requiring prompt leeway (Durand *et al.*, 2019).

The two most well-known advances today are internet of things and blockchain. Has the ability to detect that gadget of interconnection is an IoT, measure the condition of ecological pointers and activate dependent on info gave. It can help make keen arrangements that improve personal satisfaction of individuals. In like manner, blockchain is dispersed data set frameworks that guarantee significant degree of safety and least exchange overhead with in-form accessibility. To foster a smart waste management system (SWMS) to unite these two advancements we endeavor, in this proposal. They produce the measure of waste ac according to utilization off Administration for pay clients need for example is weight based in the SWMS. Smart contracts managed by a custom digital currency made utilizing are installments and by a DOA through a thoroughly robotics, exceptionally secure interaction by can be subsidized the whole SWMS. blockchain can help bring down the infiltration and administration cost which can be uncommonly useful to agricultural nesting, are not ingenious where government.

This IoT garbage monitoring system is an incredibly imaginative plan that will help urban areas lift rapidly. This task is appropriate to be used in the shining city. This plan filters the waste container and notifies the core level of the waste collected in the waste containers using a site page. For this, the frame uses ultrasonic sensors placed on the outputs to identify the tank level and the contrast and depth of the tank containers. Using the frame brand Arduino Uno, LCD monitor, ESP8266 module, LCD, and light emitting diode (LED) to enter the situation of the amount of waste collected in the container.

The sensor is used to detect data that the Wi-Fi module monitors. The waste volume is predicted by the database. The location of the bin is determined using GPS and GSM modules, and this information is sent to the administrator and worker. The workers, according to the facts, are cleaning up rubbish. When several bins are added, sorting techniques such as the Dijkstra algorithm are employed to determine the shortest path. When the bin is over 85% full, the node can be run. As a result, the shortest path is determined, allowing the truck driver to collect the garbage in a timely manner.

In non-industrial nations, trash the board has become a tremendous test. The photos of spilling over trash containers are regularly seen in our everyday life, bringing about contamination. That the trash receptacles at public spots flood well ahead of time before the beginning of the following cleaning measure is the major question of insufficient waste administration.

IoT is assuming a significant part in the present-day situation. IoT is utilized in families, farming, banking, medical services and keen urban areas. We have utilized the ideas of IoT in our undertaking to make keen urban areas. This undertaking will be extremely useful for the civil division to clean the urban areas utilizing IoT checking administrations. In this way, we need a framework which can decrease the issue to a degree. With the innovation inside our hands, we can make answers for these issues. The brilliant dustbin is the solitary answer for the waste administration.

A mobile phone application is used to display the level to the client being audited. The applications will provide a graphic view of the waste containers and display the collected waste to show the level of collected waste. It is shown on the LCD monitor. The frame will be placed on the LED when the level of collected garbage crosses the boundary of the game. Subsequently, this frame helps to keep the city clean by advising on the soul level of the container bin by giving a graphical picture of the containers through the portable application (Islam *et al.*, 2019; Kanta *et al.*, 2017; Latchoumi *et al.*, 2010; Mahzan *et al.*, 2018; Memon *et al.*, 2019).

2. Related Works

Numerous nations including India face the increasing pace of human populace and urbanization as a portion of the current difficulties. There result colossal huge loads of squanders because of the gigantic advancement occurring for what it's worth, the waste administration all throughout the planet is executed in an indiscriminate way. In spite of the presence of a few waste plants to set burning the squanders or reuse the trash, it at last outcomes in different types of squanders as its side-effects. Here there is a helpless framework to control and screen these waste materials. The transportation of waste can be made simpler starting with one end then onto the next with blockchain. Blockchain in squander the executives can genuinely change the entire interaction to a practical one (Lamichhane, *et al.*, 2018). By interconnecting diverse IoT sensors, and further incorporating them to the decentralized organization can help continuously following and age of information comparing to squanders conveyed.

Based on an extensive set of equipment, an intelligent waste container would be mounted on the lid of the waste container to monitor it. Containers with a rest section containing the touch hub entered into the next segment containing the switch. And part three includes the Android app with the base station.

There is an opportunity to improve two of its highlights using this methodology. In the beginning, the client is assisted in the use of waste characterization. At this stage, the light receptacle realizing its substance may encounter the other associated with the garbage assortment line (Ongena *et al.*, 2018; Sun *et al.*, 2016).

The solid waste management interaction can be isolated into two sections: (1) Transport and assortment and (2) Recycle and removal World Bank portrays. Waste management as the assortment of strong squanders from the place of creation to mark of removal or treatment. In created nations, the vast majority of the current waste administration frame works incorporate numerous outsider waste gatherers that waste arranged vehicle is squander containers to a reuse landfill or plant destinations. In this event of non-industrial nations, this is the inverse. The majority of the spending plan for squander the executives spent assortment of waste and just little division is spent on removal. From family and other financial services was delivered on that year that 2503 million tons of waste uncovers in 2014 in European Union by a report. Almost, burned was this waste of 47%, resured was 36% (excluding energy recuperation) burned to recuperate energy was remaining and landfilled was 10.2%. As opposed to this, the Asian nations in the vast majority, the greater part of the squanders were unloaded in go untreated was open. In untreated and open dump of waste over 60% has Vietnam, Thailand, India, Bangladesh and Nepal like nations. Over 40% of its waste is reused over just Hangkon while the greater part of their waste barn Japan and Singapore. The creators talked about the fact that IoT can directly and systematically reach countless unique and heterogeneous ending frameworks. At the same time, it is possible to select sub-sets of information for the improvement of computerized administrations. It also considered that developing a global design for the IoT is consequently a stunning task mainly. Due to the incredibly huge assortment of gadgets, connect the progress of the layer, and administrations that could be engaged with such a frame. This new model for smart waste control is presented receptacles with shiny containers added to an ultrasonic sensor. It will make it possible to identify the degrees of waste in the container, from time to time and to advance the data to the Arduino load connected to a GSM module (Loganathan *et al.*, 2017).

Likewise, on the off chance that we think about the organization of this sort of framework in agricultural nations, there are many restricting elements. Numerous legislatures in agricultural nations don't have assets to put resources into fostering a legitimate waste administration framework. Another obstacle would be the absence of appropriate installment foundation for the installment of waste administration administrations. Division of Computer Science, Stanford University, traces a few specialized, social and financial difficulties in current micropayment frameworks. One of the primary boundaries of blast of micropayments structure is the inadequacy of limiting the exchange cost according to the genuine brought about cost. In the event of cryptographic forms of money, there are no outsider association and henceforth, the exchange overhead is insignificant. Micropayments can be executed in an improved, straightforward way. An alternate way to deal with address this can be nearby local area meeting up and raising asset to put into answers for their issues. DAO is an influential idea of making association on top of blockchain innovation utilizing simple permanent PC codes. This detours the need of an outsider or government overall for legal guideline and resource security.

Since smart contracts consistently will act the manner to act before execution in which they are intended. On blockchain network one it's sent the codes can't be changed or altered. Guidelines and destinations changing the DOA will be conceivable simply by agreement (the sort of DOA upon contingent) (Mcginthy & Michaels, 2019; Petropulu *et al.*, 2019; Russell *et al.*, 2018). Like any ordinary association, speculation may require a DOA. The speculations are completely acted in digital forms of money. Digital forms of money can be bought from various trades or another DAO can be produced utilizing that can go about the national bank. By its own national bank label utilizes its own digital currency directed. According to the need the cash can flatter or swell by the bank and agreement of its administrative individuals. Apart from this, the waste insulation is completed with a moisture sensor which will detect the sorting on the moisture level and isolate accordingly. A waste audit framework using IoT is to help keep urban communities clean. The verification of waste containers and data on the degree of waste collected in the bins is carried out through a webpage by this framework. The development status of the toxic gases inside the container is also reported. The ultrasonic sensor placed the containers to recognize the level of the trash can and contrast it and the depth level of the trash can container is used by the frame for that (Stellios *et al.*, 2018).

In blockchain, information discernibility is executed through a plan system for fastened associations between time-stepping administrations and blocks, and the non-alter capacity of information is accomplished by utilizing hash work encryption. Blockchain is a rebellious innovation, which is driving another round of worldwide mechanical and modern changes, advancing the change from "data Internet" to "esteem Internet". In the blockchain, the information is put away in the "block," and each square records the entirety of its worth trade exercises during its creation. In each square, there is a field committed to recording the hash worth of the top of the past block, so the last square can highlight the past extraordinary square. Subsequently, the front and back block grouping associations structure long chains. Blockchain is a sort of blockchain data set, which is made out of blockchain through chain. The critical innovations of blockchain incorporate deviated encryption, fastened information structure, keen agreement and agreement component. Fundamentally, blockchain network is a sort of P2P organization. Every hub gets data as well as produces data, and every exchange is set apart with time stamp.

A framework can inform partnerships to deliver the cartridge on time. In this frame, a sensor is put on top of the garbage container to distinguish the relation to the full size of the container for this. When the garbage reaches the highest level, a warning will be issued from the partnership office. After which officials can make another movement to purge the receptacle. This framework will make it possible to clean the city up better. Individuals do not need to physically check all frameworks because they will receive a notification when the container is filled using that framework (Wu et al., 2019).

Sensor mounted in the cover (locater range) that utilizations a smart garbage bin or base (sensor weight) of SGB that can detect the measure of things stored in SGB. In the ascertaining the measure of waste present in SGB for ascertaining for thought the very strategy into adopts their paper. With Experimentation of the end goal, utilized a reenactment of SGB. Organization to genuine world is appropriate for previously mentioned approach. Empowered utilizing RFID innovation is now set up of various sorts of waste is particular arranging where another methodology. The utilizations of their methodology can be altogether improved by the nature of waste created. In our framework is presently unrealistic at source innovatively arranging to perform model. The utilizations of sensors installed in the SGB by the receptable to check the filling utilized are remote sensor networks. A decision support server to which empowers long reach transmission of information to data transfer nodes to these sensors feed information. Aside from a mix of RFID and WSN innovation, a methodology dependent on picture preparing that takes ideal depiction of waste level in SGBs and the degree of waste to distinguish to microcontroller utilizing them cycles, GSM module has been set up to the focal office utilizing send data. A strong waste containers checking framework utilizing GSM/GPRS and Zigbee advertisements. Three level is separated in the whole design. The lower level comprises of containers with sensors feed the situation with the receptade to center level. Synthetic sensor, moistness, temperature, weight and limit uses the proposed model. A contact between lower and upper level goes about center level. The activity cost and outflow diminish that can help the framework utilizes energy proficient detecting calculation. In a waste container while zeroed in on the checking of strong waste.

A blockchain methodology for consulting electronic waste is proposed (Beerens et al., 2020). The blockchain is the innovation that makes it possible for us to conclude agreements. Smart chords are auto executable PC codes that make indicated movements when certain conditions are met in reality.

MQTT was created as transfer speed effective and power monetary convention to screen the oil pipeline through the desert as the gadgets were associated with costly satellite connection. It is a distribute/buy in based convention where a hub/gadget that needs to send some information, pushes the information to a representative, which the transmissions the got information to all buying in gadgets. It utilizes TCP/IP convention stack. A portion of it's key highlights are asyncronicity, open norm and multiplexing numerous endorsers through a solitary channel. It additionally gives diverse degree of QoS dependent on the sort of message conveyance administration required. MQTT is included three parts, specifically: Subscriber, Broker, and Publisher. They are associated with one another over TCP.

The proposed framework using smart agreements will provide more coordination among manufacturers, shippers, retailers, and e-wastage recyclers. It will give the public authority control over the assortment and reuse of electronic waste. It will also reduce the asymmetry between coordinated and chaotic areas, resulting in increased correctness throughout the cycle. The current blockchain-based responses to waste frameworks and further the success of these arrangements in the trend to challenges examined by the waste management industry are studied (Jiang *et al.*, 2020; Paes *et al.*, 2020; Pan *et al.*, 2018).

3. Proposed Architecture

Some of the current challenges in several countries mainly in India are facing the rising rate of urbanization and human population. Around the world, a huge amount of waste occurs due to great development, then the waste is managed and well done at random. The waste control and surveillance system are in bad shape. Blockchain transfers waste all over the place. It also ensures that waste management is a sustainable process. In real-time, the process of tracking and generating data for the transported waste can be realized by linking various IoT sensors and integrity to the decentralized network. The structure of the proposed waste monitoring system is illustrated in Figure 1.

The ultrasound sensor is used to detect data which is monitored by the Wi-Fi module. The database forecasts the volume of waste. Details on the

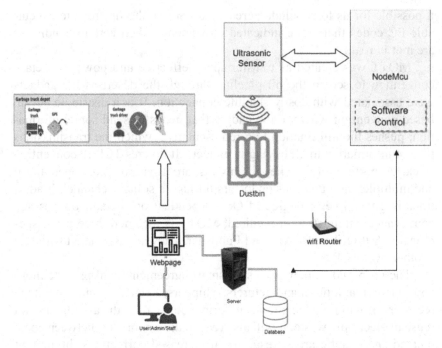

Figure 1.   Proposed Intelligent Waste Surveillance System Architecture

location of the bin are carried out by GPS and GSM modules so that this data will be received by the admin and worker. Based on the details, the workers are picking up the garbage. Sorting algorithms such as the Dijkstra algorithm are used to check the easiest route when multiple bins are added. The node can be executed when the bin is loaded at over 85%. So, the shortest route is analyzed and makes the truck driver to collect the waste in a short time. Figure 2 shows the full garbage collection scenario.

Partnerships can be guided by a framework in order to deliver the cartridge on time. A sensor is placed on top of the garbage container in this frame to distinguish the relation to the container's full size. The partnership office will issue a warning when the garbage level reaches the maximum level. After that, officials can move to purge the receptacle once more. This framework will allow the city to be cleaned up more effectively. Individuals do not need to physically check all frameworks because they will be notified when the container using that framework is filled.

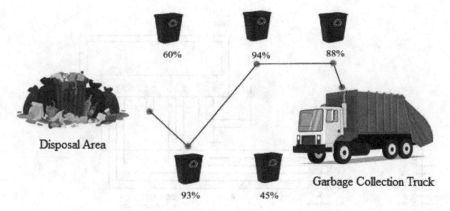

Figure 2.   Scenario for Collecting Completed Waste

A blockchain account is created for contracts, customers, and management. This account helps make an application for the collection of waste that can be completed by municipal authorities or clients. Details of the collection site as well as types of waste like industrial, solid, liquid, biodegradable can be added. The application can be authenticated by adding details like consumer name and address ID evidence and it is verified by blockchain. The customer may make the payment using E-wallets or a web application when the customer's request is successfully added to the blockchain.

The clean-up initiative is suggested to drivers through intelligent contracts when demand in the blockchain is examined by officials. Truckers are assigned by authorities to collect garbage and dispose of waste from assigned sites. Blockchain has truck and driver details for monitoring and surveillance. The condition of the bin and its location are transmitted by IoT sensors.

3.1 *Waste management systems*

In several projects, technologies such as Radio Frequency Identification (RFID), Wireless Sensor Network (WSN), IoT are used as a solution. The smart bin was patented by Junaith Ahemed Shahabdeen in which the sensors are mounted in the bottom (weight sensor) or cover (search range) to detect the items that are deposited. The Standard Generating Body (SGB) assesses the level of waste in dustbins. The SGB simulation is used for

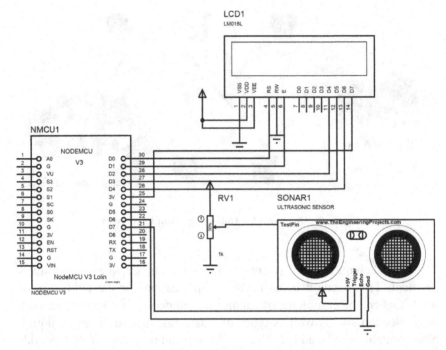

Figure 3.   Pin Diagram

experiments. Figure 3 is the pin diagram which depicts the above said methodology. In the real world, the approach mentioned above is a good one. RFID technology permits selective waste separation. It improves the quality of the waste produced. Currently, template sort cannot be completed. The sensors embedded in SGB control the filling process through WSNs. The data is fed by these sensors to the data transfer nodes in which the data is transmitted over a long distance is enabled to the decision-making server. Method of image processing captures the snapshot of waste level in SGBs and it is processed by the microcontroller to verify the waste level and the data is sent through Global System for Mobile Communication (GSM) modules to the central office. This method is used rather than combining RFID with WSN. Using GSM/General Packet Radio Service (GPRS) and Zigbee technology, a control tray system for solid waste is offered.

3.1.1 *Components used*

In the IoT environment, the open-source is NodeMCU. It concerns the firmware which runs on ESP8266 Wi-Fi SoC from the express system if and hardware depends mainly on the ESP12 module. NodeMCU mentioned firmware as opposed to developing default kits. The Lua language for the script is utilized by the firmware. That depends on the eLua method and the configuration of ESP8266 on expressive Non-OS SDK. Free methods such as Spiffs and Lua-Cjson are utilized.

Since NodeMCU is a modified version of ESP8266 that has better programming, voltage stability, and great reliability, it links various sensors to wireless controllers by Wi-Fi.

Ultrasonic sensor: An ultrasonic sensor is an electronic device used to assess the target distance by transmitting an ultrasonic signal or sound waves. The signal or electric wave is transformed into reflective sound. Sound can be heard from human movements inferior to signals or ultrasonic waves. Sensors comprise transmitters and receivers. Via piezoelectric crystals, the sound is emitted by the transmitter and received by the target receivers, as shown in Figure 4. In automation and instrumentation, engineering applications, robots, these sensors are used.

Working of Ultrasonic Sensor: An ultrasonic sensor like HC-SR04 is a 4Pin module such as echo, trigger, ground, and Vcc. In several applications, the distance measurement or the object used for detection is needed for this sensor. The system consists of two parts, an ultrasonic transmitter, and an ultrasonic receiver. These sensors operate under the Equation 1 given below,

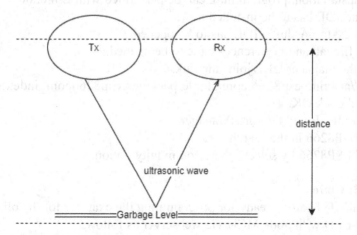

Figure 4. Garbage Level Calculation Using Ultrasonic Sensor

$$\text{Distance} = \text{Speed} \times \text{Time} \tag{1}$$

An ultrasonic transmitter is used to transmit signals or waves circulating in the air and is received by the receiver in which the waves are reflected from an obstacle. The distance can be calculated if the hour and velocity are known. The sensor has a universal velocity of 330 m/s at the condition of the part. The module has integrated a circuit to calculate the time taken for the wave that is received by rotating on the echo spindle to be in the high position. The distance can therefore be calculated with a microprocessor or a microcontroller.

3.1.2 *Algorithm*

Step 1: Firmware Installation

Initially, the firmware has to be installed on the board.

The folder of NodeMCU flashes a master has to be opened. Next, open the win32/win64 directory. Now the version folder should be opened, then flash ESP8266 should be double-clicked.

Forward to config tab.

Open the downloaded software by clicking on the small gear.

Switch to the advanced tab and the desired baud speed needs to be selected.

Forward to the operation tab and select the flash button.

Step 2: Arduino IDE Preparation

After installation, programming can be performed with ESP8266.

Arduino IDE has to be installed now.

From desktop Arduino IDE has to be opened.

Select file tab and preferences have to be opened.

Also, the manager URL joins the link.

(http://arduino.esp8266.com/stable/package_esp8266com_index.json) and click OK.

Goto Tools>Boards>BoardsManager.

Type ESP8266 in the search area.

Install ESP8266 by selecting the community option.

Step 3: Code

Node MCU board is ready for programming the example for the blinking of LED with node MCU via webserver as follows.

In arduino IDE goto tools>Boards>select NODEMCU 1.0 (ESP — 12EModule).

Move to tools and click port.

From the following code, the Wi-Fi name and Wi-Fi password have to be changed.

Select the upload button so that the code has to be uploaded.

The pin D9 of the board is connected to the positive leg of the led and the negative is connected to the ground of code.

Connect the board to the power supply and serial monitored has to be opened for Arduino IDE.

The IP address will be shown when the Wi-Fi is connected.

The shown address has to be entered on the web browser (chrome, edge, firefox, etc.).

Now the web page will be opened. Thus the LED status can be changed by selecting it ON/OFF.

3.1.3 *Geth*

Any machine can be carried out with the erythreum node using the tool as a command-line called Geth. The implementation of Geth releases version 1.5.8. The node is configurable by Geth. Two erythreum blockchain networks are used in our methodology. The erythreum properties are inherited across a blockchain network is erythreum private network, but the nodes are not interconnected with the erythreum main network or test network. Nodes used in the private network are not required to download blocks from the main network. To verify erythreum, few machines can perform nodes for internal purposes. Manual configuration of the private network required to implement. Smart contracts can be executed using the JSON-RPC interface.

3.1.4 *BLYNK App*

Using iOS and Android devices, hardware projects are controlled and monitored by the building interface via Blynk. Once the Blynk application is uploaded, create a dashboard project and arrange buttons, graphics, sliders, and widgets remaining on the screen. Widgets let turn pins on/off or data can be displayed from the sensors. Mainly hardware interfaces can be constructed easily while the software part is challenging. This portion of the software can be constructed easily as the hardware using blynk.

The system depends on the NodeMCU board on an IoT system. Through Wi-Fi, the internet is connected from a smartphone with the help of a hotspot to node MCU which has an ESP8266 circuit for internet connection.

Knowing the hotspot name, passcode, and token code, the blynk server connects the MCU node to the Smartphone. The computer transfers the code to the MCU node of the Arduino IDE to create the blynk server project application for the MCU-smart phone node connection is shown in Figure 5. Blynk libraries are zip files that are imported in the lib of the Arduino IDE after downloading it from the Github site.

Blynk server checks internet connection, hotspot connection of MCU node that has token code, hotspot name, and password. The data supplied must be matched to allow ESP8266 connection with Wi-Fi to exchange orders. The other processes only send orders between them as shown in Figure 6. The output is delivered from the MCU kit from the node to the blynk application.

Figure 5.   BLYNK Application

Figure 6. Bin Level Indication

Manufacturers, shippers, merchants, and e-waste recyclers will be better able to coordinate under the proposed smart agreement structure. It will give the government jurisdiction over the collection and recycling of electronic trash. It will also lessen the imbalance between coordinated and chaotic zones, resulting in improved cycle accuracy. The existing block-chain-based solutions to waste frameworks and the success of these arrangements in the waste management industry's tendency to issues.

3.2 *Smart garbage management schema*

```
var SGMSchema = new Schema({
location : {
type : { type : String },
coordinates : [ Number, Number ]
},
```

```
minimum_balance_required : { type : Number, default:
0.05 },
owner_type : {
type: String,
enum: ["PRIVATE", "GOVERNMENTAL", "COMMUNITY", "JOINT_
VENTURE"]
},
max_capacity : { type: Number, required: true},
current_state : { type: Number, default: 0.00 },
owner_account : { type: String, required: true},
fixed_unit_cost : { type: Number, required: true}
});
```

The ultrasonic sensor is used to detect data that the Wi-Fi module monitors. The waste volume is predicted by the database. The location of the bin is determined using GPS and GSM modules, and this information is sent to the administrator and worker. The workers, according to the facts, are cleaning up rubbish. When several bins are added, sorting techniques such as the Dijkstra algorithm are employed to determine the shortest path. When the bin is over 85% full, the node can be run. As a result, the shortest path is determined, allowing the truck driver to collect the garbage in a timely manner.

4. Experimental Results

An interface builder that is perfectly engineered is the blynk app that runs on both Android and iOS.

5. Conclusion

Depending on the population, the management of garbage and garbage that is generated each week by people is a central point of this document. In smart cities and municipalities, waste management can be easy to use. If the dustbin is loaded fully, an alert message is sent to the worker and admin instantly for clearance using a garbage system monitoring process that is based on blockchain technology and IoT. In the real world, the proposed support methods describe the need to roll out the waste management system. With a minimum of overheads, smart contracts and micro-payments can be treated as a payment infrastructure using blockchain technology. In the future, a garbage collection system based on the blockchain is used mainly in multi-story industries and apartments since it provides a secured connection to the holder of an account and micropayments which are based on the garbage weight formed by the user.

References

Beerens, R., Thissen, S. C. N., Pancras, W. C. M., Gommans, T. M. P., van de Wouw, N., & Heemels, W. P. M. H. (2020). Control allocation for an industrial high-precision transportation and positioning system. *IEEE Transactions on Control Systems Technology, 29*(2), 876–883.

Durand, T. G., Visagie, L., & Booysen, M. J. (2019). Evaluation of next-generation low-power communication technology to replace GSM in IoT-applications. *IET Communications, 13*(16), 2533–2540.

Islam, M. M., Tonmoy, S. S., Quayum, S., Sarker, A. R., Hani, S. U., & Mannan, M. A. (January, 2019). Smart poultry farm incorporating GSM and IoT. In *2019 International Conference on Robotics, Electrical and Signal Processing Techniques (ICREST)* (pp. 277–280). IEEE, Bangaladesh.

Jiang, X., Pang, Z., Luvisotto, M., Candell, R., Dzung, D., & Fischione, C. (September, 2020). Delay optimization for industrial wireless control systems based on channel characterization. *IEEE Transactions on Industrial Informatics, 16*(9), 5855–5865.

Kanta, S., Jash, S., & Saha, H. N. (2017, August). Internet of Things based garbage monitoring system. In *2017 8th Annual Industrial Automation and Electromechanical Engineering Conference (IEMECON)* (pp. 127–130). IEEE.

Khan, M. A., & Salah, K. (2018). IoT security: Review, blockchain solutions, and open challenges. *Future Generation Computer Systems, 82*, 395–411.

Lamichhane, M. (2017). A smart waste management system using IoT and blockchain technology.

Latchoumi, T. P., & Sunitha, R. (2010, September). Multi-agent systems in distributed data warehousing. In *2010 International Conference on Computer and Communication Technology (ICCCT)* (pp. 442–447).

Loganathan, J., Janakiraman, S., & Latchoumi, T. P. (2017). A novel architecture for next generation cellular network using opportunistic spectrum access scheme. *Journal of Advanced Research in Dynamical and Control Systems, 12*(12), 1388–1400.

Mahzan, N. N., Enzai, N. M., Zin, N. M., & Noh, K. S. S. K. M. (2018, June). Design of an Arduino-based home fire alarm system with GSM module. *Journal of Physics: Conference Series, 1019*(1), 012079, IOP Publishing.

Mcginthy, J. M., & Michaels, A. J. (2019, March). Secure industrial internet of things critical infrastructure node design. *IEEE Internet of Things Journal, 6*(5), 8021–8037.

Memon, S. K., Shaikh, F. K., Mahoto, N. A., & Memon, A. A. (2019, January). IoT-based smart garbage monitoring & collection system using WeMos & Ultrasonic sensors. In *2019 2nd International Conference on Computing, Mathematics and Engineering Technologies (iCoMET)* (pp. 1–6). IEEE.

Ongena, G., Smit, K., Boksebeld, J., Adams, G., Roelofs, Y., & Ravesteyn, P. (2018, June). Blockchain-based smart contracts in waste management: A silver bullet? In *Bled eConference* (p. 19).

Paes, R., Mazur, D. C., Venne, B. K., & Ostrzenski, J. (2020, March/April). A guide to securing industrial control networks: Integrating it and OT systems. *IEEE Industry Applications Magazine, 26*(2), 47–53.

Pan, F., Pang, Z., Luvisotto, M., Xiao, M., & Wen, H. (2018, December). Physical-layer security for industrial wireless control systems: Basics and future directions. *IEEE Industrial Electronics Magazine, 12*(4), 18–27.

Petropulu, A., Diamantaras, K. I., Han, Z., Niyato, D., & Zonouz, S. (2019, March). Contactless monitoring of critical infrastructure [from the guest editors]. *IEEE Signal Processing Magazine, 36*(2), 19–21.

Russell, L., Goubran, R., Kwamena, F., & Knoefel, F. (2018, March). Agile IoT for critical infrastructure resilience: Cross-modal sensing as part of a situational awareness approach. *IEEE Internet of Things Journal, 5*(6), 4454–4465.

Stellios, I., Kotzanikolaou, P., Psarakis, M., Alcaraz, C., & Lopez, J. (2018). A survey of IoT-enabled cyberattacks: Assessing attack paths to critical infrastructures and services. *IEEE Communications Surveys and Tutorials, 20*(4), 3453–3495.

Sun, J., Yan, J., & Zhang, K. Z. (2016). Blockchain-based sharing services: What blockchain technology can contribute to smart cities. *Financial Innovation, 2*(1), 1–9.

Wu, Y., Hu, F., Min, G., & Zomaya, A. (2017). *Big Data and Computational Intelligence in Networking*. Hoboken, NJ, USA: CRC Press.

Wu, Y., Huang, H., Wang, C.-X., & Pan, Y. (2019). *5G-Enabled Internet of Things*. Hoboken, NJ, USA: CRC Press.

Chapter 10

Industrial IoT with Light-Weighted Supporting Hierarchical Storage in Distributed Co-operative Network for Blockchain Technology

K. Rohini[*,**], R. Kala[†,††], C. Kavitha[‡,‡‡], R. Hema[§,§§], and
P. Praveen Kumar[¶,¶¶]

[*]*Department of Information Technology, Vels Institute of Science Technology and Advanced Studies, Chennai, India*

[†]*Department of Computer Science New Prince Shri Bhavani Arts and Science College, Chennai, India*

[‡]*Department of Computer Science, MKU College, Madurai, India*

[§]*Department of Computer Science, Institute of Distance Education, University of Madras, Chennai, India*

[¶]*Department of Computer Applications, Thiruthangal Nadar College, Selavsyal, Chennai, India*

[**]*rrohini16@gmail.com*

[††]*kalamca05@gmail.com*

[‡‡]*kkavitha009@gmail.com*

[§§]*hemaramji@gmail.com*

[¶¶]*praveenctr@gmail.com*

201

Abstract

An innovation in the Industrial Internet of Things (IIoT) gives a promising chance to incorporate huge scopes to interfere with various heterogeneous gadgets in the Web. Most existing IIoT frameworks rely on a unified architecture as a cooperative network, which is simpler for executives at the same time cannot adequately support undeniable and immutable administrations between the various gatherings. The ideal strengths for a large-scale IIoT foundation like reliability, dispersed co-activity, identifiability, and permanence are given by blockchain innovation. This chapter proposed the concept of the IIoT that relies on a blockchain to assist immutable and indisputable administrations. The issue of capacity is trending in this chapter by offering a structure based on the hierarchical blockchain. Exceptionally, the proposed design consists of a graded storage structure where most of the blockchain is placed in mist. While the latest blocks are put away in the overlay organization of the people IoT networks. Consistently, the proposed design links the blockchain, IIoT, and cloud overlay organization. Together through the blockchain connector and the cloud connector, to develop the various blockchain capabilities graded. In layering organizations, blockchain connector constructs impede blockchain from information produced in IIoT organizations. And the cloud connectors fix blockchain synchronization issues between fogs and overlay organizations. In this chapter, the co-employable ownership and access control system is proposed for lightweight IoT devices and is hardware to countless situations. An experimental result provides in this paper is to demonstrate the efficiency of the proposed hierarchy blockchain storage in a practical IIoT case.

Keywords: Blockchain technology, Distributed cooperative, IIoT, Hierarchical storage, Lightweight security

1. Introduction

In the growth of applications, the blockchain enhancement has a colossal potential and the Gig-Blockchain growth has a huge potential with a set of jobs and gives numerous institutions great opportunities. When coordinating monetary transactions between parties using blockchain, confidence is broadened as it eliminates the likelihood of theft and thus allows a database of activities (Yaga *et al.*, 2019). Blockchain creates resolved quality because of its decentralized properties and eliminates the contrast encountered while trying to join a market at the same time as another social case. Voice calls, video calls, text, and images are a direct route through the network between the sender and the recipient. To do that, people need to trust an untouchable in a traditional system as it is similar to the money exchange (Kushch & Prieto-Castrillo, 2019). In any case, it will provide ideal protection back into the blockchain example. A block must register any exchange to be used as a booklet. A block goes into the blockchain as a data collection immutable at the time when a transaction is carried out. A clean glossy block is built into it if a block is finished or a new block is newly manufactured from the container. An old block hash is transferred to each block (Li *et al.*, 2015, 2019; Loganathan *et al.*, 2017; Vasanth *et al.*, 2017).

With the rapid development of the Industrial Internet of Things (IIoT), the topology of the dispersed IIoT and the limits of embedded computing resources are becoming more and more important. It creates new obstacles for the traditional storage, transportation, and security of information. Distributed IIoT is ideal for distributed confidence and a ledger dedicated to blockchain technology, which will also be an elective approach for cutting-edge applications. It contains a limited resource and implementation technique for the Layered Lightweight Blockchain Framework (LLBF). A limited resource layer (RCL) and a wide blockchain resource layer (REL) are used in the IIoT framework. The structure and size of the blocks are being restructured to accommodate IIoT aircraft computing devices. To improve blockchain performance and reduce the number of transactions validated in new blocks, a light consensus.

Moreover, blockchain wells, as these advances are regularly altered to validate, support, and survey data provided by the machines. Furthermore, due to its decentralized existence, it specifies the need to trust the untouchable within and does not have a single excuse for dissatisfaction (Li *et al.*, 2020; Zheng *et al.*, 2019). Blockchain may be a thought that plans to decentralize as a well-being effort, contains an opportunity to form a general record for all trades that exist during a given framework, and makes them perpetual. Blockchain may be a thought which plans to decentralize as a wellness effort. It permits consensus and trust, without untouchables, indirect communication between two social occasions (Battula *et al.*, 2020; Loganathan *et al.*, 2017; Wang *et al.*, 2019).

The Communicating Things Network (CTN) is the newest advance in the development of smart technologies. It is a collection of physical devices which can retrieve and share digital data. Its goal is to create smart gadgets that enhance productivity and deliver real-time data faster than any structure or network that depends on human intervention. The networked physical parts of the system communicate with each other and monitor and analyze their environment to facilitate intelligent decision-making. CTNs are playing an increasingly important part in daily operations in today's world, enabling significant cost savings as well as enhanced visibility and efficiency in all aspects of enterprises and individuals. In this chapter, we examined one of the most important applications of the CTN (Internet of Things) and developed a secure industrial IoT framework based on the blockchain method.

A hybrid industrial architecture is an architecture in which the many divisions of a company are distributed in many countries. While IoT devices are widely used in many companies and can help lower manufacturing costs while improving quality, they can also be vulnerable to attacks by many invaders. Intruders may access IoT devices and use them for malicious operations. For example, a corporate employee can steal a product or sleep during working hours. To avoid such issues, blockchain technology is widely regarded as the most effective method for maintaining confidentiality and protecting the control system in real-time. In this chapter, we employed a blockchain technique to extract data from IoT devices and store the extracted records on the blockchain to ensure transparency among several users in different locations. In addition, the suggested architecture was tested against the internal communication of blockchain, where several hackers pirated IoT devices. A correct dynamic confidence algorithm and algorithm are devised. High-speed management is used to maintain the equilibrium of the transaction workload of the blockchain.

Blockchain is creating energy for each mechanical part to use the blockchain advancement for its inspirations, for example, secure arrangements, currency exchanges, sharing information on prosperity, at this point (Sahoo *et al.*, 2019; Wang *et al.*, 2018; Yang *et al.*, 2019). While it had first been developed to assess the digital forms of money, for example, Bit-piece. It's critical that Bit-coin is by and by treated as stock in Wall Street and monetary promote while its inspiration and certified worth are yet to arise, and its future isn't clear. It is beautiful that blockchain is a PC appearing to give widespread correspondence during a common arrangement of endorsers where trades are clear among the social occasions referring to Zheng *et al.* (2019). Critical investigations must be focused on measuring the security of blockchain, insurance concerns and impediments should also be examined. Asymmetric cryptography, or public-key cryptography, is one of the lifeblood of blockchain innovation.

This kind of cryptography allows everyone to confirm the honesty of the exchanges, protect the assets of programmers, and much more. In Bitcoin and other blockchain, computerized marks are for the most part utilized in the exchange cycle as a path for somebody to demonstrate their possession, without uncovering their private key (Chen *et al.*, 2020). blockchain is reliant on hashing. Hashing is a cryptographic technique that transforms all information into a string of characters. Just as providing security through encryption, hashing makes storing information more efficient, because hashing is of a fixed size.

2. Related Works

A couple of review work is here in connection with blockchain. Certain customary tasks are currently being considered and discussed. Within the review work, blockchain progress has been used. Such progress is the imaginable destiny of the preparation of trade. Also, it is used in informed arrangements on the web identified with money. In the review work, they additionally offered an insight identified with the blockchain ahead. The benefits of this progress need to be looked at to disrupt the money portion. To achieve this, the general cash reimbursement is a working environment (Petropulu *et al.*, 2019; Russell *et al.*, 2018). Also, the clever, modernized cash arrangements linked to a record also as the resources advanced was considered further to be in their work. In the area of research, the analysts conducted an efficient planning study. Also, it was clear that their goal was to upgrade the current state of blockchain. Reviewed issues with upcoming course identified with blockchain advancement (Mcginthy & Michaels, 2019; Stellios *et al.*, 2018; Wu *et al.*, 2019).

Universities are now integrating numerous technologies into their processes to improve the services and processes of their members as research and innovation centers. The Internet of Things, for example, is a leading-edge technology that collects data about the environment and people using a number of devices. Cloud-based models and Big Data architectures are used to process these data and generate knowledge through data analysis. These findings are used to improve processes and make better settlement decisions, which translates into better services. The integration of technology allows to create a sustainable environment that seeks the coherence between the population and the environment, ensuring an economic growth respectful of the environment. However, any technology must keep processes and data safe, and for that reason, a new technology called blockchain. It has been integrated, which seeks to address two requirements: process security and agility. The study of blockchain components to build a new layer that fits the architecture of a university campus is needed to integrate this technology into a university. It ensures that the information is safeguarded. This ensures that the data is kept cryptographically secret to avoid exposure, and that the overall procedure is double-checked by many blocks.

The reliability of the information by applying the play plan of blockchain. It is no longer understood that the blockchain is a fairly new progression. At this time, several perspectives were made in 2009. It was portrayed as an open disk identified with all Bit-coin exchanges. Besides, the specialists have also studied blockchain. The evaluation was carried out based on the processing, retrieval, and sharing of files within the decentralized system. It mulled over the data integrity. Such progress is proposed to guarantee and make the correctness in the exchanges.

To deliver secure data transmission in IIoT for smart urban applications, a lightweight data consensus algorithm for the Industrial Internet of Things (IIoT) based on blockchain technology is presented. The method relies on a registry that spans many boundaries. A bi-directional transmission approach is used to ensure consistent data during data transmission. Compared to traditional blockchain technology, the lightweight data block format is a refinement. The results of the simulations show that the suggested consensus algorithm minimizes the average number of data bounces, reducing the risk of data theft. Data accuracy, as well as low energy consumption and latency have been verified. It is essentially invulnerable to blackouts with revision limitation as well as capacity. It reduces the chances of disrupting associations and attributing inventive patterns.

Advancements are imaginative and innovative. To keep a decent key means of dangerous glare as well as to give signs of openness to progress, tacticians, organizers are needed to focus now (Beerens *et al.* 2020; Wu *et al.* 2017). It should construct the design pattern identified with blockchain. A blockchain-based on information logging, they clarified the fairness of executive design. To select the problems that exist in the past construction, logging information related to the blockchain was proposed. Similarly, the evaluation between the introduction of the proposed work and the existing frameworks was conducted in the same manner. In the evaluation work, planning was examined in the same way as future models. The reviewers forwarded the examination identified with the blockchain framework first. The latter is used two or three blockchain. Similarly, specific problems relating to the resumption of progress are also recorded in the evaluation work (Jiang *et al.*, 2020; Pan *et al.*, 2018).

By supplying applications with redundancy, immutable storage and encryption, the new blockchain technology has the potential to revolutionize industrial systems and the Internet of Things (IoT). A lot more IoT (IIoT) industrial applications and blockchain technologies have emerged in recent years. It sparked the interest of industrial and university researchers. The combination of blockchain with IIoT industrial foresight is the topic of this chapter. The author presents an IIoT framework activated by the blockchain that includes core concepts. Applications and issues of greatest importance are also discussed. With the approved IIoT blockchain, a full analysis of the latest research trends and open inquiries is provided.

The evaluation work was made together to analyze the blockchain. The review work demonstrated that the glossary could be useful for a new framework going forward. Blockchain security with issues, and approaches (Paes *et al.*, 2020). In their work, they clarified the improved blockchain and its wonderful exploration plans. Also, they examined and clarified the usage of blockchain security.

3. Proposed Architecture

Therefore, the safety of the device is essential for ensuring the well-being and adequacy of the system framework. The storage of the device is dependent upon the innovation of distributed computing and the idea of a public blockchain. When compared to a valid, state-of-the-art blockchain strategy, the survey results and the hierarchy of the proposed component are shown in Figure 1. The proposed blockchain-based IoT design includes hierarchical layers using the Merkle Root Tree Hash algorithm, e.g., IoT neighborhood organizations, the co-usable blockchain network, and mists. To depict the vital parts of each layer, we first adopt a base-up strategy and afterward present the plan subtleties of the proposed hierarchical blockchain design to alleviate the issue of storage ability.

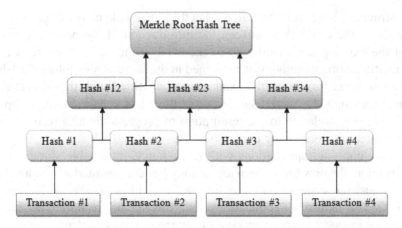

Figure 1.　Merkle Root Hash Tree Structure

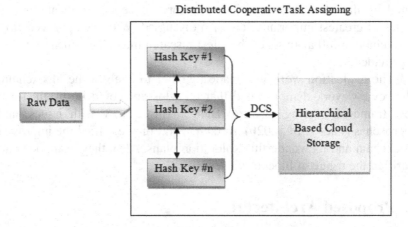

Figure 2.　Hierarchical Based Cloud Storage

3.1 *System architecture*

IoT: Notwithstanding standard storage, get-ready transactions from the monstrous raw information gathered from the organization is the key added assignment of neighborhood IoT organization as shown in Figure 2. Because of the uses in neighborhood IoT organizations and the heterogeneity of gadgets, in the stable, the information needs to be organized and scrambled. The tasks are done primarily through the information engine. The proposed design uses a blockchain connector to move as an interface between the overlay organization and the IoT organization, to continuously gather exchanges in the blocks. To obtain transactions and manage access devices, functions, and components given by the blockchain connector.

Comparing the existing framework to the proposed framework, it was found that the proposed framework prioritized delivery over the existing framework. In an open environment, it provides a new technique for dealing with data suppression, trade execution, capacity execution and confidence building. It is widely acknowledged as a revolutionary development in cryptography and digital security. Verification, confidentiality, security, and access control lists (ACL), as well as the information and source of assets, are all part of the administrations of the square chain. All of these regimes are essential for modern applications today, especially given the vast amount of data managed by systems and the use of distributed computing.

Methodology Because blockchain involves validation, inspection and responsibility, it can serve as a promising tool to provide a secure exchange of information on the system. The validation confirms that the customer is who he pretends to be. Unauthorized clients will not have access to the information as it is protected by confidentiality. Clients are able to control and protect access to their personal information. Provenance tracks information and assets, along with owners and how they are used in the system. The information's reliability is checked to see if it hasn't been tampered with. Currently, centralized controllers, such as a reporting authority, monitor these jurisdictions. Similarly, authorities frequently target the embedded controller.

Once again, blockchain has been assured, and records have been revealed that can assist in the resolution of numerous problems associated with centralization. From a security perspective, the square chain is created and maintained using a distributed overlay system, which is secured by decentralized cryptography and swarm handling. Blockchain is an innovative technique for managing data storage, trade execution, capability performance and building trust in an open environment. Many people see the square chain as a revolutionary advance in cryptography and digital security, with applications based on frameworks of digital money transmitted globally. Based on the capacity of the server farm, a distributed decentralized storage system was introduced with a number of benefits. Distributed storage organizations, such as traditional arrangements, use client-side encryption to ensure data security.

From the IoT gadgets approved by transmitting a security step to ensure the legitimacy of the raw information that can be accomplished within the IoT organization. For example, in Emerson's blockchain task, he uses the Mocana security stage, which depends on the organization that is reliable to ensure that security exchanges. Note that the IoT design which is a blockchain-based we proposed expects that getting and moving the crude information into exchanges occurred in the nearby IoT network by using the security stage. Through the security stage in a private and concentrated way, the security and trust of nearby exchanges can be ensured. The prepared exchanges are dispatched off the overlay network by the passage as a co-usable-based organization. To do, confirm and change the block together is the obligation of the network overlay after the trades are acquired.

New network computing technologies are now available for industrial IoT (IIoT) terminals. However, in unstable and scattered IIoT environments, this promising system of service delivery runs into issues since service providers or malicious clients may refuse to offer services or use them for their own gain. Traditional repudiation methods are no longer available in IIoT systems due to third-party trust requirements or prohibitive administration costs. Fortunately, the blockchain revolution is fueling creative thinking. We propose a blockchain-based fair repudiation service delivery system for IIoT scenarios in which the blockchain serves as both a service publisher and a proof recorder in this study. Each service is delivered in its own fashion, both online and offline, with mandatory evidence for non-repudiation. In addition, a service verification method based on homomorphism hashing is designed to work only with string proofs. To solve disagreements, an intelligent and impartial contract is put in place. The reliability of the safety analysis is proven and the effectiveness and efficiency of the evaluations are established.

Overlay Network: To frame blockchain hubs in the co-usable-based network overlay is able after exchanges are distributed through the passages of nearby IIoT organizations. Some attractive highlights can be given using co-employable-based organization overlays such as high accessibility, adaptability, and self-study. A productive transfer to developing the blocks from the exchanges is given through the blockchain connectors where the doors of the neighborhood to IIoT networks are coordinated as co-employable of the agreeable overlay. The engineering, we proposed expects that the predetermined blockchain agreement convention are trailed by overlay network example Proof-of-Stake (PoS) or

Proof-of-Work (PoW) or Byzantine Fault Tolerance (BFT) plans relying upon different IoT applications. Generally speaking,

BFT conventions make more sense for IIoT because they don't have two spending problems. The IIoT situations normally include the framework that is permitted which forces the stricter access control and is worked by known elements. In the blockchain permission, BFT-type agreements were generally examined with beating PoW as a point while guaranteeing a faster conclusion of exchanges and sufficient adaptation to internal failure. To accomplish agreement measure we accept the overlay network embraces a BFT convention, for example, the danger model follows the definition and versatile BFT for mechanical secure metering, i.e., 1/3 of the all-out taking part hubs are more than Byzantine hubs.

Clouds: For automatic needs (such as cycle capacity, restricted storage size, and correspondence data transmission) are compensated by cloud capacity assets and essentially unrestricted processing. Neighborhood IoT networks on mists are combined by the network of blockchain overlays in the design we have proposed. To interface the overlay organization to the cloud easily, other than the cloud administration layer fundamental functionalities (e.g., information the executives, information storage, and so on,) alluded as cloud connector were the issues between the mists and overlay organizations of the cloud connector in the blocks and synchronization.

In our design, the mists are not kept up by a solitary gathering or element. Instead of mists being coordinated as a proper co-usable, distributed storage where the single administrator does not exist. To deal with the mists, the parcel needs a co-usable means of transport of storage distributed between the mists to guarantee the coherence of the information. For capacity wholesaler hubs, Storage Network provides powerful object storage that scrambles, fragments, and appropriates information as a promising up-and-comer. The capacity of the consulting stage gives various key points like a conveyed co-activity, safety and protection, and Byzantine adaptation to non-critical failure. Conditions before assigned storage address key highlights.

3.2 *Hierarchical storage structure of blockchain*

Storage is a fundamental problem in large-scale IoT applications. Each sharing node stores local all blocks in the blockchain foreground. To solve the capability problem, another build should be formulated and when applying to a huge range of IoT applications, this storage instrument is restrictive. The primary reason for this paper is to address the issue of capacity through a variety of graded structures. The assumption on the overlay network is made before we present the progressive storage structure that we suggested for blockchain.

For instance, the BFT convention ought to be powerful enough which we embraced to manage the proportion of Byzantine hubs is under 1/3 and countless taking part hubs accepting that BFT calculation as the basic blockchain agreement convention. We embrace a various leveled storage structure where the chain of blocks or the blockchain information is tended to by the proposed blockchain-based IoT engineering storage issue are put away independently at two areas: the most recent segment in the co-employable hubs of the overlay organization and the greater part in the distributed storage. To store or download the blockchain, the nearby IoT network has the capacity, but in this design, we recommend that it is not necessary. To gather the crude information created from IoT gadgets and exchanges that are developed is accepted as the primary undertaking of the nearby IoT organization. The capacity prerequisite is diminished by the overlay hubs as they just store the most recent segment of the blockchain locally and have the remainder of the blocks in blockchain put away in the mists. The outline of the proposed blocks in structure appears in Figure 3.

It comprises of three significant parts: the initial segment is to manage the concentrated and private way exchanges (model: data preparing indoors); the subsequent part is to shape the blocks as per the new blocks in a co-employable based overlay organization (model: following agreement protocol); the last part is the blocks put away in the mists as a lion's share. Cloud information can be obtained by approved congregations and give different IoT applications brilliant administrations.

The different graded storage techniques that we have proposed, while guaranteeing their consistency in different mists, the blocks can be transferred and put aside (or we can say synchronized). To meet the capacity limit required by applications for a huge range of IoT is the main point of use of the cloud to store blockchain information. On the off chance that we accept most mists are straightforward, that assaults can be forestalled by putting away the blocks in different mists, where the information is altered in a specific cloud. The capacity is used by the proposed conspire, a circulating and pleasant distributed storage stage to monitor and scatter information blocks into the mists. Additionally, other employable

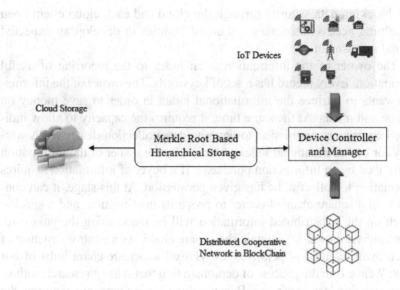

Figure 3. Distributed Cooperative Network in Blockchain Using Merkle Root Hierarchical Storage

dispersed distributed storage steps can be used as a likely arrangement, for example, the IPFS registration framework, to process the information.

Algorithm for System Registration in Blockchain

```
Parameters: blockchain, storage
begin /* to check the given system id is exists or not
in blockchain*/
if(system_id = true(blockchain)) then
return()/* if exists then return error*/
else

register_new_system_id(id,blockchain) /* register new
id in blockchain*/
end:
```

Administration taking the main cloud clients and will partake, cloud clients, themselves and approximating different advanced money for instance Bitcoin to get financial motivations to verify and put into the resolved record. Cloud clients confirm the use of a private key. Along

SLA blocking data security through the cloud and each cloud client open to, helping access customers and cloud bundles to develop an expected normal assessment.

The owner of the information is an index to the reporting of useful information. Every record has a set of keywords. The owner of the information wants to retrieve the informational index in order to save money on storage and media. At the same time, it requires the capacity to allow individual consumers permission to have its data collection dispersed. A warranty for the informational index proposed by the owner of the information is provided by an information purchaser. If a buyer of information acquires information to collect it, he has given permission. At this stage, it can connect with a square channel center to prove its qualification, and a specific search on the redistributed information will be made using the password. These hubs are used to maintain the square chain. As a control structure of government, cloud co-operatives are viewed as square-chain hubs in our work. Weave is in the process of demonstrating that it has a research authority specializing in square poles. Because diverse supporters are common, the qualification check should be held secret in order to protect Bob's privacy.

To make things even safer, the square chain can only certify that one of the followers is Bob, but it cannot take Bob's character out of the equation. Square intersections should also be unable to determine if two pieces of evidence were created by the same individual. Bob should be able to search for a password to retrieve important records from the unified cloud instead of downloading the entire information index. The introduction of the coin bit, a decentralized cryptographic money for the web, is inextricably related to the advancement of square chain innovation. The square chain has been successfully deployed in a variety of major applications since it was first introduced in 2008. The square chain consists of squares, with hash pointers which allow them to interact with each other. Squares are immutable in a trustworthy manner, thanks to updated cryptographic hashing abilities. One does not require a central power source in a square chain. Or maybe it's spread all over the system. Bit piece had open admin tools when he presented the square chain idea. Anyone who has a Web connection, especially on purpose, has access to square channel data. Our methodology analyzes the scenario of a square channel licensing framework rather than the less consent requirements. Undisputed cloud professional organizations with opposite interests are substances that approach the square chain. In terms of distribution, security, and operating costs, this model offers different points of interest on the less consent approach.

Blockchain allows the cloud turning out consortium, developing cloud-based that helps encourage customers, having the blockchain app have Swarm next to the handle, showing exquisite abilities and block-chain. Reactive, operational, and essentially accessible transportation to maintain all aspects of the required obligation and opportunities to regulate the supplier Baas. In a roundabout way receiving blockchain innovation for business purposes to a large portion of the endeavors to arrange blockchain is an interesting improvement, which lessons speculation cost and procedure for business exchange. The weaving of the platform as a service portrays its binding instrument while in transit in this way. The administration strategy through making total access notwithstanding to define the base ok place of the blockchain service is there a significant goal. Blockchain methodology conceals four highlights of the above-indicated technique: executive the relationship, oversight visual, unmistakable middle layer hand automated abuse evaluation framework, scripting, and dealing, executive checking, pertinent relationship adjusting, utilization of dissemination to offer fused support to electronic misuse objective introducing. The system that maintains the frameworks, establishing the essential system and the charging system relationship at the time of execution is the important work of the setup.

4. Experimental Results and Analysis

The cloud admin is used to obtain the cloud user layer. Cloud client as unique limits in the Cloud automation layer. The entry stage of the natural watch section inside the preconditions is formed together. Past assurance, the confidentiality requirements of its magnitude of the bundling requirement commits to what type of fix the customer evaluated the plot during the access phase. The usage by the customer during the transit of the reaction is estimated simultaneousness or in the arrangement phase of the ensuring step.

The cloud framework coordinator sets out equivalent to the cloud tipping into the organization level of the blockchain. The frame is the backbone of blockchain. Cryptography, common understanding, acceptance, and openly shared ledgers are adventures. The blockchain attributes directly the whole degrees of structure be the vertebrae of this structure be the blockchain management level. Every cloud client holds an equally free open cloud. For every cloud customer support request and recording synchronization. Understanding after that achieves the chosen

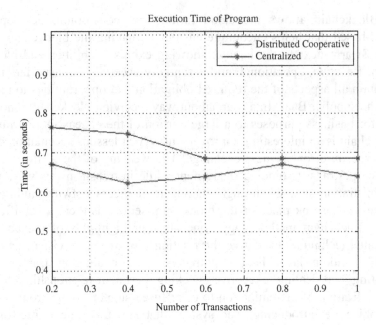

Figure 4.   Execution Time of Program

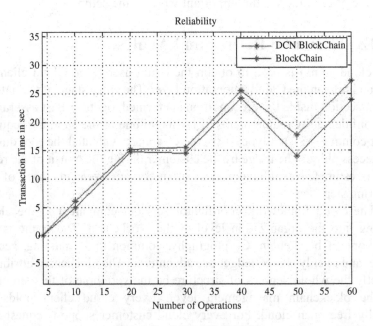

Figure 5.   System Reliability

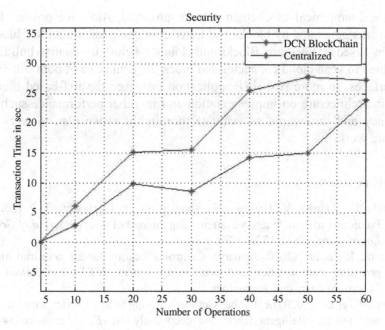

Figure 6. Lightweight Security in Blockchain

requirements, on the side of examining the state of understanding to encourage the strategy of the providers of a project quantity to an exquisite understanding. All customer incorporates blockchain amassed on own obligations. Blockchain-enabled storage capacity level data level guaranteed extra qualities of availability discover, protection with assurance provides this level accordingly. Cryptographic techniques are upgraded through the blockchain cloud within the collected measurements are shown in Figures 4–6.

5. Conclusion and Future Work

Both academic and IIoT systems as a large part of have drawn attention to application technologies and blockchain technology. IoT networks to store and manage blockchain is a difficult problem, due to IoT applications generated bulk data and IoT infrastructures as limited resources. In this chapter, the co-usable appropriation and access control system is proposed for lightweight IoT devices and it is hardware to countless situations. We provide an experimental output to show the effectiveness of the hierarchical blockchain storage proposal. Also, we present IoT networks generated by blocks and transactions to maintain an IoT blockchain-based architecture. Blocks and clouds synchronize them to build are defined to yeah cloud connector and block the connector of both software interfaces. In more real IIoT application proposed the IoT-based blockchain architecture on implementation and its other performance such as latency and throughput as evaluate thoroughly as we plan to work as future work.

References

Battula, B., Anusha, V., Praveen, N., Shankar, G., & Latchoumi, T. P. (2020). Prediction of vehicle safety system using internet of things. *Journal of Green Engineering, 10*(4), 1786–1798.

Beerens, R., *et al.*, (2020, January). Control allocation for an industrial high-precision transportation and positioning system. *IEEE Transactions on Control Systems and Technology.*

Chen, M., *et al.*, (2020, September/October). Living with I-Fabric: Smart living powered by intelligent fabric and deep analytics. *IEEE Networks, 34*(5), 156–163.

Jiang, X., Pang, Z., Luvisotto, M., Candell, R., Dzung, D., & Fischione, C. (2020, September). Delay optimization for industrial wireless control systems based on channel characterization. *IEEE Transactions on Industrial Informatics, 16*(9), 5855–5865.

Kushch, S., & Prieto-Castrillo, F. (2019, April). Blockchain for dynamic nodes in a smart city. In *2019 IEEE 5th World Forum on the Internet of Things (WF-IoT),* IEEE, (pp. 29–34). Limelack, Ireland.

Li, D., Deng, L., Cai, Z., & Souri, A. (2020). Blockchain as a service model in the Internet of Things management: Systematic review. *Transactions on Emerging Telecommunications Technologies,* e4139.

Li, S., Qin, T., & Min, G. (2019). Blockchain-based digital forensics investigation framework in the internet of things and social systems. *IEEE Transactions on Computational Social Systems, 6*(6), 1433–1441.

Liu, J., Huang, K., Rong, H., Wang, H., & Xian, M. (2015). Privacy-preserving public auditing for regenerating-code-based cloud storage. *IEEE Transactions on Information Forensics and Security, 10*(7), 1513–1528.

Loganathan, J., Janakiraman, S., & Latchoumi, T. P. (2017). A novel architecture for next generation cellular network using opportunistic spectrum access scheme. *Journal of Advanced Research in Dynamical and Control Systems,* (12), 1388–1400.

Loganathan, J., Janakiraman, S., Latchoumi, T. P., & Shanthoshini, B. (2017). Dynamic virtual server for optimized web service interaction. *International Journal of Pure and Applied Mathematics, 117*(19), 371–377.

Mcginthy, J. M., & Michaels, A. J. (2019, March). Secure industrial internet of things critical infrastructure node design. *IEEE Internet of Things Journal, 6*(5), 8021–8037.

Paes, R., Mazur, D. C., Venne, B. K., & Ostrzenski, J. (2020, March/April). A guide to securing industrial control networks: Integrating it and OT systems. *IEEE Industrial Applications Magazine, 26*(2), 47–53.

Pan, F., Pang, Z., Luvisotto, M., Xiao, M., & Wen, H. (2018, December). Physical-layer security for industrial wireless control systems: Basics and future directions. *IEEE Industrial Electronics Magazine, 12*(4), 18–27.

Petropulu, A., Diamantaras, K. I., Han, Z., Niyato, D., & Zonouz, S. (2019, March). Contactless monitoring of critical infrastructure [from the guest editors]. *IEEE Signal Processing Magazine, 36*(2), 19–21.

Russell, L., Goubran, R., Kwamena, F., & Knoefel, F. (2018, March). Agile IoT for critical infrastructure resilience: Cross-modal sensing as part of a situational awareness approach. *IEEE Internet of Things Journal, 5*(6), 4454–4465.

Sahoo, S., Fajge, A. M., Halder, R., & Cortesi, A. (2019). A hierarchical and abstraction-based blockchain model. *Applied Sciences, 9*(11), 2343.

Stellios, I., Kotzanikolaou, P., Psarakis, M., Alcaraz, C., & Lopez, J. (4th Quarterly, 2018). A survey of IoT-enabled cyberattacks: Assessing attack paths to critical infrastructures and services. *IEEE Communications Surveys and Tutorials, 20*(4), 3453–3495.

Vasanth, V., Venkatachalapathy, K., Thamarai, L., Parthiban, L., & Ezhilarasi, T. P. (2017). A survey on cache route schemes to improve QoS in AD-HOC networks. *Pakistan Journal of Biotechnology, 14*, 265–269.

Wang, G., Shi, Z., Nixon, M., & Han, S. (2019, July). Chain splitter: Towards blockchain-based industrial IoT architecture for supporting hierarchical storage. In *2019 IEEE International Conference on Blockchain (Blockchain)*, IEEE, pp. 166–175.

Wang, T., *et al.*, (2018, March). Big data reduction for a smart city's critical infrastructural health monitoring. *IEEE Communications Magazine, 56*(3), 128–133.

Wu, Y., Hu, F., Min, G., & Zomaya, A. (2017). *Big Data and Computational Intelligence in Networking*. Hoboken, NJ, USA: CRC Press.

Wu, Y., Huang, H., Wang, C.-X., & Pan, Y. (2019). *5G-Enabled Internet of Things*. Hoboken, NJ, USA: CRC Press.

Yaga, D., Mell, P., Roby, N., & Scarfone, K. (2019). Blockchain technology overview. pp. 41–50. arXiv preprint arXiv:1906.11078.

Yang, H., Yuan, J., Yao, H., Yao, Q., Yu, A., & Zhang, J. (2019). Blockchain-based hierarchical trust networking for JointCloud. *IEEE Internet of Things Journal, 7*(3), 1667–1677.

Zheng, W., Zheng, Z., Chen, X., Dai, K., Li, P., & Chen, R. (2019). Nutbaas: A blockchain-as-a-service platform. *IEEE Access, 7*, 134422–134433.

Chapter 11

Blockchain-Based Internet of Things (IoT) Security for Data Sharing in Smart City Environment

Padmavathy Thirunavukarasu Velayudham[*,§],
Vimal Kumar Maanuguru Nagaraju[†,¶], Shakunthala Masi[†,‖],
Shobana Nageswari Chandrasekaran[†,**], Rajkumar Kulandaivel[‡,††],
and Manikandan Ramachandran[‡,‡‡]

[*]*Department of ECE, R.M.K. Engineering College,
Kavaraipettai, India*

[†]*Department of Mechatronics Engineering,
Sona College of Technology, Salem, India*

[‡]*School of Computing, SASTRA Deemed University,
Thanjavur, India*

[§]*tvp.ece@rmkec.ac.in*

[¶]*mnv.ece@rmd.ac.in*

[‖]*ms.ece@rmd.ac.in*

[**]*shobana.ece@rmd.ac.in*

[††]*rajkumar@cse.sastra.edu*

[‡‡]*srmanimt75@gmail.com*

Abstract

Blockchain (BC) gained significant interest because of its undeniable nature and related advantages of security and privacy, BC has the power to solve drawback of Internet of Things (IoT) like data protection and privacy. Due to the IoT network's distributive nature and massive scale, the privacy and security of IoT have a major challenge. Blockchain has huge attention to improving audibility, IoT anonymity, security, and reliability in which billions of recently used devices are linked with internet to offer personalized services and everyday life. The most prominent issue is the scalability approach and is limited to high resource devices and must be within the wireless range of every IoT device. BC mechanism plays a vital role in safeguarding IoT-oriented applications by becoming part of a security mosaic, in the context of BC context realizes secure network over untrusted parties which is desirable in IoT with several heterogeneous devices. The BC technology has various advantages and various challenging techniques are presented to resolve the same issues in IoT. The proposed blockchain-based IoT is designed to handle mainly privacy and security threats, though consider many IoT device's resource constraints. A BC-based innovative structure is used for secure IoT data sharing and privacy preserving in a smart city environment. A smart city data exchange scenario is developed to verify the security efficacy and predict the utility of the concept proposed. Presented techniques of BC are not manageable to develop IoT applications because of complex algorithms, security overhead, throughput, and latency.

Keywords: Blockchain, IoT environment, Security, Privacy, Untrusted parties

1. Introduction

The Internet of Things (IoT) in diverse implementations is one of the fastest used inventions in last decade. In wireless or wired, smart things are related to connectivity, encoding, computation, and tracking various real-time situations. Devices are heterogeneous and have little memory and less processing capacity. Security and privacy issues come with the introduction of the IoT framework because typical current security mechanisms are not appropriate for IoT devices (Mohanta *et al.*, 2020).

In the last decade IoT is one of the most emerging developments in many applications in Figure 1. In many systems, protection and privacy

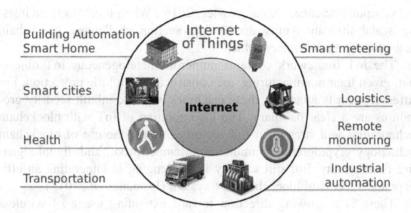

Figure 1.   IoT in Different Applications

continue to be a concern. Security and privacy concerns in IoT have already been discussed by some studies. But new technology is emerging so that the protection problem in IoT can be addressed (Atlam & Wills, 2019). Three prominent technologies, such as machine learning, blockchain, and artificial intelligence have been established.

Recently, IoT has drawn significant interest both to science and the market. IoT machines are made in vast quantities, already reaching the estimated population of the world. These smart devices are related to various environment information capture applications. Resource restriction systems are IoT devices and hence vulnerable to attackers. For IoT apps, protection and privacy concerns are important.

Blockchain technology, a distributed network, is related to one another where messages are broadcasted. Smart Contract (Mohanta *et al.*, 2018) is a self-executable software used for execution of network business logic. To reach the consensus among nodes, blockchain network uses numerous consensus algorithms (Panda *et al.*, 2019). Blockchain is a block leader that is permanent, auditable, and time stamped, used in a distributed way to store and exchange data (Kosba *et al.*, 2016). Payment history may be the data stored, for example. Bitcoin (Yue *et al.*, 2016), or contract (Wood, 2014) or even confidential information (Yue *et al.*, 2016).

In the last few years, blockchain's distinctive characteristics, which include distributed systems, suitability, immutability, and protection and confidentiality, have drawn a large amount of interest from practices and scholars across various disciplines (including law, finance, and computer science) (Abramaowicz, 2016). When it comes to addressing scalability, anonymity and IoT protection challenges, blockchain technology is the ultimate partner.

The IoT framework contains numerous heterogeneous IoT objects that, given their manufacturing, are constructed with little protection. For different security attackers, these machines with bad inbuilt security procedures are a clear hallmark. The incorporation of IoT with blockchain technologies will strengthen IoT security through the use of blockchain technology cryptography, immutability, tamper-proof, and digital signature functionality. But still security is challenging in integrating an efficient and successful blockchain IoT system (Roman *et al.*, 2013).

There is a growing direction toward extending usage of wireless networks, particularly in industrial domains, with growing implementation of IoT devices and applications. Wireless communication has several benefits, but also several security flaws including assaults, assault, and jamming (Karthikeyyan *et al.*, 2019).

Moreover, complex and specialized encryption methods cannot be used in IoT system because of space constraints in IoT computers. In the meantime, technology blockchain has its safety faults. Intelligent contracts and a decentrally autonomous association (DAO) assault have, for example, flaws in the program (Wang *et al.*, 2019). Consequently, further analysis is required to explore IoT and blockchain protection concerns.

2. IoT with Blockchain Architecture

Integrating IoT blockchain became important to solve problems with the centralized IoT architecture and to take advantage of various advantages of blockchain technology. The blockchain can be applied in various ways with IoT. This segment explores one of the ways blockchain is implemented in a couched architecture with the IoT. Basic layered IoT architecture blockchain consists of four layers, seen in Figure 2.

The first step consists of the awareness layer, which includes IoT objects and sensors, which are used to interpret the world and gather data which helped in understanding the environment. Next, performing network layer gathers relevant data which helped in understanding the climate.

Then, internet's network layer. This layer contains networking and monitoring equipment to connect and control protection. Newly added layer is called IoT blockchain framework, which includes all modules that

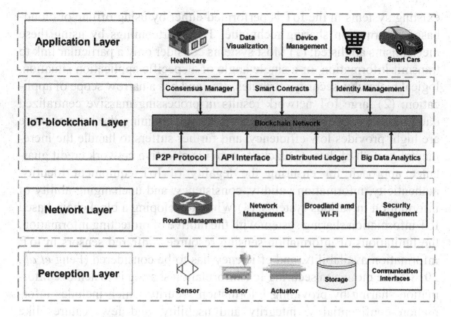

Figure 2.   Architecture of IoT with Blockchain

enable the deployment of different features of blockchain technology in IoT framework. P2P networking, distributed ledger, big data analytics, Application Programming Interface (API), smart contracts, consensus management, and identity management are all included in these features.

To allow decentralized communication between different IoT objects, P2P protocols are required. Furthermore, the API interface offers block-chain resources for IoT applications. The technology layer contains many IoT technologies that allow simulation of information to be done, creates various interactive resources, and lets decision-makers to accurately and precisely make decisions based on data gathered from physical IoT devices.

2.1 *IoT information sharing based on blockchain*

IoT lacks in maintaining effective sharing approaches which makes it more difficult to accomplish valuable data connectivity. Securing IoT information sharing is a challenging one in the field of information secu-rity and has become a hotspot (Chen *et al.*, 2018; Ferrag *et al.*, 2018; Reyna *et al.*, 2018). Interacting and transmitting information between existing systems in the IoT is performed either by using offline or cloud-based information sharing technique. The shortcomings by using these mechanisms are listed: (1) Most systems consider only a particular link to transmit information, or a single angle of a specific application situation, logical hierarchy, security attributes, etc., and has a narrow scope of application; (2) large IoT network results in processing massive centralized data; moreover the cost for investing and maintaining the infrastructure are high, provides low efficiency, and further suffers to handle the incremental growth of data; (3) lacks to provide effective network credit guarantee approach for ensuring the legality of IoT equipment Identity, authenticity, information validity, consistency, and unchanging ability of information in various systems. (4) While developing a blockchain-based IoT information sharing system with the motive of protecting information, the limitations of information sensing resources, infrared sensors in IoT, information availability, and efficiency has to be considered (Feng *et al.*, 2018). The motive to securing IoT information sharing is to achieve information sharing by providing information security which includes information confidentiality, integrity and usability, and few features like traceability, authenticity, reliability and nonrepudiation. Blockchain technology depends on the dominant computing power provided by consensus approaches namely Proof of Work (PoW) of distributed systems to protect the system from external attacks, protecting block data from faking and forging, and over double payment problems.

Integrating physical and information systems is the distinctive feature of blockchain IoT. Generally, the primary tasks are real-time monitoring and comprehensively simulating physical and information systems; integrating, sharing, and collaborating information; large-scale entity control and global optimization of system. Using blockchain in blockchain IoT transforms the energy information system from a proprietary protocol dedicated network to the standard protocol network.

The extensive use of standardized protocols and intelligent electronic devices in the blockchain IoT information system provides technical support for intelligence, however introduces several issues against network security which includes interacting with physical system and the information system itself, and among them, the internal association and cascading failure across the space.

At last, in the blockchain technology, challenges faced while providing security, strengthening the security, and improving its defense level toward threats and malicious attacks has to be significantly analyzed.

The system using blockchain technology does not depend either on third-party intermediaries or trust institutions. Every system nodes are equal, and make decisions together for ensuring the legitimacy of the transaction. Even when any of the system nodes are attacked and destroyed, no damage is caused to the blockchain system. However, blockchain ensures traceability and irreparability of information by the use of digital signatures, encryption, and other techniques.

3. Related Works

In this section, the security problems in blockchain and the IoT system are investigated (Figure 3). This survey aims to decide solution to security dilemma. Security is one of the most daunting challenges and must be effective in blockchain and IoT apps.

The authors clarify in the paper (Mohanta *et al.*, 2019) the specifics of the design in blockchain and the implementation fields. Authors defined the process and work on IoT protection in conjunction with Avec Blockchain in the paper (Banerjee *et al.*, 2018; Minoli & Occhiogrosso, 2018) as a solution approach. The Developers suggested

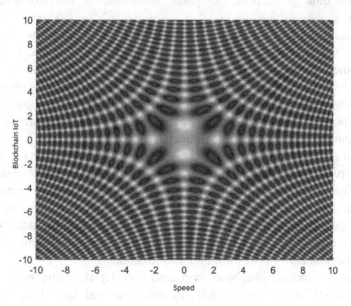

Figure 3.   Data Sharing in Blockchain IoT

a protected internet architecture based on a distributed blockchain structure (Satapathy *et al.*, 2019) for IoT applications.

In the paper (Fernández-Caramés & Fraga-Lamas, 2018), the application of blockchain technologies in IoT. Authors study various IoT security issues and effective blockchain solutions along with the deployment challenges (Khan & Salah, 2018).

The authors (Dedeoglu *et al.*, 2020) discussed the key advantages and architecture problems for integration of IoT blockchain technology. The authors (Dorri *et al.*, 2019) suggested methods for system classification by the use of machine learning algorithms on data stored in blockchain network to boost security in IoT environments by detecting unauthorized devices. In the context of a decentralized IoT system, authors (Putra *et al.*) suggested a trust protection mechanism for the protection and confidence of access control and the identification and elimination of malicious and compromised nodes. The authors (Dorri *et al.*, 2019) proposed to build a Secure Private Blockchain (SPB) platform to negotiate energy prosumers' energy price and exchange energy for a smart grid IoT application in a distributed manner.

Alfonso Panarello *et al.* (2018) have been looking at various technology domains and classified use trends in the fields of system handling or data protection, designing solutions, or the IoT-involving problems.

Blockchain-IoT protection was investigated by Mandrita Banarjee *et al.* (2018) and numerous IoT data settings that require solutions were established. Authors addressed the possible use of the blockchain in safe data sharing in IoT databases and performed extensive analysis on current IoT protection methods in terms of intrusion detection and avoidance, application classification, classification of network architectures, predictive security, and self-healing (Halim *et al.*, 2017).

Ferrag *et al.* (2018) have published a report that summarizes current surveys concerned with the use of IoT blockchain technology. Classification of a blockchain model that involves blockchain framework flaws and loopholes in IoT network blockchain protocols. New methods in the area of protection and privacy were explored and a side by side analysis was made concerning complexity, overhead communication, constraints, security priorities, and performance.

The distributed time-based consensus (DTC) algorithm is proposed by Dorri *et al.* (2019), which reduces overhead and delay mining processing. The cluster heads use the Distributed trust strategy to eventually reduce overhead of computation for checking new blocks. LSB provides a DTM algorithm to ensure that blockchain throughput does not vary substantially from total network transaction load. As a symbolic example for larger IoT implementations, we discuss our methodology in a smart home.

Qualitative reasons prove our response to many defense threats is robust. Extensive calculations demonstrate that overhead and latency of packets are minimized and the scalability of blockchains is improved relative to relevant baselines. A blockchain-based privacy-preserving device upgrade protocol was introduced by the authors (Zhao *et al.*) to conduct stable and reliable updates with a reward scheme without hindering the privacy of users concerned.

A secure blockchain platform for exchanging medical data was developed by Chen *et al.* (2018) by developing secure cloud storage for confidential medical records of patients. In this context, the storage of medical records is done using a public database that has access protection rights to the details of its members. This is stored under the chain by deploying cloud encryption.

An analysis of IoT security issues was presented by Karthikeyyan *et al.* (2019), and the blockchain was then proposed as a proposed alternative to address these problems. They also explored the possibilities of blockchain IoT integration.

Si *et al.*, (2019) introduced lightweight IoT information sharing security architecture based on blockchain technology. This model adopted a double-chain model integrating data blockchain with transaction blockchain. In the data blockchain storage and tamper-proof of data was distributed. Byzantine fault-tolerant (PBFT) approach was practically improved. The results proved that this model was secure, and effective. Moreover, it was feasible in verifying the information of the system location for protected storage devices.

4. Experimental Methodology

The experimental methodology shows the blockchain network with IoT devices is shown in Figure 4. The cloud storage system verifies the data in blockchain network. The IoT devices are communicating through gateway to blockchain network.

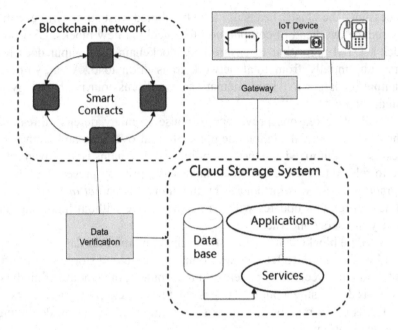

Figure 4.   Experimental Methodology Model

The data transmission among the network is secure manner. The smart city have lot of wireless devices such as camera, public telephone, etc., each device perform well with respect to data sharing.

4.1 *Blockchain network*

Blockchain technology refers to a mixture of multiple parties' transmission, collection and storing of data based on modern cryptography, distributed consistency protocols, collaboration between peer-to-peer networks and smart contracts. Main elements of proposed scheme are smart contracts. To realize the decentralized trading framework, we identify two categories of roles as follows: service request and service provider, communicating with smart contracts.

Smart contract is a self-executing computer program that, when predefined conditions are met, will autonomously execute in a verifiable manner. The blockchain offers a secure platform for intelligent contracts.

It helps participants without the need for third parties to perform traceable, permanent and protected transactions. As a transaction, users call a smart contract feature and state of smart contract will be changed.

4.2 *IoT device*

Data on real-time IoT devices are not maintained explicitly on the public blockchain. Where required, data can be encrypted until it is sent to the storage device. The raw data can then only be accessed by the device owner or others who get access from the device owner.

4.3 *Cloud storage system*

Cloud storage is used for the administration of personal data by people and the transfer and recovery of files by organizations. Some feature sets are highly valuable to organizations, but they may not apply to users. Administration and storage features are developed by organizations, for instance, that are dealing with data protection and compatibility for cloud-based files. Cloud storage helps users to store and sync data to a server online. Since files are stored not on a local disc but in the cloud, there are files on multiple computers. This helps a person to access, update, and comment on the files on various computers and mobile devices. It substitutes for jobs like emailing papers.

Cloud computing can also be used as a hard disc backup system. Cloud-based data is stored on premises and a data center run by a third-party cloud vendor in logical pools through disparate commodity servers. Cloud Storage Services protection is also a problem for consumers. These concerns have been overcome by service providers by strengthening their security capability through data protection, multi-factor authentication and enhanced physical protection.

4.4 *Data verification*

The goal of data verification is the provision of the accuracy of the obtained data and the minimization of human and instrument errors, including data analysis. Data verification is an ongoing process to begin and proceed throughout data entry and review at the data collection level.

4.4.1 *Security considerations*

The security consideration can be categorized into client privacy, secure communications, Key servers. Each category is discussed as following.

4.4.2 *Client privacy*

Blockchain is a shared directory, where anyone can access all of the transactions contained in the blocks. By creating new addresses for every purchase, a customer will protect his privacy. This helps the consumer to separate and of its purchases to make it more difficult for an attacker to merge them. Smart contracts and resource owners by default cannot see the other deal the consumer inferred.

4.4.3 *Secure communications*

Personal keys between key servers, resource servers, and clients are shared through DTLS channels. Authentication between resource servers and key server takes place via credentials, as well as through a challenge-response between clients and the key server. Blockchain transfers have signatures to maintain their legitimacy.

4.4.4 *Key server*

To sync to the blockchain, the latest nodes need to touch boot nodes. An assailant may mount MITM and direct a main server in his/her blockchain if a boot node is not authenticated, where it can freely change the background. To avoid this threat, boot nodes can use certificates to validate their validity by new nodes.

The largest problem in cloud computing is compliance criteria. Protection mechanisms can be used to avoid sensitive data reaching unauthorized users to apply data security in cloud storage environments, and at the same time approved users receive it.

Figure 5 shows that each number describes a process as follows:

1. Via the Setup algorithm, TA generates the keys. The Data Owner (DO) and Data Recipient shall use these keys (DU).
2. For the use of the cloud data. DU sends DO an application for registration.

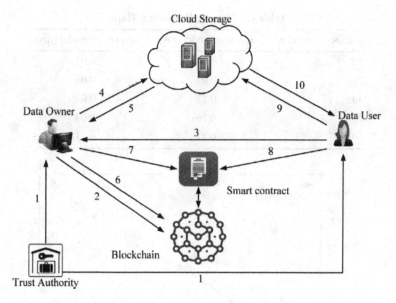

Figure 5. Proposed Network Model

3. Call encryption, and data is encrypted and transmitted to the cloud according to the access structure tree.
4. DO report the Cloud service returned location information files.
5. DO hash and insert the Information Location Files (FLI) into blockchain.
6. Do create and store in a clever deal the hashed FLI index.
7. For the use of the cloud data. In the smart contract, DU accesses the FLI index.
8. DU sends an invitation and loads data from the server to restore the data.
9. Through running the decryption DU gathers the data and checks whether the data is sent to the data holders.

5. Results and Discussion

Performance of proposed system model is calculated based on the four metrics one is average processing time for block and storage overhead, latency, encryption,, and decryption. Table 1 indicates average processing time for blocks. Data block gradually increases then the storage overhead is also gradually increased which is shown in below graph.

Table 1.   Average Processing Time

Number of blocks	Existing model (ms)	Proposed model (ms)
10	0.04	0.02
20	0.09	0.05
30	0.13	0.07
40	0.16	0.09
50	0.21	0.11

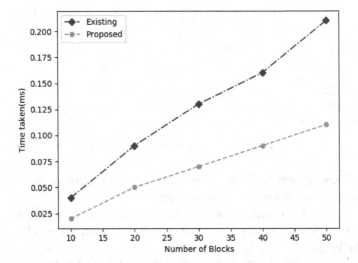

Figure 6.   Average Processing Time of Data Blocks

The above Figure 6 shows the existing and proposed model average processing time for data blocks. X and Y axis indicates number of blocks and time taken in milliseconds. The top line in the graph indicates existing model and the bottom line in the graph indicates proposed model. Proposed model achieves good results when compared to existing model.

Table 2 shows the storage overhead. The data block is gradual increases then the storage overhead is gradually decreased which is shown below graph.

Figure 7 shows that existing and proposed model storage overhead. X and Y axis shows the number of blocks and time taken in milliseconds. The top line in the graph indicates existing model and the bottom line in the graph indicates proposed model. Proposed model achieves good results when compared to existing model.

Table 2. Storage Overhead

Number of block size	Existing model (kb)	Proposed model (kb)
100	1900	700
200	1690	510
300	1390	320
400	1180	250
500	970	130

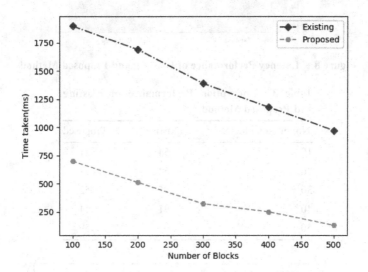

Figure 7. Storage Overhead Performance

Figure 8 shows the latency performance of existing and proposed method. X axis and Y axis indicates method used and latency values in milliseconds. Existing method achieves 18 ms and proposed method achieves 14 ms (Table 3).

Figure 9 shows that existing and proposed model encryption performance. X and Y axis shows the number of data blocks and time taken in milliseconds. The top line in the graph indicates existing model and the bottom line in the graph indicates proposed model. Proposed model achieves good results when compared to existing model (Table 4).

Figure 10 shows that existing and proposed model decryption performance. X and Y axis shows the number of data blocks and time taken in milliseconds. The top line in the graph indicates existing model and the

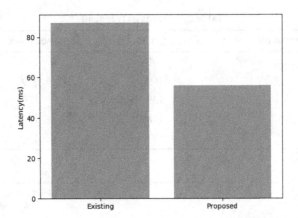

Figure 8.   Latency Performance of Existing and Proposed Method

Table 3.   Encryption Performance of Existing and Proposed Method

No. of data blocks	Existing	Proposed
10	54	21
20	64	33
30	95	52
40	91	54
50	93	59

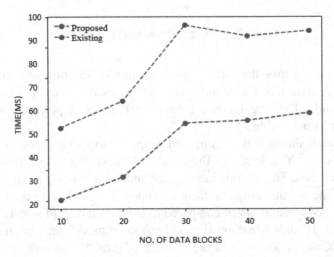

Figure 9.   Encryption Performance of Existing and Proposed Method

Table 4. Decryption Performance of Existing and Proposed Method

No. of data blocks	Existing	Proposed
10	61	18
20	67	21
30	84	46
40	87	48
50	96	49

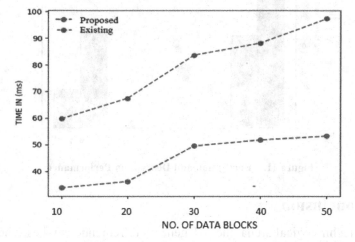

Figure 10. Decryption Performance of Existing and Proposed Method

bottom line in the graph indicates proposed model. Proposed model achieves good results when compared to existing model.

Table 5 indicates encryption and decryption performance of existing and proposed method. The graph is shown in Figure 11.

Figure 11 presented encryption and decryption performance of existing and proposed method. X axis and Y axis shows the Encryption, decryption and values obtained in millisecond. The first bar indicates encryption and the second bar indicates decryption. Existing model achieves encryption 90 ms, decryption 48 ms and proposed model achieves encryption 45 ms, decryption 19 ms. When compared to existing method proposed method achieves good results.

Table 5.   Encryption and Decryption Performance of Existing and Proposed Method

Parameters	Existing model	Proposed model
Encryption	90 ms	45 ms
Decryption	48 ms	19 ms

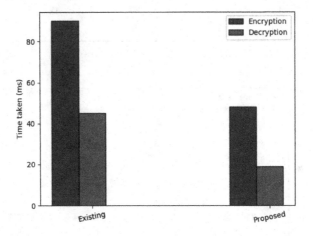

Figure 11.   Encryption and Decryption Performance

6. Conclusion

In the technological arena, the IoT generated tremendous vibes. The provision of cutting-edge solutions in different fields has been important. Smart houses, intelligent communities, fitness, transport, and logistics are some of the implementations. IoT shares data on wired and wireless networks in real-time and no protocols for managing the flow of information within the device are established. There is also a big problem in the security and access management of IoT. Nowadays, scholars have recognized the encryption and verification ability of the blockchain. The decentralized design of blockchain makes it more especially suited for IoT integration. The model suggested is an alternative model for IoT networks that use blockchain technologies to increase security over the brief period of IoT. This model would provide accurate and scalable strategies for elements of data protection in the ever-growing IoT environment. The convergence of blockchain and IoT opens the door to the creation of new technologies since computers in the IoT are real-world touch points.

It will have a clearer image of blockchain systems' success and help determine which technology fits better for any IoT-based use which is became reliable and mature.

References

Abramaowicz, M. (2016). Cryptocurrency-based law, *Ariz. L. Rev. 58*, 359.

Atlam, H. F., & Wills, G. B. (2019). IoT security, privacy, safety and ethics. In *Intelligent Sensing, Instrumentation and Measurements* (pp. 123–149). Berlin, Germany: Springer Science and Business Media LLC.

Banerjee, M., Lee, J., & Choo, K. K. R. (2018). A blockchain future for internet of things security: A position paper. *Digital Communications and Networks*, *4*(3), 149–160.

Chen, M., Lu, S., & Liu, Q. (2018) Global regularity for a 2D model of electrokinetic fluid in a bounded domain. *Acta Mathematicae Applicatae Sinica, English Series, 34*(2), 398–403.

Chen, Y., Ding, S., Xu, Z., Zheng, H., & Yang, S. (2018). Blockchain-based medical records secure storage and medical service framework. *The Journal of Medical Systems, 43*, 5.

Dedeoglu, V., Jurdak, R., Dorri, A., Lunardi, R., Michelin, R., Zorzo, A., & Kanhere, S. (2020). Blockchain technologies for IoT. In: *Advanced Applications of Blockchain Technology* (pp. 55–89). Springer, Singapore.

Dorri, A., Kanhere, S. S., Jurdak, R., *et al.*, (2019). LSB: A lightweight scalable blockchain for IoT security and anonymity. *Journal of Parallel and Distributed Computing, 134*, 180–197.

Dorri, A., Luo, F., Kanhere, S. S., Jurdak, R., & Dong, Z. Y. (2019). SPB: A secure private blockchain-based solution for distributed energy trading. *IEEE Communications Magazine, 57*(7), 120–126.

Dorri, A., Roulin, C., Jurdak, R., & Kanhere, S. S. (2019). On the activity privacy of blockchain for IoT. In: *2019 IEEE 44th Conference on Local Computer Networks (LCN)*, IEEE, pp. 258–261.

Feng, G., Zhu, L., & Meng, S. (2018). A blockchain-based privacy-preserving payment mechanism for vehicle-to-grid networks. *IEEE Network, 32*(6), 184–192.

Fernández-Caramés, T. M., & Fraga-Lamas, P. (2018). A review on the use of blockchain for the internet of things., *IEEE Access, 6*, 32979–33001.

Ferrag, M. A., Derdour, M., & Mukherjee, M. (2018). Blockchain technologies for the IoT: Research issues and challenges. *IEEE IoT Journal, 6*(2), 2188–2204.

Ferrag, M. A., Derdour, M., Mukherjee, M., Derhab, A., Maglaras, L., & Janicke, H. (2018). Blockchain technologies for the internet of things: Research issues and challenges. *IEEE Internet of Things Journal, 6*(2), 2188–2204.

Halim, N. S. A., Rahman, M. A., Azad, S., & Kabir, M. N. (2017). Blockchain security hole: Issues and solutions. In *Proceeding of the International Conference of Reliable Information and Communication Technology*, pp. 739–746.

Karthikeyyan, P., & Velliangiri, S., & Irwin Thanakumar Joseph, S. (2019, July 5–6). Review of blockchain based IoT application and its security issues. In *Proceedings of the 2019 2nd International Conference on Intelligent Computing, Instrumentation and Control Technologies (ICICICT)*, Kannur, India, pp. 6–11.

Khan, M. A., & Salah, K. (2018). IoT security: Review, blockchain solutions, and open challenges. *Future Generation Computer Systems 82*, 395–411.

Kosba, A., Miller, A., Shi, E., Wen, Z., & Papamanthou, C. (2016). Hawk: The blockchain model of cryptography and privacy-preserving smart contracts. In: *2016 IEEE Symposium on Security and privacy (SP)*, IEEE, pp. 839–858.

Minoli, D., & Occhiogrosso, B. (2018). Blockchain mechanisms for IoT security, *Internet of Things*, *1*, 1–13.

Mohanta, B. K., Jena, D., Satapathy, U., & Patnaik, S. (2020). Survey on IoT security: Challenges and solution using machine learning, artificial intelligence and blockchain technology. *Internet of Things*, *11*, 100227.

Mohanta, B. K., Jena, D., Panda, S. S., & Sobhanayak, S. (2019) Blockchain Technology: A survey on applications and security privacy challenges, *Internet of Things,* 100107.

Mohanta, B. K., Panda, S. S., & Jena, D. (2018). An overview of smart contract and use cases in blockchain technology. In *2018 9th International Conference On Computing, Communication and Networking Technologies (ICCCNT)*, IEEE, pp. 1–4.

Nakamoto, S. (2008). Bitcoin: A peer-to-peer electronic cash system. Decentralized Business Review, 21260.

Panarello, A., Tapas, N., Merlino, G., Longo, F., & Puliafito, A. (2018). Blockchain and IoT integration: A systematic survey. *Sensors*, *18*(8), 1–37.

Panda, S. S., Mohanta, B. K., Satapathy, U., Jena, D., Gountia, D., & Patra, T. K. (2019). Study of blockchain based decentralized consensus algorithms. In: *TENCON 2019–2019 IEEE Region 10 Conference (TENCON)*, IEEE, pp. 908–913.

Putra, G. D., Dedeoglu, V., Kanhere, S. S., & Jurdak, R. (2020). Trust management in decentralized IoT access control system, arXiv preprint arXiv:1912.10247.

Reyna, A., Martín, C., & Chen, J. (2018). On blockchain and its integration with IoT. Challenges and opportunities. *Future Generation Computer Systems*, *88*, 173–190.

Roman, R., Zhou, J. & Lopez, J. (2013). On the features and challenges of security and privacy in distributed internet of things. *Computer Networks*, *57*, 2266–2279.

Satapathy, U., Mohanta, B. K., Panda, S. S., Sobhanayak, S., & Jena, D. (2019). A secure framework for communication in internet of things application using hyperledger based blockchain. In: *2019 10th International Conference on Computing, Communication and Networking Technologies (ICCCNT)*, IEEE, pp. 1–7.

Si, H., Sun, C., Li, Y., *et al.*, (2019). IoT information sharing security mechanism based on blockchain technology. *Future Generation Computer Systems*, *101*, 1028–1040. doi: https://doi.org/10.1016/j.future.2019.07.036.

Wang, X., Zha, X., Ni, W., Liu, R. P., Guo, Y. J., Niu, X., & Zheng, K. (2019). Survey on blockchain for internet of things. *Computer Communications*, *136*, 10–29.

Wood, G. (2014). Ethereum: A secure decentralized generalised transaction ledger. *Ethereum Project Yellow Paper*, *151*, 1–32.

Yue, X., Wang, H.,. Jin, D., Li, M., & Jiang, W. (2016). Healthcare data gateways: Found healthcare intelligence on blockchain with novel privacy risk control. *The Journal of Medical Systems 40*(10), 218.

Zhao, Y., Liu, Y., Tian, A., Yu, Y., & Du, X. Blockchain based privacy preserving software updates with proof-of-delivery for internet of things. *Journal of Parallel and Distributed Computing*.

Chapter 12

Security Issues in Blockchain from Networking and Programming Perspective

Pranav Vyas[*,‡] and Sam Goundar[†,§]

*Smt. Chandaben Mohanbhai Patel Institute of Computer Applications,
Charotar University of Science and Technology, Gujarat 388421, India*

†*School of Computing, RMIT University, Hanoi, Vietnam*

‡*pranavvyas.mca@charusat.ac.in*
§*sam.goundar@gmail.com*

Abstract

As the world adopts more and more of blockchain-based technologies, it will increasingly attract malicious users who will find and exploit their vulnerabilities. Therefore, the study of these vulnerabilities and how they are exploited becomes vital. In this chapter, we have reviewed a variety of vulnerabilities of blockchain. We have looked at these vulnerabilities from networking as well as programming perspective. We have also discussed various attacks on blockchain-based systems as a case study to understand how vulnerabilities are exploited in the real world. We have also provided some tools and techniques that can help in detecting vulnerabilities and enhance security of the blockchain system.

Keywords: Blockchain, Smart contracts, Security, Vulnerabilities, Networking

1. Introduction

Starting with introduction of the bitcoin in 2009, the blockchain technology holds the promise to change applications for many industries. This has attracted academicians and industries to study, research, and apply blockchain technology to solve various problems. Bitcoin is a cryptocurrency and the first blockchain technology-based application. It was rated as best currency in 2015 (Desjardins, 2016), it was given status of best performing asset in 2016 (Adinolfi, 2016). In 2021, it had more than 350,000 transactions (Blockchain.com, 2021) each day in April. While the bitcoin keeps growing in popularity, blockchain has been applied in diverse fields like medicine (Chukwu & Garg, 2020; Hasselgren *et al.*, 2020; Tandon *et al.*, 2020), e-governance (Oliveira *et al.*, 2020; Malhotra *et al.*, 2020; Baudier *et al.*, 2021), embedded systems (Mhaisen *et al.*, 2020; Pavithran *et al.*, 2020; Wu *et al.*, 2020), and software engineering (Choo *et al.*, 2020; Lallai, *et al.*, 2020; Vacca *et al.*, 2020) to name a few. From blockchain 2.0, users are able to write their own smart contracts with the help of Turing compatible languages for blockchain programming. Smart contracts applies consensus techniques on decentralized network of nodes to bridge the trust gap between two sides enabling them to transact without the need for the mutually trusted third party. The most preferred platform for deploying smart contracts is Ethereum with over 100,000 smart contracts active as of January 2020 (Barton, 2020). Ethereum clocks more than 1,500,000 daily transactions as of May 2021 (etherscan.io, 2021).

As the blockchain adaptability increases, more malicious users will attempt to exploit various security vulnerabilities with different types of attacks. Some of the security vulnerabilities are as follows: 51% attack, double spending attack, sybil attack, etc. In his paper, Villata (2020) analyses 20,000 smart contracts and finds that more than 50% of them are vulnerable. Smart contracts are vulnerable to code-related attacks that allow malicious users to exploit them. An example of exploitation of a smart contract-based vulnerability is 2016 attack on DAO by exploiting its vulnerability of re-entrancy that resulted in losses of up to 60 million USD (Buterin, 2016). Another example is an attack on bitcoin trading platform MtGox where the attackers took advantage of transaction mutability which resulted in losses of 450 million USD and end of MtGox as an exchange (Adelstein & Stucky, 2020).

Many studies have been undertaken to analyze the security aspect of the blockchain technology, however, these studies lack in systematic evaluation of the blockchain vulnerabilities, various attack methods employed toward the exploitation of vulnerabilities and solution to the vulnerabilities. Some notable work has been done by Lin and Liao (2017), Sengupta *et al.* (2020), Zheng *et al.* (2018), and Saad *et al.* (2020).

In their paper, Lin and Liao (2017) discuss the security issues of network-related vulnerabilities and ignore vulnerabilities exploitable by code through smart contracts. Sengupta *et al.* (2020) highlight vulnerabilities only from IoT perspective. Zheng *et al.* (2018) and Saad *et al.* (2020) present a variety of security issues, but do not provide any solutions of these issues. In this chapter, we examine security vulnerabilities of the blockchain systems. We also study the real attacks on blockchain and understand vulnerabilities that the malicious users are able to exploit. We also suggest some practical solutions to the security vulnerabilities and give future direction of research.

The remaining part of this chapter is organized as follows. In Section 2, we examine various security vulnerabilities of blockchain. In Section 3, we study the real attacks on blockchain-based applications. We then provide a summary of solutions to the blockchain security vulnerabilities in Section 4. We provide some future direction for research in Section 5 and present conclusion in Section 6.

2. Blockchain Security Vulnerabilities

We can divide blockchain security vulnerabilities in two main types as shown in Table 1: (i) network-based and (ii) programming-based vulnerabilities. Next, we discuss these vulnerabilities in detail.

2.1 *Network-based vulnerabilities of blockchain*

2.1.1 *Consensus algorithm vulnerability*

One of the basic characteristics of the blockchain is bridging the trust gap between two or more untrusting parties without taking help of a trusted third party. It is achieved by applying consensus algorithm whenever different parties have to agree on a single set of transactions. Consensus algorithm depends on voting of all the nodes and hence it can be exploited to achieve desired results by a malicious user by controlling more than half of the nodes responsible for decision-making. Blockchain systems

Table 1.   Blockchain Vulnerabilities

S. No.	Type	Vulnerability	Effect
1	Network	Consensus algorithm	Network control by malicious user
		Public key infrastructure	Weak private key
		Cryptocurrency	Illegal activities
		Transaction verification	Double spending
		Transaction mapping	Reduced anonymity
		Transaction design	Loss of data privacy
2	Programming	Malicious smart contracts	Various real-life crimes
		Vulnerable smart contracts	Execution time errors
		Non-optimized smart contracts	High transaction costs
		Inexpensive operations	Denial-of-service attack

where PoW consensus mechanism is used are highly susceptible to this vulnerability. This vulnerability can be exploited in situations where the single node or miner controls 50% of the total power of the mining pool. For example, a well-known mining pool ghash.io reached 42% of total throughput of the bitcoin mining community. This resulted in few key miners dropping out of the pool and the mining pool had to issue a public statement to the community that it would never let its throughput reach 51% (Hajdarbegovic, 2014). It is also possible to exploit this vulnerability on blockchain systems having PoS-based consensus mechanism. This is done by controlling more than 50% of the total currency in circulation. The successful attack can result in the attacker having complete control to manipulate and modify the blockchain. Some major effects of this attack are as follows: (i) double spending by reversing a transaction; (ii) disruption of normal mining activity; and (iii) higher confirmation delay for genuine transactions.

2.1.2 *Public key infrastructure*

The user's private key is the gateway to the blockchain for the user. The private key is used as an identity of the user in blockchain-based systems. It is generated only once and maintained by the users of the system. A private key is necessary to create a new wallet to store bitcoin. A large number of vulnerabilities have been found by researchers (Farooq *et al.*, 2019; Kim *et al.*, 2019; Robinson & Julie, 2019; He *et al.*, 2020) in various digital signature algorithms that can enable the malicious user to recover another user's private key.

A lost private key is not recoverable and can result in unauthorized access to the user's wallet by malicious actors. Due to distributed nature of the blockchain ledger, it is not possible to track the activity by malicious actors and restore modified blockchain to its original state.

2.1.3 *Cryptocurrency*

It is possible for bitcoin users to have multiple wallet addresses. The wallet addresses are designed to mask the identity of their owner; thus it is difficult to associate a user with a wallet address. This anonymous identity may encourage all types of illegal activities. The users pay by bitcoins and other cryptocurrencies for products and services that are considered illegal in many countries of the world. Some illegal activities where cryptocurrencies are used as a mode of payment are trading in underground market places, money laundering, and ransomware-based attacks.

Many underground marketplaces exist on deep web where users are offered a variety of illegal products and services in exchange of payment in cryptocurrencies (Minnaar, 2017). These marketplaces exist on tor-based anonymous network. Some of the common services offered on these marketplaces include the following (Paganini, 2021): hacking services, stolen credit card/PayPal information, narcotics, arms and ammunitions, banned literature, counterfeit goods and tutorials, etc.

Bitcoin and other cryptocurrencies provide features like anonymity during the transaction. This makes them ideal candidates to move large amounts of money without any legal checks. This encourages use of these currencies in money laundering (Barone & Masciandaro, 2019) as bitcoin is an accepted currency for payment in many countries around the world. Wallet applications with built-in features of stealth and privacy such as dark wallet (Bedi *et al.*, 2020) may be used by the money launderers to send and receive payment that can help in hiding their tracks.

Ransomware is a new generation of software that is used for money extortion. This software has an ability to encrypt all files on a computer that can be decrypted only with a cryptographic key. A payment is asked in return for providing this key to decrypt the data. This payment is usually in the form of bitcoin or other cryptocurrencies that must be done within a specified time period. Some of the famous ransomware are WannaCry, CTB Locker, CryptoLocker, Reveton, etc. (Mohammad, 2020).

2.1.4 *Transaction verification*

The blockchain consensus algorithm is responsible for transaction validation. All transactions recorded by different nodes of the network must be validated by applying consensus algorithm. Double spending refers to the activity of paying same amount of coin to two or more different addresses and recorded as two or more different transactions. The basis of this attack is block confirmation delay time. The attacker takes advantage of the time between confirmation of two blocks and quickly spends same coins on two or more services. This type of attack is used to get service that is quick in nature. Therefore, by the time double spending is detected, the attacker has received service in response of the transaction. This attack can be understood in the following steps (Chaudhary *et al.*, 2020):

i. The attacker sends two transactions' requests TXa and TXb using the same bitcoin from their wallet. Here TXa is sent to the vendor whose wallet address is known in advance and TXb is a wallet address controlled by the attacker.
ii. The success of the attack depends on TXa depositing bitcoin in the vendor wallet, TXb is added to the blockchain after consensus is reached and services are received before the vendor detects faulty transaction TXa.
iii. In case of a successful attack, TXa is considered as invalid transaction based on consensus, and bitcoins are credited to wallet address of TXb. Thus the attacker has gained the access to the service offered by the vendor for free as the bitcoins are still in the wallet controlled by the attacker.

2.1.5 *Transaction mapping*

Permissionless blockchain like bitcoin and other cryptocurrencies are public; thus the information of transactions is accessible to anyone. This can be exploited by malicious users to get private information of the users. The transaction data can be easily plotted on a graph and visual inference and correlation can be applied to uncover the user's real identity based on transaction address. Reid and Harrigan (2013) analyze payee and payer wallet addresses in their paper to establish correlation between owners and transactions. The private information such as email address, billing address, and IP address may also be accessible by the service provider when the user makes a purchase using cryptocurrencies (Goldfeder *et al.*, 2017).

Usage of blockchain is not only limited to cryptocurrencies in this day and age. They are used in mobile cloud computing, IoT, and sensor networks which relay more information than just the number of coins and addresses. A malicious user may be able to track a single user by analyzing information coming from these sources. Meiklejohn *et al.* (2013) propose a heuristic algorithm to reduce user anonymity by classifying service providers of the users based on their public key information available by analyzing information accessible on internet forums and websites. Ron and Shamir (2013) studied 3,730,218 public keys and were able to map 2,460,814 keys to their owners. In their paper, Koshi *et al.* (2014) also find that it is possible to link wallet addresses to owners by correlating transactions with IP addresses.

2.1.6 *Transaction design*

The blockchain technology uses the Merkle tree technique making it possible to trace each and every transaction in an open and transparent manner. It is possible for a bitcoin transaction to have multiple inputs and multiple outputs. This is possible because the bitcoin system follows Unexpected Transaction Output (UTXO) transaction mode. The output of the previous transaction is utilized as the input for the current transaction and output of the current transaction is utilized as the input for the next transaction. As discussed previously, transaction data can be plotted on a graph and user's private information may be uncovered by using correlation.

A user's public key is easily available information that can be obtained from various internet forums, websites, and social media sites such as Twitter. The public key can also be used to track transactions from publically available transaction data. Reid and Martin (2013) tracked such public keys and performed transaction correlation. They calculated the wallet balance before and after transaction based on transaction correlation data. In their paper, Ober *et al.* (2013) study the relationship between exchange rate and number of active wallet addresses. They were able to establish that the increase in the exchange rate would also increase activity in wallet addresses.

2.2 *Programming-based vulnerabilities of blockchain*

2.2.1 *Malicious smart contracts*

The blockchain-based applications lack an automated mechanism for contract enforcement. In absence of such automated mechanism, two parties will need to depend on a trusted third party for contract enforcement. Involvement of the third party will result in loss of anonymity for both original parties. This problem can be solved by using smart contracts.

Smart contracts are programs written in Turing compatible languages supported by the cryptocurrencies. Smart contracts work on highly distributed systems to guarantee fair exchange of services and payments without the need for a trusted third party. It guarantees payment for the services provided and services as a result of the payment. Due to the nature of smart contract, it will support any criminal activity where criminal activities will be carried out for a payment. Usage of smart contracts for criminal purpose was first mentioned in Juels *et al.* (2015). For example, a malicious contract can be used with following steps to expose a private key of a certificate authority (Juels *et al.*, 2015):

i.   A node M generates a pair of a public and private keys SK_M and PK_M where SK_M is a secret key of node M and PK_M is a public key of node M.

ii. It begins by providing input of PK_M and PK_C where PK_C is a public key of certificate authority.

iii. After the publication and execution, the contract looks for an input from malicious user Q. It looks for two parameters X and Y. Here X is a zero knowledge proof of $Y = \text{Encrypt}(SK_C) PK_Q$.

iv. The contract will verify X. If the verification is successful, it will send reward to Q.

v.   It can now download and decrypt Y to get the SK_C.

The zero knowledge proof of X may be implemented as Succinct Non-Interactive Argument of Knowledge (Bitansky *et al.*, 2013). Techniques from privacy preserving smart contracts (Kosba *et al.*, 2016) can be applied to enhance the overall security.

2.2.2 *Vulnerable smart contracts*

Smart contracts are programs running in background that form the backbone of modern blockchain systems. However, since the smart contracts

Table 2. Smart Contract Vulnerabilities in Ethereum

S. No.	Vulnerability	Description
1	Call to the unknown	Calling a contract that does not exist
2	Sending with insufficient gas	Transaction failure due to insufficient gas to execute byte code
3	Exception handling	Unordered exception handling
4	Type casting	Type conversion errors during execution
5	Re-entrancy	Re-execution of function before termination
6	Information disclosure	Disclosure of private information
7	Immutation	Alteration of deployed contract
8	Ether loss	Permanent loss of ether
9	Stack memory size	Exceeding the given stack memory space

are programs, they also suffer from vulnerabilities introduced by the programming. Atzei *et al.* (2017) find vulnerabilities in Ethereum-based smart contracts that are introduced by programming errors in their paper as shown in Table 2.

2.2.2.1 Call to the unknown

Blockchain applications based on Ethereum framework have a facility that if an incoming function call does not match the signature of any existing functions in a contract, it is redirected to a fallback function of the recipient.

For example, consider the following contracts:

```
Contract Alice {Function Foo(decimal) returns(decimal)}
Contract Bob {Function Bar (Alice A) {A.Foo (2.50)};)
```

Here, we have a declared contract for Alice that includes a function Foo that takes a decimal type of parameter as input and returns a decimal type of value. Bob's contract has function Bar that takes Alice's contract as an input parameter. Therefore, whenever Bob's contract is executed, it indirectly executes Alice's contract. Assuming that by a typing error the interface of Alice's contract is declared as float instead of decimal, then Bob's contract will not find the function with appropriate signature which will result in execution of Alice's fallback function.

This vulnerability can be exploited when the amount is transferred in the recipient's account, but the function interface called from the smart contract does not match the function signature on the recipient side resulting in failure to receive the service.

2.2.2.2 Sending with insufficient gas

In Ethereum framework a cost is associated with transaction instruction. This cost is measured in units called "gas." When executing a transaction, the user must provide sufficient amount of gas so that cost of all instructions in the transaction is covered. The minimum gas value required for execution of a transaction with basic instructions is 2300. Assuming that a user attempts to execute a complicated contract with minimum gas value, this will result in gas being used, but the state of contract will not change as it requires execution of further instructions. This vulnerability can be exploited to perform denial-of-service type of attack when the recipient has inexpensive fallback function.

2.2.2.3 Exception handling

The Ethereum framework-based applications throw exception in cases of contract execution when (i) the caller runs out of gas to execute remaining instructions; (ii) stack is overflowing; and (iii) throw command is encountered resulting in user-defined exception. However, Ethereum handles exceptions differently based on its context. For example, consider the following contracts:

```
Contract   Alice   {function   Foo   (decimal)   return
(decimal)}
Contract Bob {int X = 0; function Bar (Alice A) {X=1;
A.Foo (2.5); X=2;}}
```

In the above contract, if Bob's contract calls Alice's contract which throws an exception for some reason, then the whole transaction will be marked as failed and X will return to its original value 0. Now assume that Bob calls Alice's contract directly and an error occurs on Alice's side, then Bob will receive a false value, however, the transaction will continue to execute and X will be assigned value 2.

This vulnerability may be exploited by leading Bob to believe that the transaction was successful and consuming the gas value for the transaction when in reality the transaction has failed.

2.2.2.4 Type casting

The Ethereum framework compiler is able to detect some basic type of casting errors such as casting from integer to string. However, during the direct calls between the smart contracts, the compiler can only check for the type of the parameter and match interface signature to the original function signature.

This can mislead the programmers into believing that compiler is checking for invalid type of casting. However, in case of invalid typecasting, the contract is not known to throw runtime exceptions. One of the three possibilities may stand true in case of invalid type casting: (i) if the parameter is not an address, no code in the contract is executed and the call is returned; (ii) there exists a function with matching signature which is executed and appropriate value is returned; and (iii) no function with matching signature is found and recipient's fallback function is executed. However, no exception is thrown making user believe that the transaction was successful and consuming the gas.

2.2.2.5 Re-entrancy

The programmers assume that the smart contracts have built-in atomicity and sequencing properties. Therefore, the programmers believe that when a non-recursive function is invoked, it will not be re-entered until it is terminated. This is not true in case of applications based on Ethereum framework. An attacker can make use of fallback feature of the framework to re-enter the function before its termination. This can result in unforeseen behavior and consumption of all gas.

This attack can continue until either the stack is full or all gas is used for instruction execution. An exception is thrown in both cases, however, this results in invalidation of only the last call that caused the exception, all other calls before the last are considered valid and charged for appropriate gas units.

This vulnerability was exploited in the famous DAO attack in June 2016.

2.2.2.6 Information disclosure

A smart contract can contain fields of information that are either public or private in nature. However, an attacker can still access the information stored in private fields. The attacker exploits the public nature of blockchain to read private information stored in the transaction. The miners are responsible for setting data to the fields of the transaction and then publishing it on the blockchain. The attacker simply extrapolates the data from the published transactions.

The contracts used for trading in the share markets may be required to keep future selling and asking price a private information until suitable conditions occur. The attacker may gain huge advantage by knowing this private information in advance.

2.2.2.7 Immutation

The users of blockchain systems assume that if a published contract implements its intended functionality, then during the runtime it will behave as per the expectation. This is guaranteed by the consensus protocol. This belief is also reinforced by the fact that once a contract is published, it cannot be modified. However, if a bug is found in a published contract, there is no way to patch it. This can be exploited by sending the ether to an unusable address from which it cannot be recovered. Therefore, the programmers have to find new and innovative ways to modify or terminate contract while designing and build the necessary functionality into the contract (Marino & Juels, 2016).

2.2.2.8 Ether loss

An address is a unique identity of the user that is used to send and receive the ether, a currency in Ethereum framework-based applications. These addresses are 160 bits long. However, all addresses are not associated with a user and such addresses are known as orphan addresses. Ether sent to these addresses is permanently lost and there is no technique to establish if an address is orphan or not. Therefore, it is responsibility of the programmers to verify the address manually in the program.

2.2.2.9 Stack memory size

The stack is used to store data of a calling contract when a contract is invoking another contract. Whenever such a call is made, the stack frame value is increased by one. The stack memory frames are fixed at 1024. The contract throws a stack overflow exception when the frame value goes over 1024.

This vulnerability can be exploited to halt the execution of a smart contract and perform a denial-of-service type of attack. This vulnerability was found in Ethereum framework-based applications (Swende, 2016).

It was patched with a hard fork in 2016, where gas cost for several instructions was changed. This resulted in call depth to be always less than 1024.

2.2.3 *Non-optimized smart contract*

The execution of smart contract is chargeable. In Ethereum framework applications, it is charged in form of gas. Using non-optimized smart contracts for transaction can result in higher gas consumption compared to optimized smart contracts. Chan *et al.* (2017) find seven patterns in non-optimized smart contracts that they term as gas-costly patterns. They have also developed a tool named Gasper. This tool is able to detect three gas-costly patterns, namely Dead code, Opaque predicate, and Expensive loop operation. The gas-costly patterns are shown in Table 3.

Table 3. Gas-Costly Patterns

S. No	Pattern name	Description
1	Dead code	Never executing code block
2	Opaque predicate	Predictable outcome of the condition
3	Expensive loop operation	Instructions with high gas cost in a loop
4	Constant outcome of a loop	A loop code block with static output
5	Loop fusion	Merging of several unnecessary loops into a single loop
6	Repeated computations in loop	Same expression outcome in multiple loops
7	Comparison of unilateral expression in the loop	Conditional expression evaluation with same outcome

2.2.3.1 Dead code

A dead code refers to a statement in code which will never execute under any condition. For example, consider the following code:

```
If (1==0)
{
    Print ("True")
}
```

   In the above example, you will never get output as true as the condition will never be satisfied for execution of the print statement. Here, the line with print statement is considered as dead code.

2.2.3.2 Opaque predicate

An opaque predicate in the code is an outcome of conditional statement that is already known without a condition check. Consider the following code to understand this:

```
If (a MOD 6==0)
{
    If (a MOD 3==0)
        Print ("True")
}
```

   In the above example, all values which will have reminder 0 when divided by 6 will also have reminder 0 when divided by 3. Hence, the outcome of the condition will always be true. Therefore, the second If condition is an opaque predicate in this example.

2.2.3.3 Expensive loop operation

In Ethereum network, an operation consists of one or more instructions. At EVM level, each instruction has a fixed charge for execution. Therefore, depending on the instructions in an operation, it may be charged higher or lower. An operation inside the loop may execute multiple times and if the operation is consisting of many instructions it may result in high execution expense. Moving the expensive operations out of the loop will result in lower execution expense.

2.2.3.4 Constant outcome of a loop

A loop in code may give same output every time it is executed. It is possible to assume such output at compile time resulting in gas saving by not executing the loop statements.

2.2.3.5 Loop fusion

Sometimes in the code, multiple loop statements are present, but are not necessary. It may be possible to fuse these statements together by making a common single loop performing functions of all loops. This process of replacing multiple loops with a single loop is loop fusion.

2.2.3.6 Repeated computations in loop

In some smart contract codes, there may be expressions inside loops that produce static outcome regardless of the iteration. This results in gas cost even when the output is going to remain the same.

2.2.3.7 Comparison of unilateral expression in the loop

Inside the loop a condition is present that can check the expression and return true or false value. This pattern is found when the expression is evaluated to same result regardless of the iteration.

2.2.4 *Inexpensive operations*

We know that in Ethereum, an operation consists of one or more instructions and each instruction has a pre-defined execution cost associated with it. This cost is charged by the EVM for executing the instruction. This cost is calculated in unit of gas. The execution cost can be defined by many parameters, such as: memory requirement, expected execution time, available bandwidth, queue size, etc. However, it is not possible to measure the exact cost of each instruction accurately. Hence, it is possible that some instructions that are resource intensive may have very low cost associated with them. Due to the low cost associated with resource-intensive instructions, an attacker may use these instructions and its related operations during denial-of-service type of attack. Instructions EXTCODESIZE (Gautham, 2016) and SUICIDE (Souptacular, 2015) are some examples where this vulnerability was exploited. This was corrected with Ethernet hard fork where the gas values for certain vulnerable instructions were adjusted (vbuterin, 2016).

3. Attack Cases

In this section, we present several attack scenarios that have been used to exploit various vulnerabilities and attack blockchain-based systems. Atazi *et al.* (2017) describe some of the lesser known attacks that exploit various smart contract vulnerabilities. These attacks are listed in Table 4.

3.1 *DAO attack*

DAO is a smart contract in the Ethereum framework. It is used for crowd-funding platforms. It was attacked soon after its deployment. Before the attack, DAO had raised around 150 million USD for various crowd-funding initiatives. The attack resulted in loss of approximately 60 million USD. During the investigation into the attack, it was revealed that the attacker exploited re-entrancy vulnerability of DAO smart contract.

3.2 *BGP poisoning*

The border gateway protocol is a protocol from IP family that aids in routing of IP packets toward their destination. For this type of attack, vulnerabilities of BGP protocol are exploited to manipulate the packet routing function. According to Apostolaki *et al.* (2017), the attackers would

Table 4.   **Attacks Exploiting Smart Contract Vulnerabilities**

S. No.	Attack name	Exploited vulnerabilities
1	King of the ether throne	Sending with insufficient gas, exception handling
2	Multi-player games	Information disclosure
3	Rubixi attack	Immutation
4	Governmental attack	Immutation, stack memory size, arbitrary state, timestamps
5	Dynamic libraries attack	Arbitrary state

usually target large mining pools for bitcoin. This method of attack can leave high impact as most bitcoin mining pools are highly centralized. This attack will delay new block propagation and confirmation time slowing the whole network.

According to Secure Works report (Stewart, 2014), the attackers will interrupt the connection between the clients and mining pool server. They would reroute the client's requests to a private pool resulting in higher throughput of the attacker's pool and loss to the miners.

BGP security is often ignored, therefore the attacks are difficult to detect (Yan *et al.*, 2009). BGP attack thwarting is also a time-consuming process as it will take significant time to alter the connection configuration and disconnecting attackers from the network (Guest, 2008).

3.3 *Connection hijacking*

In a connection hijacking attack, as the name suggests, the attacker will take control of all the connections of the victim (Singh, 2006). Now the attacker has control on which packets will pass to the victim and which will be blocked. The attacker can use this connection to obstruct the victim's view of the blockchain. This will result in victim utilizing its computing power on an obsolete view of the blockchain. According to Heilman *et al.* (2015), this attack can be done in two ways: (i) infrastructure-based connection hijacking and (ii) botnet-based connection hijacking. An attack can be said to be infrastructure based if the attacking nodes have contiguous IP addresses. If the attacking IP addresses are from a wide range and are scattered, that can be categorized as botnet-based connection hijacking. Few variations in connection to hijacking attacks are described in the following sections.

3.3.1 *Black races*

In this type of attacks, the victim is led to believe that an orphan block is the main block in the blockchain and the victim tries to mine the orphan block.

3.3.2 *Majority control*

Here the majority of the nodes of a mining pool are under control of the attacker. The attacker can use this condition to include the transactions in block that are beneficial to the attacker.

3.3.3 *Selfish mining*

Here the attacker takes advantage of decentralized nature of blockchain. The attacker's aim here is to waste the computing power of honest miners who are mining on the public blockchain (Solat & Potop-Butucaru, 2016). The attacker maintains a private blockchain that is one block shorter than the public blockchain (Eyal & Sirer, 2014). The attacker will try to mine the blocks before honest miners, but mined blocks will be hidden from the public miners. The mined block will be published by the attacker just as the honest miners find the new block, resulting in honest miners getting no rewards for mining.

3.4 *Liveness attack*

The liveness attack aims to delay new block confirmation. Liveness attack was first mentioned by Kiayias and Panagiotakos (2017) in their paper. The authors describe this attack in three phases as follows: (i) attack preparation phase, (ii) transaction denial phase, and (iii) blockchain retarder phase.

The activities in the attack preparation phase are similar to selfish attack where the attacker tries to gain some advantage over honest miners. This is achieved by having knowledge of some transactions, but not passing this information to honest nodes. In the second phase, the attacker prepares a block with the transaction, but does not publically share the block. This will give the attacker a chance to deny the transaction. In the third phase, the attacker will publish the transaction on the public blockchain. Now in some blockchain-based systems, the depth of the block is greater than a constant value, therefore transactions from that block will be considered valid automatically. The attacker will take advantage of this fact to keep building blocks on a private chain and publishing them to slow down public blockchain growth rate.

3.5 *Balance attack*

This type of attack exploits vulnerabilities of PoW-based blockchain systems. This attack was first identified by Natoli and Gramoli (2016). It is mainly launched from nodes with low mining power. It has an ability to temporarily halt the communication between different subgroups having near similar mining power. In this attack, the attacker records transactions in one subgroup, but mines the block in the other subgroup, increasing the weight of the second subgroup. The attack can be used to perform double spending type of attack. The authors (Natoli & Gramoli, 2016) were able to demonstrate this attack on R3 consortium-based blockchain with control of approximately 5% of computing power.

4. Security Enhancement

4.1 *Oyante*

This tool is proposed by Luu *et al.* (2017) for detecting various smart contract vulnerabilities in Ethereum-based applications. This tool follows execution pattern of EVM and analyzes the operation instructions from the bytecode of the contract. This tool is especially useful in analysis of smart contracts that are already deployed.

Oyante consists of CFG builder, explorer, analyzer, validator, and visualizer modules. CFG builder module is named as it creates Controlled Flow Graph by analyzing the bytecode of the smart contract. The explorer module takes the current Ethereum state and performs the simulated execution of the smart contract. During the simulated execution phase, the CFG may change as some part of execution may be of dynamic nature. The analysis module uses various algorithms to analyze the code of the smart contract for various vulnerabilities. This information is then passed to a validator module that will validate the findings of analyzers and mark the code paths. The visualizer gets this information from the validator and presents it to the user for further action.

4.2 *Hawk*

Hawk framework is developed by Koshba *et al.* (2016). This is a privacy-focused framework. Smart contracts written with this framework do not need to use cryptographic techniques or other data hiding techniques. As an additional feature, hawk-based smart contract will not store private financial information in the blockchain. There are two parts of hawk-based contract: (i) public contract and (ii) private contract. Data can be stored and processed publically if it is public information. In case of private information, it is stored into private contract and processed privately. The compiler divides a hawk-based contract code into three components as follows: (i) code that will execute as a normal Ethereum smart contract;

(ii) code executable only by the users of the smart contract; and (iii) code-only executable by the hawk's manager component inside the Intel SGX environment. Another feature of this framework is that due to the nature of the manager component, it will not only protect private information from public blockchain, but also protect information from other hawk contracts. In this framework, even if the manager is compromised and attempts at aborting, the users will be compensated.

4.3 *Town crier*

Town crier system is developed with keeping in mind the need of smart contracts to communicate with external data sources. The town crier system is proposed by Zhang *et al.* (2016). The smart contract that wants to access data from an external data source has to use HTTP protocol to access the external data source. The town crier acts as a bridge between the external data source and the smart contract. The town crier takes requests from smart contracts deployed in the block-chain system for external data and fetches data by executing requests in Intel SGX-based environment via a relay module. Once data is fetched, it returns the data in a form of signed blockchain messages to ensure authenticity.

4.4 *Quantities framework*

It is a simulation and analysis model proposed by Gervais *et al.* (2016). This model has simulation components that require input of consensus protocol and network model parameters to mimic execution of the block-chain. A variety of information is gathered by this simulation, such as: throughput, block propagation delay, block size, stale block, connection delay, etc. Throughput refers to a number of transactions that blockchain can handle per second. Block propagation delay is time it takes for infor-mation of a new block to travel from one end of the network to the other. Block size is determined by a number of transactions in each block. Stale block denotes a block that has been proposed by a node, but has not been written in the blockchain. Stale block rate can determine the double spending and selfish mining attacks in blockchain. The analysis of these parameters can aid in optimizing the attack response and enhancing security of blockchain.

4.5 *Smartpool*

Smartpool is a solution proposed by Luu *et al.* (2017) to address the problem of centralization of mining in bitcoin. This smart contract is based on Ethereum framework. Here, the smartpool gets their transactions from various Ethereum clients (Ethereum, n.d.; Schoedon, 2018). These transactions contain mining task information. The miners perform hashing-related computations on the task information and return the tasks to a smartpool client. The smartpool client keeps a count of number of tasks submitted by miners. Once it reaches a predefined limit, these tasks are committed to the contract and to the blockchain in turn. Once the tasks are committed, the smartpool analyzes the contributions of miners in submitting completed tasks and share rewards. The miners of smartpool need to connect to the Ethereum chain to get data from its clients. Instead of developing its own consensus mechanism, it can utilize Ethereum's consensus mechanism. Also, the state of mining pool is maintained by the Ethereum, therefore, removing need of the pool operator.

Additionally, smartpool miners can submit their shares in parts making the process faster. Smartpool also provides additional security by applying a novel data structure, which will detect and flag attackers submitting shares in different batches. Honest miners are promised due reward irrespective of malicious miners existing in the pool.

5. Future Directions

Here, we list a few areas which may interest readers who are looking to explore this topic in further detail. The first area is of consensus mechanism. The most popular consensus mechanism is PoW used in bitcoin. This consensus algorithm is known for wasting resources. There are many alternative mechanisms proposed, such as Proof of Stake, Proof of Capacity, Proof of Identity, Proof of Elapsed Time, etc. Researchers look at improving current consensus algorithms or proposing better consensus algorithms.

The second area of research can be privacy. Increased usage of blockchain applications is contributing to popularity of distributed applications. Some techniques for prevention of private information leakage are trusted execution environment (Intel SGX), code obfuscation, and use of cryptography techniques.

Third area which may interest researchers is identification of redundancy in smart contracts and removal of unutilized smart contracts. There are many smart contracts on Ethereum system that have exactly the same code, therefore, a method or tool can be developed for identification and removal of such smart contracts. During the process of recording transaction on a blockchain, large amount of data is generated. Not all data generated during this process is useful and hence, there is a need for a framework or technique to analyze this data and remove unnecessary data. This will improve the performance of the blockchain systems.

6. Conclusion

In this chapter, we focused on security aspect of the blockchain systems. We divided various vulnerabilities into two main types as follows: network-based and programming-based vulnerabilities. We then discussed each vulnerability in detail to understand how it can be exploited. We also demonstrated how each vulnerability is damaging to the blochchain system. We reviewed real attacks and identified how one or more vulnerabilities were exploited to make a successful attack. We examined some tools and techniques that can be used to identify and patch vulnerabilities and strengthen the overall blockchain-based systems. Finally, we presented some future directions for interested readers to pursue for their research.

References

Adelstein, J., & Stucky, N.-K. (August 6, 2020). *Behind the biggest bitcoin heist in history: Inside the implosion of Mt. Gox.* (thedailybeast.com) Retrieved May 4, 2021, from https://www.thedailybeast.com/behind-the-biggest-bitcoin-heist-in-history-inside-the-implosion-of-mt-gox.

Adinolfi, J. (December 25, 2016). *And 2016's best-performing commodity is ... bitcoin?* (Market Watch) Retrieved May 4, 2021, from https://www.market-watch.com/story/and-2016s-best-performing-commodity-is-bitcoin-2016-12-22.

Apostolaki, M., Zohar, A., & Vanbever, L. (2017). Hijacking bitcoin: Routing attacks on cryptocurrencies. *IEEE Symposium on Security and Privacy (SP)*.

Atzei, N., Bartoletti, M., & Cimoli, T. (2017). A survey of attacks on ethereum smart contracts (sok). *International Conference on Principles of Security and Trust*.

Barone, R., & Masciandaro, D. (2019). Cryptocurrency or usury? Crime and alternative money laundering techniques. *European Journal of Law and Economics, 47*(2), 233–254.

Barton, J. (2020, January 27). *How many Ethereum smart contracts are there?* (Coindiligent.com) Retrieved May 4, 2021, from https://coindiligent.com/how-many-ethereum-smart-contracts#:~:text=At%20the%20time%20of%20writing%2C%20there%20are%20over,Why%20are%20there%20so%20many%20Ethereum%20smart%20contracts%3F.

Baudier, P., Kondrateva, G., Ammi, C., & Seulliet, E. (2021). Peace engineering: The contribution of blockchain systems to the e-voting process. *Technological Forecasting and Social Change, 162*, 1–11.

Bedi, P., Gupta, N., & Jindal, V. (2020). Dark web: A boon or a bane. *Encyclopedia of Criminal Activities and the Deep Web*, 152–164.

Bitansky, N., Chiesa, A., Ishai, Y., Paneth, O., & Ostrovsky, R. (2013). Succinct non-interactive arguments via linear interactive proofs. *Theory of Cryptography Conference*.

Blockchain.com. (May 12, 2021). *Confirmed transactions per day*. (Blockchain.com) Retrieved May 12, 2021, from https://www.blockchain.com/charts/n-transactions.

Buterin, V. (June 17, 2016). *CRITICAL UPDATE Re: DAO vulnerability*. (ethereum.org), Retrieved May 5, 2021, from https://blog.ethereum.org/2016/06/17/critical-update-re-dao-vulnerability/.

Chaudhary, K. C., Chand, V., & Fehnker, A. (2020). Double-spending analysis of bitcoin. *PACIS 2020 Proceedings*.

Chen, T., Li, X., Luo, X., & Zhang, X. (2017). Under-optimized smart contracts devour your money. *IEEE 24th International Conference on Software Analysis, Evolution and Reengineering (SANER)*.

Choo, K.-K. R., Dehghantanha, A., & Parizi, R. M. (2020). *Blockchain Cybersecurity, Trust and Privacy*. Springer International Publishing.

Chukwu, E., & Garg, L. (2020). A systematic review of blockchain in healthcare: Frameworks, prototypes, and implementations. *IEEE Access, 8*, 21196–21214.

Desjardins, J. (2016, January 5). *It's official: Bitcoin was the top performing currency of 2015*. (Visual Capitalist) Retrieved May 6, 2021, from http://money.visualcapitalist.com/its-official-bitcoin-was-the-top-performing-currency-of-2015/

Ethereum, G. (n.d.). *Go Ethereum*. (Ethereum.org), Retrieved May 10, 2021, from https://geth.ethereum.org/.

etherscan.io. (May 5, 2021). *Ethereum daily transaction chart*. (etherscan.io), Retrieved May 5, 2021, from https://etherscan.io/chart/tx?ref=hackernoon.com.

Eyal, I., & Sirer, E. G. (2014). Majority is not enough: Bitcoin mining is vulnerable. *International Conference on Financial Cryptography and Data Security*.

Farooq, S. M., Hussain, S. S., & Ustun, T. S. (2019). Elliptic curve digital signature algorithm (ECDSA) certificate based authentication scheme for advanced metering infrastructure. *Innovations in Power and Advanced Computing Technologies, 1*, 1–6.

Gautham. (2016). *Ethereum network comes across yet another DOS attack.* (newsbtc.com) Retrieved May 6, 2021, from https://www.newsbtc.com/news/ethereum-dao-attack-attack-platforms-credibility/.

Gervais, A., Karame, G. O., Wüst, K., Glykantzis, V., Ritzdorf, H., & Capkun, S. (2016). On the security and performance of proof of work blockchains. *Proceedings of the 2016 ACM SIGSAC Conference on Computer and Communications Security.*

Goldfeder, S., Kalodner, H., Reisman, D., & Narayanan, A. (2017). When the cookie meets the blockchain: Privacy risks of web payments via cryptocurrencies. *arXiv preprint. Proceedings on Privacy Enhancing Technologies, 2018*(4), 179–199, ISSN: 2299-0984, 2018, October.

Guest, D. (February 24, 2008). *Pakistan hijacks YouTube.* (Oracle.com) Retrieved May 8, 2021, from https://blogs.oracle.com/internetintelligence/pakistan-hijacks-youtube.

Hajdarbegovic, N. (January 9, 2014). *Bitcoin miners ditch* Ghash.io *pool over fears of 51% attack.* (coindesk.com) Retrieved May 4, 2021, from https://www.coindesk.com/bitcoin-miners-ditch-ghash-io-pool-51-attack.

Hasselgren, A., Kralevska, K., Gligoroski, D., Pedersen, S. A., & Faxvaag, A. (2020). Blockchain in healthcare and health sciences — A scoping review. *International Journal of Medical Informatics, 134*(1).

He, D., Deng, Z., Zhang, Y., Chan, S., Cheng, Y., & Guizani, N. (2020). Smart contract vulnerability analysis and security audit. *IEEE Network, 34*(5), 276–282.

Heilman, E., Kendler, A., Zohar, A., & Goldberg, S. (2015). Eclipse attacks on bitcoin's peer-to-peer network. *24th {USENIX} Security Symposium ({USENIX} Security '15).*

Juels, A., Kosba, A., & Shi, E. (2015). The ring of gyges: Using smart contracts for crime. *Aries, 40*(54).

Kiayias, A., & Panagiotakos, G. (2017). On trees, chains and fast transactions in the blockchain. *International Conference on Cryptology and Information Security in Latin America.*

Kim, S.-K., Kim, U.-M., & Huh, J.-H. (2019). A study on improvement of blockchain application to overcome vulnerability of IoT multiplatform security. *Energies, 3*(12).

Kosba, A., Miller, A., Shi, E., Wen, Z., & Papamanthou, C. (2016). Hawk: The blockchain model of cryptography and privacy-preserving smart contracts. *IEEE Symposium on Security and Privacy (SP).*

Koshy, P., Koshy, D., & McDaniel, P. (2014). An analysis of anonymity in bitcoin using p2p network traffic. *International Conference on Financial Cryptography and Data Security.*

Lallai, G., Pinna, A., Marchesi, M., Tonelli, R., Chiaraluce, F., & Mostarda, L. (2020). Software engineering for DApp smart contracts managing workers contracts. *DLT@ ITASEC*.

Lin, I.-C., & Liao, T.-C. (2017). A survey of blockchain security issues and challenges. *IJ Network Security*, 653–659.

Luu, L., Velner, Y., Teutsch, J., & Saxena, P. (2017). Smartpool: Practical decentralized pooled mining. *26th {USENIX} Security Symposium ({USENIX} Security '17)*.

Malhotra, J., Jadhav, N. N., Sachdeo-Bedi, R., Sugandhi, R., & Sarode, S. (2020). Redefining trust and disinter-mediation with blockchain in E-governance. *Cross-Industry Use of Blockchain Technology and Opportunities for the Future*, 18–38.

Marino, B., & Juels, A. (2016). Setting standards for altering and undoing smart contracts. *International Symposium on Rules and Rule Markup Languages for the Semantic Web*.

Meiklejohn, S., Pomarole, M., Jordan, G., Levchenko, K., McCoy, D., Voelker, G. M., & Savage, S. (2013). A fistful of bitcoins: Characterizing payments among men with no names. *Proceedings of the 2013 Conference on Internet Measurement Conference*, pp. 127–140.

Mhaisen, N., Fetais, N., Erbad, A., Mohamed, A., & Guizani, M. (2020). To chain or not to chain: A reinforcement learning approach for blockchain-enabled IoT monitoring applications. *Future Generation Computer Systems, 111*, 39–51.

Minnaar, A. (2017). Online 'underground' marketplaces for illicit drugs: The prototype case of the dark web website '*Silk Road. Acta Criminologica: African Journal of Criminology and Victimology, 30*(1), 23–47.

Mohammad, A. H. (2020). Analysis of ransomware on Windows platform. *IJCSNS, 20*(6), 21.

Natoli, C., & Gramoli, V. (2016). The balance attack against proof-of-work blockchains: The R3 testbed as an example. arXiv preprint arXiv: 1612.09426.

Ober, M., Katzenbeisser, S., & Hamacher, K. (2013). Structure and anonymity of the bitcoin transaction graph. *Future internet, 5*(2), 237–250.

Oliveira, T. A., Oliver, M., & Ramalhinho, H. (2020). Challenges for connecting citizens and smart cities: ICT, e-governance and blockchain. *Sustainability, 12*(7).

Paganini, P. (2021, January 11). *Hacking communities in the deep web*. (infosec institute.com), Retrieved May 5, 2021, from https://resources.infosecinstitute. com/topic/hacking-communities-in-the-deep-web/.

Pavithran, D., Shaalan, K., Al-Karaki, J. N., & Gawanmeh, A. (2020). Towards building a blockchain framework for IoT. *Cluster Computing, 23*(3), 2089–2103.

Reid, F., & Harrigan, M. (2013). An analysis of anonymity in the bitcoin system. *Security and Privacy in Social Networks*, 197–233.

Robinson, Y. H., & Julie, E. G. (2019). MTPKM: Multipart trust based public key management technique to reduce security vulnerability in mobile ad-hoc networks. *Wireless Personal Communications, 2*(109), 739–760.

Ron, D., & Shamir, A. (2013). Quantitative analysis of the full bitcoin transaction graph. *International Conference on Financial Cryptography and Data Security.*

Saad, M., Spaulding, J., Njilla, L., Kamhoua, C., Shetty, S., Nyang, D., & Mohaisen, D. (2020). Exploring the attack surface of blockchain: A comprehensive survey. *IEEE Communications Surveys & Tutorials,* 1977–2008.

Schoedon, A. (June 18, 2018). *Parity-Ethereum//v2.0.0-beta.* (parity.io) Retrieved May 10, 2021, from https://www.parity.io/parity-ethereum-2-0/#:~:text= Parity%20Ethereum%20is%20a%20full-node%20client%20powering%20 Ethereum,community%20by%20renaming%20the%20client%20to%20 Parity%20Ethereum.

Sengupta, J., Ruj, S., & Bit, S. D. (2020). A comprehensive survey on attacks, security issues and blockchain solutions for IoT and IIoT. *Journal of Network and Computer Applications.*

Singh, A. (2006). Eclipse attacks on overlay networks: Threats and defenses. *IEEE INFOCOM. 2006.*

Solat, S., & Potop-Butucaru, M. (2016). Zeroblock: Preventing selfish mining in bitcoin. arXiv preprint arXiv:1605.02435.

Souptacular. (December 1, 2015). *Changing SUICIDE variable.* (Ethereum) Retrieved May 6, 2021, from https://github.com/ethereum/EIPs/pull/42.

Stewart, J. (August 7, 2014). *BGP hijacking for cryptocurrency profit.* (Secure Works.com) Retrieved May 6, 2021, from https://www.secureworks.com/ research/bgp-hijacking-for-cryptocurrency-profit.

Swende, M. (October 16, 2016). *Announcement of imminent hard fork for EIP150 gas cost changes.* (ethereum.org) Retrieved May 6, 2021, from https://blog.ethereum.org/2016/10/13/announcement-imminent-hard-fork-eip150-gas-cost-changes/.

Tandon, A., Dhir, A., Islam, N., & Mäntymäki, M. (2020). Blockchain in healthcare: A systematic literature review, synthesizing framework and future research agenda. *Computers in Industry, 122.*

Vacca, A., Sorbo, A. D., Visaggio, C. A., & Canfora, G. (2020). A systematic literature review of blockchain and smart contract development: Techniques, tools, and open challenges. *Journal of Systems and Software.*

vbuterin. (September 24, 2016). *Long-term gas cost changes for IO-heavy operations to mitigate transaction spam attacks.* (Ethereum.org), Retrieved May 6, 2021, from https://github.com/ethereum/EIPs/issues/150.

Villata, S. (2020). Digital enforceable contracts (DEC): Making smart contracts smarter. *The Thirty-Third Annual Conference,* Brno.

Wu, J., Dong, M., Ota, K., Li, J., & Yang, W. (2020). Application-aware consensus management for software-defined intelligent blockchain in IoT. *IEEE Network, 34*(1), 69–75.

Yan, H., Oliveira, R., Burnett, K., Matthews, D., Zhang, L., & Massey, D. (2009). BGPmon: A real-time, scalable, extensible monitoring system. *Cybersecurity Applications & Technology Conference for Homeland Security.*

Zhang, F., Cecchetti, E., Croman, K., Juels, & Shi, E. (2016). Town crier: An authenticated data feed for smart contracts. *Proceedings of the 2016 ACM SIGSAC Conference on Computer and Communications Security.*

Zheng, Z., Xie, S., Dai, H.-N. C., & Wang, H. (2018). Blockchain challenges and opportunities: A survey. *International Journal of Web and Grid Services,* 352–375.

https://doi.org/10.1142/9789811225079_0013

Chapter 13

Enhancing Security and Privacy in Pharmacovigilance with Blockchain

Maithili Devi Reddy[*,§] and Latha Parthiban[†,‡]

*Department of Computer Science and Engineering,
Bharath Institute of Higher Education and Research, Tamil Nadu, India

†Department of Computer Science,
Pondicherry University Community College, Puducherry, India

§maithilidumpa@gmail.com

‡lathaparthiban@yahoo.com

Abstract

Blockchain provides privacy and security without centralized authority. This work analyzes cryptography applications in blockchain and analyzes efficient sharing of health records using Attribute-Based Encryption (ABE). Secure data sharing of sensitive information stored in cloud is very important as anybody can access it from anywhere in the world. This work aims to provide a secure sharing of medical records in cloud using enhanced Ciphertext Policy (CP-ABE) and Key Policy (KP-ABE) techniques along with data owner specifying the access control policies. In an open-networked system, machine learning algorithms are effectively used in pharmacovigilance to find the Adverse Drug Reaction (ADR). Securing this sensitive data in cloud is very important as PHRs privacy concern is very important.

Keywords: ADR, Pharmacovigilance, Machine learning, Artificial intelligence, ABE, PHR, Bloom filter, Cloud, Ciphertext policy

1. Introduction

With outsourcing of secure data in cloud, there is a need for securing this data using various encryption technique. Attribute-Based Encryption (ABE) works in the principle of bilinear maps (pairing) and can be used efficiently for PHR encryption. In Cipher text-Policy attribute-based encryption (CP-ABE), a user's private key is linked with an attribute set with cipher text defining the access policy. In KP-ABE, cipher texts defines attribute set with private keys defining access structures.

The concept of ABE scheme is shown in Figure 1. The attributes of the file from PHR are encrypted and outsourced to the cloud server. In the proposed scheme, the private key is created from this attribute set and cipher text defines the access policy. Attribute-based keyword search (ABKS) has been used as an efficient technique to search keywords in cloud.

2. Literature Survey

Muhib *et al.* (2014) have used ABE, with user access defined by read and write. The proposed system achieves data confidentiality with facility for emergency access. Its main advantage is its high minimization of key management overhead and it enhances the privacy guarantee but has

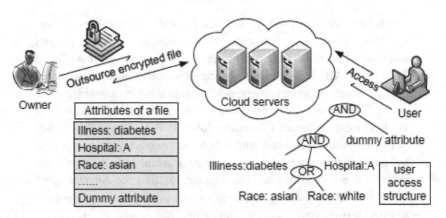

Figure 1.   Attribute-Based Encryption Scheme

inefficient key search. Kaitai *et al.* (2015) have used ABE with keyword update suited for real time implementation. This scheme has high flexible keyword update services. The main disadvantage is its less expressive keyword search where owner does not create access rights and overhead in proxy re-encryption.

Saibai *et al.* (2014) have used remote location for secure data storage and search done without decryption. Its main advantage is secure and efficient search operation for encrypted words with main disadvantage being less expressive user defined access policy. Danan *et al.* (2014) have attempted to implement mobile telecare in cloud computing. The main advantage is efficient data sharing and handles user revocation problem. The disadvantage is over headed security protocol. Ming Li *et al.* (2010) have given fine-grained access control to PHR with reduced complexity of key management. The disadvantage is less expressive user defined access policy.

3. Proposed Methodology

In this section, implementation of CP-ABE and KP-ABE is done.

3.1 (*a*) *System architecture of CP-ABE*

In CP-ABE, the following steps are carried out:

- PHR owner initially authorizes a Central Authority (CA).
- CA is responsible for generating Master Key (MK) and Secret Key (SK).
- CA issues MK and SK to user.
- PHR owner will Encrypt the file using ABE.
- Encrypted PHR will be outsourced to cloud server.
- Meanwhile, users provide attribute value to owner.
- User gets the write key from PHR owner.
- The user can read or write file by providing their respective access policies and secret keys.
- The encrypted file search is done using the Bloom filter.

Encryption of PHR using ABE is done by establishing cloud and storing encrypted data in cloud storage followed by implementation of Bloom filter and then decryption of PHR.

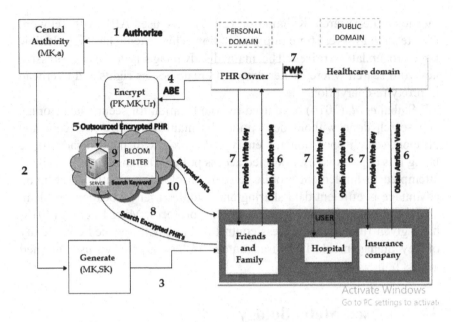

Figure 2.   CP-ABE Architecture

3.1 *(b) Encryption and decryption of PHR using CP-ABE*

The encryption of PHR is done by data owner which has the following phases (Figure 2):

In setup phase, the public parameters PK and a master/secret MK are generated.

In key generation phase, the master key MK along with a set of attributes Ur generates outputs the secret key SK.

In encryption phase, PK with message M and access structure A over the set of attributes Ur is taken and a ciphertext CT is created.

In create user phase, the public key PK, the master key MK, and user U are used to create public user key and secret keys(used during decryption) for user U.

In create authority phase, admin executes the algorithm with identifier a that outputs the secret authority key SKa.

In request attribute (SK) phase, a request for secret attribute key is given which authorizes the user U with PK for set of role attributes. Figure 3 shows the encryption of PHR's.

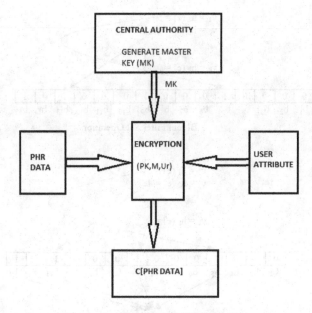

Figure 3.   Encryption of PHR's Data

During establishment of private cloud and storing encrypted data in cloud storage, the PHR data are getting stored in the cloud. At first, a private cloud storage is setup using Eucalyptus. After the cloud installation, the encrypted PHR data are sent to the cloud storage using APIs like S3curl, S3cmd and S3fs.

3.1 (c) *Bloom filter*

A Bloom filter is a data structure used for quick retrieval.

It contains array of m-bits which are set to 0 and k hash functions which in turn return a value ranging from 1 and m for setting and checking operation. Figure 4 shows Bloom filter set and checking operation.

Primary and secondary Bloom filter for finding language of words is shown in Figures 5 and 6.

Encrypted search in cloud is done which is shown in Figure 7.

From the users' private key and secret key, the cipher text is obtained. If Ur satisfies the access structure A, then decryption process happens and data is obtained as in Figure 8.

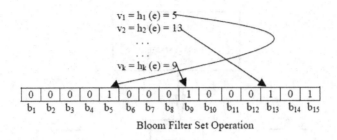

$$v_1 = h_1 (e) = 5$$
$$v_2 = h_2 (e) = 13$$
$$\ldots$$
$$\ldots$$
$$v_k = h_k (e) = 9$$

0	0	0	0	1	0	0	0	1	0	0	0	1	0	1
b_1	b_2	b_3	b_4	b_5	b_6	b_7	b_8	b_9	b_{10}	b_{11}	b_{12}	b_{13}	b_{14}	b_{15}

Bloom Filter Set Operation

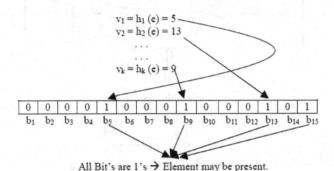

$$v_1 = h_1 (e) = 5$$
$$v_2 = h_2 (e) = 13$$
$$\ldots$$
$$\ldots$$
$$v_k = h_k (e) = 9$$

0	0	0	0	1	0	0	0	1	0	0	0	1	0	1
b_1	b_2	b_3	b_4	b_5	b_6	b_7	b_8	b_9	b_{10}	b_{11}	b_{12}	b_{13}	b_{14}	b_{15}

All Bit's are 1's → Element may be present.

Checking for an Element Presence

Figure 4.   Bloom Filter Set and Checking Operation

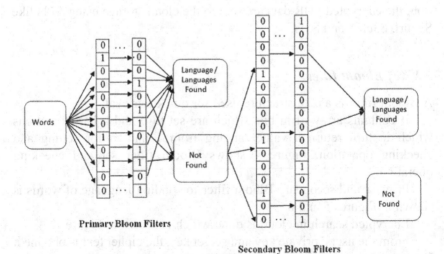

Primary Bloom Filters

Secondary Bloom Filters

Figure 5.   Bloom Filters for Finding Language of Words

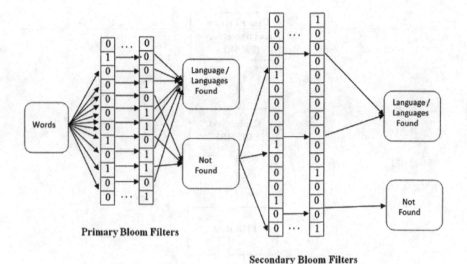

Primary Bloom Filters

Secondary Bloom Filters

Figure 6.   Process of Finding Language of Words

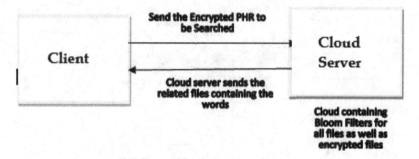

Figure 7.   Encrypted Search on Cloud

Figure 9 shows the overall system flow that depicts the working of the system.

3.2 (a) *System architecture of KP-ABE*

The proposed system was depicted in the Figure 10 and briefed as follows,

1. PHR owner initially authorizes a CA.
2. CA gets attributes from users and provides access policies to the users if attribute matches.

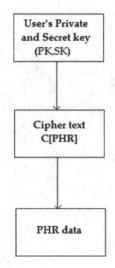

Figure 8.   Decryption of PHR

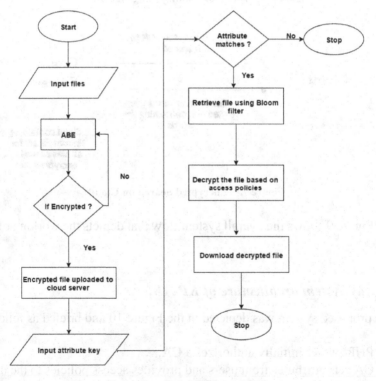

Figure 9.   Overall System Flow

3. CA is responsible for generating MK and SK.
4. PHR owner will Encrypt the file using ABE and with generated MK and SK.
5. Encrypted PHR will be outsourced to cloud server.
6. PHR owner will store the encrypted PHR in cloud.
7. User on providing MK and SK will get access policies.
8. The user can read or write file by providing their respective access policies and secret keys.
9. The encrypted file search is done using the Bloom filter.

The system architecture is shown in Figure 10.

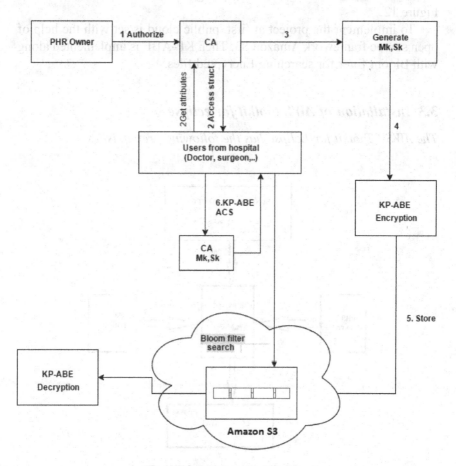

Figure 10. **System Architecture**

3.2 (b) *Modules of KP-ABE*

This research work comprises the following modules:

- Encryption of PHR using ABE.
- Establishing cloud and storing encrypted data in cloud storage.
- Implementation of Bloom filter.
- Decryption of PHR.

Encryption of PHR using ABE module deals with the encryption of PHR's by data owner as in Figure 11.

Bloom filter setting and checking operation is shown in the Figure 12.

To implement the project at first, public cloud is set with the help of open source framework Amazon S3. Then KP-ABE is implemented along with Bloom filter for searching Encrypted files.

3.3 *Installation of AWS toolkit for eclipse*

The AWS "Toolkit for Eclipse has the following prerequisites

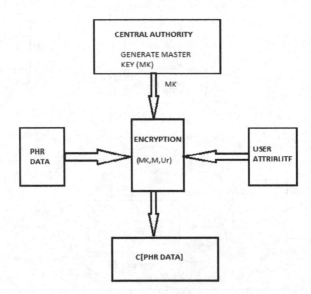

Figure 11.   Encryption of PHR Data

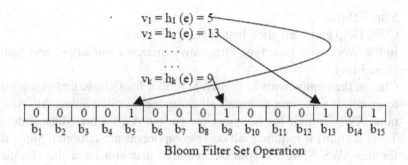

Bloom Filter Set Operation

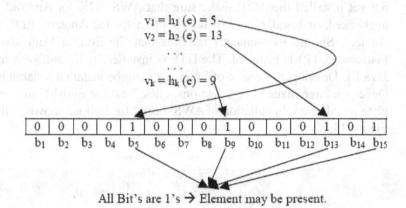

All Bit's are 1's → Element may be present.

Checking for an Element Presence

Figure 12. Bloom Filter Set and Checking Operation

An Amazon Web Services account to obtain an AWS account, go to the AWS home page and click Sign Up Now. Signing up will enable you to use all of the services offered by AWS.

A supported operating system The AWS Toolkit for Eclipse is supported on Windows, Linux, OS X or unix.

Java 1.6 or later.

Eclipse IDE for Java Developers 3.6 or later. We attempt to keep the AWS Toolkit for Eclipse current with the default version available on the Eclipse download page.

To install the AWS Toolkit for Eclipse from the AWS website using the Eclipse user interface

1. Start Eclipse.
2. Click Help and then click Install New Software.
3. In the Work with box, type https://aws.amazon.com/eclipse and then press Enter.
4. Choose the components of the AWS Toolkit for Eclipse that you want to install. If you want to install all components, click Select All. Also note: AWS Toolkit for Eclipse Core (in the AWS Core Management Tools section) is required; all other components are optional. Support for the AWS SDK for Android requires that you have the Google Android Developer Tools (ADT) for Eclipse installed first. If you have not yet installed the ADT, make sure that AWS SDK for Android is unchecked, or installation will fail. Support for the Amazon RDS or Amazon SimpleDB managers requires that the Eclipse Data Tools Platform (DTP) is installed. The DTP is installed by default with the Java EE Developers version of Eclipse, or can be installed separately.
5. Once you have made your selections, click Next (or Finish)" to complete installation. Installation of AWS toolkit for Eclipse shown in the Figure 13.

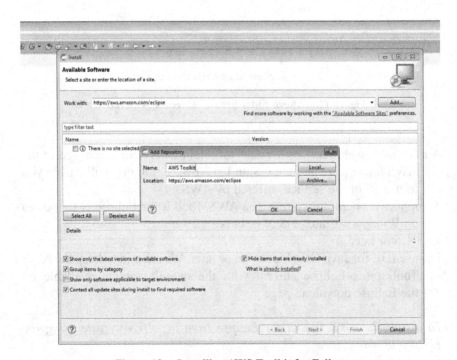

Figure 13.   Installing AWS Toolkit for Eclipse

Once AWS Toolkit for Eclipse installation completed, AWS Credentials need to be configured as shown in the Figure 14.

4. Implementation of CP-ABE

First install the tarball of libbswabe, and then run cpabe-setup for enabling master key and public key generation as in Figure 15.

File master key is used to produce private keys for Sara and Kevin using cpabe-keygen (Figure 16).

If someone wants to encrypt a secret document, then public key can be use cpabe-enc as in Figure 17. Decryption can be done using

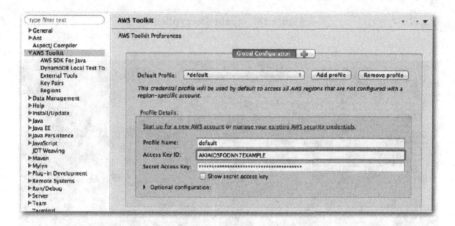

Figure 14. **AWS Credential Configuration**

```
$ cpabe-setup
$ ls
master_key  pub_key
```

Figure 15. cpabe-setup

```
$ cpabe-keygen -o sara_priv_key pub_key master_key \
    sysadmin it_department 'office = 1431' 'hire_date = `date +%s`
$ cpabe-keygen -o kevin_priv_key pub_key master_key \
    business_staff strategy_team 'executive_level = 7' \
    'office = 2362' 'hire_date = `date +%s`
$ ls
master_key  pub_key  sara_priv_key  kevin_priv_key
```

Figure 16. **cpabe-keygen**

```
$ ls
pub_key  security_report.pdf
$ cpabe-enc pub_key security_report.pdf
    (sysadmin and (hire_date < 946702800 or security_team)) or
    (business_staff and 2 of (executive_level >= 5, audit_group, strategy_team))
^D
$ ls
pub_key  security_report.pdf.cpabe
```

Figure 17.   cpabe-Encryption

```
$ ls
pub_key kevin_priv_key security_report.pdf.cpabe
$ cpabe-dec pub_key kevin_priv_key security_report.pdf.cpabe
$ ls
pub_key  kevin_priv_key  security_report.pdf
```

Figure 18.   cpabe-Decryption

Figure 19.   Implementation of CP-ABE — Allowing Kevin to Decrypt

cpabe-decryption as in Figure 18. Attributes of Kevins key satisfy the policy and Saras do not as in Figures 19 and 20.

The storage of encrypted data in cloud is done with Walrus service, where buckets are created in the /var/lib/eucalyptus/bukkits location. Using this command, a bucket named storage is created as shown in Figure 21.

Figure 20.   Implementation of CP-ABE — Not Allowing Sara to Decrypt

Figure 21.   Data Storage in Cloud

4.1 *Implementation of KP-ABE*

The setup algorithm takes no input other than the implicit security parameter. It generates the public parameters PK and a master/secret key MK generated by each CA. The Nth CA defines a disjoint set of role attributes Ur,

```
run:
Setup over!
Files containing Public Paramaters and Master Key have been generated
Type of Mapping: Type A Tate NAF Miller Projective Pairing


Element from G1:

4870477202084249368874320542634362671420123910995921428674985220549912


Element from GT:

4682016085644192589537929350332362429255631390458614167017521738650109


Random Member from Integer Group in Master Key:

1431758583354571552680065660099333336180442489897
BUILD SUCCESSFUL [total time: 2 seconds)
```

Figure 22.   Setting up CA

Name	Date modified	Type	Size
Ciphertext	4/6/2016 11:09 PM	File folder	
attribute	4/6/2016 5:46 PM	Text Document	2 KB
attribute1	4/6/2016 4:39 PM	Text Document	1 KB
MskFile	6/6/2016 2:08 PM	SER File	4 KB
PubParamFile	6/6/2016 2:08 PM	SER File	11 KB

Figure 23.   Generating MK and SK

which are fairly common for public users. These attributes are classified on the basis of their profession as shown in the Figure 22.

4.1.1 *Key generation*

The key generation algorithm uses the master key "MK and a set of attributes Ur that describe the key, and outputs a secret key SK for user U. SK should contain at least one attribute from every type of attributes governed by CA which is shown in Figure 23.

4.1.2 *Encryption* (*MK, M, Ur*)

The encryption algorithm takes as input the master key MK, a message, M and an access structure A over a set of attributes Ur. It will encrypt M,

```
run:
Please enter the name of PHR input file:
p1
Please enter the number of attributes to be used for encryption:
2
Please enter attribute 1:
neurosurgeon
Please enter attribute 2:
oncologist
KP ABE is complete and file has been encrypted
BUILD SUCCESSFUL (total time: 22 seconds)
```

Figure 24.   Encryption of PHR

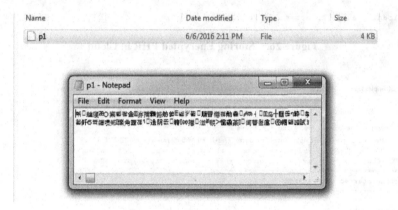

Figure 25.   The Encrypted PHR

and produce a cipher text CT such that only a user who possesses the set of attributes satisfying the access structure will be able to decrypt CT which is depicted in Figures 24 and 25.

4.1.3 *Establishing public cloud and storing encrypted data in cloud storage*

This module describes how the PHR data are getting stored in the cloud. At first we have to setup a public cloud. After the cloud installation, the encrypted PHR data are sent to the cloud storage using APIs like AWS toolkit. AWS toolkit setup and installation has been discussed earlier. The storing and downloading of PHR files is shown in the Figures 26–28.

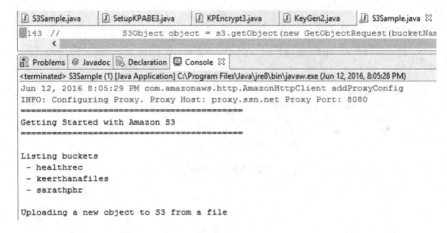

Figure 26.   Storing Encrypted PHR in Cloud

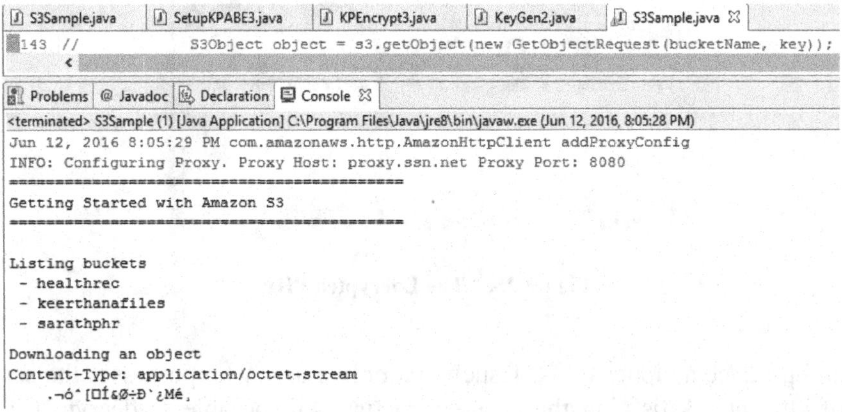

Figure 27.   Downloading Encrypted PHR in Cloud

📄 p1	6/6/2016 6:40 PM	File
📄 p1EncryptedPHR	6/12/2016 8:05 PM	File

Figure 28.   Downloaded Encrypted PHR

4.1.4 *Decryption* (*MK, CT, SK*)

The decryption algorithm takes as input master key MK, a cipher text CT, which was obtained for set of attributes Ur, and a private key SK for Ur.

If Ur satisfies the access structure A, then the algorithm will decrypt the cipher text and return a message which is shown in Figure 29.

4.1.5 *Bloom Filter for file searching*

Bloomfilter is designed as an array (A) of m bits. Initially all these bits are set to 0.

To add item
In order to add any item, it needs to be feed through k hash functions. Each hash function will generate a number which can be treated as a

```
run:
Please enter the name of PHR input file:
p1
Please enter the access structure of user:
neurosurgeon oncologist 1of2
Created key success!!
Decryption Complete!
Contents of PHR:
Name: MHVTESTVETERAN, ONE A          Date of Birth: 01 Mar 1948

----------------------- DOWNLOAD REQUEST SUMMARY -----------------------

System Request Date/Time:   05 Nov 2014 @ 0827
File Name:                  mhv_MHVTESTVETERAN_20141105_0827.txt

Date Range Selected:        05 Nov 2009 to 05 Nov 2014
Data Types Selected:
  My HealtheVet Account Summary
  Self Reported Demographics
  VA Demographics
  Self Reported Health Care Providers
  Self Reported Treatment Facilities
  Self Reported Health Insurance
  VA Wellness Reminders
  VA Appointments (Future)
  VA Appointments (Limited to past 2 years)
  VA Allergies
  Self Reported Allergies
  VA Medication History
  Self Reported Medications and Supplements
  VA Problem List
  VA Admissions and Discharges
  VA Notes
  Self Reported Medical Events
  VA Immunizations
```

Figure 29. Decryption of PHR

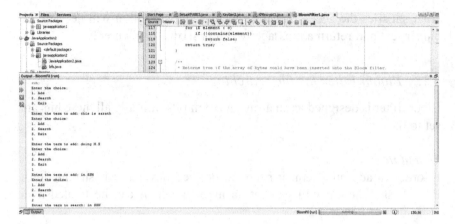

Figure 30.   Bloom Filter for Insertion of a Keyword

position of the bit array (hash modulo array length can give us the index of the array) and we shall set that value of that position to 1. Bloom filter insertion is shown in Figure 30. For example first hash function (hash1) on item I produce a bit position x, similarly second and third hash functions produce position y and z. So we shall set,

$$A[x] = A[y] = A[z] = 1$$

To find item
Similar process will be repeated, item will be hashed three times through three different hash functions. Each hash function will produce an integer which will be treated as a position of the array. We shall inspect those x, y, z positions of the bit array and see if they are set to 1 or not. If no, for sure no one ever tried to add this item into Bloom filter, but if all the bits are set, it could be a false positive. Bloom filter searching is shown in Figures 31 and 32.

Things to tune
From the above explanation, it becomes clear that to design a good Bloom filter, we need to keep track of the following things:

- Good hash functions that can generate wide range of hash values as quickly as possible.

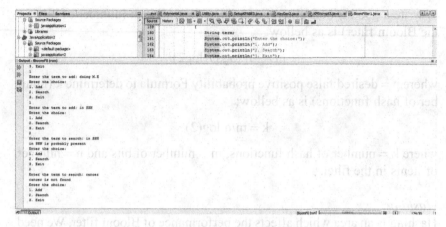

Figure 31. Searching Plain Text in PHR Files

Figure 32. Searching Encrypted PHR Files in Cloud

- The value of m (size of the bit array) is very important. If the size is too small, all the bits will be set to 1 quickly and false positives will grow largely.
- Number of hash functions (k) is also important so that the values get distributed evenly.

If we can estimate how many items we are planning to keep in the Bloom filter, we can calculate the optimal values of k and m. Skipping the mathematical details, the formula to calculate k and m are enough for us to write a good Bloom filter. Formula to determine m (number of bits for the Bloom filter) is as bellow:

$$m = -n \log p/(\log 2)^2$$

where p = desired false positive probability Formula to determine k (number of hash functions) is as bellow:

$$k = m/n \log(2)$$

where k = number of hash functions, m = number of bits and n = number of items in the filter.

Hashing
Hashing is an area which affects the performance of Bloom filter. We need to choose a hash function that is effective yet not time consuming. In the chapter, Less Hashing, Same Performance: Building a Better Bloom filter, it is discussed how we can use two hash functions to generate K number of hash functions. First we need to calculate two hash function h1(x) and h2(x). Next, we can use these two hash functions to simulate k hash functions of the nature. Gi(x) = h1(x) + ih2(x) where i can range from 1…k. Bloom filter implementation, the hashing logic is outlined here:

```
long hash64 = ; //calculate a 64 bit hash function //split it in two halves
of 32 bit hash values
int hash1 = (int) hash64;
int hash2 = (int) (hash64 ¿¿¿ 32);

//Generate k different hash functions with a simple loop for (int i = 1; i
¡ = numHashFunctions; i++)
int nextHash = hash1 + i * hash2;
```

5. Application in Pharmacovigilance

Machine learning (ML) is defined as the subset of artificial intelligence (AI) which has been emerged from pattern recognition to identify the data structure as well as to learn the methods used by customers. It is capable of providing solution for a computer program by applying the historical information for solving the given issue is an automated manner which leads to enhance the program efficiency including the computation. Recently, several ML domain has been proposed such as methods used for classifying novel astronomical structures, prediction of mischievous

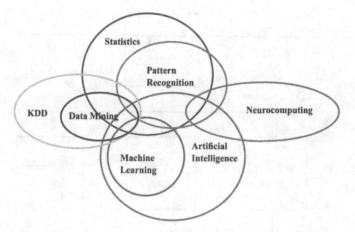

Figure 33.   Representation of Degree of Similarities between Various Fields

events in banking sectors, data-filtering process which understands the learning priority of customer, neurobiological studies, independent vehicles which helps to drive on highways. Simultaneously, there is an evolution of significant process as well as techniques to create basic ML models. Figure 33 denotes the similar degrees as well as variations of different application of computer science.

The traditional method of processing has been fixed to explicit rules which are employed by machines to resolve any type of existing issues. While comparing with conventional type of processing, ML techniques aids in building methods from available information, as well to form an automatic decision-making task which depends upon the input data. Hence, such kind of methods discovers the patterns present within data and to offer diverse DM tools, respectively.

Nowadays, every technical user consumes the benefits generate from ML. The model of facial analysis enables social network to tag the corresponding users. Here, recommendation system provides the suggestion of which movie can be watched on the basis of customer priority. Optical Character Recognition (OCR) framework transforms textual image into readable format. The mechanism of car driving is based on ML method which provides navigation and routes for desired location to be reached. Hence, ML has been frequently developed for solving required problems. There are four main types of ML-based techniques, namely Supervised, Unsupervised, Semi-supervised, and Reinforcement learning models.

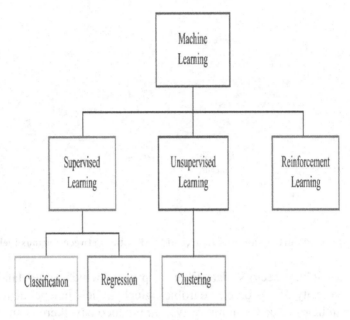

Figure 34.   Classification of Machine Learning Algorithms

Initially, supervised learning is further classified into two levels, namely classification and regression. Classification is used to predict a nominal class label, and regression is applied to forecast the numerical measure of class label. Creating a regression method is used to identify the correlation among class label as well as input detector. In case of mathematical form, predictors are said to be attributes (Lian Duan *et al.*, 2013). While statistical way, predictors are termed as independent variables, and class label is named as dependent variable. Here, the regression technique is used to denote the association between dependent as well as independent variables. After learning at the time of training phase, a novel data has been induced within the relationship curve in order to identify detection process. It tends in minimizing the ML issues such as mathematical function. The wider classification of Machine Learning is shown in Figure 34.

Rui Zhang *et al.* (2019) as divided the layers of blockchain as in Figure 35. Numerous methods have been developed to classify the data for ADR. In Sarker & Gonzalez (2015), the authors proposed the link classification approach. In Al Alkeem *et al.* (2017), secure system for

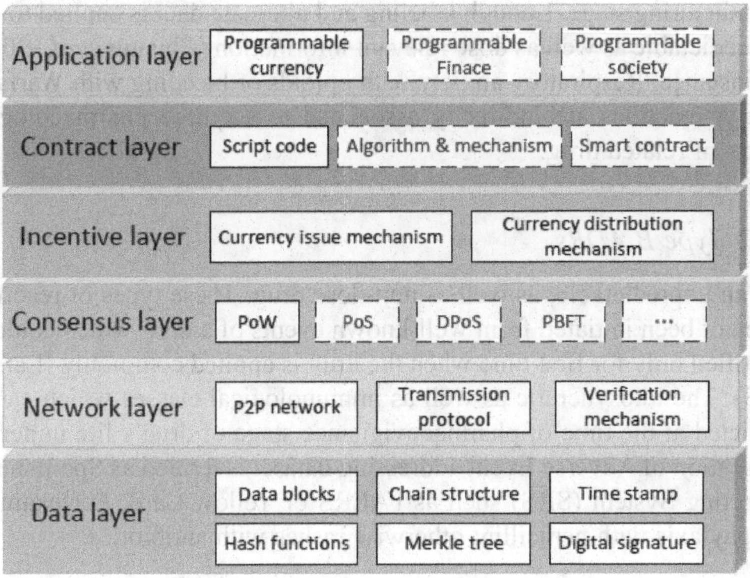

Figure 35. Layers of Blockchain

healthcare using cloud of things was proposed. In Manimala *et al.* (2011), an effective feature selection algorithm with optimization technique was proposed. In Ke *et al.* (2008), ACO with rough set theory was used for feature selection. In Lian Duan *et al.* (2013) various efficient methodologies to deduct ADR in drugs are proposed. Proposed research methodology overcomes the challenges stated above which is designed for the proper accurate analysis of drug effects.

5.1 *Types of ADR*

ADR defines the side effects generated by a drug which is classified on the basis of cause of ADR (Santana *et al.*, 2010). The information and learning is essential for physicians to observe the drug therapy as well as ADR prediction.

5.1.1 *Type A ADRs*

This kind of ADR happens by ordinary pharmacological impact and corresponding substance. In general, it is found to be present in manufacturing stage. Enough labeling and alternate data is applied to create predictable as well as dose relevant information (Chuang *et al.*, 2008). For instance, Respiratory anxiety with opioids or bleeding with Warfarin. Type A reactions are indirectly associated to acquired pharmacological effects of related drug.

5.1.2 *Type B ADRs*

It is an unpredictable, as well as non-dose drug. These types of reactions have not been initiated from well-known events of a drug which could be identified only for first time when the drug is applied commonly (Larson, 1993). The idiosyncratic as well as immunological classes which can be predicted at the time of pharmacovigilance stage of drug's life under the application of Adverse Event addressing dataset is termed as Spontaneous Reporting System (SRS) such as FAERS or Yellow Card. For example, Anaphylaxis with penicillin; otherwise rashes with antibiotics.

5.1.3 *Type C ADRs*

The cumulative toxic impact of drug has been applied across the duration results in these kinds of ADRs. Otherwise, it has a frequent response which resist in a relatively longer time interval (Liu & Chen, 2015). At this point, AE has been improved in a gradual manner. For example, Osteonecrosis of the jaw along with bisphosphonates. Here, SRS has Type C ADR information since it gathers data lifespan of drug.

5.1.4 *Type D ADRs*

In this type, the rarely applied ADRs react only for minimum duration once the treatment is over (State & Cocianu, 2007). It results in delayed reactions which makes a complex prediction. Example: Leucopoenia due to medication of Lomustine that takes nearly 6 weeks to be caused after the discontinuation of drug.

5.1.5 *Type E ADRs*

A sudden interrupt of consuming drug which has been taken for longer period results in Type E ADRs. Such ADRs are termed as "end of use" actions that happen due to immediate existence of any drug (Aghdam *et al.*, 2009). For instance, Insomnia, anxiety as well as perceptual interruptions as it have sudden retirement of Benzodiazepines. Consequently, Type A has been recommended in pre-marketing, while Type D is complex in predicting. Also, Type E could be forecasted easily as the severe result in a proof for both patient as well as a doctor. Alternatively, Type B and Type C are very hard to predict and to be examined with present available database resources (Gupta *et al.*, 2011). Type B proves in inpatient and outpatient settings and type C often detects the outpatient settings, as the default behavior is predefined. Few gathered information in SRS is composed of Type B and Type C drug responses.

5.2 *Experimental results*

Two sets of experiment were done on FAERS dataset which was downloaded from US food and drug administration website. An experimental analysis was first done by using the openvigil 2 on pharmacovigilance data on the drugs ACETAMINOPHEN and IBUPROFEN and the results obtained are tabulated. Table 1 shows the report of ADR on both drugs. Figure 36 shows the Percentage of drug interaction of Acetaminophen and Ibuprofen. Table 2 shows the disproportionality analysis of the drugs.

The attributes in Table 3 represents the following:

- count_ACETAMINOPHEN:raw counts for all reports with usage of drug 1 but not drug 2.
- count_IBUOPROFEN raw counts for all reports with usage of drug 2 but not drug 1.
- count_both_drugs:raw counts for all reports with usage of drug 1 and drug 2.

Table 1. Total Number of Reports due to Both Drugs

Number of reports [results.term]	value [results.value]
ACETAMINOPHEN alone *(with second drug)*	208936 *(229230)*
IBUPROFEN alone *(with first drug)*	89325 *(109619)*
All reports for both drugs simultaneously	20294
Total current number of reports in database	7747303

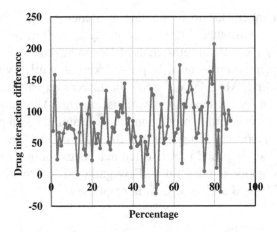

Figure 36.   Percent of Drug Interaction of Acetaminophen and Ibuprofen

Table 2.   Disproportionality Analysis for Both Drugs Acetaminophen and Ibuprofen

Event	count_Acetaminophen	count_Ibuprofen	count_both_drugs	rrr_Acetaminophen	rrr_Ibuprofen	delta_vs_rrr_both	Event_total	delta_rate_1vs2	rate_both
Nausea	15111	5026	1539	1.69842	1.32134	−0.27101	329902	1.60571	7.58352
Drug ineffective	14673	8929	1338	1.23987	1.76482	0.33833	438813	−2.97336	6.59308
Pain	12507	4933	1882	2.10164	1.93891	−1.23563	220664	0.46351	9.27368
Fatigue	12149	3961	1247	1.60714	1.22563	−0.28196	280301	1.38033	6.14467
Headache	11125	4295	1409	1.60213	1.44677	−0.56462	257478	0.51631	6.94294
Dyspnoea	10278	3327	1058	1.63968	1.24149	−0.29715	232427	1.19461	5.21336
Diarrhea	9951	2967	908	1.61862	1.12885	−0.14685	227960	1.44112	4.47423
Vomiting	9766	3570	1013	1.81787	1.55437	−0.25522	199201	0.67752	4.99162
Dizziness	8682	3542	927	1.4851	1.41718	−0.18139	216771	0.19004	4.56785

- rrr_ ACETAMINOPHEN: RRR for drug 1 and the adverse event in this line.
- rrr_ IBUPROFEN:RRR for drug 2 and the adverse event in this line.

Table 3. Adverse Drug Reaction Dataset (Ibuprofen) Classifier Performance Evaluation

Dataset	Methods	MAE	RMSE	Precision	Recall	Accuracy	F-Score	ROC	Kappa
Ibuprofen adverse drug reaction	Ensemble method	0.09	0.22	0.96	0.95	95.50	0.95	0.99	0.91
	Concept matching	0.16	0.31	0.88	0.88	88.70	0.88	0.69	0.46
	Logistic regression	0.19	0.30	0.86	0.86	87.52	0.84	0.81	0.18
	Random Forest	0.18	0.32	0.82	0.85	85.18	0.83	0.78	0.17
	RBFNetwork	0.17	0.41	0.82	0.83	83.05	0.83	0.61	0.22
	J48	0.54	0.74	0.84	0.45	45.17	0.51	0.62	0.09

- delta_vs_rrr_both: Difference mean(rrr_DRUGNAME1 and r_ DRUGNAME2) and rrr_both.
- event_total: Counts for this event (Ex).
- delta_rate_1vs2: Differences of rates.
- rate_both: Rate (percentage) D1D2Ex/D1D.

The second set of experiment was done on Ibuprofen ADR dataset using five different classification methods available in the literature. Using the ensemble method, best results were obtained for different metrics like MAE, RMSE, Precision, Recall, Accuracy, F-score, ROC, and Kappa.

6. Conclusions

Secure sharing of medical records in cloud using ABE along with data owner specifying the access control policies has been efficiently obtained using CPABE and KPABE algorithm. Also reduction in the size of the search key token and search time has been achieved while searching on encrypted data using Bloom filter. Cryptography along with blockchain is used for providing privacy and security for PHRs of patients. As an application in Pharmacovigilance, ADRs are identified from this PHRs. Also ADR of two important drugs Acetaminophen and Ibuprofen were analyzed. Ensemble classification accuracy was found to be best for ADR dataset. Future work will concentrate on computational techniques to reduce ADR and feature selection based classification algorithms for big datasets.

References

Aghdam, M. H., Ghasem-Aghaee, N., & Basiri, M. E. (2009). Text feature selection using ant colony optimization. *Expert Systems with Applications*, *36*(3, Part 2), 6843–6853.

Al Alkeem, E., Shehada, D., Yeun, C. Y., Zemerly, M. J., & Hu, J. (2017). New secure healthcare system using cloud of things. *Cluster Computing*, *20*(3), 2211–2229.

Chuang, L. Y., Chang, H. W., Tu, C. J., & Yang, C. H. (2008). Improved binary PSO for feature selection using gene expression data. *Computational Biology and Chemistry*, *32*(29), 29–38.

Gupta, S., Kumar, D., & Sharma, A. (2011). Performance analysis of various data mining classification techniques on healthcare data. *International Journal of Computer Science & Information Technology, 3*(4), 155–169.

Ke, L., Feng, Z., & Ren, Z. (2008). An efficient ant colony optimization approach to attribute reduction in rough set theory. *Pattern Recognition Letters, 29*(9),1351–1357.

Larson, E. B. (1993). Adverse drug effects: The harder we look, the more we find. *Journal of General Internal Medicine, 8*, 342–343.

Li, M., Yu, S., Ren, K., & Lou, W. (2010). Securing personal health records in cloud computing: Patient-centric and fine-grained data access control in multi-owner settings. In: Jajodia S., Zhou J. (Eds.) *Security and Privacy in Communication Networks*. Lecture Notes of the Institute for Computer Sciences, Social Informatics and Telecommunications Engineering, Vol. 50. Springer, Berlin, Heidelberg. https://doi.org/10.1007/978-3-642-16161-2_6.

Lian Duan, L., Khoshneshin, M., Street, W. N., & Liu, M. (2013, March). Adverse drug effect *detection. IEEE Journal of Biomedical and Health Informatics, 17*(2), 305–311.

Liang, K., & Susilo, W. (2015). Searchable Attribute-Based Mechanism With Efficient Data Sharing for Secure Cloud Storage. In *IEEE Transactions on Information Forensics and Security*, Vol. 10, No. 9, pp. 1981–1992, 2015, September, doi: 10.1109/TIFS.2015.2442215.

Liu, X., & Chen, H. (2015). Identifying adverse drug events from patient social media: A case study for diabetes. *IEEE Intelligent Systems 30*(3), 44–51. https://doi.org/10.1109/MIS.2015.7

Manimala, K., Selvi, K., & Ahila, R. (2011). Hybrid soft computing techniques for feature selection and parameter optimization in power quality data mining. *Applied Soft Computing, 11*(8), 5485–5497.

Lambay, M. A., Jhansi Lakshmi, M., & Gamare, P. S. (2014). Sharing of personal health records securely in cloud computing with attribute based encryption. *International Journal of Computer Science and Information Technologies, 5*(5), 6864–6866.

Pal, S. K., Sardana, P. & Sardana, A. (2014). Efficient search on encrypted data using bloom filter. In *2014 International Conference on Computing for Sustainable*.

Santana, L., Silva, L., Canuto, A., Pintro, F., & Vale, K. (2010). A comparative analysis of genetic algorithm and ant colony optimization to select attributes for an heterogeneous ensemble of classifiers. 1–8. doi: 10.1109/CEC.2010. 5586080.

Sarker, A., & Gonzalez, G. (2015). Portable automatic text classification for adverse drug reaction detection via multi-corpus training. *Journal of Biomedical Informatics, 53*, 196–207.

State, L., & Cocianu, C. (2007). Data mining techniques in processing medical knowledge. *Journal of Applied Quantitative Methods, 2*(4), 524–532.

Thilakanathan, D., Calvo, R. A., Chen, S., Nepal, S., & Glozier, N. (2016). Facilitating secure sharing of personal health data in the cloud. *JMIR Med Inform. 4*(2), e15. Published 2016, May 27. doi:10.2196/medinform.4756.

Zhang, R., Xue, R., & Liu, L. (2019, July). Security and privacy on blockchain. *ACM Computing Surveys, 52*(3), Article 51, 34. https://doi.org/10.1145/3316481.

Chapter 14

Identity Management Using Blockchain in IoT Applications

Pooja Tripathi* and Aman Pradhan†

*Inderprastha Engineering College, Ghaziabad,
Uttar Pradesh, India*

*Pooja.tripathi@ipec.org.in

†Aman.pradhan@ipec.org.in

Abstract

To evaluate the efficiency of any system, a smart work monitoring system is required to ensure the accountability and reliability of each user in the process. The ever-growing pool of Internet of Things (IoT) devices poses not only new prospects and solutions as well new set of challenges for businesses in terms of security and privacy. The widespread adoption of these smart IoT-based solutions totally depends on the availability of platforms that ensure adequate sensor data integrity while ensuring adequate user privacy in organization. In light of these challenges, previous research suggests that the integration of IoT and blockchain technology is a good way to reduce data security problems arising in IoT. In this chapter, we have designed and developed a Real-Time Work Monitoring System for all RACI (Responsible, Accountable, Consultant, and Information) levels involved in the cleaning and maintenance process of Public Toilets and Community Toilet Complex (CTC). Evaluation results indicate that the proposed design will ensure tamper-resistant collection, processing, and conversion of IoT sensor data into a safe, scalable, and efficient manner.

Keywords: Blockchain, Wireless sensor network, Security, Identity management, IOT, Work monitoring, E-governance, Public toilet cleanliness system

1. Introduction

The implementation of Internet of Things (IoT)-based solutions makes innovative possibilities in many facets of our day-to-day activities, such as home mechanization for smart operations, smart conveyance system, and supply chain management (Ahmad *et al.*, 2018). IoT systems are gaining ground for the integration of various technologies (Bhattacharjee *et al.*, 2017). Generally, the IoT system comprises of hetero native devices that collect and convert, sensitive information into usable form to be used by various applications. Wireless networks are prone to outbreaks (Khan *et al.*, 2018; Sicari *et al.*, 2015) as a result of operating in a neglected environment and there is need to devise a mechanism for tamper-proof verification in addition to a fault-tolerant network of large types of IoT devices. Authors explored and evaluated blockchain (BT) as appropriate solutions having secured access control (Fernandez-Carames & Fraga-Lamas, 2018). Author proposed BT can be secure, for the distributed data as it has the power of computations by various peers who are ready to track, verify, and perform operations. This concept has already been used to conceptualize high-throughput cases for many easily accessible objects (Zheng *et al.*, 2019), such as navigation systems (Yuan & Wang, 2016), management of health records of citizens (Dubovitskaya *et al.*, 2017; Hang *et al.*, 2019; Gordon & Catalini, 2018), reorganized internet use (Paralkar *et al.*, 2018; Raval, 2016), and foretelling platforms (Brito *et al.*, 2014; MacDonald *et al.*, 2016). There are lots of benefits of blockchain such as good clarity, increased security, improved tracking, higher power, lower cost accounting, and no interventions of third party (Swan, 2015).

BT can be revolutionary in record systems and has been predicted as a growing technology that will play a major role in the visibility, scale, and, majorly in the data acquisition of IoT devices (Joshi & Gupta, 2019; Kshetri, 2017; Panarello *et al.*, 2018; Queiroz & Samuel, 2019; Wang *et al.*, 2019). The paper (George & Nikos, 2018) recommends a blockchain platform design for healthcare discussed insights in the technical requirements and challenges. Authors (Zhu & Badr, 2018) presented the perspective of blockchain generated statistics from the IoT and identified confidence requirements of such a system. Authors (Omar & Basir, 2018) focused on the identification of the need of building Identity Management (IDM) systems for IoT and then analyzing their philosophy and block-chain sovereign solutions and elaborated the challenges associated rang-ing from access control, privacy-preserving, trust, and performance. The paper (Ahmad *et al.*, 2018) handled the challenge of identity authentica-tion and developed a framework for identity creation and transfer of own-ership. Authors (Díaz *et al.*, 2016) introduced a new technique to improve IDM by introducing face recognition in blockchain in an integrated IoT cloud application. The paper (Ramakrishnan, 2017) discussed the use of IoT sensors in sending real-time information for rapid prototyping. Researchers (Nuss *et al.*, 2018) discussed the role of blockchain in addressing Identity Access Management challenges presented by IoT. The paper (Pavithran *et al.*, 2020) compared different blockchain implementa-tion and architecture and found device to device is better than gateway architecture.

The article suggests overall cleaning facilities in the society such as public toilets and sewage system (Agarwal, 2018) for the upgrading sani-tation. In this paper (Banait, 2019), the application of the various devices such as sensors for the detection of smell, amount of water in and opera-tion of exhaust in the presence of human and triggering an automatically flush for giving a comfortable experience to the user in the toilet. The author (Begam, 2019; Elavarasi, 2018) tried to enhance the cleanliness services by the use of sensors for detecting any presence of dirt or any foul smell in the toilet to raise an alarm for the management through a buzzer and an LCD and also used GSM module for location identification. The researcher has tried to use technologies for separation and recycling pur-poses of wastes and reuse as fertilizers and it has also suggested various ideas for reducing the consumption of water without the intervention of human beings (Hashemi, 2015; Katariya, 2018; Mithya, 2019; Muntashar, 2018). These articles utilized the various technologies using urine and stool of the individual for detecting the health status of the individual (Sangwan, 2017; Sudha, 2018).

A BT-based data sharing enables to track the change management of the data. Numerous copies are available of the Blocks, hence multiple users can validate the transactions and the block created for the changes on all data can be maintained in a network without the involvement of any mediator with proper privacy and security (Agyekum *et al.*, 2019; Cachin, 2016; Chen *et al.*, 2018; Kim & Laskowski, 2018; Li *et al.*, 2018, 2019;

Liang *et al.*, 2019; Lu & Xu, 2017; Nizamuddin *et al.*, 2019; Wu *et al.*, 2019; Zhu *et al.*, 2019). BT solves issues like traceability, transparency, trust, and accountability (Dai *et al.*, 2018; Nizamuddin *et al.*, 2019; Panescu & Manta, 2018; Wang *et al.*, 2018).

These papers contributions can be summarized as the adoption of the blockchain to authenticate the supervision and management of the cleanliness system of the public conveniences and ensure the usage of blockchain for enhanced accountability for the evaluation process. The IoT and blockchain have helped to achieve the identity of the consumers involved in the feedback evaluation system of real-time work monitoring. It adopts a max-min algorithm for the normalization of the feedbacks and directly evaluates and courses the collected reports about Toilets which helps in the classification of Toilets as Clean and Unclean.

2. Method

As part of the Swachh Bharat Mission, a lot of emphasis has been taken on cleanliness and to restrict open urination and Faeces. The government is constructing public toilets in major cities across the country. Approximately 57,000 toilets are already constructed and tagged on Google maps in 2,300 cities across India, making accessibility to public toilets much easier. Cleanliness and hygienic conditions maintained in the Toilets can avoid infections that can spread through the usage of dirty and infectious toilets. Public toilets at various locations have a huge amount of disease spreading viruses which can be a major concern for public safety. Public toilets may look clean, but they are full of germs that can cause health problems. As the infrastructure is in place now the major challenge for the government is to keep the maintenance of the Toilets and to monitor the real-time working of the Caretakers deputed for the same. To ensure that the toilet is kept clean while ensuring that management performs its functions efficiently; IoT devices are used to capture the real-time condition of the Toilets through aroma sensor and the turbidity sensor that detect any bad odor and dirty water. These sensors are connected to a NodeMCU microcontroller that monitors changes and feeds them to a database that can be accessed by administrators via the mobile app. This is done using a Wi-Fi module. In this way, toilet monitoring is done effectively and the availability of collected data can be easily analyzed for further action.

The basic architecture of the Real-time work Authentication System is shown in Figure 1.

As Figure 1 shows, the Design Architecture of the Real-time work Monitoring System through Permissioned Chain framework. The system composes of different types of entities (Care Taker, User, Supervisor) and consists of Five modules (Sensor Node, Client App, Caretaker App, Supervisor App, and Central Monitoring System) based on the permissioned BT structure. To understand the required system, the Architecture of the BT in a Real-time Work Authentication System is shown in Figure 2.

2.1 *Permissioned blockchain*

The structure based on permissioned BT consists of various nodes demonstrating multiple users and regulatory nodes. Registered users acquire different authorizations and permissions including caretakers, Clients, supervisors, and regulators generate Ecerts.

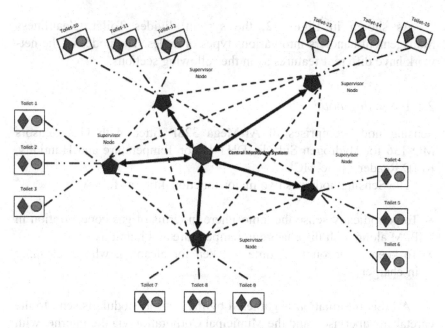

Figure 1. The Design Architecture of the Real-Time Work Monitoring System Using BT

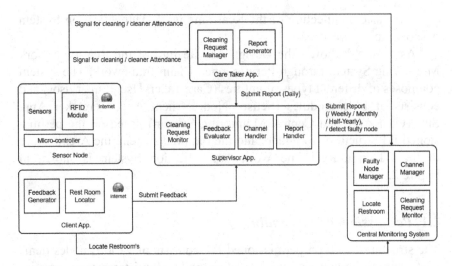

Figure 2. System Architecture of the Blockchain Technology in Real-Time Work Authentication System

As shown in Figure 2, the system divides Toilet Cleanliness Management handlers into various types of nodes. The nodes of the network have different features as in the following sections.

2.1.1 *Sensing node*

Sensing node comprises of AT-Mega 328P fitted with Gas Sensors MQ-136 for Hydrogen Sulfide, DHT-11 for Temperature and Humidity, RFID Reader, Node-MCU.

The Sensing node has two major functionalities as follows:

- To periodically sense the atmosphere in terms of gas concentration in PPM along with the change in temperature and humidity.
- To keep an account of, time is taken for cleaning, who is cleaning in-charger.

All this information is gathered by the Sensor Module is send to the caretaker, supervisor, and the Municipal Corporation via the internet with help of Node-MCU.

2.1.2 *Client/user application*

Client applications provided with two functionalities:

a. Feedback Generator: The application will focus majorly on users' given rating about the restroom they have used. The user has to give the feedback based on four major parameters: restroom order, availability of soap, and properly lilted or not. Users have the option that they feel missing/inappropriate. Users can also give feedback on cleanliness of the mirror, cleanliness of the floor, disposable garbage bags empty or not, and the sink is clean or not and so on.

b. Restroom Locator: User can also locate the nearest restroom from their place, and can also check the usability status of the restroom, availability of amenities (like soap, water, sanitary napkins, etc.).

2.1.3 *Care taker application*

Care Taker's applications have two major components:

a. Cleanliness Request Manager: It receives the cleaning token from its respective restroom whenever the presence of Ammonia and Hydrogen Sulfide reaches its threshold values. Whenever the application receives the token, it displays the details of the cleaner who is the in-charge of cleaning.

b. Report Generator: This component helps to generate a cleanliness report of the restroom in following parameters — major parameters: restroom order, availability of soap, availability of soap, and properly lilted or not and minor parameters: cleanliness of the mirror, cleanliness of the floor, disposable garbage bags empty or not, the and the sink is clean or not on daily bases and send to its respective supervisor.

2.1.4 *Supervisor application*

Supervisor application is consisting of four major modules:

a. *Cleaning Request Monitor*: It receives the cleaning token from different restrooms that are under its jurisdiction and keep a record of that.

Along with that to keep an account of, time is taken for cleaning and who is cleaning in-charge for further requirements.

b. *Feedback Evaluator*: It's a part of report handler. To evaluate the feedback, send by the user for each restroom, we are proposing a model to classify the restroom based on usability. This module takes user feedback in terms of the following parameters: restroom order, availability of soap, availability of soap, and properly lilted or not.

c. *Channel Manager*: This module is used to handle and manage this application in the permissioned blockchain channel (hyper ledger), perform consensus, add a block in the blockchain, and other permissioned blockchain operations.

d. *Report Handler*: It uses to generate weekly/monthly/half-yearly report about the restroom comes under its jurisdiction.

2.1.5 *Central monitoring system*

a. *Faulty Node Manager*: It's a part of Channel Manager. It helps to handle the faulty nodes in the permissioned blockchain channel (hyper ledger).

b. *Channel Manager*: It monitors the permissioned blockchain channel and manages the activities involved in it, like creating channels, providing membership, providing certificates, handle faulty nodes, etc.

c. *Locate Restroom*: This module will give the location of the restroom to the user.

d. *Cleaning Request Monitor*: it receives the cleaning token from different restrooms that are under its jurisdiction and keep a record of that. Along with that to keep an account of, time is taken for cleaning and who is cleaning in-charger, for further requirements.

The blockchain-based system has many advantages compared to traditional methods, such as distributional, detestable, security, transparency, and tracking facilities have been used in real-time work monitoring and authentication system. It provides the following capabilities for the decision-making process:

1. Transparency and alter resistance: BT has a list of ever-expanding records, called blocks, connected and protected using cryptography. Each block typically contains a hash pointer such as a previous

block link, timestamp. All transaction information is kept in blocks that are publically available to administrators and cannot be transformed.

2. Answerability and confidentiality: The block-based work monitoring and authentication system provides a reliable platform for collecting information from the users and caretakers. The identity of the users is not known during the screening process. So they do not have to worry about their identity being disclosed or the content of their ideas being mature.

3. Authorization and consent: BT features can offer unique control permissions through contracts. Central Monitoring Nodes gain higher authority than standard nodes in permissioned blockchain-based system, building it better for users to monitor and manage.

4. Chaincode: The permissioned network provides system logic for smart contracts as chain codes. Smart contracts run on a BT-based node and can be done automatically by calling chaincode. In the process, users complete transactions and validate via chaincode at a very low cost.

3. Implementation of Work Monitoring System

3.1 *Feedback evaluation module*

It is part of the Supervisor Application. This module uses to evaluate the feedback given by the user, who had accessed the restrooms. Feedback form is provided to the user in their User Application.

Users are provided with eight parameters, among them four are major parameters and four are minor parameters, and the user has to select only those parameters, which they feel are worst/not appropriate.

Major parameters	Minor parameters
Order of the restroom, availability of water, availability of soap, and properly lited or not.	The garbage bag is empty or not, the floor is clean and dry, the sink is clean and empty, and the mirror is clean and wiped.

Feedback Evaluation Module has three phases: 1. Feedback Gathering Phase, 2. Feedback Normalization and Report Evaluation, Phase 3. Restroom Classification Phase.

3.2 *Phase I: Feedback gathering phase*

The user using user Application can give feedback on any restroom she/ he had used. When they give feedback, the feedback will be received by the nearest supervisor application server to the user in format. After receiving the request, the application server will check, whether the feedback belongs to the restroom, comes under its jurisdiction or not, with help of ToiletID attached to it. If it comes under it accepts the feedback send it for further processing and if it is not, then search for the supervisor under which that restroom belongs and propagates the feedback to that supervisor application server via the blockchain channel (as shown in Figure 3).

3.3 *Phase II: Feedback normalization and report evaluation phase*

After receiving feedback and checking its destination, feedbacks are transferred to Phase II Feedback Normalization and Report Evaluation Phase. This Phase has two major functionalities. A. Feedback Normalization and B. Report Evaluation Phase.

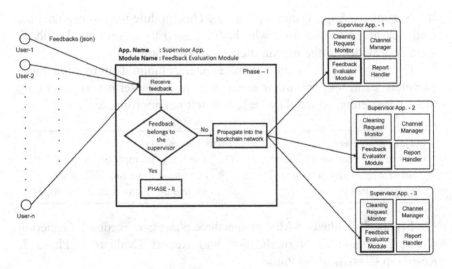

Figure 3.   Phase I: Feedback Gathering Phase

3.3.1 *Feedback normalization*

Feedbacks that the supervisor application server receives are in Boolean format, which means if the user is not satisfied with the service then only, they will select the parameter (i.e., parameter = 1) otherwise leaves unchecked (i.e., parameter = 0). If we consider that only 10% out of 50,000 users of public toilets gave feedback, then also, we will receive 5,000 feedbacks, consisting of 5,000 arrays of Boolean data (0/1) from one restroom on daily basis. So, to manage the huge amount of data, we need to normalize it to ease our calculation. To do so, we had used max-min normalization and normalize each parameter (major-minor) within the range of 0–10.

3.3.2 *Report evaluation phase*

There we make a comparison between the rating given by the user for the restroom and the rating given by the caretaker for the same, for each cleanliness parameter (major-minor). And to do so we have generated the formula as shown in Figure 4.

By this, we add a flag of accept/reject, to each parameter. And then we pass this to the next phase for the classification of the restroom.

3.4 *Phase III: Restroom classification phase through feedback evaluation module*

Here we receive the parameter status of all the restrooms, from the above phase, and based on the status of each parameter we classify the restroom

```
 1   if ((((Tpi - Upi) - Epi) > 1)
 2        Accept
 3
 4   else      if ((((Tpi - Upi) - Epi) =< 1 && ((Upi - Epi) > 2 || (Upi - Epi) > -2))
 5                   Reject
 6             else
 7                   Accept
 8
 9   //  Tpi = maximum range for the 'ith' parameter
10   //  Upi = rating given by user for the 'ith' parameter
11   //  Tpi = rating given by care taker for the 'ith' parameter
12
```

Figure 4.   Snippet of Formulae Used to Implement the Functions of the Feedback Evaluation Phase

```
1    if (Tp1 == accept && Tp2 == accept && Tp3 == accept && Tp4 == accept)
2        restroom_tag = "usbale";
3    else
4        restroom_tag = "not usbale";
5
6    //   Tp1 = order of the restroom,
7    //   Tp2 = availability of water,
8    //   Tp3 = availability of soap, and
9    //   Tp4 = properly lilted or not.
10
```

Figure 5.   Snippet of Formulae Used to Implement the Functions of the Classification of Toilets.

into usable and non-usable, and to do so we use the logic as shown in Figure 5.

After classifying the restrooms, we persist this information in the database.

4. Implementation of the Permissioned Blockchain for Real-Time Work Authentication System

Permissioned BT helps to maintain the Integrity, Correctness, and Immutability of Data through distributed control and information distribution platform that empowers multiple commanding domains, which may or may not know each other, to cooperate, coordinate, and cooperate in a rational decision-making process. Along with that, it also ensures the availability of data, since it uses distributed architectural design.

Two types of network participants are going to perform transactions in the blockchain. The details of network participants (also called Peer Nodes) with their functionalities are as follows (Figure 6):

Supervisor — Supervisor Application Server with functionalities as generating Report on a weekly, daily basis, Receive Report (from caretaker) on daily basis, Validate Report from user feedback on weekly basis, Execute consensuses, Update new participants of the network (validated by CMS) (Figure 7).

Municipal Corporation — Central Monitoring System (CMS): Its major functions are acting as Membership Service Provider (MSP), Acting as Network Certificate Authority (CA), Handling Faulty Peer nodes, Creating blockchain's block. For performing all the blockchain activates shown at the CMS, we had introduced a Channel Manager module, in the CMS (Figure 8).

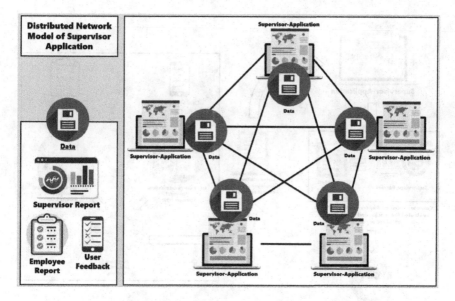

Figure 6. Distributed Network Model of Supervisor

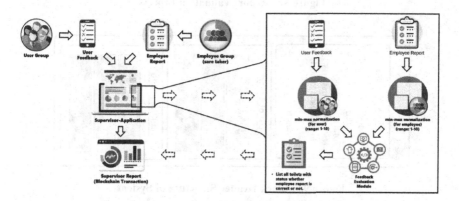

Figure 7. Feedback Collection Process

4.1 *Block structure*

It is a data structure, which carries the supervisor's report for inclusion in the public ledger, known as a blockchain. The block comprises a block header; containing various information regarding the data, followed by a long list of the report submitted by different supervisors and a list of faults detected in the reports.

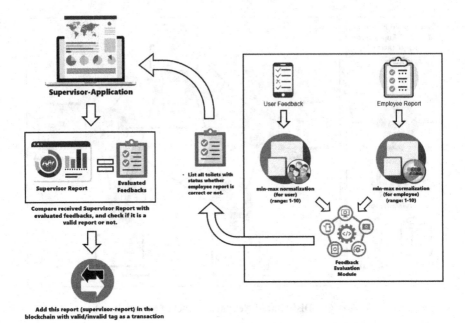

Figure 8.   Report Validation Process

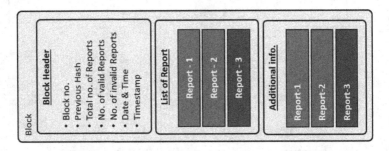

Figure 9.   Block Header Structure of System

4.2 *Block header*

The block header comprises two sets of block data (Figure 9).

In the first set of data, there is the hash of the current block and, a mention to a preceding block hash, which ties this block to the preceding block, lying in the blockchain. And, the next set of metadata relates to the validation status of reports, date and time of block generation, and time-stamp (time taken to develop a block).

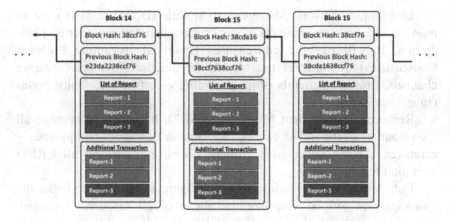

Figure 10. Blockchain Structure of the Developed System

4.3 *Blockchain structure*

All nodes connected in peer preserve a replica of the blockchain locally, starting from the beginning block (Figure 10). The local copy of the blockchain constantly updates as new blocks are discovered and added on the chain. As a chain figures the addition of new blocks from the network, it will certify these blocks first, whether the block came from the legitimate node or not, and then tie them to the present blockchain.

5. Results and Discussion

Real-Time work Authentication system will serve the municipality officials, to keep an eye on the operations and maintenances work of toilet/restrooms, work authenticity of their human resource, etc. For providing these facilities, it has the following modules.

Token Management Module (TMM), Resource Management Module (RMM-2), Distributed Network Management Module (DNMM), and Data Visualization Module (DVM).

Token Management Module (TMM): It will receive a cleaning token from its respective restroom whenever the presence of Ammonia and Hydrogen Sulfide reaches its threshold values. As soon as the application receives the token, it displays the details of the cleaner who is the in-charge of cleaning.

Distributed Network Management Module (DNMM): It is used to monitor and manage a network of supervisors that comes under its jurisdiction. It will run the consensuses (Practical Byzantine Problem Consensuses). It manages the blockchain functionalities like creating channels, providing membership, providing e-certificates, faulty nodes (supervisor), etc.

Resource Management Module (RMM-2): It is used to manage all the resources of the public toilets, like Human Resources (Employee — caretaker, cleaner, supervisor), Toilets, Users, etc. perform all CRUD operation for them.

Data Visualization Module (DVM) (Figure 11): it uses to make the municipalities official visualize the status of all resources engaged. Like the number of clean–unclean toilets, vailed–invalid reports made by the supervisor, caretaker, improvement in sanitary rate week-by-week, month-by-month, and year-by-year.

All supervisor applications are the participant of this permissioned blockchain network called Node which is operated under the central monitoring unit (CMU). To update the records, CMU runs the consensuses mechanism. CMU selects one node (supervisor application) from the

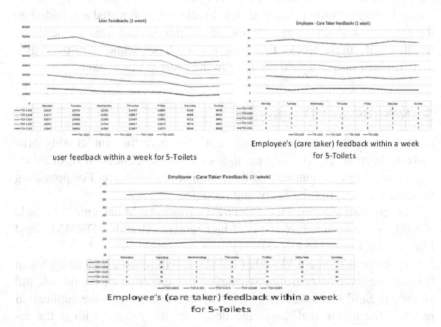

Figure 11.   Data Visualization Tool

TOI-1321   TOI-1322   TOI-1323

TOI-1324   TOI-1321

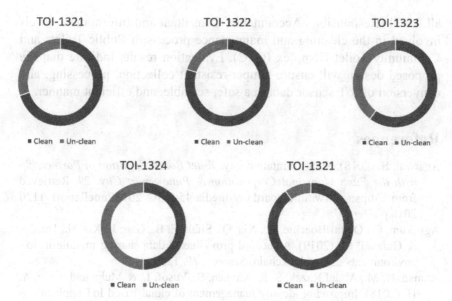

Figure 12.   Number of Clean/Unclean Toilets under a Supervisor

network and asks it to generate a new block. The committer node (select supervisor applications) and other nodes (remaining supervisor application) will share Data that consists of their components, supervisor report, user feedback, and employee (caretaker) feedbacks among each other. This data will be sent to Feedback Management Module (FMM) where Feedback Evaluation System (FES) take these data as an input, process it and list of toilets with a tag of valid/invalid report as an output.

After getting the output, every supervisor application will prepare a General Report (except supervisor application/committer node) and sent it to the committer node back. Then the committer node with help of the Distributed Network Management Module (DNMM), will include these General Reports output in the block as a transaction. After adding all the transaction in the block it adds the block its blockchain and broadcast that block into the network (to CMS also) and let the participant add that block into their blockchain (Figure 12).

6. Conclusions

This chapter presents the BT-based secure data distribution structure. We design and develop a Real-Time Work Monitoring System (RTWMS) for all RACI (Responsible, Accountable, Consultant and Information) levels involved in the cleaning and maintenance process of Public Toilets and Community Toilet Complex (CTC). Evaluation results indicate that the proposed design will ensure tamper-resistant collection, processing, and conversion of IoT sensor data in a safe, scalable, and efficient manner.

References

Agarwal, S. (2018). Smart sanitation city. *Toilet Board Coalition in Partnership with the Pune Municipal Corporation & Pune Smart City*, 29. Retrieved from https://www.toiletboard.org/media/45-TBC_2018PuneReport_1120 2018.pdf?v=1.0.1.

Agyekum, O., Opuni-Boachie, K., Xia, Q., Sifah, E. B., Gao, J., Xia, H., Du, X., & Guizani, M. (2019). A secured proxy-based data sharing module in IoT environments using blockchain. *Sensors*, *19*, 1235.

Ahmad, N. M., Abdul Razak, S. F., Kannan, S., Yusof, I., & Muhamad Amin, A. H. (2018). Improving identity management of cloud-based IoT applications using blockchain. *2018 International Conference on Intelligent and Advanced System (ICIAS)*, Kuala Lumpur, pp. 1–6, doi: 10.1109/ICIAS.2018.8540564.

Ahmad, S., Hang, L., & Kim, D. H. (2018). Design and implementation of cloud-centric configuration repository for DIY IoT applications. *Sensors*, *18*, 474.

Banait, P. (2019). Automatic washroom cleaning system. *International Journal of Scientific Research in Computer Science, Engineering and Information Technology*, *3*.

Begam, S. A. (2019). Design of smart washroom system for clean and green environment. *International Journal of Research in Advent Technology*, *7*.

Bhattacharjee, S., Salimitari, M., Chatterjee, M., Kwiat, K., & Kamhoua, C. (November 6–10, 2017). Preserving data integrity in IoT networks under opportunistic data manipulation. In *Proceedings of the 15th IEEE International Conference on Dependable, Autonomic and Secure Computing, 15th International Conference on Pervasive Intelligence & Computing, 3rd International Conference on Big Data Intelligence and Computing and Cyber Science and Technology Congress* (DASC/PiCom/DataCom/ CyberSciTech), Orlando, FL, USA, pp. 446–453.

Brito, J., Shadab, H. B., Castillo O'Sullivan, A. (2014). Bitcoin financial regulation: Securities, derivatives, prediction markets, and gambling. *The Columbia Science and Technology Law Review (STLR)*.

Cachin, C. (July 25–29, 2016). Architecture of the hyperledger blockchain fabric. In *Proceedings of the Workshop on Distributed Cryptocurrencies and Consensus Ledgers*, Chicago, IL, USA.

Chen, H., Li, S., Wu, P., Yi, N., Li, S., & Huang, X. (2018). Fine-grained sentiment analysis of Chinese reviews using LSTM network. *The Journal of Engineering Science and Technology Review (JESTR)*, *11*, 5.

Dai, M., Zhang, S., Wang, H., & Jin, S. (2018). A low storage room requirement framework for distributed ledger in the blockchain. *IEEE Access*, *6*, 22970–22975.

Díaz, M., Martín, C., & Rubio, B. (2016). State-of-the-art, challenges, and open issues in the integration of internet of things and cloud computing. *The Journal of Network and Computer Applications*, *67*, 99–117.

Dubovitskaya, A., Xu, Z., Ryu, S., Schumacher, M., & Wang, F. (November 4–8, 2017). Secure and trustable electronic medical records sharing using blockchain. In *Proceedings of the AMIA 2017*. American Medical Informatics Association Annual Symposium: Washington, DC, USA.

Elavarasi, K. (2018). Developing smart toilets using IoT. *International Journal of Pure and Applied Mathematics*, *7*.

Fernandez-Carames, T. M., & Fraga-Lamas, P. (2018). A review on the use of blockchain for the internet of things. *IEEE Access*, *6*, 32979–33001.

Gordon, W. J., & Catalini, C. (2018). Blockchain technology for healthcare: Facilitating the transition to patient-driven interoperability. *Computational and Structural Biotechnology Journal*, *16*, 224–230.

Hang, L., Choi, E., & Kim, D.-H. (2019). A novel EMR integrity management based on a medical blockchain platform in hospital. *Electronics*, *8*, 467.

Hashemi, S. (2015). Innovative toilet technologies for smart and green cities. In *8th Conference of the International Forum on Urbanism*, *7*.

Joshi, A. D., & Gupta, S. M. (2019). Evaluation of design alternatives of end-of-life products using the internet of things. *International Journal of Production Economics*, *208*, 281–293.

Katariya, D. (2018). Smart toilet. *International Journal of Electrical, Electronics, and Data Communication*, *4*.

Khan, M. A., & Salah, K. (2018). IoT security: Review, blockchain solutions, and open challenges. *Future Generation Computer Systems*, *82*, 395–411.

Kim, H. M., & Laskowski, M. (2018). Toward an ontology-driven blockchain design for supply-chain provenance. *Intelligent Systems in Accounting Finance and Management*, *25*, 18–27.

Kshetri, N. (2017). Can blockchain strengthen the internet of things? *IT Professional*, *19*, 68–72.

Li, J., Wang, X., Huang, Z., Wang, L., & Xiang, Y. (2019). Multi-level multi-secret sharing scheme for decentralized e-voting in cloud computing. *Journal of Parallel and Distributed Computing*, *130*, 91–97.

Li, J., Wu, J., & Chen, L. (2018). Block-secure: Blockchain-based scheme for secure P2P cloud storage. *Information Sciences*, *465*, 219–231.

Liang, W., Tang, M., Long, J., Peng, X., Xu, J., & Li, K. C. (2019). A secure fabric blockchain-based data transmission technique for industrial internet-of-things. *IEEE Transactions on Industrial Informatics, 15*, 358–3592.

Lu, Q., & Xu, X. (2017). Adaptable blockchain-based systems: A case study for product traceability. *IEEE Software, 34*, 21–27.

MacDonald, T. J., Allen, D. W. E., & Potts, J. (2016). Blockchains and the boundaries of self-organized economies: Predictions for the future of banking. In *Banking Beyond Banks and Money*. Tasca, P., Aste, T., Pelizzon, L., & Perony, N., (Eds.), Springer: Cham, Switzerland, pp. 279–296.

Mithya, V. (2019). Smart toilets using turbidity sensor. *International Journal of Innovative Technology and Exploring Engineering (IJITEE), 5*.

Muntashar, N. (2018). Smart urinal mechautomatic flush. *Journal of Emerging Technologies and Innovative Research (JETIR), 4*.

Nizamuddin, N., Hasan, H., Salah, K., & Iqbal, R. (2019). Blockchain-based framework for protecting author royalty of digital assets. *Arabian Journal for Science and Engineering, 44*, 3849–3866.

Nizamuddin, N., Salah, K., Azad, M. A., Arshad, J., & Rehman, M. H. (2019). Decentralized document version control using ethereum blockchain and IPFS. *Computers & Electrical Engineering, 76*, 183–197.

Nuss, M., Puchta, A., & Kunz, M. (2018). Towards blockchain-based identity and access management for the internet of things in enterprises. In *Proceedings of the International Conference on Trust and Privacy in Digital Business*. Springer International Publishing, Cham, 167–181.

Omar, A. S., & Basir, O. (2018). Identity management in IoT networks using blockchain and smart contracts. In *2018 IEEE International Conference on Internet of Things (iThings) and IEEE Green Computing and Communications (GreenCom) and IEEE Cyber, Physical and Social Computing (CPSCom) and IEEE Smart Data (SmartData)*, Halifax, NS, Canada, pp. 994–1000, doi: 10.1109/Cybermatics_2018.2018.00187.

Panarello, A., Tapas, N., Merlino, G., Longo, F., & Puliafito, A. (2018). Blockchain and IoT integration: A systematic survey. *Sensors, 18*, 2575.

Panescu, A. T., & Manta, V. (2018). Smart contracts for research data rights management over the ethereum blockchain network. *Science and Technology Libraries, 37*, 235–245.

Paralkar, K., Yadav, S., Kumari, S., Kulkarni, A., & Pingat, S. P. (2018). Photogroup: Decentralized web application using ethereum blockchain. *International Research Journal of Engineering and Technology, 5*, 489–492.

Pavithran, D., Shaalan, K., Al-Karaki, J. N. *et al.* (2020). Towards building a blockchain framework for IoT. *Cluster Computing*. https://doi.org/10.1007/s10586-020-03059-5.

Polyzos, G. C., & Fotiou, N. (2017). Blockchain-assisted information distribution for the internet of things. In *2017 IEEE International Conference on Information Reuse and Integration (IRI)*, pp. 75–78, doi: 10.1109/IRI.2017.83.

Queiroz, M. M., & Samuel, F. W. (2019). Blockchain adoption challenges in the supply chain: An empirical investigation of the main drivers in India and the USA. *International Journal of Information and Management, 46*, 70–82.

Ramakrishnan R., (2017). Innovation in product design: IoT objects driven new product innovation and prototyping using 3D printers. *The Internet of Things in the Modern Business Environment*, 189–209. doi: 10.4018/978-1-5225-2104-4.ch010.

Raval, S. (2016). *Decentralized Applications: Harnessing Bitcoin's Blockchain Technology*, O'Reilly Media, Inc.: Sebastopol, CA, USA.

Sangwan, S. (2017). Smart toilet — An IoT solution. *International Journal of Advanced Research in Science and Engineering, 5*.

Sicari, S., Rizzardi, A., Grieco, L. A., & Coen-Porisini, A. (2015). Security privacy, and trust in the internet of things: The road ahead. *Computer Networks, 76*, 146–164.

Sudha, V. (2018). A survey on the modern technologies used in public toilets. *International Journal of Recent Technology and Engineering (IJRTE), 2*.

Swan, M. (2015). *Blockchain: Blueprint for a New Economy*. O'Reilly Media, Inc.: Sebastopol, CA, USA.

Wang, S., Zhang, Y., & Zhang, Y. (2018). A blockchain-based framework for data sharing with fine-grained access control in decentralized storage systems. *IEEE Access, 6*, 38437–38450.

Wang, Y., Singgih, M., Wang, J., & Rit, M. (2019). Making sense of blockchain technology: How will it transform supply chains? *International Journal of Production Economics, 211*, 221–236.

Wu, A., Zhang, Y., Zheng, X., Guo, R., Zhao, Q., & Zheng, D. (2019). Efficient and privacy-preserving traceable attribute-based encryption in the blockchain. *Annals of Telecommunications, 74*, 401–411.

Yuan, Y., & Wang, F. Y. (November 1–4, 2016). Towards blockchain-based intelligent transportation systems. In *Proceedings of the 2016 IEEE 19th International Conference on Intelligent Transportation Systems (ITSC)*, Rio de Janeiro, Brazil, pp. 2663–2668.

Zheng, Z., Xie, S., Dai, H. N., & Wang, H. (2018). Blockchain challenges and opportunities: A survey. *International Journal Web and Grid Services, 14*(4), 352–375.

Zhu, L., Wu, Y., Gai, K., & Choo, K. K. R. (2019). Controllable, and trustworthy blockchain-based cloud data management. *Future Generation Computer Systems, 91*, 527–535.

Zhu, X., & Badr, Y. (2018). Identity management systems for the internet of things: A survey towards blockchain solutions. *Sensors, 18*(12), 4215; https://doi.org/10.3390/s18124215.

Zonyin Shae, & Jeffrey J. P. Tsai (2017). On the design of a blockchain platform for clinical trial and precision medicine. In *IEEE 37th International Conference on Distributed Computing Systems (ICDCS)*.

Chapter 15

Digital Anonymity in Decentralized Environment

Ashish Seth[*,‡] and Kirti Seth[†,§]

Inha University, Incheon, South Korea
†Inha University in Tashkent, Tashkent, Uzbekistan

‡*ashish_may13@rediffmail.com*

§*k.seth@inha.uz*

Abstract

Privacy has become a huge point of contention in recent days with tech organizations, such as Google and Facebook, which make a great deal of revenue from monetizing user data, coming into conflict with regulatory bodies such as the European Data Protection Board. So, there may be two research questions that can be raised in terms of privacy and user experience. First, what are the tradeoffs when using efficient and integrated centralized systems in exchange for giving up vast amounts of personal information? Second, how does this apply to cryptocurrencies and blockchains? In blockchains, each person has a set of identities with which they interact with the blockchain. This means that a user's privacy will be reduced if their virtual identities can be linked to their real one. Hence, one can increase their privacy through anonymity, masking their identity; can gain access to some service while minimizing how much information they reveal about their real identity.

Keywords: Decentralization, Blockchain, Anonymity, Privacy, Mixing

1. Introduction to Decentralized Environment

Any software system comprises of three basic entities: an application, data, and the infrastructure. In general, the centralized environment keep holds on the applications, the data that is used in the application and the infrastructure on which the entire application runs. It means all the components or entities of a system are governed or controlled by the central authority. On the other hand, decentralization, in general has been applied to management science, political science, law and public administration, economics, group dynamics, and technology. It is the process by which the activities of an organization, particularly those regarding planning and decision making are distributed or delegated away from a central, authoritative location, or group. Figure 1, shows how centralized and decentralized systems differ from each other.

Decentralization can mean a different thing to a lot of different people. In the context of computing, it has been refereed frequently with blockchain and cryptocurrencies. In this perspective, "decentralized" refer to things such as access authorization, organizational governance, process computation, fintech, wealth instruments, etc. In this chapter, we take it in perspective of computing resources, user rights, privacy, security, and access privileges. According to Eric Elliott (2013), Computing is decentralized when critical application services are carried out by individual computing devices or nodes on a distributed network, with no central location. If you can't point to a single service address and disable

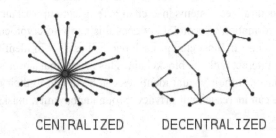

CENTRALIZED   DECENTRALIZED

Figure 1. Centralized Systems and Decentralized Systems

it to shut down core application functionality for all users, then you have a decentralized computing architecture.

To gain some perspective, let's look at the origin of Bitcoin and block-chain. We know that cypherpunks were individuals who advocated for privacy using cryptography, and that Satoshi Nakamoto appealed to this mentality with the publishing of the Bitcoin whitepaper in 2008 and subsequent release in 2009. Bitcoin was designed as the first ever decentralized, pseudonymous, and trustless system for transactions, and the way it achieved that was with a blockchain.

Initially, in designing Bitcoin, its creators wanted to get as far as possible from having any central entity, so they intended for every entity in Bitcoin to have the ability to be just as powerful as anyone else. They allowed anyone to store the blockchain. This means that everyone has everyone's data. Users can see which addresses interact with each other, how much cryptocurrency each address has, and the like. Considering the normal user which may not go out of their way to obfuscate their digital identity and activities with additional protection, it's easy to see how their transaction history and balance can be exposed to their detriment.

2. Anonymity and Pseudo-Anonymity in Digital World

When we talk about anonymity, we generally talk about hiding illicit information. But in the context of cryptography or computing, it actually means about data protection. Anonymity refers to situation where any related information and the person neither can be linked nor identified. There arise few questions that are to be answered. Following are the questions:

- Does anonymity is desired by criminals and rebels or it is also a need of common individual in today's internet world?
- Is anonymity only good for buying drugs?
- For any legal business or legal financial transaction, does still makes sense to remain anonymous?

Let's look at the situation, for example, two friends Anna and Bobby went to a restaurant for lunch. All the bills are paid by Anna. After coming back the two friends decided to divide the bill among themselves and so Bobby give cryptocurrency to Anna equivalent to his share. After some days when Anna tried to use this digital currency, he was shocked to know that his payment was denied by the vendor. Further, he was also informed by the vendor that this cryptocurrency was generated from some illegal source. Now this is definitely not a good situation for two obvious reasons as follows:

1. Anna have a doubt about his friend Bobby's transactions.
2. It also raised a question about fungibility of the digital currency.

Fungibility provides the equivalency among the two different currencies. It means that every unit of currency must be equal in value to every other unit. For example, consider dealing in cash, a dollar is a dollar. Fungibility is a crucial property of currency; in the above-mentioned scenario, we probably want to enable anonymity when vendors refuse to accept one unit of cryptocurrency over another, it reduces the fungibility of the currency and makes life harder for us.

Pseudo-anonymity refers to abstract identity, which means an individual wish to retain a reputation against anonymity. Blockchains are not anonymous by default. Fundamentally, blockchains take a central database and distribute it. However, this now means that you no longer have strong access control over your own data. All of the data stored in the blockchain is public by default, so everyone sees everything which means that there's no sense of guaranteed privacy. Private or permissioned blockchains are slightly more anonymous since read access to the database can be restricted.

Since the challenges of privacy in publicly readable databases are much more difficult and novel. Most blockchains are pseudoanymous, we use a publicly viewable but arbitrary identifier such as your Bitcoin address. These identifiers are called pseudonyms. However, keeping your real name out of your identifier does not guarantee anonymity.

A pseudonym only implies that a user is not using their real identity, such as their name, email, or other personally identifying information. As such, it is very well possible to have this pseudonym linked to some real-world identity. For example, because all transactions are public on the blockchain, if even a single transaction by some Bitcoin address is linked to an actual identity, all other transactions conducted under that pseudonym are now connected to the real identity as well. All histories of transactions and any other activity that has been recorded on the blockchain all originally had no connection to a real person and only to a pseudonym.

Most blockchains, including Bitcoin, are pseudonymous. If we design our blockchain system to be decentralized, then what that means is that more of your data is in the network, for people to publicly access. We know decentralization implies everyone has equal control of everything. So, more people will see your pseudonym. The more of your data that is on the network though, the more data that's available to possibly deanonymize you. This seems to show a slight paradox, where security and anonymity and privacy are harder and harder to ensure, if we really want to be decentralized. However, with one single connection between a pseudonym and a real life identity, everything in their history can now be linked to the person that identity belongs to.

3. Anonymity in Blockchain

Cryptocurrencies offer the advantage of privacy, it mainly offers three advantages over fiat money:

1.   Censorship resistance
2.   Decentralized control
3.   User privacy

Throughout the years, many conversations within the space seem to have been focused on issues that affect all users, such as global scalability, and enterprise blockchain solutions rather than placing an emphasis on privacy. We have seen that the Cypherpunks, though great inspiration for the principles of Bitcoin, aren't as often referenced as enterprise leaders when talking about cryptocurrencies and blockchain. Arguably, extensive privacy has always held a place within a more niche audience because of its difficulty to directly monetize.

Scalable cryptocurrency is the need of the day. Scalability is needed to make technology usable and accessible on a big scale, but it is observed that users do not want to sacrifice privacy for performance

For example, we can have a number of users who want to use cryptocurrency but out of these users how many will reveal their identity at first place? It is necessary to evaluate and analyze the advantage and cost of privacy. Cryptocurrency and blockchain can enhance privacy for their users.

Here are some recent quotes from influential people in the whole space of crypto for privacy.

Some Interesting Quotes

"I think Satoshi would barf or at least work on a replacement for Bitcoin as he first described it in 2008–2009." — Timothy May

"Privacy isn't a thing you achieve; it's a constant cat-and-mouse battle" — Riccardo Spagni

"You have a permanent record of everything taking place. If, down the road, someone finds a vulnerability that you can reveal what happened in the past, you may still be at risk." — Nicolas Christin

---

This is true in that you just don't simply achieve privacy — or it's not that likely that you can just achieve privacy. That's a pretty pessimistic outlook, but that's from the perspective of crypto anarchists. And while that cause was the motivating factor for creating Bitcoin in the first place, the average user probably doesn't strongly align that ideology.

Privacy is a major challenge. But in general, it's actually more of a matter of security than of privacy. Privacy has become a huge point of contention in recent days with tech organizations such as Google and Facebook, which make a great deal of revenue from monetizing user data, coming into conflict with regulatory bodies such as the European Data Protection Board. So clearly, there exist questions in terms of privacy and user experience.

1. What are the tradeoffs when using efficient and integrated centralized systems in exchange for giving up vast amounts of personal information?
2. How does this apply to cryptocurrencies and blockchains?

In blockchains, each person has a set of identities with which they interact with the blockchain. This means that a user's privacy will be reduced if their virtual identities can be linked to their real one.

Hence, they can increase their privacy through anonymity, masking their identity, allowing them to gain access to some service while minimizing how much information they reveal about their real identity.

Now let's consider an example. Assume Andy is very rich, and while making payment via cryptocurrency, store cashier noticed that you're wallet contains approx. $60 million Bitcoin. This greedy cashier may plan to kidnap Andy's family member and he knows exactly how much money to blackmail Andy for. Though this is imaginary situation but this is very much possible to happen in this real world. Even though Andy did nothing wrong, the exposure of the information about his transaction history and financial standing put him in danger.

4. Deanonymization: Link between Virtual Identities and the Real-World Entity

In Bitcoin, and some other blockchain platforms, it's generally best practice not to reuse pseudonyms. You could generate a new address every time you receive Bitcoin without much cost. With a different address for each transaction, there will be no way to link each of these Bitcoin addresses together. This separates the activity of each pseudonym. Hence, for someone to figure out all your Bitcoin activity, they'd have to connect you to each of your pseudonyms, not just an individual one.

This would be like creating a new account every time you leave a comment. Although it is more inconvenient to do so, it increases the difficulty of linking your accounts together, making it much harder for others to track your activity. This does introduce the slight hitch that one would have to keep track of each of these identities, but that can be easily resolved using wallet software, which often performs this by default. Just generate a new address every time you receive any cryptocurrency, or each time you use any sort of blockchain application! While this technique might be possible in Bitcoin and some other blockchain applications, it's not possible in Ethereum. And that's because Ethereum is account based, not UTXO based.

In Bitcoin, you could just generate a new address per UTXO every time you receive Bitcoin. It's much harder to do that in Ethereum and other account-based blockchains. And also, unfortunately, it turns out that basic analysis renders this technique of regenerating pseudonyms ineffective. Similar to a lock on a front door, generating new pseudonyms for every transaction does keep away naive attackers, but a determined opponent can probably find a way to link your activity together. The term "linking" in the context of anonymity is the act of associating a real-world identity to a pseudonym. Linking is also sometimes called deanonymization.

In Bitcoin, advanced linking can associate a real-world identity to an address. And same goes in Ethereum, where a real-world identity could be linked to an externally owned account. Most of these blockchain technologies are fairly secure though for the most part, since linking as we'll see takes a nontrivial amount of effort. So as long as a user isn't reckless with how they manage their online identities, they can assume that most people aren't going to try to deanonymize them.

The underlying technology might be anonymous or pseudonymous, but we still have to consider human factors. People make mistakes and need to understand that anonymity is not absolute which is not a clear "yes" or clear "no" instead, it's on a spectrum. We refer to an entity's degree, or level of anonymity, as the difficulty of associating that entity's pseudonym with their real-world identity. A high degree of anonymity allows one to reasonably expect having achieved privacy.

To deal with the question again of how anonymous cryptocurrencies can indeed be used for money laundering and online drug purchases. We could have a partial solution, where the interfaces between cryptocurrencies and fiat currencies are highly regulated. For example, we might want to be able to trade cryptocurrencies almost anonymously, but not be able to touch fiat currency without a picture of your passport. Also, it's worth mentioning that it's immensely hard to implement a sense of "morality" at a technological level. Moral and immoral use cases look identical from a technological standpoint. At the end of the day, one might want to also consider whether the positive benefits of anonymity to society might outweigh the costs.

For example, consider Tor. Tor was created by the U.S. government, but now is used by many to make it difficult for government officials to monitor their web traffic — though there are still some ways to deanonymize even this. And some users of Tor might be drug dealers or operating black markets. On the other hand, Tor has enabled free speech, for example, for reporters in oppressive regimes.

As anonymous as we think we are, there are tactics that can be used to deanonymize us. We repeatedly cite Bitcoin as "pseudonymous," and the reason is because user privacy is not black and white. There are various data science approaches for observing information on the blockchain to gather patterns and draw conclusions. Bitcoin does not provide the anonymity that most users assume they gain from using cryptocurrencies. One of the biggest issues with anonymity in public and traceable blockchains such as Bitcoin is that they are not anonymous at all in their design.

5. Techniques of Anonymity

Let's have look on a very popular techniques of anonymity which is known as based on Mixing & Transaction Graphs.

6. Mixing and Transaction Graphs

It is a technique to enhance user privacy and achieve anonymity through a strategy known as mixing. The big concern about decentralization that we look at in regards to deanonymization is that now, we can go back in the blockchain's history to reveal information about a particular pseudonym, which is simply just inspecting the transaction history in the blockchain to derive useful information known as transaction graph analysis.

On a transaction graph, see Figure 2, each node is a pseudonym, and each edge is a transaction conducted between pseudonyms. From a transaction graph, you might be able to see some pseudonyms make transactions more than others, or are paid more than others, or perhaps make certain transactions with certain other pseudonyms.

7. Analyzing Transaction Graph

There are two popular heuristics used to analyze the transaction graph, they are as follows:

1. Clustering
2. Change address

7.1 *Clustering*

One way of analyzing the transaction graph is by clustering, or attributing a cluster of addresses or pseudonyms to the same real-world entity.

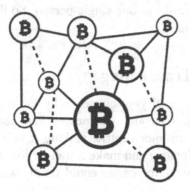

Figure 2.   Graphical Representation

Taking what we know so far, we can identify two main heuristics in associating addresses together. The first is the merging of transaction outputs, and that occurs when there are multiple inputs to a transaction. For example, consider Bob, who wants to buy a coffee that costs 0.05 BTC, and has two outputs, one with 0.02 BTC and the other with 0.03 BTC. He merges the two outputs into one that's 0.05 BTC, enough to pay for his coffee. This is a fairly reasonable heuristic because it's often the case that outputs are merged by the same entity. Rarely do people conduct joint payments.

7.2 *Change addresses*

Another heuristic is that of change addresses. Say Bob wants to buy the same 0.05 BTC coffee the next day, but only has an output worth 1 whole BTC. Bob would send 0.05 BTC to the coffee shop, and the rest of the 0.95 BTC to himself at a change address. This is fairly reasonable because in looking at Bob's transaction history, one of his two outputs must have been to a change address, unless he had purchased two items at the same time. And also, we could also look at whether addresses have been associated with any previous transactions. As per best practice, change addresses are usually newly generated, so when Bob makes the transaction to buy coffee, he would be sending his change back to an address never before seen on the blockchain — something that we can easily identify.

In both cases, of merging transaction outputs or of change addresses, if we know that Bob owns one address, we can guess with high confidence that Bob owns the other associated address. So we use these two heuristics to link all these addresses to one single person. So through this way, we could identify clusters.

8. Tagging by Transacting

Other technique for identifying cluster is by linking clusters with their real-world identities. Consider Businesses that accept cryptocurrency payments and are consumer centric, making it easy to go to an online service (such as Coinbase) and make a transaction with them. Since we know our own public addresses, we could simply wait for the transaction we made to show up within a cluster, or be merged into a cluster, and that cluster would likely be that of the business. This tactic is called tagging by transacting. On the other hand, there's a much more passive approach. We could just look at the graph and infer by looking at transaction activity.

For instance, SatoshiDice was a gambling site that allowed users to gamble with small denominations of Bitcoin. This allow large customer for making transactions, these transactions were visible in the graph, it's easy to see the transaction volume and find those transaction whose frequency was quite high. And this is true for any business or identity for which you can leverage some pre-existing knowledge. If you have some leads on transaction volume or frequency or timing, then you could look at transaction graphs and make solid linking inferences. As for identifying individuals, there are similar ways to deanonymize them. An easy way is to send them Bitcoin. If you can manage to get them to reveal their address, it's not that difficult to track them from there. This may require some social engineering if the other party is suspicious or particularly cautious.

Another way is to watch online activity, particularly forums. It's possible that an individual might post their address on a forum for convenience carelessly in order to get donations from general people or even provide services. Anyone who is watching, however, can now link that pseudonym with any other activity. Finally, several service providers, such as Coinalytics, offer services to deanonymize funds obtained through illicit means, using data analytics to discover your real identity.

9. Taint Analysis

Taint analysis is one way of easily tracing the movement of funds through the Bitcoin network. Taint analysis allows one to tag a "bad" address and trace its associated activity. It was this type of strategy that ruined Ross Ulbricht's defense by demonstrating that a majority of his funds originated from suspicious origins. Any other address in the Bitcoin space will have a certain amount of taint depending on what proportion of its funds came from a dirty address. One might think that they can circumvent getting caught by sending their tokens to a bunch of random addresses. However, by design of taint analysis, that won't work at all.

10. Money Laundering

For large institutions in traditional financial systems, some of these mixing practices may even be illegal. This is simply an intellectual exercise to understand how it may be possible to anonymize your funds to make it more difficult for someone else to track your activity. To better understand mixing's mechanics, let's examine a traditional scenario where money's origins are obfuscated such as money laundering.

Money laundering is the very illegal activity of moving large amounts of undetected money between countries or between the underground and legitimate economy. Traditional money laundering uses hundreds of fake "shell" companies, called shells because they don't do anything or own any assets. The reason why money laundering serves as a good base is because their goals are the same. However, they appear to in order to successfully serve as money laundering devices for tax purposes.

Stages of money laundering

– Placement
– Layering
– Integration

10.1 *Placement*

The first step to money laundering is placement. Over time, the "dirty" funds, or funds obtained through illicit means, are placed into these shell companies. The shell corporations write off the deposits as purchases, investments, services provided, etc., in order to make the appearance of legitimate money entering the business through legitimate means.

10.2 *Layering*

The next step is layering; in this step shell companies further pass their money through other shell companies in order to further complicate the financial supply chain to hide the true origin of the money. This step of the process is what mixing will simulate.

10.3 *Integration*

The final step of the process is Integration; this refers to when the clean money is reintroduced into the legitimate economy through the purchase of luxury goods, the end goal of all this money laundering. Mixing will attempt to simulate this process of money obfuscation by sending coins through several complicated processes.

To better understand what it means to be anonymous in this context, let's formally define something known as anonymity set. This will be defined as the set of pseudonyms between which an entity cannot be distinguished from their counterparts. In other words, it is impossible to do anything better than guess when trying to choose an address within an anonymity set to associate with some given entity. The goal of mixing, then, is to maximize this anonymity set with our resources. Let's say that mixing when done correctly now makes your entity indistinguishable within a set of N peers. This means that the anonymity set's size after one round is N. Done again with another unique N peers for each address, the anonymity size is now N squared after the second round. It becomes N cubed after three rounds and so on.

However, we do have to keep real-world constraints in mind, such as however many resources are available along with the implications of mixing. Matters such as plausible deniability and trustlessness of mixing also come into play since mixing alone isn't enough to absolve someone of suspicion. First off, trustlessness is desirable. Clearly, given the nature of the blockchain space, we want to ensure that there's no counter party risk. If someone else participates in a coin mixing process, they shouldn't be able to deny our services.

Additionally, we want to avoid our funds from being stolen. Second, we want to maintain plausible deniability. It shouldn't stand out from one's transaction history or any other data sources that you're mixing. If that's the case, then your activities will fall under much more scrutiny, even if you've done nothing wrong. These are properties we'll seek after building up some basic examples of mixing. To make clear, there's a fundamental idea behind mixing: the larger the anonymity set, the harder it is to link pseudonyms to real identities.

There are several different types of mixers. These include the following:

- centralized mixers,
- altcoin exchanges,

- decentralized mixing protocols, and
- privacy-focused altcoins.

10.4 *Centralized mixers*

The simplest kind of mixer, the easiest to design, is a centralized one, particularly a protocol known as Third Party Protocol, or TPP. By understanding a central solution first, we can then explore how other protocols may build off of this main design. With TPP, a centralized mixing service will have a set of UTXOs, referred to here as a slush fund. Whenever someone sends an input to this mixer, the mixing service operator will choose a set of UTXOs to return back to a new address also controlled by person "A." At the end, this person "A" now has "cleaned" funds minus the fee the mixing service kept. It's not hard to see some of the issues with this centralized service.

One of these issues comes down to counterparty risk: in this case, you have to trust the central service providing coin mixing services for you. There's hardly anything stopping them beyond reputation from withholding tokens from you. Additionally, you have to trust that the mixer is not keeping logs on your information. It's possible that the central party, in order to blackmail certain users or for some other purpose, is keeping a list of users who provided dirty inputs as well as the eventual cleaned funds they claimed. Finally, a centralization risk exists as well. Because of a single point of failure, which can be brought down by hacking or by a government institution demanding the shutdown of the service, it's not guaranteed that the mixer will operate as expected. Additionally, if the only UTXOs being sent to the centralized mixer are dirty coins, those dirty coins will end up becoming the new outputs for later users.

Without enough clean coins being cycled into the slush fund, it could cause the mixing to do little for cleaning your coins. A couple examples of centralized mixing services include Mixcoin, which came out of Princeton research, and Blindcoin, which came out of UMD and UPenn.

10.5 *Altcoin exchange mixing*

The next category of mixing to examine is altcoin exchange mixing. Rather than relying on a specific central service to perform the exclusive act of centrally mixing your coins, one can use a series of exchanges to bring money from Bitcoin to several other cryptocurrencies, such as Ether and Zcash, before finally coming back to Bitcoin. In this case, the cost of mixing coins is not a central mixing fee, but rather the exchange fees between each cryptocurrency used. The benefits of this approach are that the attacker now has to trace the transaction chain through several disparate blockchains and exchanges rather than simply examining a single blockchain. Additionally, this process provides better plausible deniability, since the activity looks like normal currency exchanging. However, you need to rely on exchanges not to reveal the links between your inputs and the outputs you receive on the other end.

Additionally, there still remains counterparty risk: if the exchange happens to get hacked or otherwise freezes services during your mixing process, you'll lose whatever money you had in transit. Finally, most exchanges in the United States are required to keep personally identifiable information and follow KYC/AML laws meaning that such activity may appear suspicious to exchanges, especially if done repeatedly. Thus far, proposed solutions have leveraged either a single centralized entity or several at a time. Is there a decentralized solution that will allow us to remove counterparty risk and avoid fees? One idea is to create a network of peers outside the Bitcoin network who can cooperate to make transactions which mix their coins without the need for any trusted third party.

How could we go about doing this?

Before we start diving deeper into the details of mixing protocols, let's take a step back to understand what we're working with and how to recognize a good decentralized mixing protocol.

First, let's pinpoint exactly what a mix is: it's a set of inputs and outputs each of equal size. The goal of mixing is to hide the mapping from each input to its respective output. To define correctness of a mixing protocol, let's place the following intuitive requirements.

- First, coins must not be lost, stolen, or double spent, naturally.
- Second, the mixing must be truly random and must eventually succeed in mixing. If unsuccessful, the coins should be sent back to the honest users, making the protocol resistant to DoS attacks.

To better understand the threats the protocol is up against, let's clearly categorize the possible types of adversarial models we're facing as well. These adversarial models pop up all the time when talking about computer security.

- The first type is a passive adversary. This actor is not part of the mix and may seek to use surface-level information as accessible to any other user to learn about the mapping. In this scenario, ideally, basic anonymity will prevent passive adversaries from connecting the inputs to outputs.
- The second type is a semi-honest adversary. This type of adversary is part of the mix. Though they correctly follow the protocol, they may use information gained during the process to attempt to deanonymize their peers.
- Finally, the last kind is a malicious actor, also part of the mix. As you might expect, they're able to deviate from the protocol specifications and may also attempt to steal funds from their peers in the mix. They may send false messages or withhold messages entirely in order to achieve some goal. This may remind you of fail-stop faults versus byzantine faults.

As with distributed systems, this adversarial model system lies on a spectrum. We'll make another reference to some old concepts by introducing the old concept of Sybil resistance. Because decentralized mixing is another distributed protocol, it's also susceptible to Sybil attacks. Hence, we need to ensure Sybil resistance, which has a two part definition in the context of decentralized mixing.

First, there needs to be a resistance to stealing funds. This means that we're not able to rely on partial threshold cryptography, such as m-of-n multi-signature transactions. Additionally, we need to maintain a resistance to deanonymization. A weak definition of this resistance is that participants outside the mix are not able to determine the mapping of inputs to outputs, but participants within still are. A strong definition of this is that even participants within the mix are not able to determine the mapping of inputs to outputs. However, we still need to acknowledge that a high proportion of Sybil peers will greatly reduce the anonymity set, as there are fewer unique entities within the mix.

Finally, there are a few additional caveats to consider in the context of mixing protocols.

- First, there are side channel attacks. For this reason, we'd want to user Tor for everything. Tor is a protocol developed by the U.S. government to anonymize your internet activity by restricting the knowledge of traffic to first-hop routers. Assuming that the Tor exit nodes you're using aren't adversary controlled, this will allow you to securely send messages to peers without detection.

- Second, we want to make sure that it's not obvious given the transaction amounts which input corresponds to which output. Else, our scheme would be trivially breakable. The solution is to use uniform transaction amounts across the board to ensure all inputs resemble each other, and all outputs are indistinguishable from each other.
- Finally, we want to ensure that transaction propagation does not unintentionally reveal our identities. This is known as network-level deanonymization. The first node to inform the network of a transaction is likely the source of it in almost all instances. Hence, we need a way to get around this problem as well.

10.6 *CoinJoin*

The first popularized decentralized mixing scheme was known as CoinJoin back in 2011. In this, coins are mixed together in what's known as an n-of-n multisig transaction. Each entity is required to sign off on the transaction input for the transaction to go through. One of the big benefits here that we achieve over other protocols is that it's trustless: funds cannot be stolen, since all users are signing off on the CoinJoin transaction. However, it does come with quite a few coin. First, anonymity is not secure against even a passive adversary, such as a mix facilitator. Since the best way to implement this protocol is through a centralized server, it assumes that private and anonymous communication exists for submitting output addresses. This makes it vulnerable to traffic analysis, where attackers can record and analyze network traffic.

Additionally, participating in this mixing procedure is not plausibly deniable. It's very easy to spot on the blockchain since it's an n-of-n multisignature transaction, which is unusually large. Though this can be fixed with Schnorr signatures, which combine several signatures into one piece of data, this currently does not exist on Bitcoin. Finally, it is not DoS resistant. Since it requires an n-of-n transaction sign-off, even one node disconnecting or intentionally disrupting the process can cause the entire mix to fail. So, our next question hopefully will be, "Can we do better?" Thankfully, the answer is yes.

CoinShuffle is the sequel to CoinJoin, using a decryption mixnet to jointly compute the input/output shuffling, where a mixnet is a routing protocol using cryptography to obfuscate the information trail.

One of the benefits to this protocol is that it uses an "Accountable Anonymous Group Messaging" protocol known as Dissent to resolve any traffic analysis issues. Additionally, it achieves anonymity against the mix facilitator because communications are now decentralized.

Finally, with this decryption mixnet, it provides strong Sybil resistance against deanonymization. However, it still suffers from the drawbacks of CoinJoin. Though Sybil resistance is stronger, it is not absolute. It's still possible to deanonymize someone via a Sybil attack. Additionally, like CoinJoin, CoinShuffle is vulnerable to DoS attacks as well. A drawback new to CoinShuffle is the ability of the last peer in the decryption mixnet to determine the outcome of the input/output shuffling, possibly giving this person the ability to manipulate the ordering in their favor.

To get a better understanding of the significance of CoinShuffle's decryption mixnet, let's dive into an overview. The purpose of the mixnet is to prevent anyone from knowing which message was sent by which individual except for the individuals themselves. The first step in this process is to encrypt the messages, in our case the output addresses of the transaction, with the public keys of each of the participating peers. From here, each of the messages has been decrypted in the same order. Say Red is the first to unravel a layer of decryption from each of the messages. Red, after decrypting the layer of encryption generated via Red's own public key, will randomly scramble the message order. Red cannot tell which input positions will correspond to which final output positions, and no one knows what Red did with the messages assuming Red does not disclose that information. Red will then pass it onto Blue, and so on, until all the layers are peeled off.

The issue with this protocol is that the final decision for ordering the output addresses with full knowledge of the final result lies with whichever peer is at the end of the process, allowing them to determine the final shuffle permutation. As mentioned briefly earlier, there is a liquidity problem with each of these solutions: they all are likely only to be used by others with dirty coins. What's the point in mixing coins if all you get back are dirty coins? Well, why not provide clean coins for mixing for a small fee? Due to the small risk, these market makers can charge a small fee for their services. However, there are still some issues. One is that the anonymity set is fairly small if using known liquidity providers. Another is that, according to a research paper published in June 2016, an attack with a recoverable investment of only $32,000 USD (at the time) would succeed with 90% likelihood to deanonymize the entire system. Another issue is that of plausible deniability.

10.7 *Coinparty*

Coinparty is a protocol designed to do exactly that, at the cost of some protocol security. The CoinParty protocol has three stages: commitment, shuffling, and the final transaction. During the commitment step, peers will generate an escrow address each. These escrow addresses require ⅔ consensus in order to spend. During the shuffling step, the peers perform a secure multi-party shuffle to scramble the output address ordering. Finally, during the transaction step, the peers will agree to transfer out of the escrow addresses to their designated outputs.

10.8 *Fair exchange mixers*

Fair exchange mixers are a different category of mixer. They build upon the traditional fair exchange protocol to no longer require a trusted third party to participate as part of the protocol. Instead, some party A pays another party B through an untrusted intermediary T.

Suppose you have two parties, Anna and Bobby, who wish to trade (cryptographic) "items" somehow. Consider a scenario that Anna transfer the item to Bobby and Bobby also receives the same, but Bobby didn't send his item to Anna. Now this exchange is nowhere a fair exchange. As one party got the item but other didn't. Fair exchange protocols seek to ensure that such situation never occurs, rather protocol itself ensures that either both party must transfer to each other else the transaction stands null and void.

In this scenario, what are being traded are coins for a voucher. Alice can deposit her coins and receive a voucher to redeem a comparable amount of coin later. She can then redeem clean coins at her discretion, cleaning her assets. However, this style of mixer assumes that enough transactions are passing through the mixer at the same time such that distinguishing which inputs match to which outputs is incredibly difficult.

10.9 *CoinSwap*

CoinSwap uses hash-locked 2-of-2 multi-signature transactions to do exactly this. It allows you to securely swap your coins with someone else without linking your transactions. The benefits are that it's trustless, since no party can steal your funds, and has decent plausible deniability. However, it also comes with the drawback that it's not secure against a mix-passive intermediary. Though, this intermediary can also be the person you're swapping with. Additionally, it's expensive, as it requires four transactions per swap. The way it looks on the blockchain is like Alice is paying some address and Bob is paying some other address, but there is no direct connection between the original coins and the new ones.

11. XIM

XIM, a protocol similar to CoinSwap, also uses an untrusted intermediary to create a fair-exchange mixer. This builds on earlier work on fair exchange and uses fees to prevent DoS and Sybil attacks. XIM creates a secure group-forming protocol for finding parties to participate in a mix. The issue with XIM is that it takes several hours to run because of the group-forming protocol. Blindly Signed Contracts build further off XIM to prevent the group forming process, instead using anonymous fee vouchers to deter DoS and Sybil attacks. The issue is that implementing BSC would require scripting functionality not currently provided by Bitcoin.

Mixing is something that a user would consciously have to do. Every time a user wants to be anonymous, they'd have to go out of their way mix them. What if the platform itself automatically anonymized or mixed coins to preserve privacy by default? This way, privacy is but a one-time choice for the user, and there is no suspicion on any individual user in the platform since anonymity is integrated into the protocol. In this section, we'll cover some privacy focused altcoins and the technologies they are built upon to protect their users.

12. Dash

Dash, formerly known as DarkCoin, is a privacy focused cryptocurrency that uses a mixer called CoinJoin, which we talked about in the previous section. In Dash, in addition to traditional Proof-of-Work rewards, there's a secondary network layer of what are known as masternodes. Users who run master nodes are tasked with performing privileged actions such as voting on proposals for network governance, instantly confirming transactions, and mixing coins. The idea here is that we have better plausible deniability because everyone is forced to go through CoinJoin for mixing. So, this makes for a much larger anonymity set.

The way it works is as follows:

By default on most Dash clients, users have mixing enabled. Dash calls this PrivateSend, but it's essentially the processes of executing CoinJoin, plus some Dash platform specific formalities. When a user has PrivateSend enabled, meaning that they want to obscure the origins of their funds, their client will first prepare a transaction. The transaction inputs are broken down into standard denominations of 0.01 Dash, 0.1 Dash, 1 Dash, and 10 Dash. Then, a request is made to the masternode network, indicating that you're trying to obscure the origin of your funds. When other users send similar requests indicating that they too are trying to make private transactions, a master node mixes all the transaction inputs of all the users, and instructs all users to pay their now-transformed inputs back to themselves.

So now, all users who participated in this round of mixing now has the same amount of Dash back in their possession, minus some transaction fees. In order to fully obscure their funds of course, users need to repeat mixing with masternodes multiple times — usually between 2 and 8 rounds. Users of Dash wallets have the whole mixing process happen in the background without any intervention of the user themselves, so when it's time to make a transaction; their funds are already fully anonymized. After all, this whole process of mixing does take some time, so it should be done in advance. Also, since coins are mixed in set denominations, transactions using mixing may need to spend from more transaction outputs than those that don't use mixing. And spending from more transaction outputs at time leads to larger transaction sizes, so users would have to spend more on transaction fees than usual. Some pros about Dash are that first, it solves the main issue with plausible deniability we saw earlier.

Everyone takes part in the CoinJoin mixing process. Also, since Dash uses decentralized mixing with CoinJoin, it's trustless on that end. However, there is the main con though those users have to trust both the main Dash network and also its network of masternodes. In order to become a masternode initially, users post 1000 Dash bond. And after that, masternodes also earn interest and standard income through a proportion of the block reward. If there's an entity with enough capital, they could purchase enough masternodes to subvert the Dash masternode network and potentially deanonymize the network. Unlike a lot of other altcoins, especially earlier privacy focused altcoins, that were forks of Bitcoin.

13. Zcash

Zcash is an altcoin where transactions reveal nothing about input and output addresses and also the input and output values of transactions as well — allowing for fully anonymous payments. And the way it does this is by using zero-knowledge Succinct Non-interactive ARguments of Knowledge zk-SNARKS for short. zk-SNARKS are a way of proving that you know something without revealing what you actually know. One side note is that UC Berkeley's own Professor Alessandro Chiesa is co-founder of Zcash, and co-inventor of its underlying protocol, ZeroCash. Both of these technologies rely on zk-SNARKS as we mentioned before, and Professor Chiesa is also the author of libsnark, the C++ implementation of zk-SNARKS.

Let's see that what you can do with zk-SNARKS implemented at the protocol layer is that you can first have a normal publically viewable base coin, such as Bitcoin. You can then mint it into some black box coin, which you can then keep in total anonymity and make a series of transactions. There's no way to correlate or distinguish coins and values while in this black box. Then, to get your base coin back, there's a procedure called pour.

If you recall in Bitcoin, or any payment network, you need to prove three things in order to conduct a valid transaction as follows:

- First, you have to prove that the input you're spending from hasn't previously been spent — or more generally, that you have sufficient funds for the payment.
- Second, you have to prove ownership of the coins you're spending from.
- Third, you have to prove that the sum of your transaction inputs is equal to the sum of your transaction outputs.

In Bitcoin, proof that coins haven't been spent previously is information obtained from the ledger itself, and requires no effort by the transaction sender. The sender proves ownership of the coins they want to send by digitally signing the transaction using their private key. To allow this signature to be publically verified, the sending address must be disclosed. The recipient address also has to be disclosed, in order for the recipient to then be able to spend the coins that they have received. In Bitcoin, it's easy to see that the verification of transaction inputs and outputs is trivial, since so much information is disclosed and publicly available.

On the other hand, Zcash uses zk-SNARKs to prove the same three facts — that inputs haven't been spent, that coins are being spent by their correct owners, and that the sum of inputs is equal to the sum of transaction outputs. And this is all done with zero knowledge — without revealing any information about the sender, recipient, or the assets that are being transferred. Each valid transaction is sent with an accompanying zk-SNARK, which prove the three facts we previously stated. Transaction inputs are proofs of validity for the transaction, and outputs are the details required to construct a zero knowledge proof, encrypted of course with the recipient's public key. The information required to spend the transaction outputs is also attached to the transaction which are again encrypted and keep details how to construct a new zk-SNARK that enables spending.

Zcash has two layers, a transparent layer and a zero-knowledge security layer. And users transfer their assets between these two layers using the mint and pour transactions, as we mentioned before. The reason for having these two separate layers is because at its core, the fundamental innovation of Zcash was its implementation of the zero knowledge security layer; its transparent layer started simply as a fork of the Bitcoin codebase.

Users are generally more likely to be comfortable with transparent cryptocurrencies they've seen or used in the past — like Bitcoin — so if users like that, then Zcash shouldn't take that away. Also, enabling Bitcoin-style transparent transactions also make it simple to integrate with Zcash using existing tools and infrastructure that were originally built to support Bitcoin. So now, a fun technical aside, zk-SNARKs are built on top of homomorphic encryption functions.

They have the following properties: First, given an output, it's hard to find the input. Also, different inputs should lead to different outputs. Where this starts to get interesting though, is that now, rather than wanting homomorphic functions to be random, we want to be able to perform operations on outputs of homomorphic functions. For example, if we know the outputs of a homomorphic encryption function on two different input values, we can find the output of the function on some arithmetic combination of the two inputs — all without knowing the input values themselves.

One pro is that Zcash is fully anonymous. Assuming the underlying cryptography is secure; transactions conducted in Zcash's blackbox zero-knowledge security layer are fully anonymous. Their anonymity set is the entire blackbox history. Also, another pro is that of modularity. Zcash was originally implemented on top of a fork of Bitcoin for convenience and also integration with existing tools. However, it can also be integrated with any other consensus mechanism. On the other hand, Zcash is very resource intensive. And that's due to the fact that zk-SNARK proof systems in use require about 4 GB of RAM and 40 seconds of computation on modern CPUs in order to generate proofs for pour transactions. Also, proofs require a semi-trusted one-time setup.

Adversaries with malicious setup parameters can mint coins without spending base coins. This can be somewhat mitigated with a secure multiparty computation setup, but that's out of scope for this course.

It is an interesting challenge in integrating such technologies into blockchain though, so it's definitely worth checking out. Now that we've gone through all these anonymity techniques, separating them category by category, there are some novel anonymity tactics that don't fall into the mixing or altcoin tactics but are features of blockchain protocols themselves.

14. Prospective Techniques of Anonymity

In traditional cypherpunk fashion, there was a proposal published in July 2016. Here, you can see the opening lines of the very mysterious MimbleWimble proposal. It simply read: "hi, i have an idea for improving privacy in bitcoin. My friend who knows technology says this channel would have interest..." followed by a txt file proposal. The proposal was written by a user with the pseudonym Tom Elvis Jedusor, Voldemort's French name in the Harry Potter series. The proposal was called Mimblewimble, which was also a Harry Potter reference — specifically a curse that was used to keep people from talking about a specific subject. The MimbleWimble proposal posed a design for a blockchain-based ledger system that used a cryptographic protocol more scalable and private than that of Bitcoin. By modifying transaction types in Bitcoin, Mimblewimble aims to be as low-functionality as possible, while maintaining high privacy and high scalability.

Because of this drastic change from normal Bitcoin, it aims to be implemented as an alternate blockchain (a side chain or altcoin perhaps) that supports a different type of transaction than what Bitcoin uses currently. On the privacy size, Mimblewimble builds upon Confidential Transactions, an earlier proposal by Greg Maxell, by implementing range proofs, homomorphic commitments, Pedersen commitments, and other cryptographic primitives. Also, all values in a transaction are encrypted with so called "blinding factors," secondary elliptic curves used solely for privacy's sake. Also it bundles many transactions into larger transactions in order to scramble inputs and outputs — to obfuscate the origin and destination of Bitcoins — and also for scalability reasons as well.

With Mimblewimble, you can treat each block as one large transaction. And you can also merge transactions across blocks. Joining transactions across blocks could extend all the way from the genesis block to the latest block. So, Mimblewimble can thus reduce the need to maintain entire blockchain history since the genesis block. The original proposal pointed out that to get to the current version of the blockchain, one must start from the genesis block and start block verification from there.

And as of July 2016, the time of publication, 150 million transactions must be replayed to produce a set of only 4 million unspent transaction outputs. Mimblewimble promises to half the size of the blockchain: while still maintaining confidential transactions and obscured transaction graphs. Also, Mimblewimble simplifies the current Bitcoin model to transactions that don't need extra functionality other than simply transferring value from sender to recipient. It does this by eliminating Bitcoin script. And that's the price one must pay to enable such privacy that Mimblewimble promises to provide. Currently, Mimblewimble is under active development, and it's most popular implementation is called Grin. Now, it's important for us to reflect, to see how far we've come with privacy and anonymity.

15. Summary

Fundamentally, it's easy to see with privacy, you could have the most secure system in the world, but the moment one part fails, or it's shown that a part of your system can possibly be broken or exploited, then you've lost. Privacy can be seen as a subset of security; privacy is the act of protecting confidential information, where security is the protecting. Clearly, centralized mixers and master node mixer networks sacrifice decentralization for privacy and security. On the other hand, multi-layer blockchain protocols such as Dash's master node network and Zcash's zero-knowledge security layer have associated overhead that may hinder performance — not to mention other protocol-specific scalability hits. Also, often times, in regards to mixing, it's said that mixing should be done in advance so as to spread out mixing overhead. This unfortunately is not possible if a user is sending many small transactions, where each incurs a non-negligible mixing fee. And if they run out of pre-mixed funds, that incurs mixing overhead. Really, there is no perfect all around blockchain system. Instead, each is designed for its specific goal and use case.

Bibliography

Aggarwal, A. H., & Singla, A. R. (2013). Framework for business values chain activities using SOA and cloud. *International Journal of Information Technology, Communications and Convergence, 2*(4), 281–294.

Androulaki, E. *et al.* (2013). Evaluating user privacy in bitcoin. *Proceedings of FC, LNCS 7859*, 34–51. https://doi.org/10.1007/978-3-642-39884-1_4.

Dorri, A., Kanhere, S. S., Jurdak, R., & Gauravaram, P. (2017). Blockchain for IoT security and privacy: The case study of a smart home. In *2nd IEEE PERCOM Workshop on Security Privacy and Trust in the Internet of Things* (pp. 618–623). (IEEE), Kona, HI, USA.

Elliott, E. (2019). A brief history of decentralized computing and how we can build a better future. https://medium.com/the-challenge/a-brief-history-of-decentralized-computing-d0d665783bcf.

Green, M., & Miers, I. (2017). Bolt: Anonymous payment channels for decentralized currencies. *Proceedings of CCS*, 473. DOI: 10.1145/3133956.3134093. https://par.nsf.gov/servlets/purl/10112772.

Koshy, P., Koshy D., & McDaniel, P. D. (2014). An analysis of anonymity in bitcoin using P2P network traffic. *Proceedings of FC, LNCS, 8437*, 469–485. https://doi.org/10.1007/978-3-662-45472-5_30.

Mukhopadhyay, U. A. S. (2016). *A Brief Survey of Cryptocurrency Systems*. Piscataway, NJ: IEEE.

Nakamoto, S. (2008). Bitcoin: A peer-to-peer electronic cash system. https://bitcoin.org/bitcoin.pdf [accessed: November 13, 2019].

Owen, R. D. (2015). A next generation reputation system based on the blockchain. *Internet Technology and Secured Transactions*. London, UK: ICITST.

Seth, A., Agarwal, H., & Singla, A. (2012). Unified modeling language for describing business value chain activities. In *International Conference on Advances in Computer Applications*. Proceedings published by *International Journal of Computer Applications (IJCA)*.

Zhang, K., Zhu, Y., Maharjan, S., & Zhang, Y. (2019). Edge intelligence and blockchain empowered 5G beyond for the industrial internet of things. *IEEE Network, 33*(5), 12–19.

https://doi.org/10.1142/9789811225079_0016

Chapter 16

Block Edge Computing: Blockchain-Edge Platform for Industrial IoT Networking

T. Nathiya[*,‖], B. Mahalakshmi[†,**], K. Kavitha[‡,††],
Jabeen T. Nusrat[§,‡‡], and K. Maheswari[§,§§]

[*]*Department of Computer Science,
New Prince Shri Bhavani Arts and Science College, Chennai, India*

[†]*New Prince Shri Bhavani Arts and Science College, Chennai, India*

[‡]*Department of Computer Science,
Mother Teresa Women's University, Kodaikanal, India*

[§]*Department of Computer Science,
Anna Adarsh College for Women, Chennai, India*

[‖]*tnathiya17@gmail.com*

[**]*maha.karthik921@gmail.com*

[††]*kavitha.urc@gmail.com*

[‡‡]*nusratjabeen@annaadarsh.edu.in*

[§§]*k.maheswari@annaadarsh.edu.in*

Abstract

The rapid growth of Industrial Internet of Things (IIoT) architecture presents a unique scope for developing a broad field of networking to connect multiple interconnected nodes to the Internet. The majority of current IIoT technologies are focused on unified architecture, which is easier to maintain but cannot leverage to facilitate immutable and verifiable networks between different groups. The blockchain framework is built on many desirable features for large-scale IIoT technologies, such as centralization, reliability, tracking ability, and immutability. This chapter proposes an IIoT blockchain-based infrastructure designed to encourage unchanging and empirical transactions. Nevertheless, while abandoning blockchain technology to the IIoT framework, the necessary storage space is subject to a subsidizing challenge to the cluster-based IIoT architecture. The proposed frame has a centralized storage structure where most of the blockchain settles into clouds, such as Global, Fog, and Edge. Nearly all notable nodes are processed in the superimposed network of independent industrial IoT networks. The proposed framework constantly links low-level IIoT networks, blockchain overlay networks, and combined cloud architecture through two connectors. The blockchain interface and fog interface port are interconnected for continuous data transmission. The blockchain interface in the stacked network extends blockchain blocks from the information gathered in IIoT nodes. And the cloud interface reconciles the constraints of optimizing the blockchain between the overlay network and the clouds. This is a test case to be provided to demonstrate the efficiency of the Edge Central Network Repository proposed in a practical example of IIoT.

Keywords: Edge computing, Blockchain technology, Fog computing, Industrial IoT

1. Introduction

With the advent of the 5G mobile networks, the latest development of emerging technology connected to the IoT, the modern environment is undergoing a major digital transition from mostly all domains of everyday life (Yaga *et al.*, 2019). These technical challenges play a crucial role in facilitating a range of important application areas, such as factory automation, healthcare, travel, finance, and smart home automation, including others. In Industrial Internet of Things (IIoT), sensor data is extracted from a growing portion of innovative smart equipment, providing large amounts of data to analyse, sometimes with special requirements. For example, the industrial sector is extremely time limit and thus needs very prompt intervention to ensure that the required procedures are carried out in an optimal, safe and reliable manner. Furthermore, in this type of industrial scenario, the analysis and interpretation of the data sources collected and the resulting intelligent decision-making generally require a lot of computational power.

Standard unified cloud methods are likely suitable for IIoT applications requiring high computing efficiency and are related to latency. Public services include, for example, universally open information repositories and highly managed computing functions, large-scale data collection, unnecessary analysis, and choice in real-time. However, because of the multitude of relatively small bandwidth networks, it will be optional to perform both computation and information storage functions in clustered clouds (Kushch & Prieto-Castrillo, 2019).

Fog computing has been among the closest and most important ideas. However, fog networks will be considered closer despite resources/capabilities compared to the periphery. Fog networks should be considered a wide range of technologies and services required to bring cloud computing applications closer to IoT clusters (Li *et al.*, 2019). Compared to existing approaches to edge calculation and fog, information protection protocols, stability, and reliability criteria support local edge calculation strategies (concepts such as edge or extreme edge). In recent times, blockchain is increasingly a hot topic because of its significant potential application to many banks and financial fields, for example, crypto currencies such as Bitcoin. However, blockchain as a traditional trustworthy platform for distributed and decentralized environments can also be used in a range of other promising applications (Loganathan *et al.*, 2017). In these, IIoT applications is a popular area in which blockchain may be considered the enabling technology for a range of primary prominences.

IIoT setups are increasing massively and their full rollout will pose numerous threats related to, for example, maintaining the CIA to enhance data access and transparency (Liu *et al.*, 2015). Blockchain will be part of these criteria and play an important role in providing safe and quantifiable data access and management solutions (Vasanth *et al.*, 2017). IIoT applications have common criteria to ensure data integrity security and trust between multiple parties involved concerning different sections of the supply chain (e.g., raw material supply, shipping, storage, manufacturing and processing, and customer implementation). In some of these settings, criteria such as the control of each phase and the preservation of the file of each task are predominant (Zheng *et al.*, 2019).

Edge computing is used to obtain less runtime in terms of capabilities, while blockchain is crucial to ensure safe and effective information exchange, availability, and node tracking/monitoring. Accordingly, this report focuses on the importance of the co-existence of blockchain-Edge system using the IIoT scenario that is under consideration for the Industrial Edge Project (Li *et al.*, 2020). The report therefore build on the currently presented design by incorporating blockchain and some other core features. Propose the blockchain-Edge system from this current image and evaluate any specifications and obstacles relaunched in this architecture for IIoT applications.

In this perspective, it is important to identify optimal approaches for manufacturing operations and inventory distribution and assembling logistics organization that will promote increased performance, quantifiability, and ability while retaining less maintenance and expenditure in the supply chain (Battula *et al.*, 2020; Loganathan *et al.*, 2017; Sahoo *et al.*, 2019; Wang *et al.*, 2019; Yang *et al.*, 2019). From a working perspective, blockchain has served as an important technology enabling the substantiation of decentralized consistency of various systems, such as supply, production chains, and logistics end products. This knowledge is used to improve the logistic chain and output performance, to properly control the consistency of the logistic chain, and to track faults and share equal revenue among the others (Chen *et al.*, 2020; Petropulu *et al.*, 2019; Wang *et al.*, 2018). Case studies involve identification of the origin of the sources and data, circumstances during shipment and depository, turnaround time, representation of the supply materials to the finished goods, tracking of the production process, final product, determination, and advice on electronic fabrication at the industrial site.

Objectives of the chapter:

- The chapter suggests an IT structure based on blockchain for commercial IoT applications.
- Develop future system architecture and identify critical technical specifications.
- Assess the sustainability of our proposed system by analyzing effectiveness and matching targets with ongoing work.

2. Related Works

2.1 *Blockchain for IIoT*

IIoT is the current revolutionary change for industrial and transformation companies in addressing the digitalization of companies through the diffusion of IoT. IIoT is commonly used in a range of business enterprises, including generation, electricity, distribution, logistics, healthcare, and utilities. IIoT is typically a variety of IoT instruments distributed throughout the developed system (Mcginthy & Michaels, 2019; Russell *et al.*, 2018; Stellios *et al.*, 2018; Wu *et al.*, 2019). These IIoT tools gather huge contextual data that are used to recognize compatibility issues in the systems, to fix system failure effectively, and to diagnose the abnormal operating behavior of the systems (Wu *et al.*, 2017). Such IIoT architecture will offer enormous benefits, such as efficient quality management, better customer operation, better monitoring of devices, detectable supply chains, streamlined production, and operating costs (Beerens *et al.*, 2020).

Even then, IIoT programs face a variety of issues that must be addressed before IIoT is systematically implemented in various areas. These obstacles include enhanced stability, a high degree of protection and safety, accelerated adaptability, increased scalability and reliability of IIoT information processing, improved confidence, minimum operating expenses, and a time-critical less bandwidth IoT port.

2.2 *Edge computing for IIoT*

Due to the overwhelming need for large-scale IIoT-based low-latency computing, traditional cloud technologies may not be ideal for automotive use. Edge computing emerged as an aspiring technological approach in the current situation, importing some of the cloud computing tools that allow edge networks. It will have crucial advantages with the aim to maintain less bandwidth and high performance. We suggest a broad reinforcement of the Q learning framework focused on automated computer transfer for devices that demonstrate overall success in computer transfer. Also, the authors in Jiang *et al.* (2020) and Pan *et al.* (2018) provided the conceptual comparison of the different accessible IoT nodes are shown in Figure 1.

The effective use of edge frameworks in different IIoT technology contexts has already been discussed in the research: several problems are

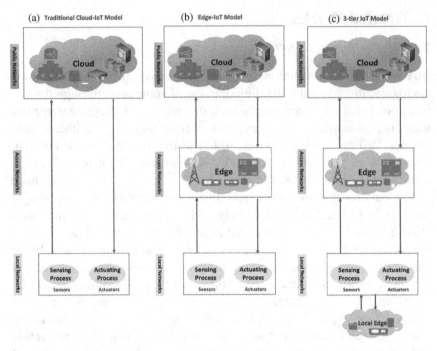

Figure 1.   Various IoT Frameworks: (a) Traditional Cloud-IoT Model, (b) Edge-IoT Model, and (c) Three-Tier Edge-IoT Model

arising in the IIoT world in 5G cyber-physical production networks to accomplish maximum spectral efficiency, maximum reliability, more convergence, and less turnaround time. Edge computing has also been used to resolve problems in computing information, secure repositories, efficient retrieval of information, and complex information gathering in the IIoT. The suggested edge configuration input for the industrial IoT uses several cooperative Microcontroller Units (MCU). Multi-MCU peripheral nodes are capable of efficient network control, integrated information collection, and network connectivity, reducing the practical use of resources and demonstrating optimization. The work described in Paes *et al.* (2020) provides an improved and secure integrated solution for IIoT onboard systems.

2.3 *Blockchain-edge integration for IIoT*

Implementing blockchain and edge computing unlocks a range of prospects for Industry 4.0 implementations and solves current vulnerabilities in IIoT devices, like the increased quantitative approach of operation and functionality, shared trust, strengthened protection and safety, production, effective resource management, smoother police/rules implementation, and continues monitoring among others.

3. Proposed Architecture

3.1 *IIoT smart building construction*

The main purpose of convenience and simplicity of interpretation, we select only one contractor and its related sub-contractors, i.e. "Log-House" contractor, as seen in Figure 2. The provision and manufacturing chain of the log-house building manufacture goes through different stages, from the production of trees in the forest to the supply and installation of fabricated logs at the building site. By this example poses a view of a device with more criteria for controlling the consistency of manufactured goods and stakeholders' material and maintaining quality supply chain mapping, packaging, and interfacing.

Processing and Shipping: The freight company will be responsible for harvesting and shipping harvested raw materials/trees from the forest area to the production facility. All data, starting with collection to distribution, are tracked in the transportation provider and exchanged with other network sub-coordinators.

Manufacturing: The processing plant generates logs from the harvested raw material. Various technologies, computers, and devices are expected

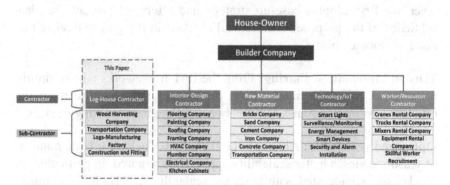

Figure 2.   Smart Building Construction Framework

to contribute to the mission. This step involves minimum bandwidth, as well as control of each procedure, to ensure the protection, safety, and reliability of the entire project.

Storage: The production contractor shall store man-made logs in the warehouse and supply tracking functionality as acceptable storage priorities. This sub-task should ensure that logs are properly packed before the transportation contractor collects and transports materials from the plant to the original construction site.

Construction: This step shall be carried out by the building firm, which shall render the needed fittings and new essential tasks start the timber logs made. The construction company and the homeowner will trace/monitor all steps through the Common Register. In the case of consistency problems, the blockchain needs to recognize the flawed processes that could have triggered the issue and to identify the responsible problem.

3.2 *Requirements of the use case*

Minimum bandwidth network: The key criteria for the selected IIoT usage scenario are to maintain the distribution of minimum bandwidth services/resources to the critical elements of the network. When compared to a valid, state-of-the-art blockchain strategy, the survey results and the hierarchy of the proposed component are shown in Figure 1. The proposed blockchain-based IoT design includes hierarchical layers using the Merkle Root Tree Hash algorithm, e.g., IoT neighborhood organizations, the co-usable blockchain network, and mists. To depict the vital parts of each layer, we first adopt a base-up strategy and afterward present the plan subtleties of the proposed hierarchical blockchain design to alleviate the issue of storage ability.

Trusted information sharing: From the IIoT frameworks take of multiple network titles, the main criteria of this architecture are to maintain efficient information transactions between different networking devices.

Optimized scalability: Although the IIoT networks have a large number of sensors/nodes, a better scalability approach is required. In particular, as blockchain is integrated with IIoT, the scalability criteria become much more important.

Validation and port control: The IIoT example would include miscellaneous sensors/nodes that will need safe entry to the different existing devices; therefore light validation and entry protection are essential criteria to be considered by the system.

3.3 *Key network elements*

Earlier explaining the existent projected BlockEdge framework, we clarify quite, in brief, the main network properties and their position.

IIoT nodes: This involves a range of IoT devices (i.e., sensors, nodes, Radio-frequency ID tags, monitors, location image monitoring nodes, and production infrastructure nodes) accessible at the owned system level.

IoT clusters: Through this IIoT block, there is a sub-contractor, i.e., a wood processing firm, is a sub-contractor who performs transactions in compliance with arrangement along with contractor "Log-house contractor." Therefore, the IIoT node presents a sub-contractor with a variety of IIoT clusters/links which are necessary to work collectively to perform various independently assigned calculations.

Edge nodes: Edge clusters/links are less powerful than clusters/actuators in IIoT nodes and are accessible close to IoT devices. The data obtained from the IoT cluster (i.e., sub-contractor) has been sent to the corresponding edge node for further analysis of the data and to ensure that the necessary low-latency-dependent operations are carried out.

Fog nodes: These clusters are stronger given capital and computing capacities than the edge nodes. A fog net refers to the contractor in the system. Fog equipment have the required services (IT, storage) for the number of IoT blocks/related chain nodes.

3.4 *Architecture overview*

Local network: They could likewise be referred to as "IoT-Edge networks" as they contain separate IoT clusters, and all of those are linked to various edge links as noted in Figure 3. As mentioned above, IoT blocks are mostly limited resources, so we merge IoT blocks calculation edge

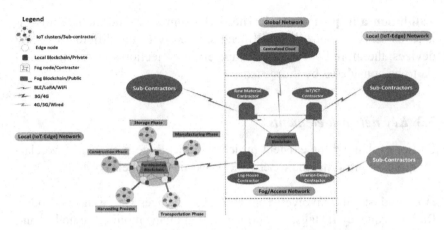

Figure 3.   Blockchain-Edge Architecture for IIoT Applications

links via maximum capacity links/systems or a gateway. We expect a relevant/permissible thin blockchain on IoT-edge nodes which are able to allow stable and reliable exchange of important data between variable IoT-edge domains (i.e., owned by sub-contractors in the IoT-edge network). In the example of log-house usage, every sub-contractor is expected to exchange some details. Blockchain is a valid method of monitoring and controlling supply chains and products on local networks.

Fog network: The fog network is comparatively resourced in view of computing, holding of data and transmission capacities with reference to availability networks. In a fog node, we meant that a contractor, such as a log-house contractor or a material driven contractor, who represents for controlling/maintaining the associated IoT cluster (applicable sub-contractors) and supplying facilities.

Many fog nodes (contractors) should share appropriate information about current operations with each other. We are waiting without permission or blockchain shared on the fog network and sharing little knowledge on the network. Blockchain for Fog network devices could produce a business base for provider I that it could sell services like computer training and processing to produce money for the customer.

Global network: Global/centralized network will have the maximum resource capability in contrast to the two networks listed above. It follows classical centralized cloud computing techniques that provide a global infrastructure network for high-repository applications and computer efficiency. Here, blockchain task is to monitor the overall design process at the above levels. Transactions between different layers and organizations are added to the blockchain as prominent nodes, which ensure that it can be traced to a given factor across the entire supply chain. Blockchain also provides a forum to process logical reports in the transfer category or to make purchases when certain requirements are met.

A number of elements of the infrastructure, depending on the nature of the operation of the IoT critical infrastructure, are vulnerable to cyber-attacks, including the following.

(1) Industrial instruments: Many devices are already in service and are difficult to update or repair. Essential infrastructure too rigid to effectively manage vulnerabilities and potential attacks. However, because new IoT gadgets are linked to the Network, they are vulnerable to cyber attacks and can be readily hacked.

(2) Overhead distribution: Connected systems can now interact with one another. Other IoT, compute, and storage devices can be added with independent exchange such as mobile and Wi-Fi connectivity that use open standard protocols. The communication infrastructure is vulnerable to hacking as well, and the communication is audible.

(3) IT infrastructure: Critical infrastructures rely on centralized cloud computing, where all data must be sent to a cloud data center for processing. This raises the possibility that there may be data breaches.

The proposed solutions for Industry 4.0 critical infrastructure must consider the following factors to address the above problems.

(1) Security: To protect IoT devices, IT infrastructure, communication infrastructure, and the various data circulating in these infrastructures, appropriate security mechanisms must be in place.

(2) Confidentiality: Data is used to make numerous control and maintenance decisions, such as predicting, detecting and locating failures, which are performed using various advanced data analysis methods. Sensitive data shall not be transmitted outside the LAN region and the use of the data shall be transparent.

(3) Scalability: Data analysis techniques are based on the gathering, storage, and processing of information. The time required to complete these processes must meet the stringent requirements of critical infrastructure and be scalable as the infrastructure expands.

Aside from the security concerns that surround IIoT critical infrastructure, scaling has hampered IIoT adoption. IIoT scalability can be improved by incorporating information technology and blockchain. To start with, edge computing can deliver blockchain and IIoT nodes with ubiquitous computer installations. Second, blockchain can improve the safety and confidentiality of both ECN and Industrial IoT by acting as a middleware between various IIoT systems. This section focuses on two aspects of IIoT critical infrastructure scalability as follows: (1) the inherent sustainability of IIoT and (2) the parallelization of the blockchain.

In critical infrastructures, IIoT has a strict evolutionary requirement, with the vision of prevalent links and stretchy connect directly for it all. IIoT scalability is hampered by heterogeneous IoT systems, diverse IIoT networks, and IIoT metadata. RFID labels, detectors, remotes, and robots are examples of IIoT devices that are connected via wired or wireless networks. A variety of IIoT devices are demonstrated using devices (e.g., ICs and detectors) and operating systems (e.g., software) (e.g., software and firmware). In addition to heterogeneous IIoT devices, networks connecting various IIoT devices use multiple methods all throughout physical layer. Near-field, back broadcast, and Bluetooth, for example, have all been widely used for short-range communications. Wi-Fi, low-power wide area networks, and active surface (e.g., 4G and 5G) were used to communicate IoT devices over large durations. Furthermore, the large amount of structured and unstructured IIoT data makes data storage and analysis more difficult.

IIoT scalability problems can be solved by combining edge computing, network softwaring, and blockchain technology. For starters, recent advances in advanced computing and network softwarization may be able to deal with key IIoT infrastructure scalability issues. In particular, the work of has introduced a certification system for IoT appliances based on edge computing. The scalability of a prototype throughout the system has been demonstrated. In the meantime, unlike traditional centralized SDN solutions, a decentralized SDN has been introduced to reach the scalability of large-scale networks. Existing SDN solutions experience bottlenecks in network controllers, which often have limited computer power. The work proposed integrating embedded and cloud computing hardware to overcome SDN controller IT bottlenecks in order to address this issue. Latency is a key proxy for scalability. A recent study on the integration of SDN, NFV, and network slicing to achieve ultra-low latency in 5G networks has been published. On the core network, embedded and cloud installations were also deployed to improve computing capabilities and reduce delays. The work also included an optimization diagram for network slicing recovery and reconfiguration that improved system reliability and scalability. To ensure the effective and safe execution of the different steps in the log home example, it is essential that each level/cluster operates collaboratively at each point in the value chain. For example, minimal data analysis and decision-making for portions of activities that can be performed by resource-constrained local area networks. The mist node supports the associated IoT edge nodes by providing the necessary tools and installations. For example, IoT edge nodes can provide high-computing critical security services/resources to ensure that appropriate security mechanisms are enabled on local networks to perform various tasks.

When a service/resource is requested from the corresponding edge node by the IoT cluster, the message agent would transfer the message to the relevant utility cluster to calculate the next level. Afterwards, it aims to verify if the desired network or hardware is present for local depository. Unless the check is effective, the authorized users will be checked via the logical node and the appropriate cluster will be forwarded to the link message agent. In the event that the required node may be accessible at the

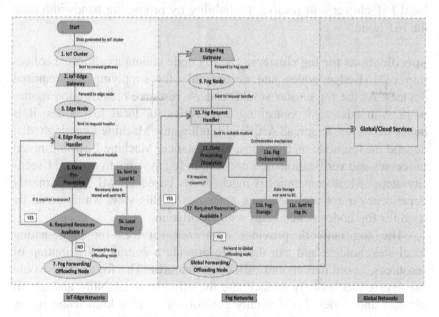

Figure 4.   High-Level Workflow of the Projected Architecture

cluster (that present services at the edge node may not satisfy the specifications of the required clusters), the message is transferred to fog networks through the fog loading node.

Depending on the type of services required, the Fog Research Manager transfers the information to the relevant calculation node installation. Tests whether the concerned node can be accessed through the Fog repository or not. Based on an effective cluster node, a volatile index on mist networks verifies the privileges available in a specific edge cluster. Based on the specified information is not shared, it then sends the packet to the above layers across the dump node of the variable is shown in Figure 4. As the sub-stratified network is the environmentally friendly in reference to energy, it offers the necessary bundles available for the fog node.

4. Technical Specifications for Projected Architecture

Specifications for local clusters: The apparent criterion for industrialized activities on the local cluster is to guarantee a minimal bandwidth distribution of available clusters/nodes. The presence of the Edge Node in the local IoT cluster will resolve the liability by promoting bandwidth near the IoT node.

Specifications for fog clusters: The fog node maintains allocated collection of IoT-edge nodes and accountable for supplying the required devices. As the fog cluster would render a resource orchestration framework with advanced controlling capabilities for local IoT nodes, it is hence necessary to spread Artificial Intelligence/Machine Learning (ML) depend on fog node mechanisms. For instance, Machine Learning-based processes and verification are important in fog systems to ensure IT security steps. Most conventional mechanisms based on ML are primarily dependent on common teaching strategies in this view which could be used for fog nodes which helps with calculation.

The fog network provides optimized services for participating local stakeholders and can therefore provide a complex distribution of resources, coordination, and offloading features. The fog system would use layered technology to facilitate the efficient availability and use of clusters and nodes. For mobility control and cluster knowledge in the fog network are important reasons of the distribution of the necessary services/tools to mobile users and the restricted capacities of local nodes/devices. Another critical requirement of the fog network is connectivity because of the accessibility of an extremely heterogeneous framework that requires a complex range of services.

Specifications for global clusters: Even though local layers interact with the supply of efficient resources and capabilities, it also needs a maximum range of devices for computing, storage and computing. Having considered the case scenario used in our log-house building, the key objectives of the local layers plan is to, allocate and oversee the entire production economy, allocate and support the depository and various services necessary is shown in Figure 5. Execute a given method and guarantee the

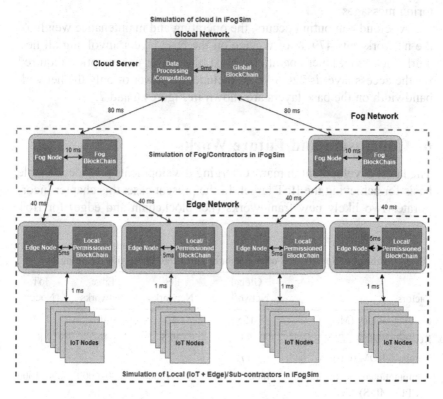

Figure 5.   Cluster-Level Framework of Block Edge in Fog Sim

availability and ease of use of intensive services. A key criterion is to ensure the secure connection of the local layers to the different layers of the device.

5. Results and Discussions

Contrasted here the main efficiency factors, i.e. bandwidth, resource utilization, and cluster utilization, in a dual display channel, i.e., when blockchain cannot be implemented and used within IIoT frameworks.

For convenience, we have just acquired a sub-contractor/IoT-edge networking in one of the cluster networks is shown in Table 1. One example of installation is the use of the convenient audio-biased knot control of a wood cutter. The main considerations in this case are the bandwidth, there will be a minimum pause in the video stream and monitoring messages.

As cloud computing occurs, the operating and maintenance weight of the network puts 479 W of voltage on the base layers, involving all network and kernel layer operations. Next, the power consumption required for the access layer is 220.3 W, so include the power of only the network bandwidth on the base layers are shown in Figures 6 and 7.

6. Conclusion and Future Works

The latest development in many emerging developments provides a stable basis for achieving the IIoT target. In the present case, this chapter incorporates two likely new frameworks (i.e. blockchain and edge) for IIoT

Table 1.　Specificities of Blockchain and Edge Protection Training

Factors	Global Networks	Fog Networks	Edge Networks	IoT Nodes
Sending latency (MBps)	155	80	40	13.5
Receiving latency (MBps)	85	39.5	16	8
Database/ROM (GB)	17	7	3	2
Computational specifications/ CPU (MIPS)	14000–21000	9000–10000	2000–6000	600–1600
Transfer rate (ms)	144	48	4	2

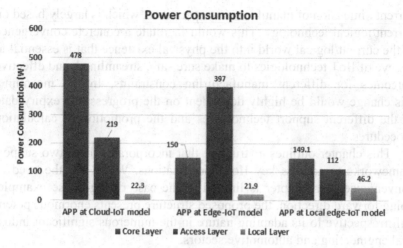

Figure 6.　Power Consumption: Without Blockchain

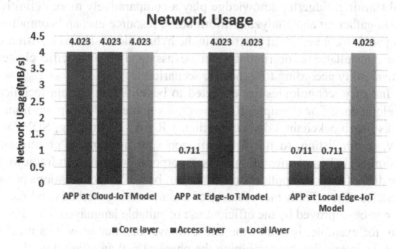

Figure 7.　Network Usage: With Blockchain

implementations in order to satisfy the necessary specifications. All these IIoT criteria generally involve: minimal bandwidth issues, centralized throughput, protection, and methods that track/control. IIoT is supposed to change the current treatment and control paths of manufacturing and our own systems by transforming them completely cryptic, toned, and flexible according to various needs. This transformation will alter the current dimension of manufacturing operations, which is largely based on current/logical technology. This would facilitate a concrete convergence of the current/logical world into the physical existence that is essential to the eye of IIoT technologies to make sure safe, streamlined, and effective outcomes for different manufacturing constraints. In the meantime, this change would be highly dependent on the progress and expiry date of the different support technologies and the promotion of calculation procedures.

This chapter outlines a structure that incorporates these two support frameworks to address key IIoT specifications. While, for the need of convenience, this chapter is limited to the case of log-house example, going forward direction, the proposed structure presents enormous potential irrespective to its adapting nature in the numerous significant industrial engineering and automotive sectors.

Usage of Artificial Intelligence in coming years, IIoT implementations would be critical for manufacturing automotive and conscious practical learning. Edge/fog knowledge play a comparatively more definitive role in gathering and analyzing information, resource use, and computing compared to conventional practices in the hybrid cloud scenario. Different zones, installations, or runtime can be assigned to a specific cluster/system/entity according to a specific scenario.

Industry technologies are expected to benefit from current technical developments. For example, IIoT integrates numerous disruptive frameworks like blockchain, edge computing, VR/AR, 3D printing, SDN, and NFV, in our listing, to fulfill the mission specifications of present and upcoming IIoT implementations. The incorporation of a given framework may differ from one application to the next, based on specifications or use scenarios. The effectiveness factors of manufacturing methods and facilities can be improved by the efficient use of suitable languages. The digital twin, for example, is one of the latest innovations that provide a mechanism for interaction by combining the physical/real and digital worlds.

IIoT systems worldwide will be complex due to the growing demand for hosting application platforms and the convergence of multiple frameworks allowed. Meanwhile, these technical advances give opponents a much wider scope for incorporating different firewalls. IIoT applications include a complex, analytical, and responsive security monitoring system that can identify and eliminate potential security threats on each network. One potential promising area of research in this area is to suggest a security orchestration mechanism capable of controlling security criteria.

In relation to adaptive safety management mechanisms, new distributed and integrated confidence models are expected to deal in the upcoming dynamic IIoT implementations of a wide range of network participants and diverse stakeholders/service vendors.

References

Battula, B., Anusha, V., Praveen, N., Shankar, G., & Latchoumi, T. P. (2020). Prediction of vehicle safety system using internet of things. *Journal of Green Engineering, 10*(4), 1786–1798.

Beerens, R., *et al.*, (2020, January). Control allocation for an industrial high-precision transportation and positioning system. *IEEE Transactions on Control Systems Technology 29*(2), 876–883.

Chen, M., *et al.*, (2020, September/October). Living with I-fabric: Smart living powered by intelligent fabric and deep analytics. *IEEE Network, 34*(5), 156–163.

Jiang, X., Pang, Z., Luvisotto, M., Candell, R., Dzung, D., & Fischione, C. (2020, September). Delay optimization for industrial wireless control systems based on channel characterization. *IEEE Transactions on Industrial Informatics, 16*(9), 5855–5865.

Kushch, S., & Prieto-Castrillo, F. (2019, April). Blockchain for dynamic nodes in a smart city. In *2019 IEEE 5th World Forum on Internet of Things (WF-IoT)*, Limerick, Ireland, (pp. 29–34). IEEE.

Li, D., Deng, L., Cai, Z., & Souri, A. (2020). Blockchain as a service model in the internet of things management: Systematic review. *Transactions on Emerging Telecommunications Technologies*, e4139.

Li, S., Qin, T., & Min, G. (2019). Blockchain-based digital forensics investigation framework in the internet of things and social systems. *IEEE Transactions on Computational Social Systems, 6*(6), 1433–1441.

Liu, J., Huang, K., Rong, H., Wang, H., & Xian, M. (2015). Privacy-preserving public auditing for regenerating-code-based cloud storage. *IEEE Transactions on Information Forensics and Security, 10*(7), 1513–1528.

Loganathan, J., Janakiraman, S., & Latchoumi, T. P. (2017). A novel architecture for next generation cellular network using opportunistic spectrum access scheme. *Journal of Advanced Research in Dynamical and Control Systems, 9*(12), 1388–1400.

Loganathan, J., Janakiraman, S., Latchoumi, T. P., & Shanthoshini, B. (2017). Dynamic virtual server for optimized web service interaction. *International Journal of Pure and Applied Mathematics, 117*(19), 371–377.

Mcginthy, J. M., & Michaels, A. J. (2019, March). Secure industrial internet of things critical infrastructure node design, *IEEE Internet of Things Journal, 6*(5), 8021–8037.

Paes, R., Mazur, D. C., Venne, B. K., & Ostrzenski, J. (2020, March/April). A guide to securing industrial control networks: Integrating it and OT systems. *IEEE Industry Applications Magazine, 26*(2), 47–53.

Pan, F., Pang, Z., Luvisotto, M., Xiao, M. & Wen, H. (2018, December). Physical-layer security for industrial wireless control systems: Basics and future directions. *IEEE Industrial Electronics Magazine, 12*(4), 18–27.

Petropulu, A., Diamantaras, K. I., Han, Z., Niyato, D., & Zonouz, S. (2019, March). Contactless monitoring of critical infrastructure [from the guest editors]. *IEEE Signal Processing Magazine, 36*(2), 19–21.

Russell, L., Goubran, R., Kwamena, F., & Knoefel, F. (2018, March). Agile IoT for critical infrastructure resilience: Cross-modal sensing as part of a situational awareness approach. *IEEE Internet of Things Journal, 5*(6), 4454–4465.

Sahoo, S., Fajge, A. M., Halder, R., & Cortesi, A. (2019). A hierarchical and abstraction-based blockchain model. *Applied Sciences, 9*(11), 2343.

Stellios, I., Kotzanikolaou, P., Psarakis, M., Alcaraz, C., & Lopez, J. (2018). A survey of IoT-enabled cyberattacks: Assessing attack paths to critical infrastructures and services. *IEEE Communications Surveys and Tutorials, 20*(4), 3453–3495.

Vasanth, V., Venkatachalapathy, K., Thamarai, L., Parthiban, L., & Ezhilarasi, T. P. (2017). A survey on cache route schemes to improve QoS in AD-HOC networks. *Pakistan Journal of Biotechnology, 14*, 265–269.

Wang, G., Shi, Z., Nixon, M., & Han, S. (2019, July). Chain splitter: Towards blockchain-based industrial IoT architecture for supporting hierarchical storage. In *2019 IEEE International Conference on Blockchain (Blockchain)* (pp. 166–175). IEEE.

Wang, T., *et al.*, (2018, March). Big data reduction for a smart city's critical infrastructural health monitoring. *IEEE Communications Magazine, 56*(3), 128–133.

Wu, Y., Hu, F., Min, G., & Zomaya, A. (2017). *Big Data and Computational Intelligence in Networking*. Hoboken, NJ: CRC Press.

Wu, Y., Huang, H., Wang, C.-X., & Pan, Y. (2019). *5G-Enabled Internet of Things*. Hoboken, NJ: CRC Press.

Yaga, D., Mell, P., Roby, N., & Scarfone, K. (2019). Blockchain technology overview. arXiv preprint arXiv:1906.11078.

Yang, H., Yuan, J., Yao, H., Yao, Q., Yu, A., & Zhang, J. (2019). Blockchain-based hierarchical trust networking for JointCloud. *IEEE Internet of Things Journal, 7*(3), 1667–1677.

Zheng, W., Zheng, Z., Chen, X., Dai, K., Li, P., & Chen, R. (2019). Nutbaas: A blockchain-as-a-service platform. *IEEE Access, 7*, 134422–134433.

Chapter 17

Strengthening Omnichannel Retail Supply Chain with Blockchain Technology

Rahul Gupta

*Amity Business School, Amity University, Gautam Budh Nagar,
Uttar Pradesh, India*

Abstract

The last few decades have seen the transformation of the modern supply chain from a simple (inflexible, linear, and reactive) to a complex (flexible, multi-echelon, and proactive) supply chain. The supply chain encompasses a global network of third-party service providers (Logistic, IT, Customer support, Warehousing), practicing numerous procedures and policies. The complex management of retailers, buyers' and suppliers' relations are susceptible to quite a few challenges (transparency, trust, security). Blockchain is an advanced technology with features like distributed notes, storage mechanism, consensus algorithm, decentralized structure, smart contracting, and asymmetric encryption, which helps to ensure supply chain network prominence, security, trust, and transparency. Blockchain technology turbocharges the profitability and efficiency of the supply chain. The level of security like physical management is complemented by process enhancements and technological leverages. Blockchain provides shared ledgers with error-free decentralized digital records, while every participating member act as a catalyst, by maintaining his data set for the transaction. Digitalization eliminates the need for traditional third-party verification; participants may self-verify the transactions. The information once entered is inconvertible and can never be obliterated. Transacted data is stored in time-stamped blocks and serves as the data structure. Blockchain technology serves flawlessly with features like storage mechanism and storage nodes, smart contract, consensus algorithm, and asymmetric encryption. Blockchain technology is successfully implemented in various sectors like finance, banking, IoT, and forex transactions. Current research focuses on providing abridged details of blockchain and serves to introduce its innumerable applications emphasizing the potential to transform supply chain provenance, business process reengineering, to security enhancement for the success of omnichannel retail supply chain.

Keywords: Blockchain, Supply chain, Retail, Transparency

1. Introduction

The origin of blockchain can be traced back to the electronic transaction system proposed by Satoshi Nakamoto in 2008. It was non trusted peer-to-peer network with proof of the public history of contacts. These transactions were prone to modification by computational hacking. Primarily blockchain-supported digital currency like Bitcoin offered promising results. Successful results encouraged several other organizations like, shipping, manufacturing, finance, energy, automotive, aviation, healthcare, food and agriculture, IoT, and supply chain management to implement this technology. The retail industry encounters challenges of trust, transparency, security, and efficacy due to the involvement of multiple entities like buyers, suppliers, and other service providers. Retailers offer their products and services via brick-n-mortar stores and revolutionary electronic channels. Competitive nature of retail demands continuous improvements in their operations and offerings. These challenges can be addressed by the amalgamation of technology like blockchain with the process like supply chain. The underlying foundation is built on EDI, WWW, and network sharing methodologies, these are supported by cryptography, disruptive computing, and software. Various transaction costs are saved by using technology, as data is stored as a shared ledger on peer to peer network system (Figure 1) (Inviqa, 2019).

2. Retail

Moderns retail business is experiencing high growth and retailers wish to grow their business and revenue either by offline or online selling.

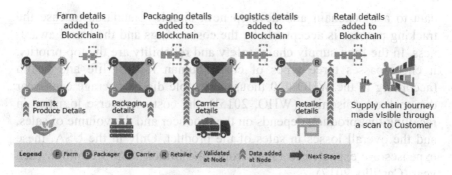

Figure 1. Retail Supply Chain and Blockchain

Globally retail business is projected to be around 26.7 trillion U.S. dollars by 2022. The share of e-retail is growing exemplary at 20% annually and will touch $5 trillion (Global Ecommerce, 2019). The profound influence of technological innovations, financial, non-financial transactions savings, buying and selling via the internet has seen tremendous growth (Chaffey, 2011; Mohapatra, 2013; Qin, 2011).

Retailers are offering their products and services via omnichannel. Brick and mortar retailers like Wal-Mart have invested in the online retail platform Flip Cart. Online retailer Amazon has invested in departmental store MORE. Corporate houses in India like TATA and Reliance are investing heavily in offering their products and services by both online and offline retail channels. While fulfilling customers' expectations, the only stumbling block these retailers face is the soiled, inflexible liner and reactive supply chain. Supply planning and inventory management are suffered by fragmented data, poor connectivity, unreliability, and transparency issues in supplies. The struggle is to offer a seamless omnichannel purchase experience and trust to customers.

3. Walmart Case

To promote food safety, IBM has worked with a group of food corporations, including Walmart, Nestlé, Kroger, and Unilever. Walmart had previously accepted blockchain technology and is now extending it to the entire group. The major goal is to reduce the expense and time it takes to recall dangerous food batches. The initial cost of migrating all data to a blockchain and develop new, simpler standards to ease the tracking process is acceptable by the cost savings and the brand awareness. In the food supply chain, safety and reliability are the top priority, it encompasses three types of costs: human loss of life and health (according to the WHO 420 thousand people die on average each year due to food poisoning (WHO, 2015)), the cost of reverse logistics in recalling that product, depends on the producer and the volume of sales, and the overall losses in sales of the product. Only in the USA, these expenses are expected to range from $4.4 billion to $93.2 billion each year (Castillo, 2017).

4. Demand Management

Demand management across the channel is a challenging task by predicting and responding at the right time and place. Required level of competency can be achieved by mutual trust, accountability, and transparency among supply partners. Digital connectivity has fueled the fire of growth

Figure 2.   Global Connectivity

by sharing responsibility at each level, focuses on problem-solving even before they erupt. Transparency and communication across the supply chain get promoted by quick decision making, forecast, and address problems beforehand (Figure 2).

World Economic Forum advocates that blockchain technology as a tool increases trust, empowers users, and checks corruption. Transaction records are saved in an incorruptible digital ledger (records of virtually everything of value) (Tapscott, 2016). Every nook and corner of retail gets revolutionized with the immense potential of blockchain technology. The role of intermediaries gets eliminated by streamlining operations. Transactional data is stored in blocks, which are unchangeable, continuous, with a single digital record and authentic verification. These blocks are connected by cryptographic value (a technique for secure communication), over a peer-to-peer network, and completely accessible to the public.

Shoppers' sensitive data is protected and guarded by potential cyber threats and results in bonding network participants with trust. Retail supply chains encounter unique challenges like security, payments, authenticity, and timely supply. Potential applications and smart contracts help in overcoming long-term and short-term challenges associated with the supply chain.

5. Payments

Blockchain-based platforms incur faster payments at a lesser cost, results in e-commerce transactions with rapid micropayments. The study suggests Ethereum' Lighting network a blockchain-based platform, handle millions of transactions per second with strong security standards better customer experience with speed, and traceability with a decentralized network, as compared to a costly and time-consuming traditional system process (Inviqa, 2019), which follows multiple stages and 2–6% processing fee (Geer, 2018). Blockchain ensures smooth cross-border transactions, overrides barriers of fees, exchange rates, and other complexities associate with international trade. Blockchain-based payment gateways as the third party, improve the functionality of traditional payment gateways. In the future, blockchain-based payment cards and digital wallets may ensure direct money transfer between buyer and seller (Mire, 2020).

6. Security

Transactional data with weak encryption stored at the cloud or centralized location is prone to hack and vulnerable to theft. Hackers with modern tools can breach by using tricks and tactics. Implementing blockchain technology, transactional data is secured in encrypted form vis network-connected computer nodes. Longer the chain of nodes ensures the impossibility of hacking. Decentralization safeguards a single point of entry into the network and restricts access to sensitive information regarding buyers & suppliers and holds the security key with reliability (Geer, 2018; Sharma, 2020). Invoice receipt and other information related to sales are stored in cryptographic form, instead of hard or soft copies, which makes it easier for customers to claim the services as promised (Market Realist, 2019). Redemption of rewards, warranties, promotional schemes, and loyalty benefits become easier to claim with reliability and authenticity (Inviqa, 2019; Post, 2019). The highest level of transparency is offered in transactions, otherwise difficult to observe, even the smallest change in the transaction is noticed, and customers track their transactions as per their wishes and requirements. Multinationals like Walmart and Unilever use blockchain technology for the smooth functioning of their supply chain and ensure their commitment to data security regulations (Market Realist, 2019; Post, 2019).

7. Material Supply

Smooth and uninterrupted supply is a dream for all retail organizations; retailers deal with numerous partners, connected through multi-echelon supply chains. All associates are spread beyond national boundaries, and practice various cultures, and bound with local procedures. Buyers at times find it difficult to trace the authenticity of the transactions, originality of supplies at every stage. These malpractices are addressed by implementing blockchain technology, which makes each stage of the supply chain accountable and transparent. The originality of the product can be traced at the customer's end by assessing real-time shipping lifecycle data (Inviqa, 2019). RFID cards and sensor technology make tracking and record-keeping easier for customers and retailers. Both track the entire timeline of products from sourcing through selling. Lesser costs are administered by eliminating superfluous intermediaries in the supply chain. Efficient use of technology in delivery and distribution saves various expenses like record keeping, follow-ups, and human resource expenses (Send & Cox, 2020).

With growing urbanization e- retail is now an essential arm of retailing, with competitiveness boost profitability for many organizations. Adding an e-retail platform in their business facilitates the development of many retailers and helps to meet the demand for more customers. Few drawbacks these e-commerce faces are not unique to India, rather the following issues are reported in other parts of the world.

- Delivery of poor-quality product.
- Suppliers commitment for efficiency and commitment.
- Ineffective management.

To encounter the issues related to these complaints various e-commerce operators take precautions including business boosting, resource handling, and data security which is in large amount. Genuine trade data affect management's decision-making. Efficient supply chain management helps organizations to be competitive in the e-commerce field (Li & Chen, 2019). Suppliers for e-commerce opt to have an operational request for implementing tools and techniques for greater operational control on data storage, movement of goods, and services (Kouvelis *et al.*, 2019). E-commerce organizations require a supply chain supported by technology, and blockchain technology comes in handy in support. Provides continuous tracking for consignments. Blockchain embedded in e-commerce platforms ensures cloud storage of data and certifies secured transitions while data handling. Blockchain technology saves transactional records on nodes and all members of the supply chain get access to these records (Figure 3).

Faster communication tools and smart technologies have boosted product and service deliveries in today's competitive environment. Firms are bound to develop innovative methods for product and service improvements. Partnering with multiple firms and assembling products via collaborations, to enhance the availability of supplies. Suppliers are better equipped with resources to tackle competitors. Efficient cost management while narrowing the gap between supply and demand, forced retailers to closely connect with their partners (Jagan Mohan Reddy *et al.*, 2019; Wong & Ngai, 2019). Product chains are managed with the development of new products and services, while transactions from supply through manufacturing to delivery deals with supply chain management.

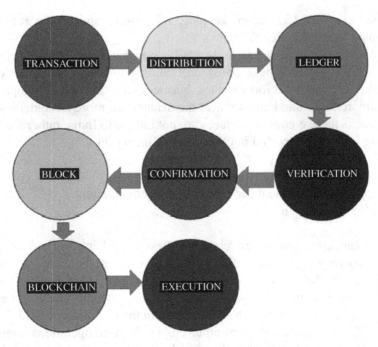

Figure 3.   Blockchain Development

So, when the production chain is handled efficiently, the management of the supply chain becomes easier for the organization. While managing all this the inherent risk of data breach needs consideration in the first place. Financial institutes follow a traditional credit ratings system and model the credit risk of the firm. Small and medium firms generally fail to show-case their absolute assessment. Contrarily shoppers assess their suppliers by vendor ratings as a broad range of operational performance. However, credit rating models for a supply chain, inclusive of an integrated vendor and financial ratings can be obtained jointly (Moretto *et al.*, 2019). Sustainability-related issues like social, economic, and environmental factors. Material quality assessment and risk are measured with an aggregated matric (Xu *et al.*, 2019). The uncertainty for demand and supply from retailers till the source studies under bullwhip effect (Braz *et al.*, 2018). This is also known as the Forrester effect, a phenomenon of upward variation in demand as we move up from customer to retailer to distributor to the manufacturer to suppliers. At each stage, the demand gets distorted to maximize profitability at the local level. The effect put a

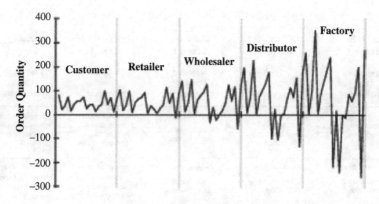

Figure 4.   Bullwhip Effect

negative impact on the performance of the supply chain. Negative impact lead to higher logistical expenses, disproportionate safety inventory, spoiled relationships, lost sales, and revenue to name a few. Major causes as studied by Lee *et al.* (1997) are order batching, price fluctuation, shortage and ration gaming, and demand forecasting.

Lack of online monitoring of these developmental phases demands robust technology. IoT, big data, cloud computing, blockchain technology, and industry 4.0, are the supportive tools for improving the product and services (Figure 4).

8. Value Chain

The transformation from raw material to work in progress, semi-finished to final product and services passes through a production process (Ellis & Santagate, 2017). All the activities in the process of transforming raw material to finish product are linked like a chain of functions. Professor M. Porter coined the value chain where each stage adds value by offering primary and secondary support activities. Today's technological enhancements like IoT, cloud computing, and blockchain technology with the support of liberalization of trade barriers, essentially recognized production as a chain of interconnected activities. Technology has efficiently facilitated in-depth analysis of each stage. Value chain deals with specific products or services while supply chain facilitates operations perspective, product chain, marketing, sales, logistics, finance, and customer service (Centobelli *et al.*, 2014). The evolution of the supply chain is depicted in Figure 5.

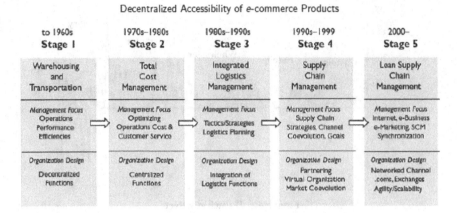

Figure 5.   Evolution of Supply Chain

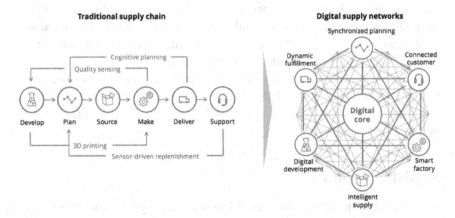

Figure 6.   Traditional versus Digital Supply Chain

Global value chains have positively impacted more than two-third of world trade, this fact was established by various organizations like WTO (World Trade Organization) and WBG (an organization for OECD (Economic C-operation and Development), and IDE-JETRO (Institute of Developing Economies) and RCGV (research center for global value chain at UIBE (the University of International Business and Economics) (Figure 6) (SAP, 2017). Governments need to support and form an environment, which is conducive to investment, upgrade skills at the local manufacturing level, and support technology providers and technology users. Hence transparent and decentralized supply chain and value chain get their way to get rid of all authentications and malicious frauds.

Understanding the feasibility of blockchain and supply chain is limited, but certainly affirms that this technology-based framework augments assurance and decreases associated risks (AEB, 2017; Lee *et al.* 1997). Products can be re-engineered and traced with smart contracts and can directly connect the value chain (Korpela *et al.*, 2017). Mean-variance is measured for analyzing global supply chain risk (Nakamoto, 2008). Food supply chain (Friedlmaier *et al.*, 2016), luxury goods (Tumasjan, 2017), and agriculture products (Kosba *et al.* 2015) have been used and get benefited from blockchain technology. Blockchain technology is also supporting industry 4.0 initiatives along with benefiting supply chain processes. Transaction records are stored in nodes which are fault tolerance, immutable with trust instead of centralized single point storage, prone to hack and failure. The Agri-food supply chain has partnered with blockchain technology and seen immense profitability (Kruijff & Weigand, 2017). IPS (industrial product-service system) has also unleashed the benefits of blockchain technology (Gallersdorfer, 2017), e-commerce is using the blockchain-based application for smooth services deliveries (Yeh *et al.*, 1994).

The above discussion supports the immense potential of blockchain in enhancing supply chain performance. Blockchain has various prominent applications in the supply chain. Some suggested uses of blockchain in the Supply chain are as follows.

Traditionally retailers were confined to their regional or national boundaries. Internationalization with diplomatic relations has boosted the trade among nations and demands better supplies, given a boost to sales across nations. The concept of global supply chains attracts attention with enhanced economic evaluations for the firm and country (Koberg & Longoni, 2018). Lack of prevention for illegal, countified products and unauthorized access results in mismanaged supply chains. Kroll reported 42% of global supply chain organizations reported at least one fraud in the last decade. IT tools come in handy in the prevention and detection of fraud along with any other supply chain incubuses, as per the report "it can also be a huge threat to a company's operations, reputation, and future business prospects" (Wailgum, 2008). These frauds are various, like bribery, kickbacks, sectioning violations, FCPA violation (Foreign Corrupt Practices Act), misapprehension of products and services (Glenn Pomerantz & Cascini, 2008).

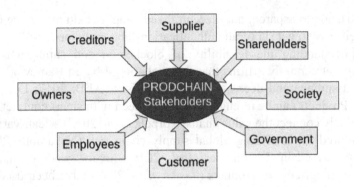

Figure 7.   PRODCHAIN

The application of supply chain has rigorously been used in agri-food (Behzadi *et al.*, 2018; Jonkman *et al.*, 2019), fashion (Wen *et al.*, 2018), healthcare, and turbines (Khosravi and Izbirak, 2019). Supply chains for all these organizations are strongly correlated with their intermediaries. Lack of trust among intermediaries' malicious perspective demolishes the significance of the supply chain. The present global business environment necessitates an approach to bridge the gap (Cole and Aitken, 2019). For better socio-economic sustainable development, a transparent approach is much needed. Blockchain technology comes in handy with integrating supply chain partners with transparent operations and decentralized resources.

"PRODCHAIN" a global platform obliquely benefits retail especially e-commerce. E-commerce has witnessed growth in terms of finance and social perspective. The objective of "PRODCHAIN" is to improve e-commerce transactions and supply chain efficiency (Figure 7).

9. Supply Chain for Tomorrow

Digitization has changed how present business models will take over traditional business models. Customers' expectations can only be met when businesses accelerate with 24/7 operational efficiency. Communication, transactions, and interactions among parterres have seen tremendous growth with upgraded technologies. Institute of Supply Chain Management proposes in their study in 2017, states that 65% of the value is generated through suppliers. Customer services, their satisfaction, and profitability are resultant of quality, delivery, and cost incurred by suppliers and supply chain partners.

The exhaustive reach of e-commerce is the resultant of hard work and performance improvement of logistical partners, meeting the high expectation of service requirements. Globalization has only increased the complexity of their working model, in fulfilling expectations at all levels. Supply disruptions like weather, delays in delivery, quality defects, natural disasters, financial stability need to be addressed. Collaboration among all stakeholders is essential to foster efficiency, innovation, and satisfaction. Lack of transparency and visibility is a challenge in collecting, processing data from various processes, sources, and systems. Greater visibility is vital in addressing challenges from the new era. Following five trends provides supports the supply chain with new advanced models.

9.1 *Distributed network*

As discussed, data is not stored at a centralized location, rather blockchain supports storing digital data at nodes, making it publicly available. Alteration is also not possible due to decentralization.

9.2 *Shared ledger*

Network participants maintain digital records of transactions serves as a public ledger. The blockchain serves as a transparent and trusted method for execution. Algorithms are run by participants for measuring the validity of transactions stored digitally. Mutually agreed common decisions for the validity of transactions are included in the blockchain, ledgers are recorded upgrades to the network.

9.3 *Digital transactions*

Blocks are structured with transactions. Every block has a cryptographic hash to the previous block in the blockchain. Transactions are structured into blocks. Each block contains a cryptologic hash to the preceding block within the blockchain. This hash provides integrity to the digital record.

9.4 *Consensus*

A protocol with all blockchain participants in the network settle around validating a transaction. Monopoly decisions are prevented as participants take decisions with the consensus of all.

9.5 *Smart contract*

Decentralized models derive efficiency and streamline operations. The smart contract regulates logistics partners and payment processes, contracts are automatically executed by predefined conditions and rules. An integrated management system is streamlined with smart contracts. Retailers are partnering with logistics and payment intermediaries by practicing smart contracts (Geer, 2018). Human resource requirements are abridged by automating certain processes and following some pre-established operating procedures (Sheil and Azmathullah, 2019). Automatic replenishment of inventories is ensured by practicing digital inventory management. Digitization ensures retailers' commitment to zero stockout situation, neither on the shelf nor on the website makes them and their customers happy (Post, 2019).

Quick response with cost-effectiveness for certain service requests is a potential benefit of blockchain technology. For example, a request for a canceled order is processed fast and saves handling of supplies, and in case of returns, it ensures timely refunds with a smart contract. The system will follow SOP and the process will be done quickly. At times customers change delivery address while the product is in transit, the smart contract ensures automatic updating of the new delivery address on the system (Market Realist, 2019). Loyalty rewards, sales incentives, and warranties are easily offered to customers with smart contracts. Visualization gets improved with series of recorded, unabridged data. Decentralization allows, stores to completely owned their assets like inventory, videos, digital signages, etc., customer possess information of product origin and components.

9.6 *Ethical standards*

Practicing Ethical Standards is the most common dilemma for any retailer, dealing either online or offline retiling (Asia Blockchain Review, 2020; Send & Cox, 2020). Unethical practices like (sub-quality standard supplies, claiming inorganic food items as organic, use of child labor in manufacturing, etc.) are followed for extra profits and to ensure timely availability of inventories. These issues can be addressed by using blockchain technology, by storing all transactional data in shared ledgers, where data is safe in encrypted form. Transparency issues are always coming under scanner, online retailer Amazon faces this issue, as per US

President's Tweet "have stated my concerns with Amazon long before the Election. Unlike others, they pay little or no taxes to state & local governments, use our Postal System as their Delivery Boy (causing tremendous loss to the U.S.), and are putting many thousands of retailers out of business! — Donald J. Trump (@realDonaldTrump) March 29, 2018".

9.7 *Transaction speed*

Removal of intermediaries ensures transactions occur on a single network, speed depends on connectivity and speed at which new blocks are generated.

9.8 *Trust and transparency*

Transparency fosters trust in the system among buyers and suppliers. Transactional data stored in shared ledgers is safe against tampering and data breaches. The system offers security, speed, visibility, and traceability.

9.9 *Process integration*

Existing and new system gets integrated for a wide range of processes, online payments, internal and external systems. Intermediaries, buyers, and suppliers served with a shared ledger with a wealth of opportunities.

9.10 *Customer reviews*

Favorable reviews are blessings while unfavorable ones are a curse. Positive reviews guide buyers and contribute to sales. Blockchain can verify and safeguards against fake reviews by customers and negative reviews by competitors. A robust foundation provides a win-win situation for all concerns.

9.11 *Personalized offerings*

The buyer's purchase history is captured by blockchain. Having full control of this information buyers are free to share with merchants of their choice. Buyer's preferential list of merchandise helps them while offering discounts and loyalty bonuses. Results can be seen in improved sales and enhanced satisfaction for their buyers.

Integration of all data sources across internal and external functions among supply chain partners. The connection also needs to ensure access to unaccounted data from outside media, IoT with traditional ERP.

9.12 Collaboration

Collaboration is essential as 50% of value comes through suppliers, and improving collaboration is essential. Internet-based networking supports multi-enterprise alliances and arrangements.

9.13 Cyber-aware

Hacking and cyber-attacks hamper the working of networks and raise the concern of reliability. Securing an online database, susceptible to cyber-attack is the biggest challenge.

9.14 Cognitively enabled

Automated operations with optimization and efficiency of the supply chain are the future. Service platform's ability to take timely decisions and opt for the next best options, understanding the impact on business and prioritizing attention based on impact.

9.15 Comprehensive

Data and real-time analytics must be scaled. The ability to outperform humans is dependent on speed.

10. Conclusion

Extensive benefits offered by blockchain embraces retailers to achieve exhaustive growth. Blockchain technology serves as a major support system for retailers while addressing buyer's dilemmas and build trust among stakeholders with a unique digital ID for every SKU. Technology serves as an ideal solution to manage buyer's data transparently and reliably. Dependency on the traditional paper-based information storage system is reduced. The retail industry faces regular and relentless breakthrough innovations with technological upgradation. The shopping experience is enhanced from personnel shopping to virtual shopping, manual search to voice search, and many more new experiences are yet to be explored. Expansion of retail activities like so is sourcing, supply of merchandise, and service management is beyond national boundaries. Fulfilling varied cultural expectations, dealing in multiple currencies, obligating regulations, forces retailers to be on their toes. Blockchain technology helps retailers to restrain, become infamous for poor quality, ingenuine, and countified items to be sold through them. Competitors adapt innovative tools-n-technologies, compulsorily motivates, and encourages all retailers to upgrade their system with the latest technological advancements. Blockchain technology is all set to become a de-facto technology to support the omnichannel retail industry.

References

AEB. (2017). *Successful Inbound Supply Chain Management*. s.l.: AEB, 2017.

Asia Blockchain Review. (2020). How blockchain has helped the business of e-commerce. *Asia Blockchain Review — Gateway to Blockchain in Asia*, January 20, 2020 [Online]. Available at: https://www.asiablockchainreview. com/how-blockchain-has-helped-the-business-of-e-commerce/ [accessed: March 23, 2020].

Behzadi, G., OâSullivan, M. J., Olsen, T. L., & Zhang, A. (2018). Agribusiness supply chain risk management: A review of quantitative decision models. *Omega, 79*, 21–42.

Braz, A. C., De Mello, A. M., de Vasconcelos Gomes, L. A., & de Souza Nascimento, P. T. (2018). The bullwhip effect in closed-loop supply chains: A systematic literature review. *Journal of Cleaner Production, 202*, 376–389.

Castillo, Michael del. (2017). Walmart, Kroger & Nestle team with IBM blockchain to fight food poisoning. Coindesk. [Online] August 22, 2017. https://www.coindesk.com/walmart-kroger-nestle-team-with-ibm-blockchain-to-fight-food-poisoning/.

Centobelli, P. *et al.* (2014). E-procurement and e-supply chain: Features and development of e-collaboration. In *IERI Procedia 6*, 8–14. Venice, Italy.

Chaffey, D. (2011). *E-Business and E-Commerce Management: Strategy, Implementation, and Practice*. Harlow (Essex): Pearson Education.

Cole, R., & Aitken, J. (2019). The role of intermediaries in establishing a sustainable supply chain. *Journal of Purchasing and Supply Management, 26*, 100533.

Ellis, S., & Santagate, J. (2017). *The digitally enabled supply chain with manufacturing use cases*. s.l: IDC US42434217.

Friedlmaier, M., Tumasjan, A., & Welpe, I. (2016). *Disrupting industries with blockchain: The industry, venture capital funding, and regional distribution of blockchain ventures*. Technische Universität München (TUM) — TUM School of Management.

Gallersdörfer, U. (2017). *Analysis of Use Cases of Blockchain Technology in Legal Transactions Master's Thesis*. Technische Universität München, Munich, Germany, 2017.

Geer, D. (2018, June). How blockchain will transform the e-commerce industry over the next few years. *The Next Web* [Online]. Available at: https://thenextweb.com/contributors/2018/06/15/how-blockchain-will-transform-the-e-.

Glenn Pomerantz, P. L. W., & Cascini, J. (2018). Supply chain fraud: Risk management for retail & consumer products companies. https://www.bdo.com/blogs/consumer-business-compass/december-2018/supply-chain-fraud [accessed December 2020].

Global Ecommerce 2019. eMarketer [Online]. Available at: https://www.emarketer.com/content/global-ecommerce-2019 [accessed: March 7, 2020].

Gregor, K. (2017). *IBM wants to make 2017 the year of blockchain enterprise deployment*. s.l.: IDC.

https://abcnews.go.com/Politics/president-trump-attacks-amazon-tweet/story?id=54093899.

https://www.freecodecamp.org/news/satoshi-nakamotos-bitcoin-whitepaper-a-walk-through-3e9e1dee71ce/.

Ignite Ltd. (February 8, 2019). How blockchain is impacting ecommerce. [Online]. Available at: https://igniteoutsourcing.com/blockchain/how-blockchain-is-impacting-ecommerce/. [accessed: March 25, 2020].

Inviqa, *An introduction to blockchain in e-commerce*, March 19, 2019. [Online]. Available at: https://inviqa.com/blog/introduction-blockchain-ecommerce [accessed: February 5, 2020].

Jagan Mohan Reddy, K., Neelakanteswara Rao, A., & Krishnanand, L. (2019). A review on supply chain performance measurement systems. *Procedia Manufacturing, 30*, 40–47, Digital manufacturing transforming industry towards sustainable growth [Online]. Available at: http://www.sciencedirect.com/science/article/pii/S235197891930037X.

Jonkman, J., Barbosa-Póvoa, A. P., & Bloemhof, J. M. (2019). Integrating harvesting decisions in the design of agro-food supply chains. *European Journal of Operational Research, 276*(1), 247–258.

Khosravi, F., & Izbirak, G. (2019). A stakeholder perspective of social sustainability measurement in healthcare supply chain management. *Sustainable Cities and Society, 50*, 101681 [Online]. Available at: http://www.sciencedirect.com/science/article/pii/S2210670719309576.

Koberg, E., & Longoni, A. (2018). A systematic review of sustainable supply chain management in global supply chains. *Journal of Cleaner Production*.

Korpela, K., Hallikas, J., & Dahlberg, T. (2017). Digital supply chain transformation toward blockchain integration. In *Proceedings of the 50th Hawaii International Conference on System Sciences (HICSS)*, Hawaii, 2017. pp. 4182–4191.

Kosba, A. *et al.* (2015). Hawk: The blockchain model of cryptography and privacy-preserving smart contracts. IACR Working Paper.

Kouvelis, P., Dong, L., & Turcic, D. (2019). *Emerging Technology & Advances in Supply Chain Finance & Risk Management.* Boston, USA: Now Foundations and Trends.

Kruijff, J. de, & Weigand, H. (2017). Towards a blockchain ontology. In *11th International Workshop on Value Modeling and Business Ontologies*. Luxembourg: Luxembourg Institute of Science and Technology.

Lee, H. L., Padmanabhan, V., & Whang, S. (1997). The bullwhip effect in supply chains. *Sloan Management Review, 38*(3), 93–102.

Li, S., & Chen, X. (2019). The role of supply chain finance in the third-party logistics industry: A case study from China. *International Journal of Logistics Research and Applications 22*, 154–171.

Market Realist. (December 16, 2019). Can blockchain change e-commerce in 2020? [Online]. Available at: https://marketrealist.com/2019/12/can-blockchain-change-e-commerce-in-2020/ [accessed: February 12, 2020].

Megahed, A., & Goetschalckx, M. (2018). Tactical supply chain planning under uncertainty with an application in the wind turbines industry. *Computers and Operations Research, 100*, 287–300.

Mire, S. (2020). Blockchain for e-commerce: 12 possible use cases. *Disruptor Daily*, March 23, 2019 [Online]. Available at: https://www.disruptordaily.com/blockchain-use-cases-ecommerce/ [accessed: March 25, 2020]. *International Journal of Advanced Science and Technology, 29*(5), 3793–3798.

Mohapatra, S. (2013). *E-Commerce Strategy: Text and Cases*. New York: Springer Science Business Media.

Moretto, A., Grassi, L., Caniato, F., Giorgino, M., & Ronchi, S. (2019). Supply chain finance: From traditional to supply chain credit rating. *Journal of Purchasing and Supply Management, 25*(2), 197–217.

Nakamoto, S. (2008). Bitcoin: A peer-to-peer electronic cash system. https://bitcoin.org/bitcoin.pdf.

Post, C. (2019). Blockchain technology to revolutionise e-commerce businesses in Australia. *Business Partner Magazine*, May 11, 2019. [Online]. Available at: https://businesspartnermagazine.com/blockchain-technology-revolutionise-e-commerce-businesses-australia/ [accessed: February 12, 2020].

Qin, Z. (2011). *Introduction to E-Commerce*. Berlin: Springer.

SAP. (2017). SAP products — ERP [Online]. https://www.sap.com/products/what-is-erp.html.

Send, D. C., & Cox, D. (March 2, 2020). Know how blockchain technology is transforming e-commerce sector. CryptoNewsZ [Online]. Available at: https://www.cryptonewsz.com/blockchain-and-e-commerce-an-inseparable-duo/ [accessed: March 23, 2020].

Send, D. C., & Cox, D. (March 3, 2020). Has the blockchain technology made e-commerce business easier? CryptoNewsZ [Online]. Available at: https://www.cryptonewsz.com/how-can-blockchain-transform-e-commerce-and-the-way-of-doing-business/ [accessed: April 5, 2020].

Sharma, T. K. (July 10, 1970). Top 10 blockchain solutions for e-commerce. Blockchain Council Blockchain council.org [Online]. Available at: https://www.blockchain-council.org/blockchain/top-10-blockchain-solutions-for-e-commerce/ [accessed: February 12, 2020].

Sheikh, H. H. S., & Azmathullah, R. M. R. (2019). A blockchain-based platform transforms e-commerce perspective into a decentralized marketplace. *International Journal of Management, Technology, and Engineering, 9*(1), 777–784. doi:16.10089. IJMTE 2019. V9I21.18.27983

Tapscott, D. (2016). *Blockchain revolution.* Penguin USA.

Tumasjan, A. (September 12, 2017). Interview on blockchain applications and current research. [Interv.] Federica Mus. Munich.

Wailgum, T. (2008). Fraud, theft risks in supply chains are everywhere. https://www.networkworld.com/article/2278876/,fraud--theft-risks-in-supply-chains-are-everywhere.html.

Wen, X., Choi, T. M., & Chung, S. H. (2019). Fashion retail supply chain management: A review of operational models. *International Journal of Production Economics, 207*, 34–55. https://doi.org/10.1016/j.ijpe.2018.10.012.

Wong, D. T. & Ngai, E. W. (2019). Critical review of supply chain innovation research (1999–2016). *Industrial Marketing Management.* Commerce-industry-over-the-next-few-years/ [accessed: March 24, 2020].

World Health Organization. (December 3, 2015) WHO's first-ever global estimates of foodborne diseases find children under 5 account for almost one-third of deaths. World Health Organization [Online]. http://www.who.int/mediacentre/news/releases/2015/foodborne-disease-estimates/en/.

Xu, X. *et al.* (2016). The blockchain as a software connector. In *Proceedings of the 13th Working IEEE/IFIP Conference on Software Architecture.* s.l.: WICSA.

Yeh, E.-C., Sun, Y., & Venkata, S. S. (1994). Design by expectation: A framework for engineering design optimization. In *Proceedings Sixth International Conference on Tools with Artificial Intelligence, TAI 94.* New Orleans: IEEE.

Chapter 18

Unmasking Counterfeit Readymade Garments in India Using Blockchain Technology

Jitendra Yadav[*,§], Madhvendra Misra[*,¶], Kuldeep Singh[†,||], and Sam Goundar[‡,**]

Department of Management Studies, Indian Institute of Information Technology, Allahabad, India

†*Department of Commerce, Koneru Lakshmaiah Education Foundation University, Guntur, India*

‡*School of Computing, RMIT University, Hanoi, Vietnam*

§*yadavjitendra.phd@gmail.com*

¶*madhvendra@iiita.ac.in*

||*kuldeepsinghcsr@gmail.com*

****sam.goundar@gmail.com*

Abstract

Counterfeit products are the replicated goods of authentic and original brands having indistinguishable packaging, labels, and trademarks on them. It is a very serious threat to economies all over the world. These products are not only causing loss to the nations at great lengths but are also, affecting the employment growth by shutting down the local industries. In the context of India, counterfeiting is no new concept even though, the apparel industry is one of the major contributors to employment and growth in the Indian economy. This chapter focuses on removing the practice of counterfeiting from the Indian apparel industry by examining the ways in which blockchain technology can be integrated with the supply chain management to provide a genuine solution for traceability along with other various contributing operational factors such as reduction in cost, damage and combating the practice of counterfeit products from the apparel industry.

Keywords: Apparel industry, Blockchain technology, Counterfeit, Readymade garments, Supply chain, Traceability

1. Introduction

Counterfeit, the term refers to products that are the replicated goods infringing trademarks and patents of big and popular brands that are of substandard quality manufactured and sold by another local and regional brand name without the consent or the authority of the original brand (Lin, 2011). Counterfeit products exist both in the physical and virtual market, i.e., online stores and this tend to be the foremost and the prime threat to the apparel industry, as this industry works on creating, designing, and imaging new designs prints, and patterns, their stealing or duplicity results in great loss to the business and violation of their copyrights. Replica products are largely impacting the brands and their associated retailers as customers get confused as they get the replica of the branded products at cheaper prices which results in a decline in sales for the authentic brands for the entire season or so on. The global market for fake goods is $1.7 trillion a year in 2018 which is estimated to grow to $2.8 billion and create 5.4 million in employment by 2022 (Shepard, 2018), with China manufacturing over 80% of all counterfeit and pirated products.

Brands spend heavy amounts to build their brand name, brand image, and position them in the market and these pirated products play havoc with the established brands, resulting in a decline in sales and market loss. In the apparel industry, counterfeit is more dominant and these pirated goods are commonly sold in markets and street corner, the dominancy of duplicate or first copy products is also prevalent in online stores and nowadays even malls and stores also sell these counterfeit products and fool customers and usually, customers do not tend to pay much attention to such minute details in the logo of brand and trademark, except few.

India has seen a subsequent rise in the counterfeit of branded garments and keeping in mind the loss faced by the brands on their sales and reputation in the market, the Government of India has also incorporated some rules to counter duplicating, piracy, counterfeiting, and smuggling of copied products. The government has revised the legal framework to address such issues and also protect the consumer from getting cheated and secure their rights. Despite such steps taken, a study conducted by the Federation of Indian Commerce & Industry shows fake goods trade activity is seen to be on the rise across the country (FICCI, 2018). To counter this dispute of counterfeit products, brands must take concrete steps to claim their originality and transparency of their products to the customers, to avoid duplicate products overpower their brand impact the brand image and customer loyalty as these counterfeit products are difficult to distinguish and are of low quality with the false brand name which leads to negative publicity of the authentic brand. Blockchain is the best technology to adopt to counter this threat and it provides transparency in the supply chain from the manufacturer cell to the retail, that is from the initial procurement of raw materials to final delivery to the customers (Yadav *et al.*, 2020a, 2020b). This technology is a boon to the apparel industry as it helps in sustainability by sincere monitoring.

The blockchain consists of databases that are interconnected through cryptography, where each block has its hash, timestamp, and transaction details, and only the approved parties can access the information that's correlated with that, and which can't be changed (Yadav *et al.*, 2020a, 2020b). Adopting blockchain technology can help counter the threat of counterfeit products and the violation of copyrights, brands must focus on how to effectively adopt this technology to provide the original and the best in the market and save their brands from the attack of counterfeit. The study intends to demonstrate the need for the adoption of blockchain technology in the apparel industry through a discussion of multiple cases.

2. Literature Review

The textile and apparel industry is one of the major contributors to employment and growth in the Indian economy after agriculture (Mehrotra *et al.*, 2014). This makes it essential for the growth of the nation, to remove all kinds of illegal and illicit trade activity from the industry to let the society and economy prosper. As India is one the fastest growing economy, this makes it an easy target to carry out practices like smuggling and counterfeiting with a significantly huge and harmful impact on the economy which is affecting the country in numerous ways. It is shutting down the local and domestic industries, creating huge loss of employment, creating suppression in investment and innovation, demoralizing the legal imports, increasing the transitional crimes, reducing the revenue that is collected by the government, and hampering the health of the citizens as well (Tracit, 2019).

Federation of Indian Commerce and Industry in its report "Invisible Enemy: Impact of Smuggling on Indian Economy and Employment" has stated that the contribution in the ready-made textile sector was around $178 billion in 2017, and 5.5% of the industry's revenue went into the export earnings in 2017–2018 (FICCI, 2019). The report also shows a significant increase in the illegal activities of the readymade garment industry which has driven huge losses to the country's economic growth, the estimates of which are given below (see Table 1).

The threat of counterfeit is continuously rising and affecting the brands they copy and duplicated, therefore blockchain technology must be adopted for transparent monitoring of supply chains in the apparel industry where from the initial process of manufacturing to the final process of selling every segment will be under strict observation under this technology. Blockchains provide many features which are most suited to such threats of fraud and counterfeit, this technology offers Immutability, that is information remains secure and unaltered, and valid which will help the brands to secure their copyrights as without permission no one has access to edit, delete or manipulate the information (Hughes *et al.*, 2019; Ismagilova *et al.*, 2020; Yadav *et al.*, 2020a, 2020b). Another feature which blockchain provides is corruption-free working, as it manages internal networking system so that hacking risks and stealing of

Table 1.   **Losses due to Counterfeit Apparels**

Readymade Garment Industry	2015–2016	2017–2018
Illicit trade practices	Rs. 3,780 crores	Rs. 5,509 crores
Total output loss (domestic)	1.88%	2.53%
Direct employment loss (domestic)	1.68 lakhs	2.49 lakhs
Total output loss (economy)	Rs. 9,960 crores	Rs. 14,516 crores
Total employment loss (economy)	2.32 lakhs	3.44 lakhs

Source: FICCI (2019).

information is prohibited (Yadav *et al.*, 2020b). Blockchains are decentralized that is the power does not lie in the hand of a single person or anyone's authority rather "group of nodes" helps the channel to remain decentralized. It can be directly accessed from the web and the information is stored it does not require many resources, this also reduces the risk of third-party intervention.

Adoption of blockchain technology by the research community can be seen in the domains of agriculture (Yadav *et al.*, 2020b), food supply chains (Queiroz *et al.*, 2020), the Indian public sector (Rana *et al.*, 2021), smart cities (Ismagilova *et al.*, 2020) but its adoption by the apparel industry researchers is at a very nascent stage. A keyword search "Blockchain" and "Apparel Industry" led to only two relevant (Bullón Pérez *et al.*, 2020; Fu *et al.*, 2018) records on Web of Science data. The limited research in the domain motivates this study to explore the probable applications of blockchain technology in the apparel industry and thus proposing an infrastructure for the same.

3. Research Methodology

The investigation's technique can be defined as hypothesis building, which involves the analysis of various qualitative assessments, and this method is becoming increasingly popular in social science research (Eisenhardt & Graebner, 2007; Kshetri, 2016; Yadav *et al.*, 2020a). As compared to a particular event, several contextual inquiries provide a more solid foundation for hypothesis development (Rowley, 2002). In comparison to quantitative analysis, subjective research requires the construction of a strong argument to protect the discovery addresses presented when there is no reliable proof of the theory suggested (Rowley, 2002). As a result, the theoretical and practical importance of the paper's investigation is contingent on the use of blockchain in the apparel industry.

3.1 *Sampling of cases*

Selection of cases is one of the crucial tasks in the final accumulation of the content, cases should be illustrative of the commonality, resemble the details and particulars in substantial measure to hypothesize testing research. Therefore, hypothetical testing must be adopted to select the cases that fit the context of the chapter most suitably, cases should be reasonable and depict the relatedness among the constructs. Cases with multiple probes should be selected over cases with a single probe as it gives a concrete base and enhances the hypothesis (Siggelkow, 2007; Yin, 2017). The cases selected must address the issues related to the chapter and provide a clear picture of the study conducted and thus cases with sufficient and reliable data are picked available from the open sources on the web.

3.2 Data collection

Previous studies have established the dimensions of data quality that are essential for collecting accurate and reliable data (Golder, 2000; Gottschalk, 1953; Yadav *et al.*, 2020a, 2020b). The study's facts and knowledge must be triangulated from various sources (Stavros & Westberg, 2009). Case studies also use a variety of data collection techniques, including documents, archival information, interviews (Cook & Campbell, 1976), and direct evaluation (Bart *et al.*, 1970). Among the numerous data sources listed (Eisenhardt & Graebner, 2007), this case study utilizes archival data sources such as newspaper articles, magazines, and records (including electronic versions), audio-visual materials, and other formats. One vital aspect of data quality is its reputation and trustworthiness, i.e., that both the source and substance of the data are trustworthy (Wang & Strong, 1996), and that the data is free of prejudice, partiality, and manipulation (Eppler, 2006). The data for the analysis was gathered from a reputable third party without relying on the organization's website profile as a portrait, thus minimizing self-serving prejudices. The data's timeliness and currency are also considered (Wang & Strong, 1996), and the cases chosen include current details and are not obsolete (Eppler, 2006). The study uses the most recent online literature accessible in the context of news stories and articles written through third-party publications.

4. Analysis of the Cases

4.1 Selling fake branded clothes in stores and online

The high-quality counterfeit goods known as "super fakes," which have been emerging more regularly in recent years, are the most visible manifestation of the increasing accessibility. Fake watches, smartphones, high-end luxury items, and other items are now manufactured to a near-exact quality. According to Ghost Data (Stroppa *et al.*, 2019), up to 20% of posts regarding top fashion labels on social media were found to contain fraudulent and/or illegal goods in 2016. In a more recent survey, they discovered that every month, over 1.6 million Stories were blatantly commercial fakes. The web recently surpassed 1 billion monthly users, providing these new counterfeiters with an audience that only seems to be increasing in size, resulting in increased counterfeit fashion production.

4.2 Counterfeit clothing products of popular brands seized by Bengaluru police

"Surprise Investigation done by Bengaluru police in 24 hours led to the detection of fraud products of clothing brands worth Rs. 2.09 crores." Recently police raided go down and seized 6,790 replicas of branded garments worth Rs. 82.48 lakhs (Krishnamachari, 2017). Some more raids were done resulting in the seizing of counterfeit clothes costing Rs. 1.27 crores, excluding Rs. 56,450 cash. The raids were also done at different locations of the state and where two of the suspects have been arrested till now. Police claim it to be a widely spread racket as the central crime bureau detected some illegal manufacturing units which were using the names of popular brands like Gas, US Polo, Diesel, Levi's, etc. which worth approximately Rs. 2 crores which is involved branded accessories of brand-named Louis Vuitton. Such activities occur on demand-supply dynamics that is the manufacturers and retailers involved. The racket of selling fraud products has been busted and go downs have been seized.

4.3 A hosiery manufacturer curbed for producing duplicate branded clothes

A hosiery manufacturer raided for producing replicated garments like tracksuits, T-shirts, and sweatshirts by the name of Puma and Adidas (Times, 2014). The manufacturer was used to operate a hosiery manufacturing cell in his home, police recovered readymade garments from the location when informed by a legal adviser of Adidas and Puma. The accused was arrested in infringement of branded products by attaching the logos of original brands and the case was filed against the hosiery owner under the copyright act, trademarks act, cheating, selling product marked with counterfeit mark.

4.4 *Company produced clothes with fake brand names got raid*

A case was reported on a company, owned by a local person that got raided by the police in a place located in Ludhiana (Punjab), India. The complaint against the company was filed by a person, who is an advocate of the brands like "Adidas, Levi's, and Puma" from New Delhi, who in his complaint accused that the manufacturing unit of this company was producing and selling fake apparel under the name of few top international brands (TNN, 2021). On which, the investigating officer later confirmed that they procured a huge number of fake products from the company's factory. The company was supplying these fake products to various distributors inside and outside of the city by applying duplicate trademarks of big brands on them. The details of the products seized by the police on their raid are given in Table.

4.5 *Market stalls caught selling duplicate apparel*

The case is from the Tibetan Market which is in Vadodara, Gujarat. The police along with the security officials of a corporate together raided the stalls of the above-mentioned market on receiving the information about the fake clothing products being sold by them in the name of international brands. The police later confirmed that nine stalls were found to be selling fake products which included shirts, pants, t-shirts, and jackets of the brand "Levi's and Superdry" and eight persons who were responsible for the act have been arrested for the same. The duplicate products seized by the police in their raid accounted for 312 pieces, the estimate of which was Rs. 4.9 lakhs (Connect Gujarat Desk, 2020).

4.6 *Fake jeans racket*

A case was reported against a showroom owner whose shop is located at a place in Bhopal. He was accused of selling fake jeans products with the label of top international brands at high prices. To which, a police officer visited the shop as a customer and purchased a pair of jeans from a branded company for Rs. 3,500 for which he did not receive a bill (Singh, 2020).

On this, the police raid the shop along with an investigator who told the police that they were selling the duplicate products in the name of highly reputed brands like "Levi's, Wrangler, Diesel, and Armani" by putting their fake labels on them. The police said that they seized 284 pairs of jeans from that store as a result of a duplicate product.

5. A General Framework of IT Architecture

Blockchain administers immutable, sheltered, and impenetrable data in a decentralized expanded ledger. The application of blockchain technology substantial and expansive and this technology is configured and prepared to revolutionize and customize transversely in different sectors, businesses, and domains (the food industry, garment industry, medicines, supply management are some of them). Blockchain technology holds expertise and is competent enough to validate the originality and efficacy of assets in such a manner that it is decentralized, credible, and unaltered with secure records of details and logs which are open to the participants who are permitted.

This study focuses to recommend a blockchain-based solution to the threats caused by counterfeiting in readymade garments along with the basic framework that will ensure promising authenticity of the products. The solution involves traceability of the supply chain at every segment involved till the final purchase by the end-user (consumer).

The blockchain-based solution consists of six major segments involved in the process, as shown in Figure 1.

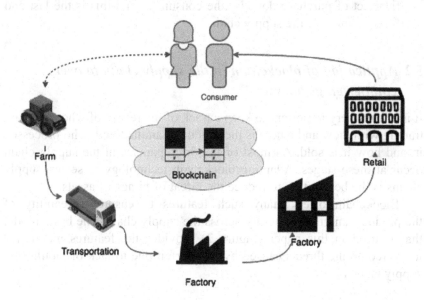

Figure 1. Overview of Segments in Supply Chain Monitoring

5.1 *Supply chain management*

Supply chain management is the process where man, machine, technology, data, and activities are involved in the mobility of any product or services from the provider to consumer. The process of supply chain initiates with the manufacturer, suppliers continuing to retailers, and then the consumer.

All manufacturing companies follow a general supply chain that majorly involves the supplier, the manufacturer (factory), retailer, and end-user.

1. Supplier — fabric, adornments (buttons, laces, brooches, etc.), and wrapping chores are done by supplier specifically in the garment industry.
2. Manufacturer (factory) — in the factory garments are manufactured (i.e., cutting, stitching, printing, patterning, and molding them to the final design) manually or by machines.
3. Retailer — they are the "Retail Branding Owner" of different brands. They serve as a middle man between the company and the consumers by buying the garments from the company and selling in the store to the consumers through various online and offline stores.
4. End-user (consumers) — the whole process was carried out from this final act of purchase done by the consumers and this is the last and final segment of the supply chain.

5.2 *Application of blockchain in the supply chain to over counterfeit garments*

It is always very important to keep a track of the record of whom you are trading with, how and where is the product manufactured, who processed it, and how it is sold. As most of the discrepancies in the supply chain occur at these stages. Adapting blockchain technology to secure supply chains is the best option to reduce the threat of piracy of assets.

Blockchain offers many such features to ensure traceability of the products and their mobility across the supply chain. The basic model that is used in this paper (Figure 2) provides the features mentioned to overcome the threats caused by counterfeit due to lack of monitoring supply chains.

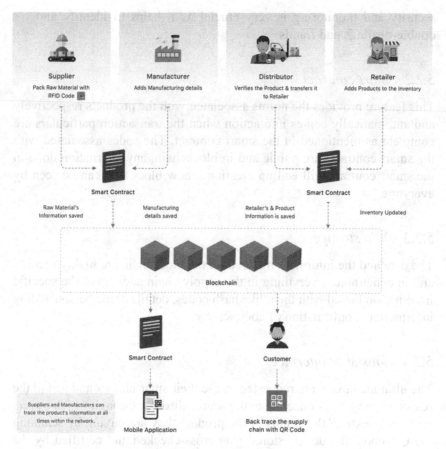

Figure 2.   Data Flow Diagram Employing Blockchain

Source: Jyoti and Chauhan (2020).

5.2.1 *Tracking history*

It is observed that many companies lack the source of their product from where it originated in the supply chains this leads to lack of traceability of expensive products and also possess the maximum chances of the product getting stolen or copied resulting in the negative portrayal of brand image and reputation because of the poor quality of the copied attire. Blockchains help to keep an unaltered and authentic record of data, information shared, mobility of the products, transaction and other details which cannot be accessed unless you are permitted to. This type of data security and monitoring is very crucial as it helps to identify and fix double-dealings and frauds.

5.2.2 *Smart contract*

This feature provides the norms associated with the products respectively and automatically comes into action when the transaction particulars are complete as mentioned in the smart contract. The codes associated with the smart contracts are public and in blockchain, any alternation done in the smart contract will end up creating a new block that can be seen by everyone.

5.2.3 *Data storage*

The data and the information stored on the blockchain are highly secured and impenetrable. Everything in the supply chain adds up to the specific information linked with them like hash codes, details of the person adding information, confirmation of contract, etc.

5.2.4 *Consumer interface*

The ultimate buyers are requested to use their smartphones and install the respective app for connecting to the source directly, through which buyers will easily extract the details of the product they are buying by scanning the QR code, the details stored gets cross-checked and certified by the blockchain integrated app thus the end-users are provided with the untouched and the authentic information of the product, which confirms that the product is not pirated or copied rather it the original one offered by the brand.

6. Discussion

The chapter focuses on the practice of counterfeiting in the Indian apparel industry with a special emphasis on the case of readymade garments by examining the loopholes of its supply chain because of which such practices become easy to conduct leading towards the negative publicity of the authentic brands. The study in the chapter shows that over the period of time there has been a drastic increase in the number of counterfeit cases in India having a significantly huge and harmful impact on the economy which is affecting the country in numerous ways. It is shutting down the local and domestic industries, creating huge loss of employment, creating suppression in investment and innovation, demoralizing the legal imports, increasing the transitional crimes, reducing the revenue that is collected by the government, and hampering the health of the citizens as well. Therefore, to overcome these issues blockchain technology has been used to provide a genuine solution for traceability by integrating it with the supply chain management in a way that the products can be traced at every segment of the supply chain. A basic model for the application of technology has been used in the chapter which mentions the features like history tracking, smart contract, data storage, blockchain, and consumer interface that will help in overcoming the issue of counterfeit from the Indian readymade garments industry. By using this framework of blockchain, customers will become able to easily identify the originality of the product also, this blockchain integrated app will be way easier to use by scanning the QR code.

The blockchain can handle this continuing issue of counterfeit that hampers the efficacy of the supply chain by offering features like transparency and traceability. With its ability to provide transparency in the supply chain to all the parties involved, it will develop a trust level easily that has been lost over the past years. Also, the inflexible system of blockchain will restrict any kind of tampering throughout the entire ecosystem of the supply chain as it provides the facility of real-time tracking of the products.

With the increasing demand by the consumers for the proof of originality of the product they buy, they are keen enough to inquire about the minute details of their products like the fabric of the garment, the authenticity of the brands they purchase from, especially when buying clothes. In case of buying the garments from online stores, customer tracks their products, their shipment, etc. to ensure that they are delivered with the right product they paid for. As the cases of counterfeit in the garment sector hiked in the markets, customers also got alert of fake and pirated products they get of the same price as the branded ones with no scope of detection because they are the replica of the original ones.

Many brands were attacked by counterfeiting, which resulted in their negative publicity because of the poor quality of the clothes, which impacted the brand image and the reputation of the brands were questioned as customer lost trust, due to fraud products they received by the names of the original ones. Various brands after facing setbacks because of counterfeiting are playing safe as of now, they are alert and using blockchain technology as the most common and the most reliable application to track their supply chain and ensure the originality of their products. Adopting blockchain also enhances the value chain and sustainability of the supply chain at a cost-friendly budget by creating the account on the platform and monitoring every segment involved in the supply chain. This technology not only provides the assurance to the brands regarding the traceability but also guarantee the customers that they are provided with what they purchased that is their product is unaltered and is original by and they can confirm it by scanning the QR code from their smartphones, which will immediately display the details that are the fabric, size, history, essential authorization, and certification associated with the product which will clear the doubt of the customer regarding the authenticity of the product along with the brand attached to it and this will eventually help the brands to retain their customers' trust, sustain their brand image and protected against such frauds.

Budget management for brand security operations has always been a challenge for most brand owners. Brand owners often have separate budgets set up for brand security and are either part of the legal budget or part of the brand marketing budget. Although using a brand security expenditure as a subset of the promotion budget makes sense (because it produces comparable outcomes in terms of sales, location, and consumer loyalty), it could be a smart choice to utilize the regulatory provisions of CSR spends for brand protection (Singh *et al.*, 2019; Singh & Misra, 2020, 2021). Many constructive and reactive brand security practices are simply expenditures by brand owners to shield customers from deception. It's just that this money has to be used in a particular way. Using CSR findings to drive sales and profitability efficiency, customer health, and brand awareness may be a clever way to get societal and corporate benefits (Singh *et al.*, 2021; Singh & Misra, 2020). Organizations can use these budgets to install and operate the blockchain-based infrastructure to protect the sanctity of their brand image and maintain their customer loyalty.

In today's era, the complaints of the consumers concerning counterfeit products are posted directly on social media and hence such actions could lead to loss of customer loyalty. To overcome the issue of misinformation and grievance redressal, the study suggests the appointment of social media influencers (Yadav *et al.*, 2021) that count educate the consumers concerning the consumes concerning the counterfeit products and use of blockchain technology for separating original from the counterfeit.

7. Limitations of the Study

The chapter is based on the collection of secondary data which has some limitations in the research. The data collected for the study is general and the sample size of the cases is small which might not be very helpful for the process of decision-making to the companies as it will be difficult for them to invest in any technology without having proper figures that focus on their specific problem.

8. Conclusion

The fraud in apparel has been spiking both in the organized and unorganized markets leading to reputation loss of the apparel manufacturers. Though the consumers demand to get an insight on the data that clarifies that the product purchased by them is not counterfeit but the required infrastructure is lacking. The study proposes the integration of blockchain technology at various touchpoints in the apparel supply chain that will enable transparency and will also contribute to maintaining the product authenticity. Future researches can be conducted on the blockchain adoption by the apparel industry from a more operational and financial perspective and thus propose an optimized infrastructure facilitating granular traceability of the product.

References

Bart, W. M., Webb, E. J., Campbell, D. T., Schwartz, R. D., & Sechrest, L. (1970). Unobtrusive measures: Nonreactive research in the social sciences. *Journal of the American Statistical Association*, *65*(331), 1413. https://doi.org/10.2307/2284316.

Bullón Pérez, J. J., Queiruga-Dios, A., Gayoso Martínez, V., & Martín del Rey, Á. (2020). Traceability of ready-to-wear clothing through blockchain technology. *Sustainability*, *12*(18), 7491. https://doi.org/10.3390/su12187491.

Connect Gujarat Desk. (2020). Vadodara PCB arrested 8 from Tibetan market for selling duplicate clothes of branded company. Retrieved November 28, 2021, from   https://connectgujarat.com/vadodara-pcb-arrested-8-from-tibetan-market-for-selling-duplicate-clothes-of-branded-company/.

Cook, T. D., & Campbell, D. T. (1976). The design and conduct of quasi-experiments and true experiments in field settings. In *Handbook of Industrial and Organizational Psychology*.

Eisenhardt, K. M., & Graebner, M. E. (2007). Theory building from cases: Opportunities and challenges. *Academy of Management Journal, 50*(1), 25–32. https://doi.org/10.5465/amj.2007.24160888.

Eppler, M. J. (2006). Managing information quality: Increasing the value of information in knowledge-intensive products and processes. In *Managing Information Quality: Increasing the Value of Information in Knowledge-intensive Products and Processes*. https://doi.org/10.1007/3-540-32225-6.

FICCI. (2018). *Fake Products: 80% of Consumers Believe They Use Genuine Ones, Say FICCI*, ETRetail.com, June 12, 2018. http://ficci.in/ficci-in-news-page.asp?nid=14577.

FICCI. (2019). Invisible Enemy: Impact of Smuggling on Indian Economy and Employment. Retrieved February 22, 2020, from https://ficci.in/publication.asp?spid=23132.

Fu, B., Shu, Z., & Liu, X. (2018). Blockchain enhanced emission trading framework in fashion apparel manufacturing industry. *Sustainability, 10*(4), 1105. https://doi.org/10.3390/su10041105.

Golder, P. N. (2000). Historical method in marketing research with new evidence on long-term market share stability. *Journal of Marketing Research, 37*(2), 156–172. https://doi.org/10.1509/jmkr.37.2.156.18732.

Gottschalk, L. R. (1953). Understanding history, a primer of historical method. *Nursing Research, 2*(1), 44. https://doi.org/10.1097/00006199-195306000-00021.

Hughes, L., Dwivedi, Y. K., Misra, S. K., Rana, N. P., Raghavan, V., & Akella, V. (2019). Blockchain research, practice and policy: Applications, benefits, limitations, emerging research themes and research agenda. *International Journal of Information Management, 49*, 114–129. https://doi.org/10.1016/j.ijinfomgt.2019.02.005.

Ismagilova, E., Hughes, L., Rana, N. P., & Dwivedi, Y. K. (2020). Security, privacy and risks within smart cities: Literature review and development of a smart city interaction framework. *Information Systems Frontiers*. https://doi.org/10.1007/s10796-020-10044-1.

Jyoti, A., & Chauhan, R. K. (2020). Block chain based data provenance in supply chain. *International Journal of Innovative Technology and Exploring Engineering, 9*(3), 317–322. https://doi.org/10.35940/ijitee.C7980.019320.

Krishnamachari, S. (2017). Fake products of clothing brands seized by Bengaluru police. Retrieved April 5, 2020, from https://www.ibtimes.co.in/fake-products-clothing-brands-seized-by-bengaluru-police-726592.

Kshetri, N. (2016). Creation, deployment, diffusion and export of Sub-Saharan Africa-originated information technology-related innovations. *International Journal of Information Management, 36*(6), 1274–1287. https://doi.org/10.1016/j.ijinfomgt.2016.09.003.

Lin, Y.-C. J. (2011). *Fake Stuff: China and the Rise of Counterfeit Goods.* Routledge, New York, https://doi.org/10.4324/9780203829752.

Mehrotra, S., Parida, J., Sinha, S., & Gandhi, A. (2014). Explaining employment trends in the indian economy: 1993-94 to 2011-12. *Economic and Political Weekly, 49*(32), 49–57.

Queiroz, M. M., Fosso Wamba, S., De Bourmont, M., & Telles, R. (2021). Blockchain adoption in operations and supply chain management: Empirical evidence from an emerging economy. *International Journal of Production Research, 59*(20), 6087–6103. https://doi.org/10.1080/00207543.2020.1803511.

Rana, N. P., Dwivedi, Y. K., & Hughes, D. L. (2021). Analysis of challenges for blockchain adoption within the Indian public sector: An interpretive structural modelling approach. *Information Technology and People*, ahead-of-print. https://doi.org/10.1108/ITP-07-2020-0460.

Rowley, J. (2002). Using case studies in research. *Management Research News, 25*(1), 16–27. https://doi.org/10.1108/01409170210782990.

Shepard, W. (2018). Meet the man fighting America's trade war against Chinese counterfeits (It's Not Trump). Retrieved June 19, 2020, from https://www.forbes.com/sites/wadeshepard/2018/03/29/meet-the-man-fighting-americas-trade-war-against-chinese-counterfeits/?sh=6ace17961c0d.

Siggelkow, N. (2007). Persuasion with case studies. *Academy of Management Journal, 50*(1), 20–24. https://doi.org/10.5465/amj.2007.24160882.

Singh, K., & Misra, M. (2020). Linking harmonious CSR and financial inclusion: The moderating effects of financial literacy and income. *The Singapore Economic Review*, 1–22. https://doi.org/10.1142/S0217590820500629.

Singh, K., & Misra, M. (2021). Linking corporate social responsibility (CSR) and organizational performance: The moderating effect of corporate reputation. *European Research on Management and Business Economics, 27*(1), 100139. https://doi.org/10.1016/j.iedeen.2020.100139.

Singh, K., Misra, M., Kumar, M., & Tiwari, V. (2019). A study on the determinants of financial performance of U.S. agricultural cooperatives. *Journal of Business Economics and Management, 20*(4), 633–647. https://doi.org/10.3846/jbem.2019.9858.

Singh, K., Misra, M., & Yadav, J. (2021). Corporate social responsibility and financial inclusion: Evaluating the moderating effect of income. *Managerial and Decision Economics, 42*(5), 1263–1274. https://doi.org/10.1002/mde.3306.

Singh, R. (2020). Bhopal Police busts fake jeans racket. Retrieved December 13, 2020, from https://www.indiatoday.in/crime/story/fakejeans-gang-racket-bhopal-1637217-2020-01-16.

Stavros, C., & Westberg, K. (2009). Using triangulation and multiple case studies to advance relationship marketing theory. *Qualitative Market Research: An International Journal*, *12*(3), 307–320. https://doi.org/10.1108/13522750910963827.

Stroppa, A., Gatto, D., Pasha, L., & Parrella, B. (2019). Instagram and counterfeiting in 2019: New features, old problems. Retrieved July 17, 2020, from https://ghostdata.io/report/Instagram_Counterfeiting_GD.pdf.

Times, H. (2014). Hosiery owner arrested for making fake branded clothes. Retrieved May 18, 2020, from https://www.hindustantimes.com/punjab/hosiery-owner-arrested-for-making-fake-branded-clothes/story-Et7icE4QYYarg5xTOmhkKI.html.

TNN. (2011). Firm raided for producing fake branded clothes | Ludhiana News - Times of India. Retrieved July 5, 2020, from https://timesofindia.indiatimes.com/city/ludhiana/firm-raided-for-producing-fake-branded-clothes/articleshow/9178231.cms.

Tracit. (2019). Mapping the impact of illicit trade on the sustainable development goals. Retrieved September 30, 2020, from https://unctad.org/meetings/en/Contribution/DITC2019_TRACIT_IllicitTradeandSDGs_fullreport_en.pdf.

Wang, R. Y., & Strong, D. M. (1996). Beyond accuracy: What data quality means to data consumers. *Journal of Management Information Systems*, *12*(4), 5–33. https://doi.org/10.1080/07421222.1996.11518099.

Yadav, J., Misra, M., & Goundar, S. (2020a). An overview of food supply chain virtualisation and granular traceability using blockchain technology. *International Journal of Blockchains and Cryptocurrencies*, *1*(2), 154. https://doi.org/10.1504/IJBC.2020.108997.

Yadav, J., Misra, M., & Goundar, S. (2020b). Autonomous agriculture marketing information system through blockchain: A case study of e-NAM adoption in India. In *Blockchain Technologies, Applications and Cryptocurrencies* (pp. 115–138). World Scientific. https://doi.org/10.1142/9789811205279_0005.

Yadav, J., Misra, M., & Singh, K. (2021). Sensitizing Netizen's behavior through influencer intervention enabled by crowdsourcing — A case of reddit. *Behaviour and Information Technology*, 1–12. https://doi.org/10.1080/0144929X.2021.1872705.

Yin, R. K. (2013). Applications of case study research. *Applied Social Research Methods Series*. https://doi.org/10.1097/FCH.0b013e31822dda9e.

Yin, R. K. (2017). *Case Study Research and Applications: Design and Methods*, Sage Publications, Newbury Park, California.

Index

A

adverse drug reactions (ADR), 271–272, 295–297, 300
agriculture, 58
artificial intelligence (AI), 100, 292
algorithm, 184, 190, 194, 198
ANN, 72
anonymity, 326–333, 337, 340–342, 344–346, 348–349
Ant Colony Optimization (ACO), 116–120, 135–136, 141
Arduino Uno, 182, 184
artificial, 93, 99
attribute-based encryption (ABE), 139, 271–273, 277, 280, 285, 300

B

Bitcoin, 1–3, 5, 7–10, 13–15, 17–19
blockchain, 93–109, 153–154, 183, 185–189, 191, 195, 197–199, 202–213, 215, 217–218, 244, 304–307, 310–312, 314–319, 326–334, 337, 339, 341, 344, 348–350, 354–358, 362–364, 368, 370, 373–379, 381, 383–389, 394–396, 397, 401–403, 405–406

blockchain's distinctive characteristics, 223
BlockEdge, 361
Bloom, 275, 279, 280
blynk, 182, 195–196, 198
business intelligence (BI), 146

C

challenges of Tokenization, 54
Clause 49, 147–148, 150–152, 154
cloud computing, 93–94, 98–99, 109, 272, 275
cloud storage services, 231
computation time, 83
control, 329
corporate governance, 146–150, 152–154
counterfeit, 393–396, 398–399, 401–402, 404–406
Ciphertext Policy (CP-ABE), 272
cryptocurrencies, 1–2, 247

D

data block, 233
data management, 45
decentralization, 95, 326, 329, 333

digitalization, 2
distributed systems, 2–4, 10, 14, 17

E
echocardiogram, 69
edge, 354–358, 362, 364–368, 370
Edwards-curve Digital Signature
   Algorithm (EdDSA), 160
electronic health records (EHR)
   credibility, 26
e-learning, 116, 120
enhanced liquidity, 52
Ethereum, 252
Ethereum technology, 35

F
Frost-filterative fuzzified
   gravitational search-based shift
   invariant deep structure feature
   learning (FFFGS-SIDSFL), 73, 75,
   82, 84–87, 90
fog, 354–355, 361–362, 366–367,
   370
food supply chain, 62

H
hash functionality, 175
hashing, 2, 12–13, 15
Hawk framework, 261
hierarchical blockchain, 202, 207,
   218
hybrid ensemble-based learning
   model, 31, 37

I
identity authentication using
   blockchain, 47
identity management, 305
industrial Internet of Things (IIoT),
   182, 202–204, 206–207, 210–211,
   217–218, 354–362, 364, 368–371

image encryption, 172
image histogram, 174
immutable, 202–203, 207, 214
infrastructure, 56
intelligent communities, 238
intelligent electronic devices, 226
internet of things (IoT), 100,
   182–183, 304–306, 320
IoT, blockchain, and AI, 45
IoT devices-based micro-payments,
   49

K
Key Policy (KP-ABE), 280

L
ledger, 2, 3
learning object (LO), 116–117,
   120–121, 136–137, 139

M
master patient index, 36
ML, 292–293

N
network-based, 245
number of pixels per change rate
   (NPCR), 160

O
official regulators, 35
omnichannel, 374–375, 389
Oyante, 261

P
pattern recognition, 83
Personal Healthcare Record (PHR),
   271–275, 277, 279–280, 300
Proof-of-Work (PoW), 246
privacy, 326–330, 332–333, 338, 344,
   346, 348–350

Q
quality of life, 57

R
readymade garments, 399, 401,
  404–405
regulatory challenges, 54
regulatory issues of stablecoins, 48
retail, 374–375, 377–379, 384, 389
retailers, 380, 383, 386–388
Radio Frequency Identification
  (RFID), 161

S
Sarbanes Oxley Law (SOX), 147
Schnorr signature, 170
security, 244, 303–305, 310
smart cities application, 56
smart contracts, 230, 250
smart trash, 182
smart waste, 182–183, 186
soft clustering concept, 31

stochastic gradient learning fuzzified
  gravitational search (SGLFGS), 76
supply chain, 373, 375–381–385,
  388, 394–397, 401–404, 406–407
supply chain transparency (SCT), 160

T
Tokenization, 50
Town crier, 262
traceability, 394, 401–403, 405–407
transparency, 373, 375, 377–378,
  385–387

U
user privacy, 329

V
vulnerabilities, 245

W
Wi-Fi module, 182–184, 189, 198
wireless, 304

Printed in the United States
by Baker & Taylor Publisher Services

Printed in the United States
by Baker & Taylor Publisher Services